Social facts a

THE LEWIS HENRY MORGAN LECTURES/1981

presented at
The University of Rochester
Rochester, New York

Social facts and fabrications
"Customary" law on Kilimanjaro, 1880–1980

SALLY FALK MOORE
Harvard University

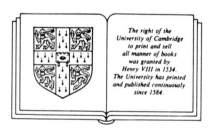

The right of the
University of Cambridge
to print and sell
all manner of books
was granted by
Henry VIII in 1534.
The University has printed
and published continuously
since 1584.

CAMBRIDGE UNIVERSITY PRESS

Cambridge
New York   Port Chester   Melbourne   Sydney

Published by the Press Syndicate of the University of Cambridge
The Pitt Building, Trumpington Street, Cambridge CB2 1RP
40 West 20th Street, New York, NY 10011, USA
10 Stamford Road, Oakleigh, Melbourne 3166, Australia

First published in 1986
Reprinted 1990

Printed in the United States of America

Library of Congress Cataloging in Publication Data
Moore, Sally Falk, 1924–
Social facts and fabrications.
1. Law, Chaga (African people)   2. Customary law –
Tanzania – Kilimanjaro.   3. Chaga (African people) –
Social life and customs.   I. Title.
LAW   349.678'26   85-7897
346.7826

ISBN 0-521-30938-7 hardback
ISBN 0-521-31201-9 paperback

British Library Cataloging-in-Publication applied for.

Contents

Contents

Tables

Illustrations

Foreword

Professor Sally Falk Moore delivered the nineteenth series of Lewis Henry Morgan Lectures at the University of Rochester in 1981 on March 17, 19, 24, and 26. All those who heard her elegantly clear exposition were aware that what she had to say was a careful distillation of her argument and of the evidence supporting it. The lectures and discussion of them indicated that there had to be more and there is, here presented in fully developed form.

The lecture titles of Professor Moore's original series, "Process in Anthropology," were:

1. Making Models That Move
2. Explaining Historical Sequence: An African Case of Early Economic Success
3. Not Very Customary Law: The Chagga of Kilimanjaro Today
4. Some Significant Sequences

Comparison of these titles with the present version's part and chapter designation makes it clear that the shape of the original has been preserved, though often what was initially a paragraph has become pages or even an entire chapter.

This study of the Chagga, based on extensive field research and augmented by the published literature in several disciplines and by archival resources, undertakes to break new ground in the study of law and social change, and has strong implications for anthropological theory in general. The account is certain to be of great interest not only to anthropologists concerned with East Africa, but to all anthropologists, especially those engaged in the study of law or change. It will also be significant for individuals with a diverse range of other concerns, such as those interested in history, social theory, economic development, and political systems.

Lewis Henry Morgan, though he did not know the Chagga, would have certainly welcomed this book and the lectures from which it developed.

In dealing anthropologically with law and with social change, Professor Moore's work unquestionably carries forward the broad tradition for which Morgan labored so hard to establish a base.

ALFRED HARRIS
Editor
The Lewis Henry Morgan Lectures

Preface

This is a book about the transformation of the way of life of an African people. It uses fieldwork data to illuminate history and the historical record to make sense of ethnography.

When I first went to Africa in 1968 to work among the Chagga of Kilimanjaro, I had three general lines of inquiry in mind. The first concerned recent history. The Chagga were reputed to be among the most modern of the rural peoples in Tanzania, being prosperous cultivators who had started one of the first African-owned cooperatives in the continent. I wanted to know how their economic transformation had come about and why. The second question had to do with their indigenous legal system. In the nineteenth century, the Chagga had permanently occupied individually held plots of land and irrigated gardens. Permanent landholding clearly meant that they had had an elaborate system of property rules. I was interested in the nature of the ongoing system of landholding, other aspects of local law, and the way these might reflect change. The third issue concerned African socialism. I wanted to see it in action, to observe at the grass-roots level the attempt to implement an ideological position. This book reflects those interests, and concentrates on the legal dimension of local affairs. Law is treated here as a categorical slice of life that includes both local practice and national policy, activities both in and out of the courts, and touches everything from politics to property, from incest to inheritance.

The fieldwork for this study was done in a series of segments in the summers of 1968 and 1969, the summer of 1973, and later visits in the winter of 1974 and the fall of 1979, and a brief visit in 1984. The longest periods of continuous contact were four-month stretches in the summers. Kiswahili and English were the languages I used. In addition to their own language, Kichagga, almost all Chagga speak Kiswahili. Kiswahili is the language of the schools, the courts, and of public affairs. A number of Chagga also speak some English, and a few speak it well, so I often had opportunities to check matters in both languages.

In order to make certain that the material I was collecting was not someone's idiosyncratic view I worked in four contiguous ex-chiefdoms, Kilema, Marangu, Mamba, and Mwika. I also made some visits to the primary courts in Keni-Mriti-Mengwe and in Moshi. The people I knew in each ex-chiefdom did not know my contacts in the others and had no way to know what I was being told elsewhere. I employed research assistants to collect some comparable materials in Machame and Uru, though, of course, they had no idea what patterns I expected the material to produce. Thus some data have been assembled from seven of the seventeen ex-chiefdoms of the mountain. Only a small part of this material is in this book.

Working in segments of time over a number of years, originally because of family reasons, not intellectual ones, eventually turned into a singular advantage. To return at intervals and to be more warmly welcomed each time is encouraging. But more important, revisiting in this way gave a time perspective on dispute histories and on political change that could not have been obtained in any other way. To know people over a dozen or more years is to see their children grow up, to have shared some of their past, to have known some of the people who have now died. That knowing-the-past changes the ways one perceives others and is perceived oneself.

Many Chagga helped me in my collection of material, some as paid research assistants, some out of friendship, others out of curiosity or ethnic pride. I cannot mention all of the many people I knew or met, but would like at least to acknowledge some by name. But for the patience and help of these persons this account could never have been assembled: Mary Makulata Nguma, Hawkins Ndesanjo Mremi and his wife Martha Makwai, the Reverend Arbogast Sekundo, Joseph Merinyo, Mapenguka son of Muchake, Petro Itosi Marealle, Sifueli N. Minja, Elinami Njiro, Aaron Z. Nkya, Epiphania Masawe, Pastor Godwin Moshi, Nicodemu Male, Stanislaus Teliani Mosha, Fidelis Merishoki, Magistrate Modesto Ngoti, Magistrate John Leana Moshi, and Cliff Mamuya. All of these persons, and a large number of others, took time from their other affairs to talk with me, to tell me things about their lives or work, and to ask me questions about mine. Crossing the great distance that lay between us was a moving experience for me, and a profoundly humbling and instructive one.

Although the studies of an academic anthropologist may seem politically insignificant from an American perspective, they are not politically colorless locally. Because of the strong ideological commitment of the Tanzanian government to detribalization, the idea that someone was writing about the way of life of the Kichagga-speaking people of Kilimanjaro had local political resonance. That layer of meaning floated behind many immediate concerns. Some individuals feared that too much might be

found out about their property dealings. Others worried that their manipulations of the bureaucracy might be discovered and reported, or some
absence of political faith recorded. To be counted trustworthy by some in
these circumstances is great good fortune. To be classified as potentially
dangerous by others would not be unreasonable. Doing fieldwork in such
a setting is a complex task. Writing about it has sometimes been more so.
But now that enough years have passed since independence the most
dedicated friends of African socialism themselves speak publicly and
more frankly of deep running problems in realizing the ideals of the
movement than in the early days.

As far as possible the field data in this book are reported as observed,
found, told. Having found corroborating materials in a variety of ex-
chiefdoms gives the specific instances chosen for description a typifying
ethnographic weight. And their specificity gives them life. But in the
interest of not harming any individual, identities have been concealed by
changing names and by omitting detailed geographical locations. But
other than concealing identities, I have not tampered with the data reported here.

This book is written for the Chagga themselves to read, and for their
children later on, as much as it is for others to learn about them. For
those interested in social theory the history of their "customary law"
poses many of the analytic and methodological questions that are problematic today. Quotation marks emphasize that the notion of "customary
law" is itself a cultural construct with political implications. The term
sounds as if it designates a straightforward set of traditional rules. But the
entity to which it refers is a set of ideas embedded in relationships that
are historically shifting. The label "customary law" has its own history in
the colonial and postcolonial worlds.

I have reason to be grateful to many individuals and a number of
institutions for having had the opportunity to explore these questions on
Kilimanjaro. First, I am grateful to the African Studies Center at the
University of California, Los Angeles, for having provided me with a
scholarship period to prepare myself before I started fieldwork. I was
thus able to learn the rudiments of Swahili before embarking, and to read
something of the history of the area. I am especially grateful to Professors
Hilda Kuper, M. G. Smith, and the late Max Gluckman for their interest,
help, and encouragement at that stage of my work. The Social Science
Research Council funded my first trip to East Africa, the National Science Foundation two subsequent ones, and most recently the Wenner
Gren Foundation made possible a side trip to Kilimanjaro when I was in
Africa on other business. Nothing would have been possible without the
financial support so generously given. I am also grateful to University
College, London, for hospitality over the years, especially for allowing

me to use its facilities between trips to Africa, and to the University of Dar es Salaam, for permitting me to be a research associate of that institution whenever I was in East Africa. At Dar my work was formally sponsored by a series of deans of the Law School to whom I owe thanks, particularly to Yash Ghai and to G. M. Fimbo, and to Professor Isaria Kimambo who made my work possible in his capacity as chief academic officer of the university during several of my visits. Recently and informally I have been encouraged by the interest and hospitality of Professor Justin Maeda and I want to acknowledge my debt to him. I also have had many reasons to be grateful to the Department of Anthropology at Harvard University over the past three years for the cheerful collegiality which made it possible for me to finish this book. I am very much indebted to Jane Trahan for processing the manuscript through its several drafts and managing its form with skill and care. To Alfred and Grace Harris at the University of Rochester I owe special thanks, since their invitation to give the Morgan Lectures and their cheery welcome at Rochester brightened a period of work that might otherwise have been less productive. And last I would like to thank my husband for being such good company and such a warm friend through so many unusual times and in so many unusual places.

Introduction:

A time-oriented anthropology: events, processes, and history

Since World War II social anthropology has become increasingly preoccupied with process over time. This historical attitude might be called the New Social Anthropology were it not for the fact that there have always been some anthropologists laboring in that vineyard even when other themes have dominated the discipline. But now there is a new urgency along with a new reflexivity in this growing interest. On the large scale the current problem is how to use yet transcend the limitations of a pair of excessively general models of change. One is the evolutionary one which puts certain abstracted social types in developmental, metatemporal sequence. The other model is an even simpler and more contemporary construct; technologically advanced societies are contrasted with all others. All significant change is interpreted to be the consequence of the self-serving activities of those dominant societies in the world economy and in world politics. Both models are founded on a gross morphology of types. To both are attached some general conceptions of the dynamics of transformation, endogenous and exogenous. The dilemma of the anthropologist is that, applied to the world of this day, both models trivialize the very variations with which anthropology is preoccupied, and about which it has something to say

Equally troublesome are the questions raised by the truism that models of society vary according to the historical moment at which they are produced. Considerable self-consciousness has been generated about the reasons for current interests and the constraints on insight these imply. How are anthropologists to understand their own time, their own theories of their time?

A less time-warped vision of social "reality" must have seemed more available in the 1870s, when Lewis Henry Morgan sat in his study in Rochester, New York, writing *Ancient Society* (1877). Without apparent hesitation or self-doubt he attempted to explain social change on the grandest possible scale. He traced its progress from what he imagined to be the earliest beginnings of group life to the nineteenth-century zenith that he was experiencing. But even for him an undistorted "reality," though presumed to be knowable, was not simple.

Morgan was ready to describe social evolution in general as "a progressive connected series," but when it came to particulars the dynamics of change he adduced were many and various (1963:58). As long as he was talking about what he saw as the three great stages of human progress, savagery, barbarism, and civilization, Morgan's causal argument was essentially that, as material conditions change, other changes follow (271-2, 351). But when it came to institutions Morgan's thesis was quite different. Government, the family, language, religion, and property, were all said to have evolved out of "a few germs of thought" that were there from the beginning. And, he said, "the evolution of these germs of thought has been guided by a natural logic which formed an essential attribute of the brain itself" (59-60). He assumed that human intelligence impelled people consciously to seek better solutions to the technical and social problems of existence, hence bringing about change. But he also asserted that the propellants of institutional change were "unconscious reformatory movements to extricate society from existing evils" (53). In Morgan's argument one sees both the operation of conscious intelligence and of "unconscious reformatory movements," both the determination of societal forms by material conditions and the capacity of an aware human intelligence to reshape these conditions (351). Morgan seems not to have seen any tension between a vision of humankind consciously striving for control of its situation, and the quite different view of individuals as relatively powerless beings swept by great forces of culture and history. Yet today the reconciliation of these two perspectives presents serious analytic challenges.

Another instance of double vision that was not problematic for him was his conception of the relationship between structure and "practice," ideology and action, which he described in two quite different ways. In some parts of his work Morgan assumes that an absence of congruence between cultural ideas and social behavior is commonplace, that it always occurs in the course of change, and that change is unending. In other parts of his writing Morgan stresses a necessary coherence between social practice and cultural order, a systematic consistency. For example, in describing the evolution of kinship systems he assumes that the forms of the family change before kinship terminology does. It follows that there are periods when terminology does not reflect current organization, but rather past organization (1963:444, 450). He seems to be arguing that circumstances of change necessarily produce an absence of isomorphism between cultural categories and social relationships. Yet when he is explaining why his good friends the Iroquois had a confederacy that was committed to liberty, equality, and fraternity, and pledged to democracy writ large, he says that the reason was simple, these were the "cardinal principles" of the basic kin groups of which the tribe was composed. The cardinal principles therefore shaped the whole society. Morgan's idea here seems to have been that large political entities grew out of small ones, and that a superordinate organization necessarily replicated the values of its sub-parts. "As the unit, so the compound" (85). The picture is of total consistency produced from the ground up. But elsewhere, the argument goes in the opposite causal direction from the large scale to the small. The family "is the creature of the social system, and will reflect its culture . . . it must change as society changes, even as it has done in the past" (499).

Morgan's eclecticism about the dynamics is attractive even when his facts are wrong, and seems much more suited to an exploratory social science than to a dogmatic one. Much more variety of argument appears in Morgan's work than in what Engels made of it (1884). Morgan adduces general causes and particular causes at many different levels. In his account, change in some social forms could be analyzed in the framework of accretion (more and more property, bigger and bigger organizations); changes in others were to be addressed as the product of experiments in relation to which conscious choices were made of better and better customs and techniques (1963:434). His argument with its mentalist and moralist streak emphasized that change was generated by the germs of thought, the capacities of human intelligence, and reformatory movements. And it stressed a materialist theme when he talked about the growth of property as "an unmanageable power" with political and economic inequality a long-term consequence of its growth (351). As Sahlins has said, "The man may be submitted to many theoretical readings" (1976:57). Terray speaks of "the different ways of reading Morgan . . . the evolutionist reading, the structuralist reading, and the Marxist reading" (1972:89). The wealth of causes Morgan mentions, and only a few have been noted here, make many subsequent explanations look impoverished.

Inherent in Morgan's evolutionary project were many interrelated analytic puzzles. He sailed through all of them more confidently than can be done today. At least three questions which did not trouble him now give considerable unease. First is the problem of determination as against improvisation, invention, construction, and choice. How can the impact of intentions be acknowledged, while giving proper weight to the determined in thought and situation? Second is the problem of system. How are the systematic connections among social practices and between these and cultural ideas to be appraised without losing sight of inconsistencies, conflicts, and disconnections? If some arrangements, activities, and ideas are less tightly interrelated than others, how are integration and nonintegration to be addressed in the same model? And last, can general trajectories of historical sequence be constructed that can be reconciled with particular histories? As he addressed his illustrative examples Morgan dealt with these three questions of determination, system, and sequence incidentally and with more panache than consistency. Many of the theoretical bogs Morgan thus traversed without stopping now seem full of daunting obstacles.

Part of the trouble comes from a central paradox in anthropological method and theory. Anthropologists are methodologically committed to observing social life at first hand, on a small scale. But the discipline has been theoretically committed to inferring from those small-scale observations something on the large scale about the character of "society" and "culture."

A generation ago society was a system. Culture had a pattern. The postulation of a coherent whole discoverable bit by bit served to expand the significance of each observed particularity. Societies could be classified as types and compared. Everyone knew that in reality boundaries were not always clear, that mixed systems and "intermediate" types were commonplace, that transformation and transition were ubiquitous, and that conflict and contradiction were inherent in social life and human thought. However ethnographically real, and often faithfully described in the literature, these "irregularities" were a theoretical public nuisance. For many decades now the very shifting picture that was once thought least amenable to systematic theorizing has become the only interesting problem for analysis. This new focus creates methodological problems. If connected social fields are varied in composition and structure, and are changing over time, then how can the significance of localized, short-term fieldwork be magnified into a picture of a social/cultural totality? The musicians are visible but where is the symphony? What method will capture the essence of a transforming, variegated entity? The project now is to understand the constitution of heterogeneity and metamorphosis, open systems and their levels of integration, to assess if possible the direction and velocity of a process of change. The leap of interpretation is from situations observed to ongoing historical processes in which the observed events are seen as episodes. Anthropology is caught between its method and its ambitions.

When, at the foot of Mount Kilimanjaro, one meets a blanket-wearing, otherwise naked, spear-carrying Maasai man on a back path in the Tanzanian bush, one notices that he has a spool from a Kodak film packet in his earlobe as an earring plug. That earring alone is sufficient to indicate that he is not a total reproducer of an integrated ancestral culture. His film spindle is made of extruded plastic manufactured in Rochester, New York, his red blanket comes from Europe, his knife is made of Sheffield steel. Dangling from a thong around his neck is a small leather container full of Tanzanian paper money, the proceeds from selling his cattle in a government-regulated market. The price of his animals varies with world inflation. The roads nearby have buses and tourists. The international economy has penetrated everywhere. Ideas and information have moved with it. All peoples live within nations and have seen the silvery sides of planes flying over their lands. The definitions of social part and social whole have changed.

This means that anthropologists have had to reconsider both the consequences of method and the perspectives of theory. The anthropological project has been redefined by its subject matter. Not only is new work now undertaken in terms of new models, but older materials are being rethought. Long-term field research has come into its own (Foster et al. 1979). There has been an intensified interest in history (Lewis 1968). As Augé has remarked, and his comment is only part hyperbole, "Anthropologists have discovered that the societies they study have a history just when historians, along with Fernand Braudel, were discovering the structural dimension of [the] historical . . . longue durée" (1982:112).

Increasingly, detailed long-term history has been addressed by persons who initially set out to do fieldwork. But they approach history in a great variety of ways. Recent work by S. J Tambiah and M. G. Smith (1978) show the eclecticism of anthropologists in choosing the theoretical frameworks on which they found historical analyses. Tambiah says of his study of Buddhism and polity in Thailand that he "uncovered, in following the trajectory from contemporary Thailand to early Buddhism, a recurrence of structures and their transformations in systematic terms" (1976:5). Tambiah abstracted a political type from the Thai material: the galactic polity. In doing so, he produced a creative advance on a Weberian maneuver. By constituting the galactic polity as a general type and then tracing it through a series of transformations in the very historical instance from which the type was distilled, Tambiah avails himself of the condensed characterizing power of social typologizing, while escaping its atemporality. The social type is constructed on a foundation of durable Thai ideas and institutions. Tambiah argues that "the systematically accountable . . . produces a historical totality that is best understood not in disaggregation but in combination . . . the passage of a totality and its 'becoming' . . . over time" (5). M. G. Smith's fascinating and problematic study of sequence is entirely different, yet it too raises issues about the tension between model and instance. The model Smith constructs is not of a type, but at an absolute level of analytic generality. His framework is purely theoretical, designed for application to any society. It does not grow out of the particular instances to which he applies it. Smith is concerned to specify the formal attributes of all corporate groups. He then puts the diagnostic elements he has identified in a hierarchical/causal order. That is to say, he argues that in corporate groups certain constitutive elements are by definition logically preconditional to others. His temporal sequential hypothesis is that change in the preconditional elements will necessarily have systematic consequences for all subordinate conditions and that these must occur in a sequence related to the logical hierarchy. He then proposes to test this thesis in a historical instance, a Hausa state from 1800 to 1958. There is a question whether definitional frameworks of this kind are "testable" at all, whether there is not an inherent circularity in making an analysis of data in terms of a logically formal framework while also considering the same analysis to be a "test" of the framework. But Smith's contribution serves important purposes beyond the ultimate theoretical goals he sets himself. The logical model of corporations serves him as a guide to particular aspects of corporate polities in historical time. Tambiah and Smith's methods are unusual and original, but their interest in history is no longer so. Even in anthropological analyses in which the objective is more comparative than historical, historical themes are recurrent, as is clear, for example, in the work of Jack Goody (1971, 1976, 1982, 1983). Comparing metamorphic sequences may eventually become a dominant methodological form.

The first step is to establish detailed accounts of particular histories assembled from an anthropological perspective. Tambiah's and Smith's are among the most ambitious of recent efforts to do so. In their work the focus has been on polities from the top down, on continuities and transformations at the centers of power. Because the problematic of this book is that of inspecting a changing African "customary law" over the better part of a century, it concentrates on the opposite dimension, on the base of the political structure rather than the top. The base is where "customary law" endured. The situation on Kilimanjaro is one in which the indigenous polity was dismantled through colonial conquest and was ultimately replaced. Old subparts were repeatedly reassembled under new governments. In such circumstances the greatest organizational and cultural continuities are found not at the highest levels of government, but at the level of domestic organization, of kinship connections and of neighborhood and parish politics. This book follows the melting down and recasting of the political organization of a group of African chiefdoms to the point where they ceased to be such at all, and their people became a localized ethnic category in a culturally plural nation, preserving for quite new reasons certain elements of their old "customary" laws.

The conceptual shift to a time-oriented anthropology which this work represents dates not only from this decade. It dates at least from the 1940s. As postwar anthropology gradually gave up the model of a stable, integrated social/cultural system as its dominant paradigm (and it did not altogether relinquish it), the fragment that was fieldwork could no longer serve as the key instance of such a system. Instead, the most salient larger entity to which fieldwork findings could be attached became the trajectory of change itself. *Fieldwork has become a peculiar form of current history.*

Consequently social anthropology in the 1980s, though a long way from Lewis Henry Morgan, is in some respects closer to his interests than it was in the 1930s or 1940s. As Sahlins says, "The great challenge to an historical anthropology is not merely to know how events are ordered by culture, but how, in that process, the culture is reordered" (Sahlins 1981:8). "The historical process unfolds as a continuous and reciprocal movement between the practice of the structure and the structure of the practice" (72). The unresolved paradoxes in the thought of Marx, Freud, and Weber have become more salient features in theory than their visionary paradigms.

What implications does this general shift of subject matter and of attitude have for the fieldwork method and for the inferences that can be made from the evidence it garners? Surely in complex settings the "culture" or the "whole society" (however those are defined) cannot be constituted out of the small part that is observed. Information about the larger "background" must be obtained through methods other than field observation. Archives, government files, census reports, agronomists' surveys, missionary records, newspapers, interviews – all the tools of the historian and the journalist become pertinent to an understanding of local events in a time context (Schapera 1962; Smith 1962).

If the "process of change" is the matter inquired into, given that the period of field study is limited, can change be *seen* in fieldwork? Furthermore many changes do not originate where the anthropologist happens to be. Can fieldwork be done with a historical attitude even in places where there is no historical record? Because the social field being observed is recognized to have penetrable economic and social boundaries and limited autonomy, what is the analytic bridge between the visible scene and the larger background? Between the limited period of fieldwork and the longer historical era? As the recording of the total ethnography of a people becomes less and less a practicable objective, what kind of inquiry can cut across these several levels of time and place?

One old technique is to concentrate on a particular institutional domain (economy, politics, law, religion), and to try to understand its social logic (Augé 1982:107–8). But this old technique is now used under new constraints. For one thing these domains are self-consciously conceived as modern Western categories, not as universal ones. To be sure, institutions partially analogous in form or function to those in the West exist in other societies, but it is precisely to discover and understand the logic of *differences* that one looks in the first place, and differences there are. A second limiting assumption stems from an awareness that even from the

point of view of the West, where these analytic categories were generated, the domains of economy, politics, and the rest are understood to be
neither discrete nor autonomous. That being so, general causal arguments
founded on the universal primacy of one domain or another have become
less than illuminating. Even a structural Marxism that alludes respectfully
to the contention that *in the last instance* the economic is determinative
finds it necessary to assert that in history, "From the first moment to the
last, the lonely hour of the 'last instance' never comes" (Althusser
1970:113).

For many anthropologists, economy nevertheless serves as the central
connecting entity around which ethnographic data are organized over
space and time. In 1961 Leach insisted that "the student of social structure must never forget that the constraints of economics are prior to the
constraints of morality and law" (1961:9). The prevalence of this attitude
suggests that Sahlins is right in his argument that the dominant symbolic
idiom of discourse in our own society is the economic. He speaks of "the
cultural scheme" as "variously inflected by a dominant site of symbolic
production, which supplies the major idiom of other relations and activities" and for us, he contends, that site is the economic, which gives all
else meaning (1976: 206, 211). Impossible to prove and difficult to refute,
the underlying point is incontrovertible, that we come to the analysis of
the thought of others with our own cultural categories and conceptions in
mind even if we use them to heighten the perception of differences.
Sahlins dolefully puts it, "Having dissociated the cultural order into subsystems of different purpose – we are forced to live forever with the intellectual consequences" (205). But it is mistaken to assume that our set of
institutional categories state, market, church is therefore a serious obstacle to analysis. It is a truism that the state is not only the site of politics
and legislation, but purchaser, seller, employer, money lender, and
manufacturer of ideology, as well as a host of other things. Religious
institutions own property and directly enter the political arena as well as
propagating philosophical ideas and performing rituals. The institutional
"subsystems of different purpose" overlap, intersect, become one another
in different situations. The discrete definition of the subsystems in terms
of function has long been seen to be impossible and theoretically useless.
Such a division may have seemed clear to Malinowski, and seemed simple
in some textbooks, and perhaps in the administrative organization of
academe. It is (and always has been) less than clear in life. The element
of cultural arbitrariness and ethnocentrism in any such classification is no
longer a surprise. Given the overlapping nature of such categories, like
most other categories used in anthropology, the task of explaining the
logic of one major institutional domain then necessarily leads outward to
the others (see Needham 1975).

That being so, in my view there are three primary routes to social analysis that in combination commend themselves to the eclectic anthropologist today: the approaches via relationships, via resources, and via "representations." By definition, those dimensions are present in every institution, in every social field, in every social situation. The elements of the triad are always intertwined, but in variable and complex ways. They are not simple reflections of one another. An approach to data made in terms of all three dimensions opens the possibility of analyzing dynamic shifts in their patterns, content, and connections over time. Doing so in terms of specific settings and specified systemic tensions is the task of the day. Within that skeptical, time-oriented and tridimensional perspective, more easily described than accomplished, law is the category of affairs used as the point of departure for this book.[1]

In anthropology law is a topic that could be said to have floated down the same theoretical stream as the rest of the discipline. There are exceptions; but the general drift is the same. It had a nineteenth-century evolutionist for a grandfather in Sir Henry Maine (1861), and evolutionary approaches have enjoyed considerable durability since. Most of the few descriptive works that were produced in the first half of this century treated the law of particular peoples in much the same way that "customs" were treated in the ethnographies of the period, as an expanded list of rules, sometimes embellished with illustrative cases (Malinowski 1926; Schapera 1938). After 1945, legal anthropology gradually moved away from that kind of description. At first there was Hoebel's totalizing, structural-functional and culture–pattern-like comparative account of several whole legal systems which sought to identify the underlying "legal postulates" of each society (1954). Virtually at the same time others generated a very different approach – small-scale case studies of dispute hearings in action (Gluckman 1955:196; Bohannan 1957; Pospisil 1958).

At first such hearings were interpreted as largely normative and standardizing, of interest because they were expressive of "traditional" ideas. That these hearings were taking place under colonial conditions was noted, but that circumstance was not the central focus of discussion. The emphasis was on the customary content of the disputes themselves and the rules and concepts employed. The ingenuity with which indigenous ideas were applied was admired, the logic which they represented was aesthetically and intellectually appreciated. But later another stream of analysis displaced this one. Disputation came to be treated primarily as it involved strategic competition between individuals. Within this approach disputing was seen as an occasion for the testing of relative power, not for the most part as an occasion for the "application" of rules (Gulliver 1973). In anthropology concentration on the rule dimension weakened as individual strategy came to the fore. The questions of choice of argument,

choice of forum of hearing, and choice of occasion became major parts of
the analysis (Collier 1973; Nader 1965). The active individual with intentions became the object of study. The unfolding of a case over time
entered the models of disputing.

Several inconsistent tendencies can be seen in the subdiscipline today.
In one stream of development the scale of the subject matter has been
reduced. Interest in describing "whole" legal systems has faded as the
focus on particular cases and disputing has increased (Fallers 1969;
Nader and Todd 1978; Comaroff and Roberts 1981). In another direction the scale has increased and the subject matter has expanded. Plural
levels of law and plural legal systems have come to enjoy stage center in
a major postcolonial spate of works (Hooker 1975; Starr 1978; Burman
and Harrell-Bond 1979). An evolutionism of sorts also has come back
(Diamond 1971; Roberts 1979; Newman 1983). At the same time the
study of coherent cultural assumptions manifest in the judicial domain
continues a durable intellectual tradition (Rosen 1980–81; Geertz 1983).
Most recently of all, building on earlier work (Kuper and Kuper 1965;
Fallers 1969; Schapera 1970), some legal anthropologists have been
newly occupied with change and legal history (Benda-Beckman 1979;
Saltman 1979; Snyder 1981; Moser 1982).

This book, in keeping with that latest of developments, analyzes the
transformation of legal and political ideas and practices among the
Kichagga-speaking people of Kilimanjaro over the past hundred years.
To the extent that this book asks the question how the distinctive legal
aspects of the way of life of the Chagga people came to be the way they
are today, the story is an account of the transformation of a tradition. But
it is also the story of the making of a new polity and economy in which
"traditional" law has come to have a very different significance from what
it once had. What has been attempted, in a broad sense, is a *metamorphic
analysis* which includes both an account of alterations within the tradition
itself and a sketch of the overwhelming changes in its political / economic
context.

Clearly tradition is one of the elements most readily available for the
bricolage of the present. From this perspective current social/cultural
"systems" like souped-up automobiles are constructions made out of new
and used parts. This composite condition is acknowledged more at some
times than others. The British, with their policy of indirect rule, were
clearly not replacing all they found in existence in the colonies. By contrast, revolutionary regimes frequently claim they will erase the past. The
former rule actually changes more than it claims, the latter less. In the
present period of applied projects and planned change, of hubris about
designed societies, the place of "used parts" in particular historical sequences is more than academically instructive. Traditional ideas and tra-

ditional relationships frequently carry heavy emotional freight, and, as all ethnic revivals have made plain, may have substantial latent momentum which can be mobilized for modern political purposes. But the tradition of the modern ethnic group, and the tradition of its past, though they have a family resemblance, are not the same thing. The story of the Chagga of Kilimanjaro makes this plain.

The Chagga are a people who have experienced more than two decades of Tanzania's African socialism with its policy of detribalization and national homogenization.[2] Independence came to Tanzania in 1961. Today, Tanzania has standardized organizational charts of party structure designed to substitute for all that went before. Earlier, the Chagga had the experience of a long period of European colonial rule (German 1896–1916, British 1916–61). They have a Western-educated leadership, a strong involvement with Christianity, and a commitment to the Western-dominated world economy to which they sell their excellent *arabica* coffee. They have been abruptly reorganized by governments several times, and more gradually rearranged by innumerable incremental forms of change. They brought a rich indigenous African culture with them into this century of Western involvement. Elements of it came to be classified by their colonial rulers as "native customary law." Part of that body of ideas and institutions still shapes their present. But so does government legislation, demographic change, and the price of coffee.

Small-scale legal "events" in the rural neighborhoods of Kilimanjaro today bear the imprint of the complex, large-scale transformations. Yet the changing place of disputes between individuals in the larger scheme of things is not by any means always self-evident. Nor is the potentially transformative role of local allocations of individual property obvious. That the connections often do not appear on the surface is particularly so when participants discuss arrangements as if all that were involved were the dictates of custom and the strategies of personal advantage. Disputes and allocations have an immediate internal logic, but they also have an external logic that depends on conditions on the large scale over long periods of time. I agree with Abel that a village is not a suitable unit of analysis for the study of a legal system (1979:225). Hence though this book provides a description of Chagga cases of dispute and allocations of property and Chagga ideas about these matters, the presentation of data is combined with a broad, historically contextualized interpretation.

The present account is divided into three sections. The first describes the state of affairs on Kilimanjaro late in the nineteenth century; the second, the great changes of this century seen on the large scale; and the third gives a picture of contemporary rural life at close range through particular lives and relationships. Some conclusions follow. Within that broad outline a number of theoretical themes are explored, earlier interpretations are revised, and new data are presented. Part I reinterprets earlier ethnographic descriptions and travelers' reports to stress the early involvement of the Kilimanjaro economy in a system of regional and long-distance trade, punctuated by various forms of raiding and warfare. The second part sketches the vast economic and political transformations that came with cash cropping and colonial rule, and indicates the parallel changes in the formal legal system. "Customary law" is seen to become a limited but important residual category, using old forms in new situations. Since 1926, numerical information shows the changing types of cases that have come to the courts, and case summaries show the logic of official decisions. Part III shows what goes on outside the official system, and puts court case records in an entirely different light. The core of Part III consists of the "legal" chronicle of the members of a particular localized Chagga patrilineage. Their story serves as an illustration of the situation of localized lineages in general. It is a tale of competition for property and progeny, a tale of perjury, posturing, and violence. The chronicle of the lineage both describes the patrilineage as it is today, and as it remembers its past, giving land plot histories, details of its allocations of property, its internal disputes, and its use of the institutions of the formal legal system. Since the story of the lineage is roughly contemporaneous to the larger-scale history described earlier, these two streams of sequence are then brought together.

At the end of the book, a theoretical epilogue briefly sketches the way in which social process and change have been addressed in anthropology since 1945, and returns to some of the general issues raised in this introduction. The argument it puts forward is that the hybrid historical / ethnographic perspective is a methodological advance. It serves as a means of overcoming the inevitable sociological and temporal myopia of the fieldworker or the villager, while simultaneously exploiting the detailed information about behavior and ideas to which only fieldwork can give access. Throughout this book the analysis depends on an oscillation back and forth from small-scale events to large-scale processes to assess the impact of one on the other. A uniquely full record can be pieced together for the Chagga, permitting these kinds of questions to be raised. An eclectic use of processual perspectives makes it possible to attempt answers.

Part I

Precolonial economy, politics, and law

Figure 1.1. Map of Tanzania. *Source:* Aylward Shorter, *East African Societies* (London: Routledge & Kegan Paul, 1974), p. 133.

I

The nineteenth century on Kilimanjaro:

Ivory, slaves, cattle, and warfare

Kilimanjaro, home of the Chagga, has long been a good place to live.[1] For centuries the great hills and gorges of the mountain have sheltered its inhabitants from all but the most intrepid raiders coming up out of the plain. The steeper slopes are arduous to climb, but there are enough relatively level places to cultivate gardens, and the volcanic soil is rich. High above the cultivated area is a forest full of animals.

Comparatively safe and well fed in the leafy fastness of their beloved Kilimanjaro, the Chagga have always looked down on the flat, hot, arid land below from a position of geographical advantage. Their climate, their soil, their water have favored them. In most years they have a good rainfall. And water also comes from streams that flow from the high forest belt, some of it descending dramatically in rushing brooks over great boulders, dropping in waterfalls into roaring pools. Tamed water too quietly moves for miles in winding narrow irrigation channels the Chagga have dug for centuries to moisten their richly productive, well-manured banana groves.

As for the world beyond the dry plain that skirts the mountain, the paths that lead to the coast 317 kilometers away have long been known to the Chagga, as have routes to the interior. Contacts between Kilimanjaro and the "outside" probably existed for millennia.[2] But to early European visitors Kilimanjaro sometimes looked inaccessible. When missionary Johannes Rebmann, the first European to reach the mountain, tramped over the trails in 1848 during the rainy season, he complained that the biggest obstacle to establishing a mission was the state of the route (Krapf 1860:245). He had much trouble with the slippery mud and the daily torrents of rain which in some seasons can still impede movement on the many dirt roads. Not until more than a hundred years later was the major access road paved (Maro 1974:233). But even in 1848, in the dry season, the trading caravans with ease regularly traversed the routes from the coast and had done so for years (Krapf 1860:251, 260).

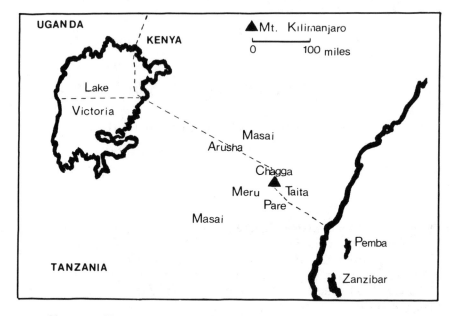

Figure 1.2. Chagga of Mount Kilimanjaro in relation to Lake Victoria and the coast. Some neighboring peoples are indicated.

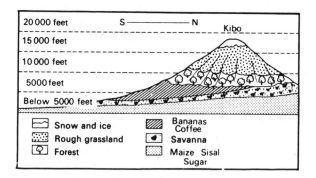

Figure 1.3. Altitude and ecology of Mount Kilimanjaro. Section from north to south.

In the mid-nineteenth century the Chagga were prosperous cattle keepers and horticulturalists. They were organized into at least two or three dozen autonomous chiefdoms. The chiefdoms were not large. More than fifty years later in the early 1900s the missionary Bruno Gutmann, chronicler of the Chagga, estimated that the population of Moshi chiefdom was 7,000 (Gutmann 1926:1; Human Relations Area Files [HRAF]:1).

Plate 1. Kibo peak of Kilimanjaro photographed from Kilema. (Photo by D. C. Moore)

According to Gutmann, there were approximately thirty-one separate chiefdoms of various sizes on Kilimanjaro in his time, having together a total population of slightly under 100,000 persons.[3] There is no way to know whether population had increased over the nineteenth century, or whether the numbers in 1900 were much as they had been in 1850.

But there are clues of substantial organizational continuity. Each chiefdom was composed of many named exogamous patrilineages, and of these one was the lineage from which chiefs came.[4] There were eighty intermarrying lineages in the Moshi chiefdom at the turn of this century. These lineages varied in size.[5] Many recognized a relationship with lineages of the same name in other chiefdoms. However, there does not seem to have been any formal organization of the lineage above the level of the chiefdom, and contact with distant branches was not necessarily maintained. The Chagga call their patrilineal kin groups *ukoo* or *kishari*. They use the same term for all levels, whether the descendants of one grandfather, a great-grandfather, or more distant lineal ancestors. Context indicates whether the allusion to "lineage" is to a narrow range of close kin, or to a wide span of more distant name relatives. In the literature in English and in the British colonial records what are called lineages here are often called "clans," but there is no difference of sense. Thus where "clan" appears in this book, in quotations or otherwise, it is not necessar-

Figure 1.4. Chiefdoms of Kilimanjaro as of 1946. Also three divisions: Hai, Vunjo, Rombo.

ily used in the technical anthropological sense to allude to a large, loosely connected category of kin having many extended and often untraceable kinship links. "Clan" is simply used here interchangeably with lineage or patriline at whatever level the context indicates.

Patrilines tended to be localized.[6] Member households occupied contiguous but separate, permanently cultivated plots of land, the boundaries of which were marked by living planted fences of dracaena.[7] What Rebmann observed in 1848 was still true in 1900. There were "no compact villages or town, but only isolated enclosures, separated from each other by open spaces extending about the eighth of a mile, and always covered with banana trees. Each yard is occupied by a single family, in several huts, protected by hedgerows of growing bushes, or of dried branches, which serve as a defence against wild beasts, more especially Hyenas" (Krapf 1860:244). The greater lineage territory included not only household plots, but sometimes also some uncultivated meadowland in it or adjoining it (Gutmann 1926:304; HRAF:272). Residence was virilocal; after marriage a woman moved from her natal lineage to live in the lineage territory of her husband. Each wife had her own hut and garden. Land was plentiful and productive.

Agnatically related kinsmen, settled in one locality, recognized common leaders. Their most senior male member led them in ritual matters and in other internal lineage affairs, and they were often represented externally by another, younger man, a "spokesman," a man gifted in oratory, with skills of leadership and judgment who was an able negotiator (Gutmann 1926:14; HRAF:11). Spokesmen dealt with the chief in tax and other matters on behalf of their agnates, and negotiated with other spokesmen when a lineage member was involved in a debt or dispute (1926:15; HRAF:12). There were also some Chagga lineages without spokesmen (1926:18; HRAF:15). The localized lineages were evidently the basic corporate units of local politics, often dealing collectively with the outside world.

Above the level of localized patrilineages, each chiefdom was divided into geographical districts (*mtaa*, sing.; *mitaa*, pl.; sometimes called parishes).[8] The *mitaa* were not merely territorial but administrative components of the chiefdom. District heads (*mchili*, sing., *wachili*, pl.) were appointed by and answerable to the chief, the *mangi*.[9] In addition to his subordinate district leaders, each chief also had a rudimentary personal staff. He had bodyguards around the clock. Service in the warrior-guard rotated among the districts (Gutmann 1926:497–8; HRAF:448). Also surrounding the chief were favored kinsmen who supervised corvée work and did other administrative tasks (1926:68; HRAF:57). He also had messengers ready to communicate his commands to the districts. It was the messenger's job to roam the hills blowing an antelope horn to call the fighting men together when an attack was impending, or to make announcements when corvée labor was needed or a meeting was called (1926:373–4, 503; HRAF:335–6, 453).[10] The chief is also said to have had a council of lineage heads he could consult or mobilize (Dundas 1924:287).

The nineteenth-century chiefdom was thus politically organized into three hierarchical levels, each progressively more inclusive: the level of the patrilineages, that of the districts, and that of the chiefdom as a whole. All were crosscut by an age-grade organization. The chief's power was founded in large part on the support of the men's age-sets. Indeed he is said to have depended on the warrior age-class for his office itself. Ideally the chiefship descended by inheritance to the first-born son of an incumbent, but if the new mangi proved to be unpopular with the warrior age-class, it could unseat him and install his next younger brother (Gutmann 1926:68; HRAF:56; on age-classes see Dundas 1924:209–11; Gutmann 1926:321; HRAF:288; Moore and Purritt 1977:29–30).

There was no paramount chief of all the Chagga, no centralized government that arched over the many small hegemonies. Some of the chiefdoms were more powerful than others, and dominated allied groups of lesser ones. The history of the area was a long sequence of small-scale wars. The many chiefdoms fought, settled their differences, and fought again.[11]

What were they fighting about? Part of the answer is quite clear. The Chagga did not spend the eighteenth and nineteenth centuries sitting under the trees waiting for the Europeans to arrive to give them their first contact with strangers. They were already deeply involved in trade exchanges with a world beyond Kilimanjaro. Coastal Africans had long preceded the Europeans. In 1848, when missionary Rebmann walked to the mountain from the coast with his umbrella and his Bible, he found a coastal Swahili resident in the entourage of a Chagga chief. The Swahili had already lived there for six years (Krapf 1860: 251). Kilimanjaro was a stopping place in the caravan trade from the coast.

In fact, when they saw missionary Rebmann, the Chagga asked him what he had come to trade. Rebmann replied through his guide that he had not come to trade anything, that all he had with him was his umbrella, that he had come to tell them the word of God that was written "in this Book" and he thumped his Bible. He promised them that all of the worldly goods they might desire and all the secrets of the universe would be theirs, if they but listened to his teachings. It puzzled him that the Chagga persisted in assuming that he must have come to trade (Krapf 1860: 239). It should not puzzle us.

The details of the history of the Chagga have been recounted heretofore as a long series of battles among the many chiefdoms for power and dominance on the mountain (Stahl 1964). In this connection nineteenth-century encounters with traders, missionaries, and travelers are treated in general as superficial instances of culture contact in which certain trivial material novelties and ideas were introduced: a few beads, some bolts of cloth, some wire for jewelry, and other bodily adornments, and now and again a steel knife or an occasional musket for good measure. These items are described as gifts to the chiefs which the chiefs often later redistributed to their favorites. But it is implied by omission that such prestige items left undisturbed all the basic forms of production and organization, that traditional Chagga patterns continued (Stahl 1964:45, 49). No particular attention has been given to the internal restructuring that might have been the consequence of trade and warfare. Not enough print has been expended on the question what the chiefs might have been fighting about, or wanting to have power over, as if expansion and conquest were a natural propensity of any political unit. Indifference to that question is not new. Warfare was once thought to be simply an irrational predilection of the Chagga. Writing in 1885 about his long stay on Kilimanjaro, Sir Harry Johnston asked, "Why, in the midst of such superb scenery, with smiling plenty on every hand could these silly savages think of nothing but mutual extermination?" (1886:177). To his eye the turmoil that was churning in East Africa was not appropriate to the lovely waterfalls and to the green and shadowy glens near his camp. But for us there is a simple answer to Sir Harry's rude question. Chagga chiefdoms were competing to control access to the long-distance trade and to the items valued in it. Once chiefdoms were organized for trading, raiding, and exacting tribute, the complex undoubtedly had a momentum that led to the events that Mrs. Stahl described so well, but did not explain (1964). Goody has put it concisely, "The impact of long distance trade on social organization . . . depends upon the degree to which productive activity is diverted to serve the purposes of external demands" (1971:24). For the Chagga one must add that the organization of manpower for destructive activity, defense, and control was another major consequence.

The interchiefdom wars were not disputes over land in its productive sense. In the nineteenth century there was no shortage of land. Each chiefdom had more land available than it could use productively, given the size of its human population. Labor was a scarce resource, not land. As far as one can tell, arable lands were never taken or occupied in these wars. Raiding was for other purposes, probably to achieve (or ward off) political dominance, tribute, and control over trade routes. But once a cycle of mutual raiding was started, vengeance may also have played a part in the fighting. There were also immediate ancillary gains. Raiding rewarded the attackers with cattle, human captives, iron, an occasional ivory tusk, and other valuables. All these were far more scarce than land. Trade and the political development associated with it, including warfare, had transformed the significance of cattle, iron, and people. From a time when these were elements figuring exclusively in the domestic productive sphere, and in local exchange, they became, in addition, major counters in the long-distance trade.

Instead of perceiving nineteenth-century Kilimanjaro as an isolate, as a divided society turned inward, a culture of exotic customs, feuding settlements, and inexplicably fierce and ambitious chiefs, Kilimanjaro can be better understood in terms of the larger political geography and history of East Africa. The significant trading region extended eastward to the Indian Ocean, and inland and north and south as far as Lakes Victoria and Tanganyika. Within this regional perspective Chagga trade can be conveniently sketched in terms of the articulation of three major geographical zones: (1) Kilimanjaro itself, that is, economic relations within and among the Chagga chiefdoms on the mountain slopes, (2) contacts between the mountain and the areas immediately surrounding it, and (3) relations between Kilimanjaro and the coast. Looking at nineteenth-century Chagga history broadly in terms of these three geographical/political zones makes much intelligible that otherwise might be hidden in a seemingly fortuitous jumble of individual chiefly careers.

Of these three zones of trade, the trade on the mountain itself is the basic

Plate 2. A marketplace in Old Moshi in 1902. (Photo from M. Merker, 1902)

Plate 3. The Mwika market in 1969. (Photo by D. C. Moore)

one into which the others feed. Travelers to Kilimanjaro saw markets there long before the colonial period. Each Chagga chiefdom had at least one marketplace and sometimes several. In 1861 C. C. von der Decken saw a market at which he estimated there were 500 women (1871:300). There must have been many others as large, run by women as they are today. These markets are now held every fourth day. The time of the market cycles of adjacent marketplaces are interlocked in such a way that every weekday there is some market held within walking distance of virtually every homestead. There is good reason to believe that the four-day cycle (without the present Sunday exception) is an old pattern.

Why, when each woman grew the same vegetable foods as any other, did anyone have anything desirable to barter? The answer is plain to anyone who has lived in the area and talked to the farmers. The ecology of Kilimanjaro is such that in the normal annual cycle at different altitudes and on different sides of the mountain, there are significant differences in the abundance and ripening times of cultivated plants. What is plentiful in one settlement at a particular date is barely available in another. In particular years there are sometimes aberrantly extreme local shortages or surpluses. There is today and was in earlier centuries good reason for interlocal trade on the basis of the normal differences in eco-zones of cultivation, let alone the occasional climatological peculiarities of particular years. In addition to these temporal and climatic variations in cultivated produce within the banana belt, there was also a marked difference between the products of the forest and those of the plain. It was desirable to have access to both. In the precolonial period this desire must have encouraged considerable exchange between settlements up and down the slopes of the mountain, encouraging "vertical" political alliances.

Another ecological consideration underlying some of the alliances between settlements higher up and settlements lower down was the system of irrigation. Localized lineages controlled most of the canals. The sources of water for the irrigation ditches were rivers and streams that had their origin in the forest, high above the settled area. Over the centuries the rivers have flowed swiftly down the slopes, cutting deep ravines. Consequently for irrigation purposes the Chagga have had to tap the streams at points much higher up on the mountain than the level of the high ridges on which their homesteads are situated. Starting from the forest streams they have dug long narrow channels through which the water is made to flow into gardens and fields (Meyer 1891:103). Secure water rights imply political understandings among settlements through whose territory, or near whose land, the water passes. Water thus constituted a major reason for alliances between chiefdoms above and below, and was a motive for amicable relations with chiefdoms on either side.

Peaceful arrangements about water control must have had the secondary consequence of ensuring conditions favorable to local trade.

Agreement on water rights bears on the process of political consolidation. Over the nineteenth century and through the first half of the twentieth, what had originally been many independent and small Chagga chiefdoms were gradually merged through precolonial conquest and alliance (and later through colonial administrative fiat) into larger and larger chiefdoms. The geographical patterning of this political aggregation shows a strong tendency for the chiefdoms to be formed "vertically," that is, up and down the slopes of the mountain.[12] "Horizontal" or "lateral" conquests and alliances also existed but the tendency toward vertical political formation was dominant. Ultimately, in British colonial times, this process culminated in the division of almost all of the mountain into broad, more or less vertical strips from the forest above to the plains below, each strip a separate colonial chiefdom. Thus early trade patterns and the political prerequisites of irrigation constituted the initial bases for the evolution of the "vertical" aspects of later local political geography. Verticality continues to have significance today.

But there were also horizontal links that crosscut vertical political units. Von der Decken reported much visiting between chiefdoms as well as much intertrading in the mountain markets when he was on Kilimanjaro in 1861. Like Rebmann twenty years earlier, he noted an active trade with the Masai and the Kahe on the southern plain, and also between Chagga and other peoples at the big market to the east at Taveta (Krapf 1860:245; Von der Decken 1871:271; to the same effect see Gutmann 1913:502). The existence of many active markets, locally linked together in the timing of their cycles, bespeak much contact and coordination among chiefdoms whatever their hostilities. Thus although the chiefdoms fought, the local trade went on, probably with interruptions, but resuming and steadily continuing over the long run.

Another evidence of interchiefdom complementarity was the placement of cattle in the custody of distant households. Cattle were important to the Chagga. Milk, blood, meat, and manure were of major significance in their domestic economy and their ritual life. Men accumulated as many beasts as they could. The care of cattle required least effort on the northeastern slopes of Kilimanjaro where cattle can graze. Such pasture land is much less available on the southeastern side. There customarily only one to three beasts could be kept by a household and these animals were stalled indoors. The women went down to the lower slopes every day or two to fetch huge headloads of grass which they carried up to their hungry animals to stall-feed them. This work is again a "vertical" economic interdependence.

In the nineteenth century, partly because of the large amount of labor

Plate 4. Women with headloads of grass to feed stalled cattle in 1902.

Plate 5. Women carrying headloads of cattle fodder in 1973. (Photo by D. C. Moore)

involved in stall-feeding, partly because it was useful to conceal assets, it was not unusual for a cattle-wealthy man to place one or several of his beasts in the custody of another family, either in his own or in another chiefdom. Cattle thus distributed in distant jurisdictions were not accessible to local chiefly levies of tribute, nor to the demands of relatives, nor was a man's whole herd endangered by a cattle raid. Nor, were the beasts, being scattered, as vulnerable to being destroyed by epidemic disease. But there were risks. The custodian might not return the animal. For such an eventuality there were legal remedies both practical and magical.[13]

This evidence on markets, on climate, on irrigation, and on animal husbandry taken together suggests that in the first trade zone, on the slopes of the mountain itself, the local variations in rainfall and temperature, the sources of water, the means of keeping cattle, and the exchange of products from forest and plain, all militated in the direction of inter-chiefdom trade and mutual political accommodation. As earlier remarks have made evident, the chiefdoms were at times politically autonomous competitors, sometimes bitter enemies, but clearly they were also often actively interlocked in significant economic interdependences vertical and horizontal.

The ecological links in the second zone of trade were no less binding than those on the first. Kilimanjaro was inextricably tied to the plain around it and to the nearby Pare mountains because Kilimanjaro has no iron, virtually no clay, and no salt. Gutmann alludes to only two places on the mountain itself where there were potters: Usseri to the extreme northeast, and Naruma and Nschara in Machame on the west. Outside of these sources, pots were obtained, as they still are, from Upare and from the plains district of Kahe (Gutmann 1909:169). Thus the mountain Chagga have long had to do business with peoples in the "lower areas" to obtain clay pots in which to cook and store food. They have also had to trade to acquire iron. They obtained unworked ingots which their own blacksmiths then fashioned into spears and hoes. They also traded to obtain *magaddi* or soda, which is the local salt substitute. Rebmann remarked on the trade in *magaddi* in 1848 (Krapf 1860:245). Archaeological evidence suggests that the trade in pots may be nearly two thousand years old (Odner 1971). The antiquity of the iron trade is less certain, but it is surely some hundreds of years old and may be much older than that. In the main, the iron came from the north Pare mountains, from Ugweno with which there are close linguistic connections (Kimambo 1969:32, 39–40, 138; Nurse 1979). But some may have come from the Kamba (Krapf 1860:358). Whether there ever was interchiefdom fighting purely over access to iron is not clear. By the time the historical record is incontrovertible, namely, in the nineteenth century, the many wars and alliances

Plate 6. Ironworking in East Africa in the 1860s. (From Carl Claus von der Decken's *Reisen in Ost-Africa,* 1871. Edited by Otto Kersten, Leipzig and Heidelberg, 281.)

between Chagga chiefdoms and Pare ones did not just concern iron; they were entangled with the traffic in ivory and slaves. But the importance of iron cannot be overemphasized; whether for tools to hew down the great trees that grow on the mountain, and to cut them into pieces and planks, whether for hoes and sickles, or to be forged into spearheads and knives, iron was essential to every household. It had another use as well. It served as a kind of currency, as it did elsewhere in East Africa (see Roberts 1970:52–53). The standard large units of exchange were cows, goats, and iron "hoes." A "hoe" may have consisted of enough unworked iron to make a hoe, rather than a finished article (see Willis 1974:79). Cloth and beads were the smaller units (Meyer 1891; Von Clemm 1963). A newly born calf was worth four goats. A goat was worth two iron hoes (Gutmann 1926:470; HRAF:422–3). Iron thus figures as a unit of exchange in commerce, and not only as a material for the manufacture of utilitarian objects. Willis has noted a similar use of iron currency by the nineteenth century in Fipa far to the west (1974:79).

Kilimanjaro's internal markets and its economic relations with the region immediately around the mountain were intertwined with a third zone of exchange: the trade with the coast. The nineteenth-century circumstances of the ivory trade, the slave trade, and the business of provisioning caravans together not only explain the probable causes of interchiefdom wars but also help elucidate the foundation and extent of Chagga chiefly power. Chagga chiefs had a monopoly on all major transactions with outsiders in the long-distance trade. All ivory taken in a chiefdom, or by its warriors, and all captives similarly acquired were the chief's to exchange. There is no clear indication that the Chagga ever held slaves. Male captives were exchanged (or "sold"?). Captive women were sometimes taken as wives and children were sometimes adopted.

Some of the ivory traded by the Chagga was obtained from elephants they hunted and trapped themselves, and it is evident that (at least in the second half of the nineteenth century) they also got tusks by purchasing them from other inland peoples (Stahl 1964:173). Ivory also might have been taken by force from passing caravans. That would have been dangerous and there is no clear evidence of Chagga piracy of this kind, but it may be worth a passing moment of speculation. When chiefs bought ivory, they paid for it largely in cattle. Whether they occasionally also used hoe blades for this purpose is not clear. A good tusk was worth forty head of cattle and forty goats. Given the exchange value of cattle, it was not only useful to raid and loot for captives, it was essential to raid for cattle. Cattle raiding was done systematically, and all the booty was turned over to the chief after the battle. One half of the beasts were the chief's share, the rest were redistributed to his warriors and favorites

(Gutmann 1926:538; HRAF:486). But the chief retained the right to re-claim beasts if he needed them.

Not nearly enough attention has been paid to the way in which the ivory and slave trades, the provisioning trade, and the raiding and trading in cattle were interlocked. There is a telling passage in the writings of missionary Krapf. He says, in 1849, that the Kamba, who traded ivory on the coast, would accept nothing other than livestock for their ivory (Krapf cited by Lamphear 1970:90, Christian Missionary Society Archives, 174:58 and 179:30). This observation has been interpreted as showing that the Kamba had such an oversupply of cloth, beads, wire, red ocher, and other ordinary coastal trade items that they did not want any more. That is possible. Clearly cloth, beads, and wire jewelry were not sumptuary items among the Chagga but in general circulation. In 1861–62 von der Decken saw 100 men and women dressed in cloth (1869:290). But it seems likely, at least in the interior, that cattle were always more valued than cloth and trinkets. Except for guns and gunpowder, none of the coastal trade items was a producer of wealth. Cattle were. Livestock multiplied. Livestock were a durable, expandable, movable form of wealth, with a high economic and symbolic value. The exigencies of war, and of the ivory trade, as well as the provisioning business, must have produced chronic shortages of cattle. There must have been frequent, sudden needs for large numbers of animals.

Chagga chiefs had to be able to demand cattle tribute from their sub-jects and allies in order to muster the herds necessary to buy tusks when there was an opportunity to do so or to pay ransom for captured relatives and subjects when necessary. They also needed to be able to demand cattle and other beasts to slaughter for the feasts that attended the arrival of important caravans, and to provision those caravans. Every patrroline-age, virtually every household, was vulnerable to the cattle demands of the chiefs. Hence a major item in the domestic economy of Chagga households was also a major item in the system of chiefly tribute and chiefly trade.

At the beginning of the nineteenth century, Orombo, a chief from the eastern side of the mountain, tried to conquer all the rest, and to put them in a tributary relationship. His career seems a clear reflection of the interlinkages between the internal and external trade and local political upheaval. He started by conquering the eastern side of the mountain and then turned his attention to the southwest. Orombo's cause was greatly enhanced by a strategic alliance he was able to make with a Chagga chiefdom some miles to the southwest of his own called Mamba. Mamba was a center of ironworking. As the spear-making center of the day it may well have served as his principal supplier of arms. There is in Upare a place called Mamba, and it is possible, since Upare was the source of much of Kilimanjaro's iron, that Mamba not only was important as the locale of blacksmithing, but also had control over much of the iron trade with Upare, as Kimambo asserts (1969:139). If that were so, it would explain why Kilimanjaro's Mamba was of political importance at the beginning of the nineteenth century and why its assistance to Orombo was crucial to his expansionist success. Mrs. Stahl says, "Orombo was the first of the empire builders on Kilimanjaro. At its zenith his empire stretched over half the inhabited area of the mountain." She argues that from the Kishingonyi hills eastward he united the lands of Rombo into a political entity, but that those lying westward of the hills, the lands of Vunjo, he used only "for purposes of exploitation," "draining them of cattle, manpower and every bit of metal" (1964:348). Using the term "empire" may be a little grand for the reality, but even if one considers the political unification to have been fairly shallow, it was remarkable that such a far-reaching military assault should have taken place at all, and that it should have had any durable effects. Why this attempt at conquest was made, and why it should have originated when and where it did, on the more pastoral side of the mountain, which is now the most economically backward, has always been an enigma. It ceases to be unintelligible if one looks at the circumstances of the ivory trade at the time. The Chagga did not carry tusks to the coast themselves, but rather traded with the Kamba, who in turn brought them to Mombasa. The northeastern side of Kilimanjaro is elephant country today and probably was a good source of ivory early in the nineteenth century. The Chagga were then "producers," the Kamba (and probably others) "middlemen" in the trade. Gray tells us that by the 1840s 70,000 pounds of ivory a year from Kilimanjaro and the Kamba was finding its way to Mombasa (1963:226). Lamphear says that "by at least as early as 1844" the Swahili residents of Mombasa were beginning to form their own trading caravans to go upcountry to Uchagga (1970:87). The trade must have been underway some decades earlier, coinciding with Orombo's expansion.

When a Chagga chief traded with outsiders, he gave his men shares of the cloth, beads, wire, and other goods he had received. Thus the chief *and* his men had a strong interest in enlarging the area of his monopoly, in making neighboring chiefdoms subservient to his own, so that they would have to supply him with any tusks they obtained. Such conquests simultaneously enlarged the sources of ivory, reduced the competition, and sometimes even supplied the chief with captives to be sold as slaves or ransomed as hostages. Capturing hostages for ransom was profitable. The ransom for one chief's wife and son are said to have been 40 head of cattle and 2 tusks (Gutmann 1926:542; HRAF:489). Interchiefdom wergeld for a chief, his brother, and his wife, his land and his cattle, was said to have been 500 head of cattle, 500 goats, and 1,000 hoe blades

(1926:436; HRAF:392). Whether or not the figures are accurate, the sense is clear. If Orombo was trading ivory with the Kamba, he had good reason to expand the area he controlled.

The hypothesis that the Kamba trade in ivory had a close relation to Orombo's briefly held dominance over the mountain is supported by what is known of the timing of Orombo's fall and the breakup of his consolidated domain. Orombo's so-called empire collapsed at just about the same time that a major shift of power occurred on the coast. In 1837 Mazrui power in Mombasa came to an end. From the 1840s on, Zanzibar to the south, not Mombasa, came to dominate the coastal trade. Instead of trading through African middlemen, many more Swahili came directly to Kilimanjaro in ever larger numbers, generally approaching from the southeast. It follows that the importance to the ivory trade of the Rombo side of the mountain, the northeastern side, declined dramatically. It is also possible that marauding Maasai made the country between the coast and the Rombo area especially difficult for caravans to traverse in this period (Lamphear 1970:88). After Orombo's fall, the ascendance of the southern chiefdoms and their dominance of the Kilimanjaro caravan trade was assured, and not challenged again. But the southern chiefdoms fought bitterly among themselves to get an ever larger share.

Not only was selling ivory, and some slaves, profitable, but so was the provisioning of caravans. Caravans making the long walk from the coast, with many dozens of porters, needed a safe place to rest and an opportunity to restock their food supply. The provisioning of caravans may have been as important in shaping the political economy of the Chagga as the direct trade in ivory (and the ancillary slave trade). In the second half of the century caravans of hundreds of men came to the southern slopes of the mountain all year around (Von der Decken 1869–71:272). Camp grounds were provided to accommodate them. For example, in the 1880s, Bishop James Hannington and 100 porters trudged seventeen days from the coast to Moshi (Hannington 1885:606–13). Hans Meyer had sixty-five porters for the trip in 1889 (1891:94). The supplies needed for such parties must have been considerable, and those mentioned here were not unusual in size. The Chagga were stocking caravans with food and beasts for the journey inland to Lake Victoria or points south, or refilling their supplies for the return journey to the coast. It must have been a big business and must have required a marked increase in Chagga food production.

Increases in food production seem to have been managed in two ways, through the chief's powers over collective labor, and by individual households. The chief normally feasted his visitors with beer and meat. If he did not want to expend his own herds, he could obtain the beasts through levies of tribute. Grain for much of the beer came from the chief's extensive eleusine fields. These were worked and irrigated by corvée labor. In addition to chiefly transactions with caravan leaders in ivory, cattle, and produce, there was a considerable petty trade between the women of ordinary households and the ordinary bearers. These women flocked to the grounds where many dozens of caravan porters camped and there conducted their own exchanges directly with the coastal visitors (Meyer 1891:108, 116). Thus some of the increased production of vegetable foods necessary for provisioning the caravan trade was undertaken by individual households, some by chiefly control of corvée labor.

The Chagga were fortunately situated with respect to increasing the production of vegetable food. They could grow more bananas with a minimum increase in effort. Had the staple crop required more labor, the Chagga might not have been able to move into the provisioning business nearly so easily as they seem to have done. It is clear that some of the provisioning trade consisted of an expansion of domestic production and an extension to new customers of the very kinds of trading the women were already engaged in in their own local markets. Hence, when coffee came in, in the twentieth century, and was planted household by household, it was hardly the first Chagga produce grown for the market.

Even though it was relatively easy to increase the production of bananas, it was difficult to increase the production of animals. A cow cannot be made to calve more often than once a year. Once the female animals are kept for breeding and only the males slaughtered, there is not much more that can be done to obtain more animals except to take them from someone else. Cattle raiding was thus as important an adjunct of the caravan-provisioning business as it was of the trade in ivory.

If a chiefdom raids others, it must expect to defend itself against counter-raids. Defenses were built by corvée labor. Long ditches were dug. Earthworks and wooden fences were constructed. Underground chambers large enough to hold cattle and people in hiding from raiders were excavated. Guards were posted at chiefdom borders. These techniques existed in 1848 and probably were in use earlier (Krapf 1860:243).

To afford traders and porters safe passage to and from the chiefdoms, and protection against attack when camped inside, a chief had to have an efficient military organization that could be summoned in a moment. He had to know that when the war horn was blown the age-grade of warriors would come running and whooping and waving its spears. The chiefs had to protect their customers. Even beyond their borders, they had to defend the routes to and from the chiefdoms, and sometimes provide escorts for the purpose.

Charles New vividly describes an anticipated attack and the measures taken against it when he was in Old Moshi in the 1870s:

Plate 7. Chagga warrior with colobus monkey fur on helmet and ostrich-feather cape. (Photo from M. Merker, 1902)

Plate 8. Two Chagga warriors. Each age-set had its own shield design. (Photo from M. Merker, 1902)

Plate 9. Two Chagga maidens before their circumcision. (Photo from M. Merker, 1902)

Presently the hills rang with the alarm of war. The Mangi [chief] happened at the time to be sitting before the tent. He puts his hand to his ear, and listened for a few seconds with great attention. Instantly his countenance changed into downright ferocity. I could as yet hear nothing. Again the Mangi listened, and grew more ferocious in aspect. Now he leaped from the ground like a tiger, gathered a piece of cloth about his waist, roared out at the top of his stentorian voice the war cry, and rushed off towards his palace, presently making his appearance with a plume of feathers upon his head . . . armed with bow and arrows, leaping and shouting like a man demented, and away he hurried to the front. By this time all was commotion, the whole country rang with the shouts of the men and the shrieks of the women; and the hills echoed and re-echoed the sounds. Presently all the paths along the mountain sides were streaming with men accoutred for war and armed to the teeth. Some carried bows and arrows, many bore the Masai spear and shield, but a large number were provided with muskets; while clubs, short swords, daggers, knives, hatchets, billhooks, flourished everywhere. The din, uproar, and excitement were tremendous . . . for five minutes he scanned the plain with his eagle eye, without uttering a word, and then said, "It's all right." Now we observed two parties below, one foes, and the other coming toward us. The latter proved to be a company of Wasuahili traders; the former were a band of Masai. The Wasuahili told us upon their arrival that the Masai were coming to attack Moche but for having met with them. "As it was," said they, "some of our men were seized, and would have been killed, only we ransomed them; and then, as we were coming in here, we paid them to go another way," so this accidental rencontre prevented what might have been a dreadful fray. . . . The incident gave me some idea of Mandara's strength. The chief said he could at any time muster at Moche some 700 spears, and from what I saw of the numbers that turned out upon this occasion, I should say he has certainly not exaggerated his force. (New 1874:388–91)

Eventually, more guns exacerbated the military competition. By 1885, the Chagga had many British Snider rifles that had been traded for ivory (Johnston 1886:252). They had had some guns much earlier. Von der Decken gave a pistol to his host-chief in Kilema in 1861 and commented that, of all his gifts to the Chagga chief, this was the only one that interested him (1871:275). In 1885 the Chagga were asking Bishop Hannington for guns (1885:611). These military activities had their economic aspects and their political consequences. Whether one looks at what seems to have been stepped-up raiding over the course of the nineteenth century, elaborated systems of defense, increased food production, more and more competition over the trade, and the development of an effective system for obtaining tribute labor and tribute cattle, all point in the direction of highly developed local chiefly power. When Rebmann arrived in 1848, chiefly authority was notable and ranking clear (Krapf 1860). Fifty years later it can only have been more entrenched. The long-distance trade was central to all of this development. It was not just an exchange of trinkets for produce with an occasional lethal gadget thrown in. The chiefs were not naive fellows easily gulled by having bright beads dangled before them by wily outsiders. There were high stakes involved of which they were fully aware.

The relative safety of Europeans once they arrived on Kilimanjaro is an indication of the importance of the continuing contact to the Chagga. Since the Chagga greatly outnumbered their Swahili or European visitors, they could easily have killed the traders and appropriated their goods. Who would be the wiser? Why were most of the strangers allowed to come and go in peace, exchanging some of their goods with one chief and some with the next? The answer is that the security of these outsiders lay in the value of the trade. In 1862 Von der Decken said to the Chagga in essence, "If you are friendly, all will be well with you. But if you show yourself to be an enemy, not only will I kill many of your men with my guns, but everywhere on the coast it will be said that in the future all caravans should avoid your chiefdom" (1871:293). According to Von der Decken that argument was persuasive. The trade was not only useful to the outsiders, it was obviously considered vital by the Chagga themselves.[14]

Given this background, the internal politics and economy of the Chagga must have been deeply reshaped by participation in the ivory trade, in the slave trade, and in the provisioning of caravans. The trade was no superficial swapping of luxuries for luxuries, of tusks for wire and trinkets, carried on by chiefs alone for their own benefit. The external trade was not discrete from the domestic economy, nor was it segregated from local politics. All agricultural production must have been increased. When the natural increase of beasts did not keep pace with the demand, cattle raiding was surely stepped up. The physical security of every household must have been intermittently threatened by the raiding. The need for military power and corvée labor for defense works and food production required a considerable degree of centralization and organization. Chiefly office and all that surrounded it must have been transformed by the role of the chief as monopolist of the major trade, as principal assembler and redistributor of wealth, as user of corvée labor, and as commander of the warrior age-grade. It was raid or be raided, conquer or be conquered once ivory, human beings, and cattle had become important items of exchange in impersonal transactions. Every Chagga household must have been involved, directly or indirectly.

It is not surprising that in the nineteenth century the "silly savages could think of nothing but mutual extermination" despite the beautiful scenery. Nor is it surprising that, when the colonial government put an end to the slave trade and the interchiefdom wars, when the ivory trade was transformed, and the caravans stopped coming through, the Chagga were ready for some other way to enter external markets. Coffee provided them with an opportunity to do so and they seized it.

2

Practical norms and mystical ideas in Chagga law

GUTMANN'S RECONSTRUCTION AND POSNER'S THEORIES

What is known of precolonial and early colonial Chagga law is largely found in the books and articles of the Lutheran missionary Dr. Bruno Gutmann, who was posted on Kilimanjaro most of the time from 1902 to 1920 (Gutmann 1926).[1] Gutmann's is a marvelously colorful and voluminous record, especially full of the ethnography of the chiefdom of Old Moshi. He was generally sympathetic to the Chagga, and frequently not to the German administration. But his view of the Chagga is deeply colored by his conception of social and moral evolution, and the way in which he thought some earlier, purer version of Chagga society was breaking down. In keeping with the style of the day, a great deal of what Gutmann wrote about Chagga "custom" and "law" is stated in terms of normative rules. This approach raises problems of interpretation.

How rule-bound were the Chagga? There is a widespread assumption outside of anthropology that preindustrial peoples are somehow more rigid about their oral rules than postindustrial ones are about their written laws. That is simply not so. Among peoples such as the Chagga, the flexibility of many supposedly rule-governed arrangements was and is a basic fact of life even as it is among ourselves. In all legal systems there is a tension between standardization through rules of general application and the negotiability and discretionary arrangement of specific affairs. Further, many rules that are stated as if they were universally "applied" are in practice selectively used. Choices about these matters exist in some form in all societies. This plasticity is no less present in a system of oral customary law than in written law. Certainly some rules are much more frequently followed than others, but in the absence of statistical data comparing rules with practices, there is no reason to be literal about rule statements. They must not be read as invariable practices in any society, nor as representing the way the system "works." Richard Posner has

38

argued that highly exact rules are more prevalent in simple societies than in sophisticated ones because such exactness operates to maximize social efficiency under primitive conditions. It is an ingenious argument.

The . . . source of law . . . that dominates primitive law is custom. It is custom that prescribes the compensation due for killing a man, the formalities for making a contract, the rules of inheritance, the obligations of kinship, the limitations on whom one may marry, and so forth. Custom (including customary law) resembles language in being a complicated, slowly changing and decentralized system of *highly exact rules*. (Posner 1980:31; italics added)

The notion that customary law consists of highly exact rules is part of Posner's economic argument that "many of the distinctive institutions of primitive society . . . can be explained as direct or indirect adaptations to the high costs of information" (1980:4). His general premise (about all legal systems) is that law is fundamentally an instrument for maximizing social wealth or efficiency. He argues that, whereas modern societies can afford broad legal standards which judges particularize through precedent, in primitive societies in the absence of judges, precedents, and writing, exact rules perform these functions. He has a second economic rationale for primitive exactitude, namely, that under archaic conditions exact rules serve as a means of avoiding the high costs of negotiation.

Unfortunately for his argument, both Posner's conception of the way "highly exact rules" operate in "primitive" societies and the idea that negotiation is avoided are not well supported by the facts.[2] Negotiation is commonplace in such societies. But it is easy to see how such a misunderstanding might arise. There is no doubt that rule statements which sound exact are often made by the peoples anthropologists study. When Gutmann reports rules, as he does by the dozen, he was surely not misrepresenting what his Chagga informants told him. Old ethnographies are full of legal rules stated as practices. For example Gutmann tells us that among the Chagga the wergild for the homicide of a man was seven steer and seven goats (1926:243; HRAF:216). But despite that apparently exact statement, anthropological knowledge of the way such matters work in practice suggests that matters were much more indefinite. What is meant by a steer? Were castrated male animals the only acceptable payment? Or was whatever Chagga term was used simply generic for cattle? Were cows ever used in payment? Could substitutions be made? And the age and sex of the goats? And what about the timing of payment – all at once, some immediately after the death, some later? Some perhaps never? What might lead to adjustment in the amount or kind of payment? And what happened if payment were delayed? Might a creditor choose to accept a few goats now rather than a calf later on? Negotiations were always necessary to answer these questions despite seemingly "exact" rules. The same kind of variability is often inherent in systems of bridewealth payment. The rules are "exact" but actual instances do not necessarily conform. Institutionalized forms of negotiation are standard adjuncts of these types of rules, demonstrating their inexactitude in practice.

Fixity of rule statement is frequently found coupled with flexibility of practice. For example, among the Chagga there were (and are) culturally standardized forms of "contract." A Chagga who places a she goat in the household of another to be fed and looked after knows the standardized terms that govern such "lendings" and "borrowings": for example, that the rule is that every third kid belongs to the borrower, that the lender receives the other two. But both lender and borrower also know that if they both agree they can modify the standard terms to suit themselves. For instance, if the lender consents, the borrower can keep an extra kid and can make a special payment or do agricultural work in return for being allowed to do so.

This adjustable relationship of standardized rules to practice is also seen among the Chagga in inheritance and *inter vivos* property allocations. There are stated rules about who should inherit the deceased man's undistributed property or be guardian of his widow and children. But the actual allocation is handled by a body of kin who have considerable discretion in whether or not to follow the "standard" conventions, the wishes of the decedent, or their own conceptions of an appropriate division.

There is an additional dimension. "Fixed" transactions can be modified after the fact. Today many allocations of property, or mutual arrangements of exchange among the Chagga, are subsequently challenged or renegotiated as the micropolitics of local alignment or other conditions change, even though, when made, they seem to have been intended to be firm and permanent (and in many cases were made under "exact" rules). This perpetually reopenable nature of what seem initially to be rulebound allocations (or transactions or decisions) is not a new characteristic of Chagga affairs. There is evidence in Gutmann of just such negotiability early in the century. It is consistent with what is known of small-group politics elsewhere, and the effect of such politics on the interpretation and manipulation of rule systems in general.

Thus at least three technical questions should be in the mind of anyone reading rule statements in old ethnographic materials like Gutmann's: (1) Is the significance of the rule as stated really exact and clear for all cases? (2) Was there in practice a social body (or individual) that could legitimately exercise discretion or make adjustments in the rules? (3) Did interested parties themselves have the capacity to negotiate (and over time renegotiate) the stated standardized terms for the type of transaction or other arrangement between or among them, or were they rule-bound.

Rules are most comprehensible as actually used in the process of social life. Outside of that matrix, stated abstractly, their practical significance is much more difficult to decipher. Instances, cases, and contexts are essential. Thus it is extremely important to know not only that a cow *could* be transferred from A to B under conditions X but how *often* such transactions took place in the society at a particular period, what alternatives there were and how important any particular course of action was in the economy, in politics, and in the strategies of individual interaction. A raw recitation of rule statements cannot reveal these matters. Without a fuller account of the lived-in context, knowledge of which is available for the present but not for the past, the "rules of law" are a kind of sociological fragment, remnants of a living society, not unlike the material remnants, the broken pieces of pottery and ruins of walls from which archaeologists try to reconstruct civilizations. That sociological fragment in a rich and fascinating form is what Gutmann has left us.

By the time Gutmann arrived on Kilimanjaro, German colonial government had been in place for sixteen years. In many chiefdoms, including Old Moshi, some of the aspects of the traditional life in which Gutmann was most interested had gone out of existence. Well aware of ongoing changes, Gutmann used the accounts of elderly informants to reconstruct the past, and was an acute and critical observer of what went on in his own time.

For the past twenty years native law has been undergoing a complete revolution. The European judicial authority (a district official with a knowledge of the Roman Law, a secretary, or a constable) has the final decision in the lawsuits of the natives. The lower court is represented by the chief who combines the functions of magistrate, preliminary examiner, justice of the peace, and expert. In addition, there are interpreters who translate the native idiom into Swahili for the benefit of the European masters.

An obvious flaw in this judiciary system is the fact that the lower and the higher courts stand in a political relationship to each other, and this political relationship is the basic one.[3] (Gutmann 1926:20–21; HRAF:18)

Gutmann goes on to say that he thought things were better in earlier times when Chagga disputes were heard by a judiciary assembly of men convened either by the district leader (*mchili*) or by the chief (*mangi*) (Gutmann 1926:590ff.; HRAF: 529ff.). He describes precolonial procedures and what seemed to him the accessibility of justice in the indigenous system. No formal fees were paid for a hearing on the district Lawn of Justice before the *mchili* and local men, though they expected some demonstration of gratitude in the form of beer. But on the chief's Lawn of Justice the plaintiff had to bring a beast to open the proceedings and the defendant had to produce one of equal value. If the defendant had no beast, he might ask to borrow one from the chief, offering a daughter as a pawn in exchange.

The role of the chief in these hearings was merely to pronounce the decision of the assembly of age-sets after it had been communicated to him. The chief might choose to intervene in the matter of the amount and kind of compensation, or the number of beasts to be provided for the feasting of the judiciary assembly, but he did not make the decision itself. Indeed, in precolonial times chiefs were not always present during the assembly discussion. Later, in German times, they did preside.

A feature of indigenous procedure about which Gutmann was particularly enthusiastic was that of representation. In precolonial days both parties to a dispute heard before the chief's judiciary assembly were represented by spokesmen. The chief also appointed a third "speaker" as a kind of chairman for the palaver. Both spokesmen-representatives and the chairman were paid fees. The payment often consisted of metal wire rings (or, in the western districts, a goat). The whole assembly was also provided with beer. Mobilizing men for a public hearing was clearly a costly affair for the parties, particularly so on the chief's Lawn of Justice. Both the district judiciary assembly and the chief's assembly continued in Gutmann's time but their character had been deeply altered. Gutmann felt that the colonial chief did not properly represent his subjects in the European court, and wanted to reinstitute a modified form of the earlier system of representation, which he considered an integral part of the indigenous "social organism."[4]

Gutmann's discussion of Chagga legal procedures and the practical organization of persons and property on Kilimanjaro is threaded with detailed descriptions of Chagga rituals and beliefs in which, as a missionary, he had a special interest. These are highly relevant to the legal system, and are as important to an understanding of the way it worked as any descriptions of cases.

Law is connected with ideas about order, about causality, and about responsibility (O'Connor 1981). In the Chagga philosophical system, like that of many other African peoples, the visible universe, including the apparently fortuitous, accidental, and random, gave evidence of the parallel and intertwined existence of an invisible and mysterious causal order. Embedded in Gutmann's mechanical but detailed descriptions of Chagga incantations and ritual manipulations, including those of "legal" rituals, are the symbolic categories of Chagga explanation. This material, combined with insights gleaned from fieldwork, reveals the outlines of their ideas of cosmic order. The ritual elements of Chagga law, and Chagga ideas about culpable harm done through mystical means were an essential part of the symbolic representation of authority, competition, and conflict.

THE MYSTICAL DIMENSION IN THE DEFINITION OF WRONGS AND IN LEGAL PROCEDURES

Chagga wrongdoers could be made accountable in many ways, not only by being called for trial-like palavers before assemblages of peers (in the lineage, in the district, or on the chief's Lawn of Justice) but also by being ritually cursed. During rituals of malediction misfortune could be legitimately and publicly wished on a wrongdoer where other strategies to make him (or her) acknowledge a debt or a wrong were impractical or unavailing. Cursing instruments for this purpose included cursing pots, iron cursing bells, and cursing stones. The theory was that a person under a curse would have to come forward to beg that the threat of misfortune be removed. Another ritual could remove the curse. Negotiations would ensue.

The symbolic significance of Chagga instruments of malediction, the words said over them and the substances used, are a manifestation of broad philosophical conceptions of cosmic order and causality. Clay, iron, and stone cannot be destroyed by fire. Pots, bells, and stones were elements in an elaborate symbolic classification of the concrete and the cosmic. They were not just mechanical magical gadgets, standing by themselves.

In Chagga ideology sexual difference was a fundamental principle of order in the universe, or a key metaphor for that order. Since the combination of the sexes generates new life, the powers of life and death were mysteriously inherent in sexual contact and sexual disorder or anomaly. Sexual organs were an important element of the design of the cursing pots and stones, and the bells were metaphorically equipped with sexual allusions.[5]

Cursing instruments used for "legal" purposes afford a glimpse of the link between the enchanted world and the practical one. The cursing stones could be used as a property-protecting device. Placed on a stick in a field, the stone guarded it, ready to bring misfortune to thieves, a part of a supernatural system of enforcement that was supposed to function where other means were not available (Gutmann 1926:659–61; HRAF: 593–4). The cursing pot could also be used to protect property, to force the return of "loaned" cattle that were being withheld. A serious problem confronted the lender of Chagga cattle placed on loan in chiefdoms other than his own if the borrower refused to return the beasts, or said an animal had died when it had not, or did not surrender a calf. The legal dilemma was one of jurisdiction. No forum in any chiefdom had jurisdiction over the citizens of another chiefdom. Only if such persons presented

themselves voluntarily, could disputes concerning them be heard. "Foreigners" appearing as plaintiffs were likely to be at a disadvantage. The
political implications of using self-help usually precluded taking forceful
action. To mount a private raid against another chiefdom was dangerous.
Recourse had to be had to some other measure. There was the cursing pot.

"You have not returned my head of cattle which you withhold from me by force.
Now I am sending the destroyer so that he may play with you. . . . " "I am
sending you the destroyer which is going to torture all your bones. May he
penetrate your bones and twist your joints so that you become a cripple of stunted
growth. And if they ask: 'What is this?' they will also answer you: 'This is that
destroyer which circulates in you and causes you to perish.' " "Should you remain
deaf and despise the law, the destroyer shall extinguish everything in your homestead." (Gutmann 1926:624–5; HRAF:559–61)

This radically abridged poem of hate (there are pages and pages of it) is
the kind of thing Gutmann reports a Chagga would say in the marketplace
as he swung the cursing pot. The market was a place of safety, an asylum.
No blood could be shed there. The curser was in no danger. The market
was also a place where women of many chiefdoms congregated. They could
be counted on to take the news home. "You woman from Sia, the neighboring district, I ask you to carry the report to him, to his homestead," said
the curser sending a message to his victim (1926:622; HRAF:558). The
cursing was announced in advance and repeated on a series of market days
in a highly public manner. Sometimes the pot was swung in secrecy at
night, but doing so was a kind of sorcery and not legitimate, unlike the
daytime, marketplace cursing (1926:652–3; HRAF: 587).

"Swinging the pot" was thus a means of forcing a party outside the
jurisdiction of one's own chief to come forward in a cattle case. It was
also a way of putting pressure on an unknown thief or a known wrongdoer in other kinds of cases. The same device could also be used to settle
a legal wager, for which purpose it was ritually activated to turn against
either accuser or accused, depending on which was telling the truth.
Gutmann says the cursing pot was effective. The moment anything went
wrong in the household of the victim, the moment one of his children or
his animals fell ill, the moment that he or one of his household stumbled
on a root or a stone, he was sure to think of the Destroyer, the power of
the cursing pot that had been awakened against him. He would begin to
worry about what worse thing might happen next, and about the cost of
giving in. Ideally the victim would eventually present himself to the curser
and ask to have the curse removed, indicating his willingness to finance
the ceremony with a sacrificial sheep and beer, as well as returning the
cow and her calves (1926:642; HRAF:577).

The cursing pots were said to be in steady demand and could be loaned by their owners (Gutmann 1926:631; HRAF:566). Many lineages were said to own cursing pots. But cursing bells belonged exclusively to the lineages of smiths whose magical powers were much feared (Dundas 1924:272). According to Gutmann, the cursing pots were more frequently used. (Gutmann, 1926:663: HRAF:596). Jealous of their powers, the chiefs are said to have tried to confiscate the cursing pots of rival lineages. Some were given up. But others were kept by individual owners. In theory the pots could not be legitimately employed without permission of the chief (1926:621; HRAF:557). Since the cursing pots represented a rival form of enforcement, chiefs tried to limit or control their use.

The transmutability of issues from the material order to the spiritual order and back was (and for many today still is) an everyday aspect of Chagga life and thought. Bourdieu argues that in precapitalist societies the enchanted world is a medium for the misrecognition of economic relations, a form of false consciousness that can disguise from the actors what is really going on in the material world (1977:171–2). He contends that it prevents them from recognizing the economy as an economy, or from seeing advantage as such. But the idea of the enchantment of the world can also have exactly the opposite effect, to exaggerate the social reality rather than mask it.

Ideas of sorcery and witchcraft and mystical manipulations operate to putatively expand the powers of others. In Chagga relations of conflict and hierarchy, the belief in the mystical domain exaggerates the capacities of individuals rather than masking them. The effectiveness of authority and the malevolence of competitors and opponents are aggrandized when mystical powers are added to mundane ones. Ascribing to others the invisible capacity to cause personal misfortune transforms social relations which objectively only involve elements of *social coercion* into relations potentially involving *physical attack*. The mystical cause is imaginary, but the violations are really experienced. Since no one can escape illness or death or some misfortune, mystically caused violence is potentially experienced by everyone. The only "legal" question is which particular individual caused which particular disaster.

In a Chagga dispute the ante could be raised, the domain of disputation changed, and this-worldly issues complicated when hostilities over material matters or questions of worldly power were translated into the realm of actual or suspected mystical harm. Misfortune and mortal danger could easily be invoked with spoken words or manipulations of magical objects or substances. Anyone who had cause to be angry not only might use such measures, but was considered likely to. Not only the living but the dead could be angry, so causality was by no means only of this world. In a dispute the domain of discourse could easily be shifted back and forth from this-worldly concerns about payments of goods or beasts to other-worldly concerns about the doing of mystical harm. Indeed, this translation from one realm to the other could even be used as a strategy in disputation. One of Gutmann's cases retold here gives the sense of this switching of levels, and one way it was done.[6] The case describes the causing of a death with words, not as often reported in the literature after the fact, after some misfortune has taken place, but before the fact. It also shows the overriding patrilineal right of a father to his child, even to kill her.

The man who put the death curse on his own child

A widow who lived in the chiefdom of Uru with her only son took into her household a young girl from a district where there was a famine. The young girl proved to be a costly companion / servant / guest. Though uncircumcised, she went to the market, and urinated there. Her action constituted a defilement for which the widow had to pay a goat of expiation to the market women. The widow also had to finance the girl's circumcision which cost her another goat. Then the girl became pregnant from having intercourse with the widow's son, and the widow had to pay a goat to the elders to perform the rites for this "wedding of disgrace."

After the marriage, the young couple continued to live with the widow, and she continued to finance their ritual expenses. After the birth of the first grandchild, the widow provided the sheep for the ritual of the newly born. The child died. The young girl had another child. The widow again furnished an animal, the fifth. Later the child became seriously ill, and the widow supplied a sixth animal for a sacrifice to restore her to health. Soon the daughter-in-law was pregnant again, and asked her mother-in-law to suckle the first surviving child. The widow reactivated her breasts and gave suck to the child.

Bad feelings subsequently developed between the daughter-in-law and mother-in-law. The son decided to set up a separate household for his wife. However, they left the grandchild with the grandmother. Taking the grandchild with her, the old widow then left Uru and the patrilineal territory of her deceased husband (and son) and went to live with her half-brother in Moshi in the territory of her natal patrilineage. After a year, the son appeared and asked for the return of the little girl since she was then old enough to look after younger siblings. (In the Chagga version of patrilineality Chagga children belong wholly to their fathers, though they may be loaned to grandmothers and others.) The grandmother refused to give up the child unless the son repaid her the six animals that she had furnished. Most of these were expenses that should have been borne by the deceased husband's patrilineage. The son was furious and cursed the child, "May it die shortly." Gutmann explains that if the son had not cursed the child he would have been at a legal disadvantage in trying to recover custody. A mediator would have told him to give up the child and would have told the grandmother in return to give up her claim to the beasts. But because of his cursing the child, the balance of advantage moved to the son. The old woman would have had to hurry up and negotiate while the child was still healthy, because if she did not, and the child died, she would become liable for the wergeld of seven cattle for having delayed, and the chief would so declare when the case was brought to him. (Gutmann 1926:689–91; HRAF:619–21)

It is not clear from Gutmann's account what the outcome actually was, or whether he was discussing a hypothetical outcome. It sounds as if the grandmother did delay and the child did die, and the dispute actually came to the chief as a suit between a son and his mother over whether the son owed the mother six small stock or the mother owed the son seven cattle, or both. But what is worthy of notice about the death curse is that it was not in itself a culpable act. The father was apparently justified in using this extreme measure in the circumstances to try to force his mother to come to terms with him. The case also involves residents of two different chiefdoms, Uru and Moshi, and hence it was suitable for the plaintiff-son from Uru to bring it before the chief of Moshi.

The conceptual intertwining of mystical and material realms was an integral part of the operation of ordinary life and of legal affairs. In such a world ordeals and oaths and conditional curses make sense. The Chagga used all three. Indeed rituals of various kinds were essential to legally effective actions and proceedings. Rituals served as markers of legal affirmation (rather the way we use signatures and oaths of office), as markers of legal status (the way we use coming of age), and figured both in processes of detection and of prevention of wrongdoing.

Ritual symbols of legal affirmation, for example, included the ceremonial transfers of bridewealth from the groom's people to the bride's people which made first marriages legally binding (Gutmann 1926:84ff.; HRAF:7off.). Other ceremonies confirmed the inheritance of widows (1926:53–4; HRAF:43). The transfer of a developed banana grove to a nonkinsman involved the pouring of libations of milk and beer, and the handing over of a banana shoot by the potential heir to mark before witnesses his relinquishment of rights (1926:305; HRAF:274). Perhaps most dramatic of all was the ceremony of collective dissociation by which a lineage assembled with the chief to expel a member. This purpose was accomplished by throwing away a yellow fruit (nduo) on which each lineage brother had spat to indicate his corroboration. The lineage thereby rid itself of any further collective liability for the acts of the expelled member. When the lineage's legal trustee made the first gesture toward throwing the fruit, it was the chief's role to intervene and ask whether the expulsion were irrevocable. If it were not, a discussion of conditions ensued. If it were irrevocable, the legal trustee of the lineage proceeded and threw the fruit (1926:20; HRAF:17).

Such ritual markers have multiple significances, but surely two of their essential functions are: (1) to indicate unambiguous *intention* to witnesses and interested parties, and (2) to mark in an unmistakable way a specific moment after which legal relationships are different from what they were before. Legal rituals in Chagga society and certain formalities in our own are dramatizations of the moment of changed legal relationships. The very extraordinariness and nonmundaneness of the acts that are used to mark such moments is part of their efficacy. It is much harder to argue later on that such an act was accidental or incidental, and was not intended to carry the conventional legal meaning. In a nonliterate culture legal rituals of this kind serve to inform many witnesses simultaneously in a manner difficult to forget that a change in rights has taken place. These are performative acts and statements.

Life crisis rituals also can serve as markers of changed legal status. Thus, for example, the circumcision of a Chagga girl was a ritual that changed her property rights. It marked the end of the period of her life during which her father was entitled to the products of her agricultural labor. After circumcision, her produce was her own (Gutmann 1926:64; HRAF:52). After the circumcision of a Chagga male, he was eligible to be called up for corvée labor, and his father could withdraw from this obligation of the household, substituting his son (1926:379; HRAF:340).

Rituals were also used as processes of detection, to discover guilt or innocence. When a man was seriously ill he, or his brothers, might consult a diviner to discover which kinsman had caused his illness. The diviner might hint that a particular brother who would profit from his sibling's death was probably responsible. The lineage then looking for confirmation or disconfirmation might then assemble to sacrifice a goat. Its intestines would be inspected for a particular sign of the man's guilt or innocence (Gutmann 1926:679–80; HRAF:611). In a more public test, ordeals were sometimes used in the presence of the chief. An accused person might walk across ritually treated ashes, or pull a stone out of a pot of hot water, or drink an herbal decoction to show his innocence or guilt. Before the accused underwent the ordeal, he and his accuser might make a legal wager before the chief indicating how many beasts would be paid by the loser. The ordeal was said to have been frequently requested by the accused as a way of demonstrating his innocence (1926:670ff.; HRAF:602ff.).

The legal wager could be used as a means of detecting the truth. Thus if two men claimed the same cow, they could resolve their dispute by agreeing to the terms of a wager that would test which claim was rightful. The cow's ear was nicked so that both claimants could partake of the beast's blood. If the cow's calf lived it belonged to X. If it died, it belonged to Y and X would have to pay an extra beast (Gutmann 1926:615; HRAF:551). Even more grim in its test, the "cursing pot" could be used in a legal wager of death. The accused person could take a small stick, or a bit of his own clothing, spit on it (thus endowing the stick with an element of his identity) and offer it to his accuser, challenging him to swing the cursing pot for him. If the accuser accepted, a formal wager was made in the presence of the chief. The stick or piece of cloth was put in the pot, and the pot was ritually activated for a specific period related to the beginning of the next agricultural cycle. If death came to persons or animals of either household (either that of the accused or the accuser) during the period specified, the death was an indication of culpability. If deaths occurred on both sides, the adversaries split the costs (1926:651ff.; HRAF:586ff.). The outcome was pronounced on the chief's Lawn of Justice.

Conditional curses could also be used to prevent trouble, and as a test of bona fides. So, for example, a conditional curse could be put on new settlers to make sure that they would not harm the community into which they were moving. A man resettling might actually be an agent from another chiefdom or district sent to kill the leaders of the host community. A woman marrying into a lineage might be spying on behalf of her male relatives. In either case rituals could be performed pronouncing conditional maledictions on the newcomer should he or she intend to betray the trust of the hosts. To be willing to undergo such a ritual was testimony of good faith (Gutmann 1926:682–3; HRAF:614).

Much has changed on Kilimanjaro in this century, and most but not all of these ideas have vanished. The mystical dimension of the social order was far more universal, far more public and more directly attached to the political system in Gutmann's time than it is now, and must have been even more so before the colonial period. Then, political leaders and contenders in dispute could legitimately and publicly deploy this-worldly and otherworldly forces to help reach their objectives, and it was assumed that they would do so. In the precolonial period all relationships between individuals and all organizations had otherworldly significance. Today, the patrilineage and the church still have these meanings, but most other organizations, governmental and economic, are energetically secular. However, competitive personal relationships between individuals, especially among kinsmen and between affines, still remain heavily charged with the possibility of mystical harm. To this day, concerns about sorcery often permeate this-worldly legal disputes between such intimates. Given the insistently secular nature of the public agencies of dispute resolution today, only an intimate knowledge of the affairs of a lineage or of individual lives can bring these nuances to the surface.

In close contact attitudes emerge about the mystical doing of harm today that with great clarity echo the past. An old woman in a Catholic area dies suddenly at night, on her way to the latrine pit. Her neighbor remarks that such a sudden death is a terrible thing. The old woman never had an opportunity to make a deathbed confession. "Who knows how many people she may have killed?" One would be tempted to think that this was a Chagga version of a Catholic attitude toward confession if one did not hear the same kinds of statements in Protestant areas in a form more like that found in Gutmann. According to Gutmann, before a family head died, he was supposed to take care to tell his heir (either his brother or son) about all the disputes in which he had been involved in his lifetime and the secret measures he had used to gain advantage. Occasionally in the interest of the well-being of his descendants the dying man would allocate a beast to repair the damage he had thus done to relations between his lineage and another. But most importantly he was under a special obligation to disclose whether he had killed anyone in order that his son and other kin could be warned never to intermarry with the lineage of the victim, lest the harm be returned and visited on some later generation (1926:718; HRAF:640–1). One can hear the same said in the rural areas today.

To observe local rural Chagga affairs now (or to inspect the "legal rules" Gutmann reports) without understanding this doing of mystical harm as a dimension of life would be to misunderstand many intimate relationships and disputes. It is often possible to report the same relationships entirely in terms of rational this-worldly economic or micropolitical rivalry, since such matters are often at stake. One might then suppose that the supernatural realm of harm-doing is just a simple representation of the competitions and coercions of this world. It is a representation, but it is not a simple one. The two worlds, material and mystical, are not completely synchronized in time. A drought strikes. A goat dies. A crop is eaten by parasites. A child falls out of a tree and is injured. A woman aborts. A man falls ill and dies. These events have an accidental and random timing as far as the events in the social world of economic and political competition and control are concerned. They are not absolutely synchronous with moments of intense disputation and competition, nor does disaster necessarily follow immediately when curses are spoken or other harm-doing measures are taken. The Chagga take this into account, and say that the effects often emerge only years later. There are thus two quite different time spans for material and mystical causality. The one is immediate, visible, and of clear effect. The other is invisible and of uncertain timing and effect.

Anthropological explanations of witchcraft accusations have often been so focused on making them rational in Western terms that some of the livelier goings-on that pervade a complex and subtle system of harm-doing like that of the Chagga are lost to view. Witchcraft with its echoes of Salem and of Joan of Arc and of religious persecution in Europe is probably a misleading term to use. Like totemism, witchcraft is a term applied to a great variety of social phenomena, the particulars of which deserve differentiation. Franz Boas's strictures on lumping apply. Even "sorcery" seems too much laden with memories of the Brothers Grimm. Harm-doing or harm-threatening through mystical means are awkward but culturally more neutral descriptions, and give more sense of the quasi-legitimacy of some of these measures.

In Chagga life today many misfortunes are attributed to such mystical harm-doing. But this retrospective attribution of causality with its hindsight socio-logic is not the only occasion of talk about mystical harm in Chagga life. People actually buy substances and say magical words to send harm as well as to protect themselves from it. The doing of mystical harm is not just a matter of retrospective supposition trotted out to explain misfortune. At coffee harvest time, when the money rolls in, the pastors preach from the pulpits that the peasants should not waste their money on such things. The church designates itself a better protection and a more just harm-doer. It asserts that God punishes only wrongdoing, not the just. These days the legitimate way to curse a rival or opponent is to say threateningly, "I leave it to God," or "You will see."[7]

Thus Chagga customary law in precolonial times was a complex system of political institutions, of semiautonomous, organized social domains that controlled persons and resources, and of a system of ideas that ranged from the most materialistic sorts of cost accounting in cattle to the most mystical notions of the causes of misfortune.

3

The powers and obligations of chiefs and commoners

INTRODUCTION

Much has been made of the political egalitarianism supposedly found in the small-scale societies of another era, and of the attractions of social order founded on consensus and reciprocity. The evidence from the Chagga obviously will not close debate on the nature of small-scale society. It is a single case. Moreover, as has been amply demonstrated, Chagga society was not a pristine instance. The chiefdoms were not untouched by peoples and events beyond their border. But the Chagga material organized here around power and obligations should help to erode what seem to be irrepressible idealizations.

To understand inequality in Chagga society, both the culturally formalized and the informally operative deserve note. Although formal "constitutional" equality existed between persons of the same age and sex, and all exogamous patrilines had formal equivalence, the operational reality for individuals was otherwise. Politically and legally elaborated inequalities existed between chief and subject, senior and junior, male and female, cattle lender and cattle client, and adult and child. Inequalities of an informal nonlegal but recognized nature existed between the cattle rich and the cattle poor, between the chief's cronies and subjects without influence, and between members of powerful lineages and members of weaker lineages, within the same patrilines and between them.

But beyond these, a much more fundamental asymmetry was inherent in the relationship between an individual and the essential groups to which the person belonged. To the extent that (all or) a substantial part of a group could be mobilized against an individual member who could not muster adequate countersupport, that member was subject to powerful controls. These ranged from psychological pressures to life-threatening actions. The deployment of force was neither unknown nor unused. The importance of common understandings and reciprocity must

52

not obscure the place of extreme measures in small-scale societies. Expulsion and violence cast their frightening shadow as remote but real possibilities in the background of mundane life. The weak might have recourse to mystical harm-doing in retaliation. But even in that domain the powerful were thought to have better resources of protection and aggression.

The political situation of Chagga individuals, whether chiefs or commoners, always involved the implied capacity for group (or action-set) mobilization. Equality/inequality in Chagga life is not comprehensible simply in terms of a system of stated rules about the relative legal position of individuals or the formal equivalence of exogamous patrilines, or the relationship of age-grades. The asymmetry of the group/individual perspective must be added. That dimension not only supplies a subtext for Gutmann's text, the whole picture adds a gloss on Dumont's discussion of hierarchy, equality, and the place of the individual. There are many more forms of symmetry and asymmetry in social relations than Dumont takes account of in his dichotomous schematization (1980).

One of the striking hallmarks of difference between certain small-scale and certain large-scale societies is in the prevalent type of asymmetrical relation between group and individual. When a group transacts with an individual *member* that relationship should be distinguished morphologically and dynamically from the instance in which a group transacts with an individual as *outsider*. The processes through which power and control are mediated often find their expression in these group/individual asymmetries. In modern Western industrial society there are vast numbers of asymmetrical transactions in which individuals deal with organizations of which they are not members, transactions in which the individual has relatively little bargaining power. In Chagga society in the late nineteenth century those transactional asymmetries were more often found between individuals and organizations of which they *were* members. In a "constitutional" sense organizations of which Chagga individuals were not members had no directly effective authority over them. Aggrieved individuals seem to have appealed to the age-grade assembly or the chief, but groups as collectivities seem not to have done so. Asymmetrical transactions of the type group versus individual seem to have been essentially a matter of the internal affairs of a Chagga group. That difference (between modern Western and nineteenth-century Chagga asymmetrical transactions) in organizational frame has continuing significance on Kilimanjaro today. Comparative analysis of this dimension of the processes of control exposes continuities in the webs of political action that are otherwise unrecognized. They are of pressing theoretical importance because they characterize fundamental systemic differences.

POWERS OF CHIEFS
The Organizational Context

The late nineteenth-century Chagga chiefdom was a closed constitutional framework which only permitted the formation of particular kinds of groups. These stood in a prescribed relation to one another. The organization of Moshi chiefdom has already been sketched. Many (most?) of its households were aggregated into small geographically localized exogamous patrilineages, and groups of these in turn constituted the subdivisions of local administrative districts (*mitaa* or parishes). Male age-classes, subdivided into age-sets, and also in a practical sense locally divided by district, formed a crosscutting structure. Apart from special-purpose groups consisting of the users of a particular irrigation canal, the simple framework of patrilineages, districts, male age-classes, and the encompassing chiefdom itself was the sum total of the formal group structure.

The basic principles of structural transformation of these groups were accretion and fission. When independent chiefdoms were conquered they often were annexed as districts of the victorious chiefdom (Gutmann 1926:431–2; HRAF:388; see also Stahl 1964). Later they sometimes seceded and regained autonomy or attached themselves to another dominant chiefdom. Parts of lineages could split off and become separate, new lineages (Gutmann 1926:5; HRAF:5). New lineages also could be founded by individuals. But in the late nineteenth century the *types* of groups that were permitted to exist were the few already mentioned, and the general principles that defined their boundaries and memberships and activities were clear. Strangers, settling locally, who were not qualified as members on the basis of birth could be attached to local units as individuals in a kind of auxiliary status, and/or could found new patrilineages.

Although there were certain "rich" individuals (men much wealthier in cattle than others because of the special patronage of the chief) these *masumba* did not form a corporate group of any kind, and merely constituted a favored category of individuals within the conventional group framework. Nor did cattle patrons and cattle clients form groups as such. Women, though divided into age-classes for corvée purposes, seem not to have been formally organized as such, nor were their markets the nucleus of any corporate group of women.

The framework surrounding the arenas of competition, collective and individual, was defined by the conventional group structure, as were the parameters of intergroup conflict. Crosscutting the boundaries of the formal structure and affecting the internal configuration of corporate groups were connections established by marriage, geographical contiguity, alliance, friendship, patron-client relationship, personal network, and the like. But the group structure was the system as officially conceived.

Offices were embedded in the formal groups. The chiefdom, the lineages, the age-sets, and the districts had their leadership positions, and some had subleaders or assistants. In multilineage chiefdoms such as Moshi, the chiefly office descended through one family branch of one of the patrilineages. Members of the chiefly lineage were sometimes in a favored position because of their greater access to the chief. But the members of the *mangi's* lineage did not constitute an aristocracy, and were not an *officially* privileged category. Internally, the chiefly patrilineage was segmented and structurally formed like the others (Gutmann 1926:68; HRAF:56).

District heads (*wachili,* pl.; *mchili,* sing.) were customarily members of patrilineages resident in the districts they administered. Appointed by the chief, they served as corvée supervisors, tax collectors, and war leaders of their respective areas. Fighting units for war, and collective labor parties for corvée work were organized by age-class and district (Gutmann 1926:310, 321, 538; HRAF:278, 288, 486).

As for councils, the age-class assemblies of the districts, which could all be summoned together to the chief's Lawn, were the principal broad-based political bodies which could be mobilized and consulted on matters ranging from extraordinary tax levies to the settlement of dispute (Gutmann 1926:381, 589; HRAF:342, 529). (No doubt all members did not come to these meetings, and it is difficult now to know what numbers actually appeared.) The chief also consulted with lineage representatives, both lineage spokesmen and lineage heads, but whether these constituted a formal council is not clear (Dundas 1924:211, 287; Gutmann 1926:13, 14; HRAF:11, 12). The chief, together with his advisers, his administrative subordinates in the districts, and his military arm, the warrior age-set, could mobilize more strength then any single lineage. But this capacity was used for a limited set of purposes. Chagga chiefdoms can be thought of as made up of many distinct, semiautonomous social domains contained within a superordinate organization of limited functions, headed by a chief.

The official allocation of all major productive and political resources and their management took place through the workings of this structure of groups and offices. Control over women was allocated through the same channels. Operationally, of course, the personal characteristics and networks of individuals greatly affected actual events within and between groups and the relative prestige and prosperity of individuals and households. But the official structure shaped the arena of their activities.

For the most part, to the extent that arrangements were negotiated, compliance to norms exacted or enforced, or disputes were settled, the official groups were the framework within which those ends were achieved. All the high offices and all the major groups were multipurpose entities functioning in the economy, in political affairs, and had ritual and religious significance. To a great extent the "living law" was the order that they made.

Chiefly power over persons: the control of force and violence

Chiefs had the power to torture and kill and used it. But they must have used it rarely and judiciously or they would have hardly remained in office long. Charles New, who visited Rindi in 1871, says that, while he sat in Rindi's tent,

a party came accusing someone of theft. Soldiers were despatched [sic] instantly to look for the thief, who was soon found. His guilt was proved, but he stoutly denied it. He was then bound, and most unmercifully beaten till he pleaded guilty and offered to restore the stolen goods. To torture him further, a stout rope was put round his temples and twisted tight with sticks, till the vein burst in his head and the blood ran from his nose and mouth. He was so severely handled that when he was led past my camp he could scarcely crawl. In the end he was taken to the frontier of Kirua. . . . . His property would be confiscated. (1874:416)

Certainly one cannot be sure how much New understood of the situation that led to this attack, but that Rindi could order it carried out, and that he used his young warriors to do the job, seems highly credible. The chief who divided his war spoils with his warriors was well served by them. Their existence gave him power over others.

Gutmann refers to torture of precisely the kind New described as one way chiefs forced men to disclose how many head of cattle they had and where they were kept. In some cases the chiefs used torture to oblige a person to pay compensation that otherwise would fall the lot of their patrilineages to pay. In other cases they used it merely to extort cattle for themselves (1926:688; HRAF:619). Chiefs sometimes approved of killings by their subjects. An instance is described in which a man tried to take advantage of the chief's greed for cattle. Expelled by his lineage he wanted vengeance so he went to the chief and informed him of the numbers and locations of his erstwhile kinsmen's cattle. (The chief could then more easily "tax" or confiscate some of these concealed beasts.) The lineage brothers were understandably angry. The informer found temporary asylum in the chief's household. But no sooner did the informer fall ill under the chief's roof, then the chief turned him over to his vengeful brothers. They seem to have killed him the next day presumably with the chief's tacit knowledge and approval (1926:237; HRAF:210).

In some circumstances a lineage might be justified in getting rid of one of its own members. A lineage member who killed or injured people not only put himself under obligation to compensate with bloodwealth the kin of those he had damaged, but also made his lineage mates liable should he not be able to pay. The contingent collective liability of a lineage for the debts of lineage members probably encouraged the Chagga to expel a brother whose killings and assaults were inconveniently expensive (Gutmann 1926:19, 247; HRAF:16, 17, 220). In some cases, rather than being expelled such a person could be killed off with the complicity of the chief.[1]

Under what other circumstances could persons other than the chief legitimately kill? Blood vengeance between lineages may have existed in the nineteenth century. Where a homicide occurred *between* lineages, the victim's kin were under pressure to avenge the death with a reciprocal killing. The decedent's spirit could trouble living kin if they did not take action. Such spirits were dangerous. They clung to fences and hedges and did not go away the way the decently dead did. But an explicit Chagga norm favored the acceptance of compensation over retaliation, "The slayer is not to be slain" (Gutmann 1926:244, 245; HRAF:217, 218). The ghost might be propitiated by the sacrifice of a beast of the bloodwealth payment. Gutmann tells us that "blood revenge was almost completely eliminated" (1926:240; HRAF:213). But he also goes on to say in an ambiguous passage, which may refer to the Chagga but possibly is a piece of Gutmann's general evolutionary speculation, "Both forms – the blood revenge and the wergild compensation were used" (Dundas 1924:292, 293; Gutmann 1926:240; HRAF:214). Gutmann says that the choice depended not only on the nature of the homicide, but also on the history of relations between the two lineages, their relative sizes, and other contingent factors (1926:241; HRAF:214). Dundas says it depended on which region of Kilimanjaro was involved and on the local development of chiefship (1924:292-3).[2]

Chagga bloodwealth for ordinary people was said to be seven head of cattle and seven goats for a slain male, eight head of cattle and eight goats for a woman (Gutmann 1926:243; HRAF:216). But bloodwealth could be much higher for a chief and his family or in war compensation between chiefdoms (1926:435; HRAF:391, 392).

In an ordinary interlineage homicide the chief's hut was a place of asylum to which a killer could flee. If he reached that place of safety, the chief then sought out the decedent's kin to arrange the bloodwealth settlement. After compensation for a homicide was paid and matters were settled, the chief presided over a ceremony of blood brotherhood in which the two enemy lineages exchanged blood and mutually pledged an end to hostilities. The chief received a fee in animals for his intervention (a cow and a sheep or goat) (Gutmann 1926:243; HRAF:216). For a killer without kinsmen, the chief himself could choose to pay the bloodwealth fee, and the man whose blood debt was thus paid became a dependent (slave?) of the chief (1926:243; HRAF:217).[3]

There were several types of homicide that did not involve liability for bloodwealth. A homicide in which the victim had committed sorcery or treason was not a culpable homicide (Gutmann 1926:246; HRAF:219, 220), nor was a punitive killing by a chief of a disobedient subject (1926:249; HRAF:222). But the last was not necessarily without political consequences for the chief. The chief endangered himself if he seriously offended a powerful lineage. And he and his kin were in supernatural danger if the killing were wrongful and the dying victim cursed him (1926:352; HRAF:318).

In aggregate, the series of normative rules relating to blood vengeance, bloodwealth, and violence put forward by Gutmann, together with the illustrations he gives, leaves the strong impression that in matters of homicide, much depended on the social situation surrounding the individual case. Was the chief disposed in favor of the killers or the killed? What was the social prominence and political strength of the lineages involved, and so on? How precarious was the chief's own political situation?[4]

The chief had the power to use force to produce compliance with his orders, and with other rules, provided he took care to discover whether he had enough political support to take action. Despite this political nuance, the successful Chagga chiefs in the second half of the nineteenth century should not be thought of as occupying a powerless office, as merely being leaders in a company of equals as some have suggested. To order men into battle is to have the right to ask them to kill others and to lay down their lives. When raids produced booty, the chief shared some of it with the warriors. But Gutmann makes it plain that the chief took half the cattle, and the warriors divided the remaining half among them (1926:538; HRAF:486). That arrangement does not show equality even if some elements of egalitarian ideology sustained the system (Iliffe 1979:59). Nor were raids and wars just momentary excursions for the chance at booty. War could and did also result in the "pacification," subjugation, or annexation of enemy chiefdoms. During the second half of the nineteenth century a number of chiefdoms enlarged themselves in this manner and came to dominate others. Is one to believe that a force usable against outsiders was never deployed at home? Chiefs must have used both the military and the economic power they had from external warfare to control some internal matters.

But their positions were not completely secure. Thus Gutmann's informant says Rindi was admonished when he was installed to be careful of his behavior as a *mangi* or he would risk removal from office.

You are the support of the country. But do not fall out with the country, for otherwise we will have to remove you and turn the country over to your brother. If you become detrimental to your country, they will not dare tell you this openly to your face. But they are going to sing you the song. . . . Understand this warning, and improve conditions. (Gutmann 1926:352; HRAF:318)

If you should disregard the advice of your men, you will not be able to keep the country which you receive from your father through our hands. (Gutmann 1926: 349; HRAF: 316)

Gutmann's work shows ambivalence about whether to describe chiefship in terms of its powers or its limitations. By the time Gutmann was on Kilimanjaro the conditions surrounding chiefship had been so profoundly changed that it must have been extremely difficult to reconstruct what the office had been in the nineteenth century.[5]

From the specific materials Gutmann collected on the chiefs' "legal" interventions and noninterventions a picture can be constructed of the domain in which chiefly power was exercised, and the purposes for which it was used. Neither a simple conception of egalitarian relations nor an exaggerated conception of autocratic power without limits is appropriate. Political astuteness was needed to manage the office, but with political acumen a chief could build strength and wealth out of the exigencies of the external trade, chronic warfare, and internal chiefdom politics.

Chiefly power over persons: taxes, tribute, corvée labor and access to women and children. The chief as "universal kinsman"

Chiefs exacted cattle, grain, beer, labor, and children from their subjects. But this was done in a kinship metaphor, an analogy to the obligation of kinsmen to one another. Any man could ask his lineage mates for contributions of beasts when he needed them for a ritual occasion. The same applied to grain for beer. Then when kinsmen slaughtered or brewed, they shared the meat and the beer within the lineage. Men also called their kin to help them with heavy work clearing fields, building houses, or with urgent harvesting in a system of exchange labor. The chief called up corvée labor using the metaphor of kinship exchange, but in his case the "exchange" was highly asymmetrical.

When the chief claimed some of his subjects' children, this, too, was based on the model of ordinary kinship rights. Chagga had (and have) clear ideas about the contingent interests of kinsfolk in one another's children. Every household was (and is) entitled to keep its first two children, but the "loan" of a third child could (and can) be requested by childless kin or aged relatives needing resident help. (This is still done.) Children could fetch water and gather firewood and fodder and carry messages. They could sweep and be useful in a thousand ways. The chief obtained third children from his subjects presumably on this analogy, both girls to serve his wives and boys to look after the goats.

It was not unusual for children of ordinary citizens to be used as pledges for unpaid debts. The child was placed in the household of the creditor until the debt was paid (Gutmann 1926:477, 478; HRAF:429, 430). For example, a child might be placed in the household of his/her maternal uncle because bridewealth for his/her mother was unpaid. A chief sometimes paid a subject's debt and took the pledge child into his own house (1926:115; HRAF:203). Sometimes pledge children were adolescents, not simply toddlers. Indeed, older children were preferred since they could work harder. Thus the chief not only was a "universal kinsman" as far as demands for beasts, produce, and labor were concerned, he could also become a "substitute creditor" by paying the debts of his subjects.

Occasionally chiefs had sudden needs for extra produce and cattle, for example, when large trading parties arrived, when captives had to be ransomed, when ivory tusks were to be bought, and when major rituals had to be mounted, as when an old chief stepped down and handed over his *mangi*-ate to his son (Dundas 1924:95; Gutmann 1926:380–95; HRAF:341–54). Then chiefs could demand grain or beasts of their subjects as needed. They sometimes made these requests to individual homesteads. But in precolonial times, the chief usually made major demands for cattle either to individuals with whom he had placed his own cattle or to a lineage through its lineage head. The lineage head in turn allocated the contributions among the member households according to the capacity to pay, past contributions, and other considerations of fairness. Chiefly taxation for beasts for slaughter was done on the model of reciprocal slaughtering obligations between lineage kinsmen. After the beast had been killed, the chief sent the neck of the animal to the owner, and the biggest slaughter share of meat to the next person from whom a beast would be demanded.

The chief was also entitled to a share of meat of any slaughtering feast held by his subjects and to a share of any beer brewed for a large beer party. The slaughterer and the brewer always distributed shares to kinsmen. By placing himself as a universal kinsman, the chief always had the means to be hospitable to visitors, and could offer them beer and meat from his ample and continuous supply. When he gave a beer party celebrating the life crisis rituals of his own family, the chief demanded contributions of eleusine from his subjects. This grain tax was also an analogy to kinship obligation in that contributions of grain were made to a kinsman who required them to brew a large quantity of beer for a marriage or a circumcision. When major chiefly beer parties were given, the whole citizenry was invited.

Persons desiring the chiefs' favor or grateful for some past favor gave occasional "voluntary" tributary gifts. The most desirable of these was a fattened castrated goat (*ndafu*). Though Gutmann does not mention it in this context, the *ndafu* goat was a customary gift of gratitude from a son to a father for having raised him.

A chief could call up his people for corvée duty as he saw fit. Gutmann estimated that men worked an average of about twenty days a year for the chief, women about ten, and children irregular amounts of time (1926:387; HRAF:348). A man was obligated to do corvée duty from the time he was circumcised until his son was circumcised and could be substituted for him (1926:379; HRAF:340). Corvée obligations included house building for the chief, defensive works and construction for the country, such as the digging of trenches along the borders, the erection of watch towers on the chief's lands, the protection of the chief's court with trenches, palisades and stone walls. Some irrigation canals were dug by corvée labor under chiefly orders (1926:374, 375; HRAF:336, 338). Labor on public works was ordinarily rewarded with beer drinks. To have sufficient harvest for his many feasting obligations, the chief also used corvée labor for his large banana groves and fields of millet.

Because chiefs had greater means with which to pay bridewealth and because it was politically desirable for a lineage to have one of its daughters married to the chief, chiefs were in a position to have more wives than their subjects. In the early colonial period the number of chiefly wives was substantial.[6] These women, in turn, had many servant girls who did their work for them. Gutmann equates the contribution of children for service in the chief's household to a tax (1926:388; HRAF: 349). Such children were demanded of the poor, whereas cattle were exacted from the rich.

Chiefly control of the external trade

As indicated elsewhere, in the late nineteenth century there was substantial chiefly control over ivory for the external trade, and on the return trade in guns and ammunition. The Chagga sold captives as slaves. Chief Mandara explained to Sir Harry Johnston who had reproached him for doing so, "What am I to do? To kill captives would be wrong. If I return them to my enemies, they would just fight me. If I kept them in my own land my people would say, 'If strangers are to occupy the soil, where is the room for our children to cultivate?' Then what can I do but sell them to the Arabs?" (Johnston 1886:180; paraphrased). Plainly the Chagga themselves did not hold slaves. There was no monopoly on small items such as cloth, knives, wire, other forms of metal, beads, and such objects, but the chief, through his control of the major external trade, had the

largest stockpile of these desirable items and redistributed them (Gutmann 1926:381; HRAF: 342). This redistribution can be read as an exchange for political and material support. To translate chiefly dominion
of the external trade into "legal" rules would be an artificial exercise. But
the chiefly role as trade monopolist and major redistributor was certainly
a regularized part of the social order.

The chiefly dominion over unoccupied lands

In theory, all land in the chiefdom was held with the chief's implied
consent. The chief could allocate unoccupied lands, and had a reversionary right to such lands if there was a failure of male issue and there were
no other local lineage heirs (Gutmann 1926:62; HRAF:50).

The chief's allocation of annual-crop land

In precolonial times, in addition to their banana gardens high on the
mountain, the Chagga cultivated large fields at the edge of the plain.
These were divided into *mitaa* shares, and subdivided into individual
strips. These fields were kept in crop rotation (maize, beans, millet) and
were said to have been redistributed annually under chiefly supervision
(Gutmann 1926:307; HRAF:275).

Arable lands of the chief

The chief had large banana groves and fields of millet cultivated by
corvée labor (Gutmann 1926:375-8; HRAF:337-9). The eleusine fields
of the chief were divided up in such a way that each district supplied
separate corvée teams to cultivate it. Each district section of the field was
subdivided into beds to be cultivated by four men per bed. Millet was a
key ingredient of beer.

The punishment of corvée evaders was sometimes undertaken by co-
workers, sometimes by the chief. Cattle might be confiscated, or the
man's banana grove devastated, or he might be forced to do extra work
or pay a fine. Evaders were warned by the chief's herald. District heads
checked on the performance of corvée duties, as did the chief's lineage
brothers. If an evader were accused before the chief of missing days of
labor, a punitive portion of work would be measured out for him. He
could escape this labor by paying the fee of one head of cattle to the chief
(Gutmann 1926:69, 376-9; HRAF:57, 338-40). Such a beast was then
slaughtered for the benefit of the corvée workers. The chief rewarded

corvée workers with beer and meat when their tasks were complete, occasionally adding a piece of cloth.

Cattle of the chief and the chief's cattle clients

Chiefs had access to a larger number of beasts than any other men through taxes (Gutmann 1926:381; HRAF:342), legal fees (1926:613; HRAF:549), confiscations (1926:570, 571; HRAF:513, 514), bridewealth of many daughters and "adopted" daughters (1926:388; HRAF:349), and through tribute and warfare (1926:537, 538; HRAF:485). Chiefs also had the heaviest obligations involving the redistribution of cattle and meat feasts. Thus any important stranger visiting a chiefdom was received with chiefly hospitality of which meat was a major feature. This demonstration of generosity also served as a security measure, and as a way of maintaining a monopoly on major items of external trade (Gutmann 1926:384, 401, 406; HRAF:345, 360, 365; Krapf 1860:238; Von der Decken 1869–71:275; New 1874:439). The chiefs offered cattle to foreign visitors for coastal goods, especially cloth, beads, metal wire, and guns. They also needed large numbers of beasts to obtain elephant tusks and to ransom captives (Gutmann 1926:381–3, 542; HRAF:342–4, 489). As chiefs subsidized the largest parties of corvée laborers, and feasted them not only with beer but sometimes with meat they also needed animals for this purpose (1926:378; HRAF: 339–40). The chief's duty to feed his people in times of famine sometimes required him to use his own animals. The efficacy of administration also depended in part on chiefly generosity with cattle. The chiefs rewarded their district supervisors, the *wachili*, with occasional presents of beasts. When the warrior age-grade heard a legal case argued on the Lawn of Justice, in which cattle were brought as a legal fee, one of the beasts taken as a fee for the lawsuit was slaughtered for consumption by the warriors (1926:501, 592, 611–12; HRAF: 451, 531, 548–9).

A chief was consequently under continuous pressure to keep himself supplied with cattle to maintain his position of political authority, and inversely a great many of his exercises of political authority were also concerned with obtaining cattle. He approached lineage heads for contributions of cattle from patrilineages (Gutmann 1926:382; HRAF:343). He sometimes assembled the whole of the warrior age-grade to announce a special levy of cattle taxes to finance the purchase of ivory (1926:381; HRAF:342). Raids were frequently undertaken to capture animals from neighboring chiefdoms, and wars often ended with subjugated peoples paying cattle tribute to the victors.[7]

Given the chief's right to the largest share of livestock booty, and his

tax and tribute powers, he was bound to acquire more animals than his
immediate household could look after. This problem was dealt with simply. The chief put his surplus livestock in the households of his subjects,
"loaning" his cattle to others (Gutmann 1926:611; HRAF:548). However, the chief retained the right to reclaim these animals on demand.
This arrangement placed the recipients of the animals, who temporarily
benefited from the milk and manure, under various counter-obligations to
the chief. Such a chiefly cattle transaction was in keeping with a normal
custom of cattle placement between commoners, but elements in the
chief's relationship with his cattle clients indicate the beginnings of strati-
fication. Among the most prominent men in the Chagga hierarchy were
those Gutmann calls *masumba,* the men who could and did regularly
contribute cattle to the chief. A cattle-wealthy man who contributed at
least one head per year to the chief, and who was willing to contribute a
beast for the entertainment of the chief's visitors on demand, was called
an *isumba* (pl. *masumba;* Gutmann 1926:442; HRAF:397).[8]

"COMMONER" CONTROL OF LIVESTOCK, LAND, WATER, AND PERSONS

The use of livestock: acquisition and disposition

Chagga ideas and practices regarding property in cattle were elaborate,
rich in symbolic meaning, and reveal in a condensed form aspects of their
economy, their political system, their relations of kinship, and their cos-
mology. The ideology of a pastoral people was intertwined with the practices and beliefs of a horticultural society. The Chagga placed a high
value on having beasts and on eating meat. To have a cow, and perhaps
some goats, stalled in the grass house in which mother and children slept,
meant fecundity, prosperity, and comfort, all under one roof. In the rainy
season, the mountain can be very cold. Animal warmth was a ready form
of central heating. The arrangements also made for a considerable degree
of intimacy, real and symbolic, between people and their beasts. For
example, the fertility or infertility of domesticated animals could be con-
tagious to human beings living under the same roof. From the start of a
marriage, a heifer was placed in the hut of a bride (Gutmann 1926:11;
HRAF:9). She was to care for it, feed it, eventually milk it, use its milk
and manure, and enjoy its warmth. Should it turn out to be an infertile
cow that calved only every third year, it had to be removed, as it could
have a pernicious effect on her procreative capacity. It could not be
housed with a childbearing woman and her young children, but had to be
looked after by an old or childless person (1926:455; HRAF:409). When
an old cow, after years of giving milk and bearing calves, was no longer

fertile, she was slaughtered. But ritual apologies had to be made to her, and those who owned her took precautions to have her killed by someone she did not know lest she recognize the persons responsible for her death (1926:459; HRAF:412). It is undoubtedly a connected phenomenon that the Chagga do not eat milk and meat at the same meal. The specific traditional meaning is uncertain, but it may be that the custom is a precaution to maintain the fertility of cows. The message that cattle are being slaughtered should not get back to the cow, through the milk, or she may cease to give milk or calves in revenge.

Most male animals were ritually slaughtered and eaten. Fertile cows were preserved for their productive and reproductive capacities. Not to have a cow or other livestock (goats or sheep) was the Chagga definition of poverty; having many beasts, and many feasts of meat, their definition of wealth. In the 1970s a Mchagga told me, rubbing his stomach, that no Chagga man feels well unless he eats meat every few days. I am sure the Chagga would have said the same a hundred years earlier. Those who could afford to do so slaughtered animals at every life-crisis ritual. Those who could not afford to do so often "borrowed" animals at critical times and put themselves into debt.

Cattle produced milk, butter, blood, manure, meat, and skins. All were considered essential. Milk, butter, and blood were important in the Chagga diet. Manure was used to fertilize the banana gardens. Butter was rubbed over the body as a cosmetic, and on skins to soften them. Skins were used for clothing, bedding, and as parts of utensils. Material usefulness was matched by ritual indispensability. To marry properly, a man needed livestock for feasting and bridewealth (Gutmann 1926:93, 94, 97, 104, 107, 121, 122, 124, 125; HRAF:78, 79, 81, 88, 91, 104, 105, 108). A week after a child was born, two goats had to be slaughtered, one for the ancestors, and one especially to supply blood and meat and fat for the young mother (1926:221; HRAF:195). If anyone was dangerously ill, a goat was slaughtered (1926:464; HRAF:417). After a man's death, to facilitate his departure from this world in the right way, animals had to be slaughtered for him. Ideally, one ox was sacrificed when the body was buried and at least one more later on when the body was exhumed (Gutmann 1909:131ff). The slaughtering of stock when there is a birth, a serious illness, or a death is still done by those who can afford it to this day. Dundas reports very lavish burial slaughtering (1924:182–92). If a widow was inherited in a leviratic marriage, the new husband sacrificed a goat to pacify his dead brother (Gutmann 1926:52; HRAF: 41–2). For the living, slaughtering feasts, regularly held, were a normal part of the ritual of patrilineage life (1926:43–6; HRAF:34-6). If a man wanted a serious favor from the chief, it was customary to present him with an animal. Chiefs taxed the lineages in beasts. There was thus a continuous need for animals, either for reproduction, milk and manure, or to be used for slaughtering and meat, or for political obligations and favors.

The acquisition of livestock was an endless preoccupation. The ordinary ways a male commoner could acquire livestock were through (1) natural increase, (2) inheritance, (3) allocation by a father or elder brother or other agnatic kinsman, or as (4) bridewealth for a sister or a daughter. The "extraordinary" ways he might acquire cattle were through (1) "borrowing" to dispose of (i.e., to use the beast for sacrificial slaughter or for payment to another) with the promise (implied or explicit) of reciprocal repayment when practicable, (2) "borrowing" cattle to keep in the household under a cattle-placement agreement, or as (3) compensation for a wrong, or as (4) a reward from the chief either in the division of war booty or for some special service. Women as well as men could have a property interest in livestock, but men were prevalently the livestock owners (Gutmann 1926:64; HRAF:52–6). Men had considerable discretion over the allocation of their stock during their lives (1926:40, 57; HRAF:32, 46). They could do nearly as they liked. However, after a man died, there was often litigation over the allocations and their finality. Stock could be placed "on loan" without being "given away." Unless a man made his intentions clear before witnesses (and even in those circumstances) the chances were that disputes would arise after his death, certain persons making claims based on genealogy, others based on allocation and possession, still others on debt, and so on. A man who had no sons and was on bad terms with his lineage could try to disinherit his kinsmen by "willing" his cattle to the chief. After his death the kinsmen were likely to put pressure on the chief to give them some of the beasts. The outcome depended on their bargaining strength (1926:62; HRAF: 51).

A woman could acquire livestock of her own through *inter vivos* gifts from her father if she had no brothers. She could also acquire beasts through her own trade, if she was industrious, canny, and fortunate (Gutmann 1926; HRAF:46, 54–5). Under unusual circumstances she might inherit a beast. During her lifetime a woman could dispose of her livestock acquired through her own efforts as she saw fit. But all stock that remained in the household on her death normally went to a son, either to the firstborn son of her first marriage, or if there was none, a son of subsequent leviratical marriage. A daughter would not receive any of the livestock unless there were no sons. If there were no children when she died, a married woman's brother inherited her own livestock but not that which had been placed in her house by her husband or his lineage (1926:64; HRAF:53). A beast placed in the hut of a married woman by her husband did not become hers to dispose of. It became part of the wealth that would pass to the children of that house, or revert to the husband and his heirs if there were no children.

Cattle "lending," the acquisition of cattle clients

In some parts of Kilimanjaro, particularly in sections of the most easterly and westerly districts, Rombo and Machame respectively, cattle in numbers could be herded and grazed with ease. In the central area of Vunjo, in which Moshi is located, there was rarely sufficient pasturage. There, a few cattle were kept in the sleeping huts. It is said that the numbers were two or three head per household, and a few goats and sheep. These were all stall-fed, a practice reported for the early 1860s that persists to this day. The maintenance of stall-fed cows required a great deal of labor. Women had to go to the plain to cut the grass for fodder and carry it up in great headloads for the cattle to eat. To supply the beasts with fluid, the cattle were fed cut-up banana stems from the grove (Von der Decken 1869–71, 1:270, 272). They were sometimes also fed bananas, particularly when the intention was to fatten an ox or a gelded goat for slaughter.

It is difficult to assess the proportion of livestock to population during the nineteenth century. Early in the twentieth century wealthy men slaughtered cattle as many as five times a year, poor men once every two or three years (Gutmann 1926:390; HRAF:350). Gutmann asserts that in precolonial times a person with no more than five head of cattle was a "poor" man (1926:382; HRAF:343). He makes no clear statement about the slaughter or possession of goats and sheep which was likely more common. Although the ideology of the Chagga was as livestock-oriented as that of any pastoral people, statements on cattle "lending" indicate that in precolonial times some households had no cattle of their own. The practice of cattle lending may have fluctuated with the availability of cattle as well as with other factors (see Iliffe 1979:124 on the rinderpest epidemic of 1891). Gutmann said that almost every Chagga had cattle placed with households in other districts, often in order to conceal assets (1926:401, 440–1; HRAF:360, 395).

For the ordinary man distant placement carried risks. If the beast was confiscated from the "borrower" for debts, or as compensation for a wrong perpetrated by the borrower, the owner could not easily stop the proceedings and had to be satisfied with taking subsequent action against the borrower. By then, the borrower might be without assets (Gutmann 1926:442–3; HRAF:397). Thus an ordinary man, who had no special status, could not, even if he knew about it, successfully interfere with the confiscation of animals secretly placed with others by declaring to the authorities that the animals were really his, not those of the debtor or wrongdoer. No one would pay attention to his statements. But the *ma-sumba*, the cattle clients of the chief, were listened to in these circumstances.

Occasionally, a powerful man undertook cattle placement precisely for the purpose of giving protection to a poor man who was already in trouble with creditors, the district leader, kinsmen, or neighbors. In such a situation, a beer feast and maximum publicity accompanied the placement of an animal in the house of the beleagured man. The public occasion was a way of saying that from then on the lender was committed to protecting his client, and it served as a warning to creditors who were troubling him. The patron declared that the client should be allowed to work off his debts to others by working in their fields and that the client's property should be left untouched (see note 8).

In addition to the purposes of saving the labor of stall-feeding and of concealing assets, a third motive for placing cattle with another was to gain a client. The relations of cattle lenders to cattle borrowers were considered to be those of superiors to inferiors (Gutmann 1926:441, 443, 448; HRAF:395, 397, 402). Not infrequently, the recipient was "poor" and therefore not in a good position to bargain with the lender. For him the use of the milk, manure, and warmth of the animal and a share in the meat of bull-calves when they were slaughtered were well worth the effort involved. In addition to looking after the cow, the effort entailed could include the obligation to give beer or grain in gratitude to the donor, or to work for him in his fields. In return the donor might occasionally share with his client some *largesse* on festive occasions. The patron might also represent the client in dealing with the chief (1926:441; HRAF:396).

The normal terms of a cow loan were that the recipient received the milk and manure. The calves belonged to the donor. If a calf was born, its birth had to be announced promptly to the owner. After the first milking, the cow keeper was supposed to bring beer or eleusine grain to show his gratitude to the owner. The owner or his family could drink no milk of the loaned cow during the period of the loan. It was said that they would die if they drank it (Gutmann 1926:450; HRAF:404). The milk belonged to the borrower who had to share it only with the calf. If the calf was a female, she was moved to another household as soon as she was weaned. A heifer could not grow up to maturity and become pregnant in the same homestead as its mother, even as Chagga daughters had to move to other households on marriage. The borrower, however, raised a bull-calf to maturity and eventually returned it to the owner for slaughtering. At the appointed time, the borrower had a right to be invited to the slaughtering feast. There, like the agnatic kinsmen of the owner, he was fed a meal of pieces of meat in blood sauce. He was also owed, as his share to take home, one leg of the beast, the neck and a pot of blood. For his wife he was given a part of the intestines, intestinal fat, the liver, the milt, and the feet, all mixed with blood. The Chagga wore skins as clothing, and used them for bedding as well. If the borrower chose, he might forgo his slaughtering share in exchange for the animal's skin (1926:451; HRAF:405). In return for the meat, the borrower was obligated to give the owner beer. If he failed to provide beer when the cow came into milk, or when he received meat, and failed to do so a number of times, then after raising three or four calves he had to pay the owner a goat instead.

The Chagga drew blood from the necks of cattle for certain ritual foods. Because this practice involved risks to the loaned animal, the recipient of the borrowed beast was not allowed to bleed it without special permission from the owner. Drawing blood was not a normal right that automatically went with the transaction of placement (Gutmann 1926: 449, HRAF:403). If after being given permission, the borrower successfully drew blood without harm to the animal, he owed the owner a quantity of beer (1926:450; HRAF:404). If, in the course of bleeding the animal was injured and died, the borrower was obligated to inform the owner and bring him a goat. The goat was slaughtered by the man who had bled the deceased beast and was then divided, the borrower receiving one front leg and the neck up to and including the point of the wound. The owner got the rest of the meat which he distributed among his agnatic kinsmen. The borrower then passed the neck on to the man who had drawn the blood. The phlebotomist (a specialist in this service) was forbidden to eat the neck but could pass it on to his children. The killer of an animal could not eat the part of the meat that contained the wound or he would die (1926:449; HRAF:403–4).

If an animal placed in agistment died from any cause, immediate notice had to be given to the owner (Gutmann 1926:452; HRAF:406). The possibilities for cheating were considerable. Animals could be reported dead or lost even though they were simply concealed in another house. Measures could be taken to require proof, but these were difficult to check. Another form of cheating was to report the birth of a bull-calf, when in fact a much more valuable cow-calf had been born. The cow-calf could then be exchanged with someone else for a bull-calf which would be shown the owner when he visited.

The owner had the right to take his cow back on demand, but it was considered improper to place a dry cow in someone else's care and then take it back again just when it came into milk. The borrower's only recourse in such a case was cursing. The correct way for an owner to compensate the borrower if he took the cow away prematurely was to give the borrower a hoe or a goat. An old cow, past further calf-bearing, was returned to the owner for slaughter (Gutmann 1926:454, 457; HRAF: 408, 411).

Cattle lending was a matter of trust, and involved considerable risk. It was possible for the owner to visit his animal in the borrower's house, and men did so. But frequent visits were considered an imposition (Gutmann 1926:455; HRAF:409). Some men who had many animals placed in other chiefdoms went on long journeys to check on their cattle (1926:456; HRAF:410).

Since placement was often with someone in another district or another chiefdom, not with a near neighbor, both making the initial arrangements and checking on the subsequent well-being and reproductivity of cattle involved much visiting between chiefdoms (Gutmann 1926:399–401; HRAF:360). Messages announcing a planned visit could be sent through the market women (1926:401; HRAF:361). Unannounced visits were also sometimes undertaken. A set of rules existed having to do with obligations of hosts and guests.

The Chagga also loaned nanny goats but on somewhat different terms. All the calves of a placed cow belonged to the original owner on the theory that the milk and manure were sufficient compensation for the caretaker. In contrast, in the case of goats because they were not milked, every third kid belonged to the borrower. After the fourth kid, the arrangement came to an end. But it could be renewed (Gutmann 1926: 460–1; HRAF:414).

Relations within the lineage regarding livestock

Shares of meat: slaughtering groups and slaughtering partners

Slaughtering feasts were (and still are) celebrations of kinship in which the men of a localized patrilineage got together, killed an animal, divided the meat, cooked and ate a little of it on the spot, consumed a good deal of beer, and then took their separate shares of meat home. Such feasts took place in connection with every wedding, every birth, and on every other imaginable occasion when someone who could afford to be host found reason to invite his agnates to share a beast. Lest the dead withhold their blessings, a sliver of every share was offered to the ancestors, as was a libation of beer. When something was wrong in the lineage, when there was an illness or some other misfortune threatened, the sacrificial element of the slaughtering feast was the central rationale. Even in good times of celebration, communication with and propitiation of the dead were always elements in the feast. But the purely gustatory side was also important. Entrails were observed for any signs from the spirit world, but haruspicy was usually only a side meaning of the event. Indeed, anything unusual on any occasion was always interpretable as a message from the dead. As the slaughtered animal passed from life to

death it could carry a message to the ancestors. The senior elder who led
the ritual aspects of the slaughtering feast sometimes explicitly addressed
a particular spirit and dedicated the animal to it. Every man present put
some of his own saliva on the forehead of the animal to be sacrificed as
part of the dedication. An ox was killed by being hit over the head at that
spot and then suffocated. Goats and sheep were stabbed in the heart.
Rings (sing. *kishongu*) were later fashioned out of the animal's skin,
particularly out of the forehead part where the death blow was given,
though other bits were used as well, to be worn by those present as
talismans on fingers or toes.[9]

The feasting complex has importance from the point of view of "law."
In form it replicates the hierarchical distribution of authority within the
lineage and the birth order of the men; in substance it deals with the most
valued scarce resource of the time, cattle. In a metaphoric way it represents relationships of succession and inheritance, and the contingent interest of kinsmen in each other's property. As lineage slaughtering feasts
persisted in 1984, it is well worth piecing together from modern and old
evidence what can be understood of the nineteenth-century practice.

It can be assumed that then as now few lineage slaughtering feasts
involved the whole of the localized patriline. Most were held for small
subsegments, the male descendants of one grandfather, or one great-
grandfather. Thus there were slaughtering groups of varying sizes and
levels which corresponded to the genealogical segmentation within the
lineage. Only occasionally were large oxen killed, or several goats killed
at one time, and only on those occasions could a large group assemble.
Most of the time slaughtering feasts were small, and confined to the male
descendants of one grandfather. Though these meat-sharing groups were
normally composed of genealogically close kin, if one branch shrank, or
there was a lone kinsman without close brothers, these oddments were
aggregated to other lines. The meat sharing taken home by each married
male participant was often divided again, and some parts might later be
sent to senior agnates of other lineage branches who had not been invited
to the slaughtering party, to affines, and to anyone else with whom the
man wanted to divide his share. Though women received meat from men
through this household distribution, meat was profoundly a male-owned
food. No woman was even supposed to untie a bundle of meat that her
husband brought home. He was supposed to undo the package (Gutmann
1926:181; HRAF:159).

Within any single group of sons of one father, there existed a system of
slaughtering partnerships. One of the fundamental rules was that no man
ever slaughtered one of his own beasts (Gutmann 1926:44; HRAF:35).
The host's slaughtering partner always did that office for him, killed the
animal, butchered it, and distributed the meat. Brothers who were

slaughtering partners were supposed to have the closest possible relationship of mutual aid in all matters, not just in slaughtering feasts. The service
was reciprocated on the next occasion when the original slaughtering
partner took his turn to be host, and the host was the slaughterer. If, for
some reason, a man was rejected as the partner of his proper patrilineal
brother, he could make someone else his slaughtering partner, preferably
his *olea*, a man related to him through common descent from two sisters
(1926:45; HRAF:36). But the normal way for slaughtering partnerships to
be divided up if there were several sons was as follows. First and last sons
were slaughtering partners. If there was an even number of middle sons,
they were also paired, eldest to youngest. If there was an odd number of
middle sons the leftover one had to find a half brother or other less closely
related kinsman to be his partner (1926:48; HRAF:38). Obviously, depending on the configuration of the family, age-distributions, and so on, a
range of alternatives could be followed or improvised.

There was a conventional way of dividing the meat and blood at a
slaughtering feast. The division was not only into the parts to be eaten at
the slaughtering place and the parts to be taken home, but also in the
allocation of particular anatomical parts to particular kin. This division
represented the metaphoric correspondence of animal anatomy to the
social body.[10]

The question this "poetry of slaughtering" raises is to what extent is it
reasonable to talk about slaughter sharing as a "legal" right? For the
precolonial period, there is evidence that nonfulfillment of the terms of
an agistment between a livestock owner and cattle borrower (i.e., between nonkin) could become a matter for litigation, and an explicit statement that the proper payment of meat from bull-calves slaughtered was
part of the usual obligation. But there is less evidence of the consequences of the improper allocation of meat shares *within a lineage*, save
that it might disqualify an heir to the lineage headship. Disputes over
slaughtering exchanges did turn up in the present fieldwork. Exclusion
from slaughtering is a sanction that is still used. Meat-sharing obligations
are taken very seriously. Today intralineage controversies over such
issues are preeminently part of the private domain that should be handled
"at home," rather than brought before public agencies. Private settlement presumably was standard in such matters in the nineteenth century;
hence the absence of discussion of such disputes in Gutmann is not surprising, nor is it necessarily an indication that they did not exist.

The cattle of bridewealth

The multiple bridewealth payments made in relation to a marriage took
place over a period of many years. For the most part, the beasts offered

in the various exchanges that preceded the couple's settling down together were slaughtered and eaten. The later payments of heifers were to
be kept for reproduction. Thus Gutmann describes a series of preliminary
bridewealth prestations involving the slaughtering of one head of cattle
(1926:97; HRAF:81) and the presentation at intervals of a number (6) of
goats and one sheep, most of which were slaughtered and eaten in the
premarriage festivities. Some years later, after the first child of the marriage was seven or eight years old, a heifer and a goat were owed by the
groom to the bride's father or brother. Subsequently, when affordable, a
heifer and a goat were owed the wife's maternal uncle (1926:121, 125;
HRAF:104, 108).

Variations in designating the recipients of bridewealth could be made.
A father sometimes paired off his sons and his daughters, so that should
the father die each of the sons would receive the bridewealth owed for a
particular daughter. If no such arrangements were made, the firstborn
son acquired all rights, standing in his father's place (Gutmann 1926:38;
HRAF:30). Or sometimes the firstborn son received all the bridewealth
of all his sisters, except for that of the youngest, which went to the
last-born son. In any case, even when the firstborn received all the bridewealth of his sisters, he was under an obligation to help his brothers with
their bridewealth needs, just as his father would have done had he lived.

Since the transfer of bridewealth from the groom's lineage to the
bride's was an ongoing burden over a period of many years, it was often
the source of quarrels and usually remained incompletely paid. If it began
to look as if the later and more valuable payments were not forthcoming,
measures could be taken. A member of the wife's lineage, her brother,
for example, could take one of her children as a debt hostage and keep
the child until the bridewealth was fully paid (Gutmann 1926:233;
HRAF:206). The firstborn son of the marriage could not be made a debt
hostage in this way. It was usually a middle son who was given to be held.
In special circumstances, a daughter might fill this role. Sometimes a male
debt hostage himself, on reaching adulthood, could redeem the debt by
acquiring cattle and paying for his own liberty. As can be imagined, the
taking of a debt hostage led to considerable complications, if the cattle
owed remained unpaid over a long period of time.

The inheritance of livestock

The rules relating to the inheritance of livestock both reflected and
helped produce the general structure of relationships between a father
and his sons and among brothers. The first principle was that the eldest
and youngest sons were favored, and middle sons were "second-class"
heirs, who received much smaller shares of everything. The second princi-

ple was that in a polygynous household the inheritance was in a marked degree divided among the households established by marriage. That is, the eldest and youngest sons of one mother became the favored heirs of beasts in her hut, and had no right to livestock in other wives' huts. Disputes sometimes arose in cases in which the husband had moved an animal from the hut of one wife to the hut of another. Moving an animal was not unusual, and the children of the wife from whom the beast had been taken had the right to reclaim it unless their father had publicly and specifically stated in tying the beast to the new wife's hut that it was for her children. The third principle was that the firstborn son of the first wife became the deceased father's positional successor as far as responsibility for and authority over family and discretion over certain family assets were concerned, even if he was younger than a son of another wife (Gutmann 1926:31–7; HRAF:23–8). If the first wife had no son, then the position of authority fell to the eldest son of the second wife (if the second wife had no son, the eldest son of the third wife, and so on). Gutmann's accounts of variations in the inheritance patterns depending on numbers of wives, numbers of sons, birth order, number of cattle in or out of the maternal household, and on the rules of particular lineages are less than clear. He seems to have been looking for firm rules where instead there clearly were elements of situational discretion exercised in the distributions.

Gutmann's informant provided some hypothetical cases in which it was assumed that by far the largest number of head of livestock were stalled in other households, under the system of cattle placement described earlier. Those beasts are said to have been counted up and divided in the *matanga,* the meeting of kin and others (notably debtors and creditors) held on the fourth day after death to divide the decedent's property and responsibilities. Each head of cattle stalled outside (i.e., not in a wife's hut) was given to a particular son. Gutmann gives several versions of the division (1926:35–6; HRAF:27, 28). The numbers of beasts and sons involved indicate that his informant must have been talking about a wealthy, polygynous man.

(1) If there are five sons and twenty head of agistment cattle:

1st son	7 head
2nd son	3 head
3d son	3 head
4th son	2 head
5th son	5 head

(2) If there are three sons and forty head of agistment cattle:

1st son	20 head
2d son	5 head
3d son	15 head

The eldest son who receives the largest number must use his inheritance not only for himself but for the benefit of his brothers as his father would have done. When given his deceased father's spear, he was admonished to keep the livestock and tend it so that it would increase and be of help to his brothers. He was warned not to give the cattle to the chief (presumably to gain political recognition) but to keep them for his brothers. Thus he was to use the beasts to provide bridewealth for them, and to provide cattle to install in their households when they began married life in independent households. In addition to the cattle he inherited for this purpose, he administered the disposition of the beasts received for any unassigned bridewealth of his sisters. Once again, he must do as his father would have done. If one of the wives of a decedent had no sons, sometimes she was "given" one of the middle sons of another wife, to make the division of the inheritance somewhat more even.

If the father had married a widow of one of his brothers, and had had sons in this marriage, these sons also had a right to a portion of the inheritance. The firstborn, positional successor of the decedent, was obligated to pay the half-brothers some of the cattle, a cow and a calf for the eldest, and a cow for the second half-brother. The new head of the family might also use this occasion to separate the half-siblings from his slaughtering feasts thenceforth, and thus also exempt them from inviting him and his siblings to their feasts, and from paying him the *kidari* (the most prized slaughter portion). More succinctly stated, the new head of family could use the occasion of the division of the outside cattle of his deceased father to segment the lineage still further. Consequently the sons of the inherited widow would not share with their half-brothers any ordinary goat-slaughtering feasts. They would continue to share beer feasts which had a wider range of guests on great occasions, and only retained their meat-eating connection on the occasion of a huge feast (e.g., one in which two head of cattle were killed and a much larger lineage segment shared in the celebration) (Gutmann 1926:43, 46; HRAF: 34, 37).

If a father thought his firstborn son was not the most judicious of his sons, he could arrange in advance that he be succeeded as family head by another son. He might convene a slaughtering feast, and give his firstborn the knife for butchering and distribution of the meat and ask him also to distribute the beer. If the other sons did not seem satisfied and did not hail the distributor as their potential family head the father could take this as a sign that he should choose another son. In fact, whether the father tested reactions at a slaughtering feast or not, he had discretion over the matter, and could pick any son he thought would be best at the job. There was a tendency to appoint the eldest, and failing a competent eldest, the next eldest, and so on down the line. But the father was not obliged to follow the sequence of seniority and could pick any one of his sons, even the youngest, to succeed him (Gutmann 1926:41; HRAF:32). If, however, when the father died, all of his sons were minors, a brother of the father, often the very one who entered a marriage with the widow, became a kind of trustee of the estate, pending the majority of the sons. This situation was one that could be readily abused by a grasping uncle, and often subsequently gave rise to litigation when the rightful heir became adult (1926:50; HRAF:40).

If the family configuration is such that inheritance is not from father to sons, but from brother to brother, a rule often stated today is that the slaughtering partnerships are the determinants of mutual inheritance. Thus, a brother inherited from a dead brother only if the decedent left no sons. But if this was the case, the pairing went according to the partnerships. The first and last sons were mutual heirs, and a pair of middle sons were mutual heirs. Gutmann's account confirms this arrangement and also makes other statements that seem inconsistent and garbled. He may not have fully understood what he was told or perhaps did not understand all the contingencies he was trying to describe (1926:49; HRAF:39). What matters is that in default of sons, adelphic inheritance does *not* follow an eldest to youngest sequence, but seesaws between paired sons. An uneven number presented a problem under this rule, and sometimes, in situations of bad relations between the middle brothers and his siblings, resulted in the disinheritance of full brothers. Thus a middle brother without a sibling (or other patrilineal kinsman) as a slaughtering partner, could designate his "substitute" slaughtering partner as the person to bury him, and could prohibit his brothers from doing so, thereby disinheriting them. And if, in these circumstances, the middle brother died without leaving offspring, a cow and a calf would be left in the homestead of the widow, but the rest of the decedent's cattle were "inherited" by the chief. This arrangement seems to bespeak a reversionary right of the chief to property in livestock in default of appropriate patrilineal heirs.

Women could own livestock, acquired as a gift from a father, or more rarely inherited, or bought with the profits from the sale of her own produce (Gutmann 1926:64–6; HRAF:53–6). Property acquired by a woman through her own efforts could be freely disposed of by the woman during her lifetime. When the husband of a cattle-owning woman died, she called her brother to help her to assert her own rights to her own cattle stalled in her hut. But if she herself died, her property passed to her son, or if she had no son, to a daughter. A daughter could ask for compensation if the father slaughtered any of the mother's livestock. If a woman died childless, her brother took such stock.

If one appealed to a chief, could he intervene in lineage affairs regarding the inheritance of cattle?[11] He could, and the instances Gutmann refers to indicate chiefly support of a decedent's wishes as against the interests of agnates.

Gutmann describes a case of a disputed inheritance which concerned the division of cattle left by Ndevero Kimaro-Ljavere of Moshi on his death.[12] Ndevero had adopted a son captured in a war with Usseri. At the *matanga* the cattle were divided among his sons, including the adopted one. The other brothers objected and appealed to the chief. After hearing the first wife testify to the deathbed statements of the decedent that he wanted his adopted son to receive cattle, the chief decided that the adopted son should be given his share (1926:41–2; HRAF:33).

A further corroboration of the existence of chiefly intervention in matters of inheritance is found in another passage. A chief could be asked to commit himself in advance to the protection of a decedent's *inter vivos* allocations. When a father wished to make unconventional allocations of cattle or land to his *daughter's* son, and to prevent his kinsmen from undoing the allocation when he died, he went to the chief and presented him with a beast, asking him to protect the grandson's interests after his death (Gutmann 1926:60; HRAF:49).

Although there were "rules" of inheritance, and although the kinsmen at the *matanga* had important allocatory powers, these instances show elements of an oral "will," and arrangements in anticipation of death in which a man could allocate his own property in a manner inconsistent with the rules and could look to the chief to protect his allocations. An oral will raises some interesting questions about Sir Henry Maine's ideas about the evolution of law, and the shift from intestate succession to testamentary disposition (1861:177, 195). Maine's general explanation concerns the progressive emancipation of the individual from the control of the kinship group. Gutmann's examples from the Chagga suggest that the oral will can appear in tandem with a general system of intestate succession and that its enforcement is connected with a certain type of political development.

Wrongs connected with livestock and the problem of stock debts

Cattle theft, according to Gutmann, was the most frequent form of theft. One method was to place a beast that did not belong to the possessor in another household on loan, thus concealing its location from the owner (1926:569; HRAF:512).[13]

The refusal to return a loaned cow on demand was another recognized wrong (Gutmann 1926:651; HRAF:585). Failure to deliver one of its calves was another. Other forms of misfeasance also were connected with cattle loaning. A bull-calf could be substituted for a cow-calf, or the death of a new-born calf could be reported when the calf, in fact, survived.

The caretaker of a borrowed cow was responsible for its well-being. He was supposed to protect it from injury, and if despite due care it was injured, the problem had to be reported promptly. Failure to take proper care or failure to report an injury could make the borrower liable to replace the animal. If he could not afford to do so, or refused to, he could send his child in its place as a debt hostage or debt slave (Gutmann 1926:477–9; HRAF:429–30).

Livestock debts are the principal debts Gutmann considers, and he has a good deal of discussion of debt. Persons who borrowed a beast for an emergency sacrifice might find themselves in debt (Gutmann 1926:472; HRAF:424). If they did so repeatedly, matters became serious for the debtor. If the debtor had no property, and was unable to repay the cow or goat, he became the "son" of the creditor to the extent that he was obligated to work for him (and/or supply him with beer and produce) until the debt was cleared (1926:231–2; HRAF:204–5).

If, on the other hand, the debtor acquired livestock and simply did not repay, another situation existed. The creditor did not have the right to help himself to a head of cattle or a goat from the debtor's homestead, unless he did so in the presence of, and with the approval of, one of the chief's representatives (Gutmann 1926:474; HRAF:426). Among other considerations, the only cow of a wife could not be taken, and had to be left untouched as "it is a Chagga principle that a house without a cow cannot support a wife" (1926:484; HRAF:435). But the creditor did have the right to take whatever he could seize from the debtor in person while the debtor was walking in the open (1926:475; HRAF:427). This form of "seizure on the way" could also be carried out against any agnaic kin of the debtor who would have been liable for his debt. It was also extended to any resident of the debtor's district (provided it was not in another chieftaincy) (1926:476; HRAF:428). Seizures were supposed to make the agnatic kin or neighbors of the debtor put pressure on him to repay. The creditor who had made the seizures did not have to release property until the debt was paid, and could refer the victims of the seizures to the debtor for redress. The more direct forms of self-help available to the creditor (and the others) against the debtor were (1) sleeping in his yard and refusing to leave, (2) extinguishing the debtor's fire every time it was lighted, and (3) excluding the debtor from the use of irrigation water (1926:476; HRAF:428).

Debts did not die with the debtor provided they were again claimed and thereby renewed at the *matanga*. A person who buried a debtor assumed his assets and obligations (Gutmann 1926:482, 483; HRAF:433, 434). If the agnatic kinsmen refused to bury the debtor because they did not want to assume his obligations, and he remained uninterred, the widow could turn to the chief. The chief might then pay off the creditors.

The children of the debtor then became liable to the chief for their father's debts when they grew up. The chief could also postpone all payments, and require the creditors to wait until the children could clear the paternal debt (1926:484–6; HRAF:435–7). If there were no children, or only one or two, and the prospects for recovery of the debt were not good, the chief could turn the burial obligations over to the creditors themselves. By burying the corpse, but leaving the associated rituals incomplete, the creditors acquired some use of the debtor's banana grove until the child or children were adult, at which time the debt could be settled, and the final ceremonial acts connected with the burial could be completed.

"Commoner" interests in land, produce, and water

Introduction

Modern commentators sometimes argue that (1) the Chagga did not "buy" and "sell" land in the precolonial period, and (2) that the Chagga did not have individual landholdings, but merely a share in patrilineal territories. There are grounds for such an argument, yet too much emphasis on the invariable existence of collective interests can be misleading. Certainly neither buying nor selling existed in the modern commercial sense. Land was not a commodity. There was no market in land, and no acknowledged variability of price, but rather a convention that a nonkinsman being given land must pay a cow and a goat in return. Social limitations existed on the free alienation of improved land that had been received from an agnate. A transfer of such land was possible only if the patrilineage had no objection. Agreement may not have been easy to obtain and may have been still harder to prove. Even if a lineage member witnessed the transfer and did not object at the time, he might raise agnatic claims later on (Gutmann 1926:306; HRAF:275). That it was difficult in advance to prevent the eventual reopening of such issues is yet another illustration of the perpetually renegotiable nature of what often started out looking like a binding transaction that conformed to normative rules.

As conditional as was the transfer of inherited land, just so simple was the acquisition of bush land. There was no shortage, and the consent of the chief was pro forma. Once he had cultivated the bush land, a man could freely alienate it. Men did so in exchange for "a cow and a goat." But more often they left such land to their sons. Thus there was a continuous process by which bush land became reclassified as lineage land as it passed from one generation to the next.

As for individual holdings, individuals had clearly marked plots in

which they had exclusive interests during any period of beneficial occupancy, and these plots were normally passed on to their lineal heirs. It
was only in default of lineal male issue that the latent residual interest of
collaterals became manifest. There were rules, which are discussed later,
for the succession of sons to father's property, and in the absence of sons,
the inheritance by brothers and/or brothers' sons, and in the absence of
these, for allocating the priorities of interest of contingent and residual
agnatic heirs. Although such rules existed as stated norms, the Chagga
had many ways in which to adjust the rules in practice.

On the day of the *matanga,* not just rules, but the wishes of the decedent and family configurations were taken into account. Patrilineage micropolitics also had an important role in the designation of an heir and
the distribution of property and guardianships. Again, inheritance is an
example of the negotiability in practice of what appear in some ethnographic statements as fixed rules. Because of this quality of negotiability,
it is probably better to conceive the rules of inheritance as "preferred
claim" or "guideline" rules rather than as enforceable rights. The role of
the patrilineage in these circumstances is quasi-administrative, that is, it is
guided by rules and declared objectives, but has considerable discretion
in applying them to particular cases.

Banana gardens and meadowland nearby

Because of the richness of Kilimanjaro's volcanic soil, the practice of
manuring (particularly with cow manure), and irrigation, the Chagga
could cultivate their banana gardens year after year indefinitely. Thus the
site of a developed banana garden, a *kihamba,* interplanted with vegetables, could be occupied permanently by a man and his descendants.
Patrilineage lands also included some fallow and some open meadow used
for grazing, both also frequently the property of individuals (Gutmann
1926:304; HRAF:272; see also Griffiths 1930:38). Full rights to dispose of
land belonged only to men, though married women and widows had
rights of occupancy and use.

The Chagga recognized that property interest in a particular banana
garden belonged (1) for life to the man who had first cleared and developed it, and subsequently (2) to his male lineal descendants (according to
a set of rules given elsewhere), and failing male descendants, to his
brothers, and failing brothers, to other agnates, but these rights of lineal
descendants and agnates were subject (3) to the rights of any holder's
surviving widow to occupy the land until her death, and subject (4) to the
rights of any occupier to whom a lineage owner had transferred the
garden with suitable ritual and with the informed consent of other lineage
members, with the transaction duly witnessed by one of them, and sub-

ject (5) to the reversionary right of the chief to reallocate it, should the land be abandoned by the lineage (Gutmann 1926:302–9; HRAF:270–6). In short, lineage members had rights in *kihamba* land as against the chief's reversionary right only so long as the lineage remained resident in the area.

A man might choose to "lend" a part of his meadow to an outsider (sometimes a son-in-law, sometimes a brother-in-law) for his occupation and use. The conditions under which such as assignment was made was normally the agreement that the occupier would pay the owner *masiro,* an annual gift of beer and produce, forever. This was an acknowledgment in perpetuity of the continuing interest of the original owner and his heirs in the land. The chief's consent was not necessary for such an arrangement. The relationship was hereditary, and both the donor and the occupier could be succeeded by their male descendants or other agnates according to the usual rules. The original holder (or his descendants) in theory retained the right to reclaim the land on demand, provided he paid compensation for any improvements.[14]

With chiefly approval, any immigrant family could settle on previously uncultivated, unclaimed land, clear it, start a banana garden, and build a hut on it. By these means new lineage segments could be founded. If the family was fortunate and multiplied, its members might then expand into contiguous uncultivated, unclaimed land, if no one objected (Gutmann 1926:303; HRAF:271). Hence many of today's localized patrilineages were immigrant segments of lineages settled in other chiefdoms a hundred years ago.[15]

As the generations passed, occupants of a banana garden were buried in it. After an initial burial in the hut, the body of a dead person was later exhumed and most of the remains reburied in the banana grove. The skulls and sometimes the arm bones were kept above ground. A special place in the grove marked with dracaena plants was reserved for the skulls of the ancestors (Gutmann 1926:308; HRAF:276). This "skull grove" of the ancestors was, of course, the best evidence of the right of a descendant to that particular banana garden (1926:302; HRAF:271). It took only one burial to start such a skull place, and two or three generations to make it venerably ancestral. The Chagga frequently did migrate and easily founded new localized patrilineal settlements as politics and other exigencies dictated. They carried with them the whole cultural apparatus for investing any new territory with supernatural beings specifically connected with a particular patrilineage. They established this connection by residence on the land, cultivation of the plot, the production in the garden of bananas and their offshoots, having a hut of children and grandchildren, and eventually burying the dead in the grove. All these, over time, produced a mystical association of patrilineal ancestors with

the land, translatable into a supernaturally protected legal right. A living
hedge of dracaena (*masale*) marked the boundaries of individual holdings. Thus the same plant that marked the skull grove of the dead ancestors was used to delineate the boundaries of the Chagga plots, boundaries
that the dead ancestors, as spirits, would protect.

Legal rights could be defended by invoking the ancestors to bring disaster on anyone who wrongfully occupied the land. If someone dared to
do so, he could expect to be plagued by misfortune, by nightmares, by
hallucinations, and worse, by crop failures, sick livestock, and illness and
death in the family. Land could be rightfully occupied by someone other
than a lineage member only if the lineage agreed to it (and the ancestors
were not opposed). But if the lineage did not agree, or the holder from
whom possession was ostensibly received, did not in fact give it, then woe
to the occupant. The lands became gardens of misfortune. With land
plentiful, as it was in the nineteenth century, and mutual assistance from
neighbors essential to social life, there was no reason to settle where one
was not wanted, and much reason not to do so.

The transfer and inheritance of kihamba land: fathers, sons, widows, and grandchildren

A man enjoyed less freedom to allocate his *kihamba* land than his
cattle. There was a strong sense that the land should descend agnatically, and that in the absence of special circumstances the claims of
agnates were always stronger than the claims of others. Within the
agnatic group clear priorities were given to kinsmen in certain genealogical relationships to the preceding holder of land. But even within
this framework a man had some discretion. He could allocate a better
plot to a son he preferred and a worse plot to one he disliked. He
could give a nearby plot to a son toward whom he had no obligation
but liked, and a distant one to a son he was obligated to care for but
disliked. He could allocate a plot to an adopted captive boy whom he
made a son. He could adopt a son-in-law. And if he hated one of his
sons, he could build a case for having the son expelled from the
lineage, and once that was done, the son could be denied any patrilineal land at all. This extreme measure was not often taken but it was
formally available (Gutmann 1926:19, 41, 235; HRAF:16, 17, 32, 33,
209). A man's preferences might have force even after his death. The
final decision on who should inherit a particular *kihamba* rested with the
lineage (1926:302; HRAF:271). The lineage decided whether to conform
to conventional rules of inheritance, whether to follow the wishes of the
decedent, or whether to use its own discretion (Moore 1981:225–48).

The preferred rules Gutmann left us regarding the patrilineal transfer of land seem to have been based on the assumption that a father would not die until after his sons were adult and at least the eldest was married. The rules seem also to assume a large family with a multiplicity of sons, which may, in demographic reality, have been unusual in the nineteenth century. The basic norms having to do with the provision of land by fathers for sons involved *inter vivos* transfers as well as inheritance. Eldest and youngest sons were favored. In large parts of Kilimanjaro, at the time that an eldest son got married, his father presented him with a developed banana grove. It was a paternal obligation. The father's own *kihamba* would eventually go to the youngest son by inheritance. Thus when the youngest son married, the youngest son built his wife's hut in his father's *kihamba* and went on living there all his life. Middle sons were not so fortunate. They were not given *vihamba*. They were supposed to clear and cultivate bush, to start their own gardens. A father could give middle sons developed banana gardens if he had them, but only if he chose to do so. He was under no obligation to provide them with developed land. Sometimes middle sons were sent to the paternal grandfather's house, to be brought up there, in the hope that *he* would provide for them (1926:60; HRAF:49). Otherwise middle sons were expected to cultivate bush, or to appeal to the chief to find them a suitable place to settle. If the population was not expanding, the number of middle sons would have been small, their problems of no great consequence.[16]

If a son predeceased his father but left children, the grandsons might inherit directly from the grandfather. If the dead son was the youngest son, no problems with respect to the *kihamba* arose, since the grandchildren already lived there. But if the dead son was an older son, and there was a surviving younger son, the grandfather might still prefer to give his *kihamba* to a grandson rather than to his own youngest son. The grandfather had the right to do so, but was under some obligation to provide a substitute *kihamba* for his own youngest (Gutmann 1926:59; HRAF:48).[17]

If an old man died leaving no sons, but left brothers with sons, his land went to his nephews. Their fathers, by definition, already being provided with *vihamba,* the particular nephews who inherited were the sons of his slaughtering-partner-brother. In theory, in all multi-son families, as in the inheritance of cattle, so with the inheritance of land, the eldest and youngest male siblings were partners and mutual heirs, and if there were two middle sons they were partners and mutual heirs. If there was an odd number of middle sons, the eldest inherited from the odd one (Dundas 1924:309; Gutmann 1926:49–50, 58; HRAF:39, 47). The eldest also inherited the *kihamba* of any widow who died without sons.

In general, widows had the right to remain for life in the banana groves allocated to them during their lifetime. A widow's youngest son and his

wife were, of course, coresidents of the *kihamba,* and remained there
with the widow until she died. If there were several widows, each would
have been allocated a separate hut and *kihamba.* The youngest son of
each wife eventually inherited her banana garden.

Widow inheritance by a brother was the standard practice, provided the
widow consented. Gutmann says the choice of brother was hers (1926:50;
HRAF:39). If she had had children with her deceased husband, she and
the children remained on the *kihamba.* If she and the widow-inheritor
subsequently had children, these were *his* children, not those of the deceased (1926:51; HRAF:40). The actual father had to provide land for his
own children. The *kihamba* of the deceased went to his own son or sons.
The inheritor of the widow could not encroach on these rights.[18] Thus
normally, when a man died leaving a widow (or widows) and sons, no
kihamba lands really changed hands. The widows continued to live where
they had before, and the sons as well.[19]

If, at his death, the father had had unoccupied lands, meadow, fallow,
or deserted groves, that unallocated land all went to the firstborn son. It
was his right and obligation to use this property as his father would have
done, to administer it for the benefit of his brothers as well as himself, to
allocate parts of it to them if they requested land. He also had the right to
allocate it to others for *masiro* if his brothers consented (Gutmann
1926:38; HRAF:29).

Cultivated land other than banana land: the maize lands and eleusine lands

In addition to their banana gardens the Chagga cultivated maize fields in
the lower areas of the mountain at the edge of the plain (Gutmann
1926:307; HRAF:275). No one lived in or near these fields. The huts of
the cultivators were in the banana belt much higher up on the mountain.
In the appropriate seasons they walked down to their *shamba* lands each
day. The chiefs organized the division, allocation, planting, rotation, and
protection of the maize fields near the plain. These were in constant
danger from animal and human predators and required guarding once the
crops had started to grow (1926:307; HRAF:275). In theory the chief
annually reallocated shares of the maize lands, holders being given the
use of the land for the year. Once a year in some areas, the chief selected
the part to be cultivated and on a particular day the land was divided up
with the help of the district heads and lineage elders (Dundas 1924:301;
Griffiths 1930:73). In the colonial period, the same shares of *shamba* land
were often reallocated to the same persons year after year. This procedure may have occurred in precolonial times as well, for as long as the
system of fallowing and shifting cultivation permitted.

Eleusine (*mbege*) was grown for beer making and was of major importance to the Chagga. It was grown in the rainy season in the lower areas
(where it was rotated with crops of maize and beans), and in the dry
season in the hill country, some of it in the bracken land between the
banana belt and the forest, some of it in the *vihamba*.[20]

Gutmann has little material on the precolonial arrangements regarding
non-*kihamba* arable lands beyond what has been noted here. Since this
land was not a scarce resource and all of it may have been part of a
system of shifting cultivation with annual or frequent reallocations, it is
not surprising that there is no legal elaboration with respect to it.

Rights in irrigation water

Irrigation on Kilimanjaro consisted of canals which tapped stream water
and brought it to planted areas in an intricate system of narrow channels.
Most canals were particularly associated with the lineage of the canal's
founder after whom they were usually named. In some cases it was the
chiefly lineage, but for the most part it was not. The head of the community of users was always chosen from the founder's lineage. But lineage
members were seldom the only users (Gutmann 1926:414; HRAF:372).
Thus the community of users of one canal constituted a local corporate
group that was not exclusively a kinship group.

The canal community head had ritual functions as well as administrative and allocatory powers. Each year after the rainy season the canals
were cleaned and repaired as a group effort on a day decided upon by the
water-community head. The sanction for failure to labor or noncompliance with his orders was withdrawal of the right to use water (Gutmann
1926:415; HRAF:373). One who could not attend was obligated to send a
substitute. The community head alone had the prerogative of making the
necessary libations and saying the appropriate prayers annually just before water was allowed to enter the newly cleaned canal. His ritual capacities were also used if and when the water level became low. In return
for his services he received from each member of the canal community an
annual bowl of eleusine grain (one of the essential ingredients of beer), or
the users brewed beer for him, and he invited his lineage to the beer
party. Beer brewing of this sort was done for the chief in the instances in
which the chief was "master" of the canal. In fact, part of the beer
brewed for an ordinary canal head was supposed to be paid to the chief as
canal tribute (1926:416; HRAF:374).

Canal users evidently argued a good deal about their use rights, which
were sometimes intricate. In some canals the water flowed continuously.
In others the water was collected in pool-like reservoirs at night, and was
then allowed to flow during the day.[21] In one pattern the man who lived

on the right side of the channel at the lowest point reached by the canal got his water first, then the next one above him, and then the one above him until about the middle of the area served by the canal. Then the pattern was repeated on the left side from the bottom up. Then the upper half started and was watered in the same manner from bottom to top, right side first. When everyone had watered his gardens once, the sequence started again. Few canals had enough water for a third series. The length of the period of watering varied with the canal, the number of its users, and the like. The canal head often had additional privileges. In some small canals the head of the canal community could draw off water for himself whenever he pleased. In others he had a right to the water all day on every market day (every fourth day). As it was more than he needed for his own use, he could allocate some of it to others, who, in return, would pay him in produce at harvest time.

Lineage and family control over persons: the allocation of property, labor, and marriage partners

From birth to death Chagga individuals, male and female, were dependent on others who often in consequence had some control over them. As children they worked for their parents. They tended animals, obtained fodder, fetched water and firewood, and ran other errands. Parents could assign their children to others. Children could be "loaned" to relatives or "pawned" to others. Old women without children in their households could request a child of a young family. The third child was particularly suitable for such placement (as were all children beyond the first two). Children were deposited as pledges for debts. Girls were particularly desirable for this purpose, as the bridewealth for a girl could then be received by the creditor in lieu of the debt when the pledge child married.

The labor situation of a young person after the age of circumcision changed. After circumcision, a girl owned the vegetable produce she had planted and harvested. Previous to circumcision, it belonged to her father. Normally the father financed the circumcision and gave his daughter a substantial gift in the celebrations that followed. Depending on his means he gave her a cow or a goat or other food, and the promise of more later. He also organized the celebration to which other gift-bearing kin came. The property received on this occasion was hers to keep. The circumcision was frequently soon followed by marriage. The father received the most substantial part of the bridewealth paid for his daughter, or if he wished, he could assign it to one of his sons. The father's consent was necessary to her marriage, and indeed, most marriages were arranged by the young couple's parents.

The basic principle governing the elders' choice was that named patrilines be exogamous. However, even on this point exceptions were made for chiefs (Gutmann 1926:72; HRAF:60). Also if two lineage branches of the same clan were considered to be distantly related, marriages were sometimes permitted. Marriage to a woman of the groom's mother's clan was considered especially desirable provided she was not a first cousin. Marriage to such first cousins was prohibited, as was marriage to a wife's sister while the wife was alive. Marriage rules, prohibitions, and preferences varied somewhat from one lineage to another. Certain lineages never intermarried. Others were said to prefer to intermarry. The senior men who had substantial control over the marriage of their sons and daughters could decide on the suitability of a particular match as they saw fit, or could declare the unsuitability of all intermarriage with a particular lineage.[22] The lineage elders also had much to say about the marital fate of widows. Widows were allocated to chosen heirs at the *matanga*. A widow could, in theory, refuse a particular partner, but may have been under pressure to accept her assignment. Children subsequently born to the widow were the children of the heir.

A young man, after circumcision, was expected to take over his father's corvée labor obligations. When a son's marriage had been arranged, his father provided him with the necessary bridewealth, and if he was the eldest son, with a plot of land of his own. (As indicated earlier, middle sons pioneered new lands, and youngest sons remained in the paternal household after marriage.) Previous to his marriage all the labor of eldest and middle sons was at the disposition of his parents. Afterward the young men expended most of their effort on their own households, on exchange labor obligations, and on obligations to the chief. They continued to owe some debts of gratitude to their fathers. The labor of the youngest son and of his wife remained at the disposition of the father.

A wife was expected to raise all the vegetable foods eaten by her family and to feed the cows stalled in her house. Any surplus produce was hers to sell in the market. Thus her labor was for the most part owed to her household. Only a small part of it was her own.

Rights to labor were enforced in various ways. In the system of exchange labor (in which men of a lineage or a neighborhood helped one another in major group tasks such as housebuilding or harvesting, or cultivating *shamba* land) reciprocity could be withdrawn. (Women were also involved in reciprocities, but on a smaller scale, often exchanging services with individuals, rather than participating in collective activities in groups.) Systems of reciprocal exchange of labor of this kind were essentially self-enforcing, and were not "legal" rights in any formal sense. But, particularly with respect to men, the accumulation of failures in these obligations over the long term could cause an individual to lose standing in the lineage, and ultimately suffer serious consequences.

Hierarchies of control existed even at the lowest levels of organization. Strong sanctions could be applied by fathers against children, husbands against wives (though they had to contend with the men of the wife's lineage), and by the lineage against a member, or senior lineage elders against juniors. Many sanctions have already been mentioned in other contexts. The many property rights men had (and wives derivatively from them) were contingent on being in good standing in the lineage. Some corvée obligations, some tribute demands, and other debts were met by the lineage collectively. Collective obligations implied the internal allocations of contributions imposed on individuals. The decision which individuals would do the work or pay and which would not was no small matter. In this as in other ways the lineage was in a position to allocate payments and penalties, not just properties and privileges.

Everyone was vulnerable to the lesser sanctions connected with the withholding of reciprocity and assistance. To run away, to try to resettle, was difficult for men, probably even more difficult if not impossible for women. Formal expulsion was a severe sanction rarely resorted to, but one that lay in the background. It was sometimes possible for an expelled man to become a retainer and dependent of the chief (Gutmann 1926:20; HRAF:17). Gutmann more than hints that lineages sometimes killed unpopular members. Probably all of these extreme measures were rare, more talked about than done, but they are representations of the coercive power of the kinship groups on which men and women were dependent.

THE SOCIAL FOUNDATIONS OF THE CHAGGA LEGAL ORDER IN PRECOLONIAL TIMES

In the main the mundane Chagga social order depended for its operation not on chiefly direction but on suborganizational arrangements within local social groups. In the precolonial period much of the negotiating, resource-allocating, rule-making, rule-administering, rule-enforcing and dispute-settling activity among the Chagga took place within the districts, the localized patrilineages, the irrigation associations, and the men's age-sets of the district and some of it in the women's markets. Each of these relatively autonomous social domains controlled important human and material resources which it could allocate and regulate. On the whole, internal disputes were disposed of internally. So necessary to the social and economic well-being of an individual were these social entities that the possibility that access to their resources could be withdrawn from a member, or that a person could be ousted, was deeply threatening. The need and the fear (to say nothing of routine) were probably sufficient to induce in most persons a reasonably effective level of compliance to the demands and decisions of the leadership and for the social order to "work." A number of examples have been touched on. In the irrigation canal associations, access to water could be refused to anyone who broke the rules, or defied an order of the canal group leader. Both potential inducements to compliance and direct sanctions were embedded in the resource control of the canal user's association itself. An age-set could punish a member who did not perform his or her share of collective corvée labor. All the principle social units of Chagga society had such autonomous means of coercing or inducing compliance from members.

As far as one can tell, neither objections to particular allocations nor other disputes over the internal administration of group affairs were lightly or easily brought to the chief for intervention. As mentioned earlier, district heads and the chief, each together with members of age-sets, did hear cases of dispute. But the chief's authority in particular seems to have been appealed to only occasionally when disputes proved to be intractable, or in situations that fell in the structural interstices, disputes between members of *different lineages* whose quarrels were not within the usual concerns of any group of which both parties were members, and disputes between residents of *different chiefdoms* and the like. Apart from the expense, for there were cattle and beer fees for hearings, there were other strong reasons not to go to the central authorities, not to try to overrule a decision made within a special domain of local control. "Going outside" was an offense against the internal hierarchy of authority, and produced ill-will that was dangerous for the future. Exit, moving to another district or chiefdom, could be a socially costly alternative. The wide distribution of lineage names over the mountain suggests that historically, in other times, this solution must have been attractive. But in periods when it was harder to move out (and over this century it has become increasingly difficult), there have been strong reasons to accept the decisions made in those domains of local control.

The Chagga often considered it "shameful" to go outside the local lineage to settle internal quarrels, and some sentiment to that effect remains to this day. Lineage elders probably did everything they could to prevent going outside since it gave their own decisions more force. The "shame" emphasized was not just a matter of washing dirty linen in public, it was also the shame of not having accepted lineage authority. The challenge to seniority implied more than a rejection of a particular decision about this-worldly material things; it implied a violation of the general spiritual and ritual order. Precolonial organizational order had ritual dimensions, and organizational leaders were also ritual leaders who were defined as ritually indispensable to the ongoing affairs of the organization. Canal group heads performed annual rituals to bless the canals. Senior elders of the lineages led the performance of lineage ritual and were intermediaries between the living and their dead ancestors. Chiefs performed rituals on behalf of the whole chiefdom. All secular power had its religious dimension. To question the decisions and persons possessed of such temporal and mystical influence as lineage elders and to go to the chief to ask him to intervene was full of risk, this-worldly and other-worldly. It was done only from time to time when the stakes were high.

The *mangi* seems to have used his authority largely to exact tribute, labor, and fighting power. His personal interests were completely intertwined with those of his office. Unless a matter concerned his chiefship or his own interests, he did not on his own initiative undertake to enforce the social order, or to intervene in disputes. When controversies came before the age-class assembly, his role was limited. But if he was appealed to personally to mediate or decide a controversy, and chose to heed the appeal, then it seems that he could and did act. But even in this quasi-judicial or mediatory capacity, the chief seems to have taken care to serve his own interests, both by collecting fees in cattle and beer, and by interposing himself profitably in relationships of debtor and creditor and guardianship. When he put his power at the service of others, it cost them something.

With his wealth, his control of the long-distance trade, and of booty, the chief was in a position to reward his district heads, his favorites, and occasionally other subjects. With his access to the services of the military age-class, he was able to threaten them.[23] The polar extremes of political division in the chiefdom seem to have been between chiefdom-wide control by the chief and local lineage control. The district head and the district age-sets occupied an interstitial position but, as Gutmann tells it, one that frequently seems to have been mobilized in the interests of the chief. District organization must also have had a local political significance to which Gutmann gives scant attention.

The law Gutmann described serves as a basis for interpreting the practical operation of these domains of power by providing a sense of the way controls over persons and material resources were managed at various levels of organization. But his use of these data was quite different from mine. The selection from and interpretation of Gutmann's work here has been structured by a knowledge of what became of Chagga ideas, politics, and law later in the century. The key is found in the organizational matrices in which norms and sanctions, discretionary decisions and negotiations, and the management and allocation of resources were carried out. It is important not to read the system only with a Western legal-professional orientation, looking for lists of rules, a particular sanction attached to a particular rule, while seeking a detailed definition of the parameters of the rules. Rule statements there were, and are, but they are not intelligible out of social context. More appropriate to an understanding of the way things worked is a focus on the asymmetrical relations between groups and individuals, on the nature of transactions between individuals, and a conception of the micropolitics of the significant groups. Chagga "law" was situated in ongoing arenas of action. It was a framework of organizations, relationships, and cultural ideas, a mix of principles, guidelines, rules of preference, and rules of prescription, together with conceptions of morality and causality, all of them completely intertwined in the web of ordinary activities.

It was not a special domain of knowledge or practice, but a body of ideas and usages known to all and used by all. What is discernible in Gutmann's rambling discourse about Chagga law and rules, Chagga ideas and customs, and Chagga chiefly history is the cultural ambience of continuous local struggles for social power, organizational and individual, enduring and transitory, structural and situational.

PART II

Twentieth-century transformations: economy, government, courts, and cases

4

The German period:

chiefs, cattle, cash, and courts

From the beginning of the colonial period the legal system on Kilimanjaro must be conceived as having two dimensions. One includes all that came under the immediate direction of government and administration, the other the residual part left to the Chagga to administer. The two were, of course, interdigitated and interrelated in reality, and each affected the other. The residual part was, obviously, historically linked to precolonial "customary law," but from the start was only a segment of the precolonial Chagga system of law-government. Attached to a political order quite differently constituted from that to which it was originally hitched, and operating in the framework of a different economy, residual "customary law" was an altered entity from the very beginning. Its development as economic, demographic and other transformations took place over the years is outlined here. To describe the process, a variety of nonlegal dimensions must be sketched. Local dispute-case records seen alone would give a misleading sense of social and cultural continuity, because the issues that were permitted to surface in local courts and the framework of concepts that legitimized them tended to have a traditional character, especially in the early years. But if one keeps in mind the drastically changing milieu in which these cases arose, the visible continuity of some normative concepts is seen in perspective. Substantial descriptions of the political, economic, and social changes that form the background of the cases is essential to understanding their content.

In 1886 Germany and Britain divided their spheres of influence in East Africa. Over the next few years Kilimanjaro came under full German control. Thirty years later, by the end of the German period (1916) every Chagga institution had been buffeted by the changes the Germans brought to the mountain. From the marriage bed to the public arena everything was disturbed and shaken. Christian missionaries extolling monogamy hammered at polygynous households. Many continued to be polygamous. All Chagga were told to dig latrine pits and to discontinue

95

their tidy habit of defecating in the banana grove. Everyone dug latrine pits, but no one used them (Gutmann 1926:324; HRAF:292).

In the public arena resistance was more difficult. When the Germans took over, they immediately abolished the military aspects of the Chagga age-grade system. Having met with armed resistance, they wanted to avoid any risk of rebellion. That abrupt change had profound structural implications. From a time when the chief's coercive authority had depended on the military age-class, a force that also could hold him in check, the chiefs ceased to be answerable to their subjects. The chiefs came to rely on the German colonial power as the source of their legitimacy and effectiveness. Uncooperative chiefs were hanged or deposed. As long as chiefs were in the favor of their masters, they held power. A misstep, and they were removed. But only the missteps that concerned their masters were at issue. The earlier constitutional framework of Chagga politics was never to be the same again.

The military defeat of the Chagga by the Germans, the stripping of the military power of the chiefdoms, and the abolition of warfare and raiding changed the roles of all men of all ages by altering the balances of functions among them. It changed altogether the character of the age-grade system, which came to function principally as a mode of classification for the purpose of calling up corvée labor and eventually disappeared. The caravan provisioning and the "protection" business of earlier times were no more. The possibility of acquiring cattle or other valuables through raiding was over. Chiefs and their clients were cut off from the economic benefits of booty that had once been distributed to chiefly favorites. The slave trade ended. The ivory trade had faded and what was left of it must have changed hands (Stuhlman 1909:792; Iliffe 1979:48–52, 130). The long-distance trade was to become a white people's province of activity. Chiefs had to find new sources of income. Everyone was concentrating on new ways to acquire cattle.

In the early period, some of the force of German authority was extended to Chief Marealle (Melyari) of Marangu. In his heyday (until 1904) the Germans made him chief over all of eastern Kilimanjaro. He became something of a subchiefmaker himself, and had a tremendous effect on internal Chagga politics. Marealle used his office to exact enormous amounts of cattle tribute from subject chiefdoms for himself and for Marangu. He also managed to extend the territory of Marangu to include *mitaa* that previously had been part of the neighboring chiefdom of Mamba. Despite the protests of the Mamba people, that annexation was confirmed both by the German administration in 1905 and later by the British (Gutmann 1926:435–9; HRAF:391–4). Marealle's activities are the most extreme example of the persistence of interchiefdom competition for dominance over territory on Kilimanjaro into colonial times. In precolonial times expansionism had been carried on through warfare and alliance. In the colonial period it continued in a new guise: administrative consolidation. Some chiefdoms swallowed others. The competition went on in a new arena, the arena of administrative reorganization. Neither warfare, nor alliance, but favor with the colonial government was the new source of power, or more accurately for most commoners, favor with the favorites of the colonial powers.

The competition for cattle also changed. It is not clear whether Chagga cattle were directly affected by the rinderpest epidemics that devastated Maasai cattle in the 1890s. However, the Chagga must at least have been indirectly affected by the disaster to the Maasai with whom they had always traded as well as fought. Some Maasai settled among them in this period and became assimilated. Gutmann in the early 1900s said that the value of cattle had greatly increased since precolonial times, and that in his time the fee of a beast required by the chief to hear a law case was much too high, even if it had been fair in earlier times (Gutmann 1926:611; HRAF:548).[1]

For chiefs, the problem of obtaining cattle in numbers without the trading-raiding-booty-agistment complex to justify taking them meant creating and increasing cattle levies. Court fees were one means. But there were others. Gutmann depicts the precolonial chief as a redistributor of cattle and other wealth for political purposes (and public benefit), and the colonial chief as much more of an accumulator of cattle and other wealth for private purposes. His account of early happy times may be somewhat exaggerated since chiefly predation and accumulations seem to have been well established before the colonial period. But there was undoubtedly basis for his contention.

In German times, apart from corvée labor, the tax collected by the chief was principally in cattle, meat, and beer. Gutmann's rough estimate of chiefly revenues was calculated on the basis of a guess that at least one head of cattle was probably paid the chief every seven-year period (1926:390–5; HRAF:350–4). (This was a lower estimate than he made elsewhere in the same book. See Gutmann 1926:383–5; HRAF:344–5.) He also figured that there was one beer payment and one meat payment per annum per household, and twenty days corvée duty. "Nowadays," he says, "the income of the chief is guaranteed by the administration, and he collects his income with less trouble than formerly" (1926:390–5; HRAF:350–4). In addition to these payments to the chief, each Chagga had to pay to the colonial government a head and hut tax of at first three rupees (later six rupees) as well as doing additional corvée labor for the colonial power. Gutmann estimated that the chief was paid seven times as much as the colonial government in this process. He counted thirty-three corvée missions done for the chief during the months of July to September 1915 in

Plate 10. Chief Marealle of Marangu. (Photo from the collection of Hans
Meyer's daughter. Meyer visited Kilimanjaro in 1887, 1888, 1889.)

Plate 11. Men and women singing and dancing. (Photo from M. Merker, 1902)

Kidia District in Old Moshi where he lived (1926:390–5; HRAF:350–4). He says that in colonial times the chiefs abused their powers egregiously, that in Uru before 1917 each young man had to pay a five-rupee fee to the chief before he could be betrothed and then owed the chief one head of cattle before the wedding. Raum cites Gutmann's saying in 1907 that in the middle of that year

> the Chagga chief Ngalelo . . . suddenly announced that the whole populace had to drink the poison ordeal "to rid the country of evil." . . . Many confessed and paid a fine in cattle, which was divided between the chief and his courtiers. In some districts of the chiefdom a fixed charge was raised, in well-to-do districts 1 rupee, in poor ones half a rupee. This ordeal was a modification of the traditional procedure: no longer was it used to determine the guilt or innocence of a suspect individual; it now served to test the loyalty of all subjects of the new chief and to provide him with a source of revenue. (Raum 1965:182, citing Gutmann, *Evangelisch-lutherisches Missionblatt,* 1907)

The process of tax collection and the enforcement of corvée duties was managed through the existing system of district (*mitaa*) supervisors (*wachili*). Each chiefdom had no fewer than eight supervisors, each with a herald (with horn) and an assistant. The supervisors in turn were supervised by a super-supervisor who acted as intermediary between them and the colonial government. The supervisors received no pay from the chief,

and probably used their offices to exact payments on the side for themselves. Exacting payments certainly was the custom later on in British
times. Gutmann says, "A great many supervisors were put in chains
because they had not fulfilled their duties conscientiously and honestly"
(1926:392; HRAF:352). Gutmann thought the chief's cattle tax should be
abolished, and he had various other proposals for restoring the public
uses of the chiefly herds. He clearly thought the redefinition of the office
of chief in German times was deleterious.

Not only the abuse of cattle taxation disturbed Gutmann, but the extremes to which chiefs took the custom of using the children of commoners as servants in their households (1926:388–9; HRAF:348–9). If
the chief requested it, he had "always" had the right to the third child of
any man. The German administration ended this form of servitude for
boys, who in earlier times had been used as goat herds. Since the chief
stopped keeping goats in colonial times, and concerned himself exclusively with collecting cattle, this loss of herd boys presented no great
problem. The collection of fodder for cows was a female task, so girls
continued to be taken into chiefly households as servants for the chief's
wives. The young girls were all children of the poor, not the wealthy.
They remained in the chiefly establishment until they married, and the
chief received the bridewealth for them. Gutmann says the girls were also
sexually available to the chief. As far as Gutmann was concerned, this
whole complex was a form of slavery (1926:388–9; HRAF:348–9). The
chief's wives were the only Chagga women who did no work at all, and
each had from five to eight girls working for her. The Moshi chief, Salema, asked Gutmann to try to help him improve the situation of these
children since he seems to have been unable to control his wives.[2] Salema
had more than 70 servant girls in the houses of his wives and his mother.
As there were altogether 1,240 girls in the chiefdom, 70 represented a
substantial percent of the total. The Chagga deeply resented this form of
servitude. Gutmann offers as proof that when, in 1917, the British arrested the chief of Kibosho and replaced him, the question raised about
the new chief by his subjects was how many wives he planned to have.
Before the installation of the new chief was ratified by his people, they
demanded to know his plans on this point, and told him he would have to
limit himself to five, because the previous incumbent had had so many
wives that the burden was intolerable (1926:388–9; HRAF:348–9).

The Germans also intervened in the use of pledge-children in the cattle
arrangements of the Chagga. In precolonial times and during the early
colonial period a great many Chagga from Moshi and Marangu had
placed cattle in agistment in Rombo, an area on the eastern side of the
mountain where there was ample grazing pasture, and cattle did not have
to be stall-fed. In return, many Rombo children were placed in Moshi

and Marangu households as debt-pledge children. The colonial government required that these children be returned to their families (Gutmann 1926:479; HRAF:430). One can only guess that the Chagga must have reclaimed their cattle, and made rearrangements as to their care.

A law case arising much later (Mwika, Case 17, 1931) alludes to this period and indicates that the then chief of Nganyeni, Lengaki Mariki, maintained a *boma,* a cattlefold, on the plain for himself and his subjects. The cattle of commoners were placed in agistment with the chief to be kept and grazed by his agents in the cattlefold in the lowlands.[3]

Who was right and who was wrong regarding the particular facts of the case is not important. What the case account implies is that in the German colonial period there was an important change in the relationship between chiefs and commoners with regard to cattle, and an altered form of the practice of placing cows in the households of others. The chief seems to have ceased to be a depositor of cattle in the households of favorites and to have become almost exclusively a collector of them. The former practice in which individual commoners placed cattle with individuals in other chiefdoms (often taking pledged children in return) had diminished or virtually ended. Some traditional rules about cattle placement were involved in the new practices. The change in the use of such customary law rules seems more important than the continuities in the framework of stated norms.[4]

Backed by the force of the colonial presence, those chiefs who were willing to cooperate with the Germans came to occupy other new roles. They became labor recruiters and tax collectors for the colonial state. Men had to be mobilized to construct buildings and roads for the colonial government, and to work the settlers' lands (Gutmann 1926:390–1; HRAF:350–7; Winter 1979:43). Pressed by hut taxes imposed from 1898 on, and by some labor obligations that could be bought off with cash, as well as tempted to buy cattle, the Chagga were rapidly drawn further into the cash economy.[5] First they sold their labor. Then little by little, following the example of the missions, they began to plant coffee bushes in their banana gardens. Eventually they sold almost anything that someone would buy including grass (for fodder) from their fallow lands (Gutmann 1926:308; HRAF:276).

The advent of the cash economy meant that commoners were not solely dependent on inheritance or cattle placement to acquire cattle but could buy them. Men began to get into trouble with cash debts by buying cattle for bridewealth or other purposes (Gutmann 1926:482; HRAF:433). Inherited money was either distributed in accordance with the customary patterns of inheritance or *used to buy cattle* (Gutmann 1926:38; HRAF:29).

The chiefs took advantage of the widespread buying of cattle by commoners to impose new taxes. They learned from colonial taxation the practice of taxing everyone equally, rich and poor alike. They adopted this practice and applied it in their own cattle taxation, imposing payment of one beast every three or four years, and imposing it on all, rather than as had been customary, only on the cattle-wealthy. Such a change was possible because "poor people" had begun to acquire animals with their wages (Gutmann 1926:383–5; HRAF:344–5).[6]

In the early years of the century not only did the German presence disturb and change the whole cattle economy but the colonial government tried to tamper directly with the women's markets. The chiefdom of Moshi had had three marketplaces in early colonial times, and presumably also precolonial times (Gutmann 1926:430–1; HRAF:387).[7] The multiplicity of these marketplaces was and is a widespread feature of local life on Kilimanjaro. But in 1911 the German government tried to discontinue all markets in all the chiefdoms from Marangu to Uru and to require the inhabitants of these chiefdoms to bring their wares to the market of the district office in Old Moshi. The women continued to maintain one of the Moshi markets in defiance of the government order. And, indeed, eventually the government saw the folly of its rule and withdrew the order. But in Old Moshi two of the old markets were not reopened in Gutmann's time.

The women, who had policed their own markets in earlier days could no longer do so. They had had means of punishing individuals who brought rotted produce or watered milk to market, or who charged exorbitant prices. Gutmann says, "Since the establishment of the colony the natives do not dare take the market law into their own hands. In consequence cheating and high prices remained unchecked. . . . You cannot buy undiluted milk there any longer" (1926:430–1; HRAF:387). He says the colonial administration took the view that all such matters should be reported to it, and the government would investigate and take appropriate action. But the women were too intimidated to use the colonial courts for these trivial matters, and were debarred from taking action themselves, so cheating was rampant.

Gutmann's sympathy for the Chagga gives a sense of the interstitial position of the missions on Kilimanjaro. Situated in the heart of the chiefdoms, in the midst of ordinary Chagga homesteads, they were close to everything that went on. The German administration arranged that the Lutherans and Catholics have local proselytizing monopolies. In most parts of Kilimanjaro the two churches were not in direct competition for the same population. The countryside was divided up between them. Consequently to this day there are distinct Catholic areas and Lutheran areas which date back to the early decades of the German presence.

In addition to religious teaching (the Lutherans in Kichagga, the Catholics in Swahili) the missions opened dispensaries, hospitals, and schools. In 1909 there were 10,000 children in Catholic mission schools, and by 1914, 9,000 in Lutheran schools (Shann 1956:25, 28, 29). The missions trained Chagga teachers and lay brothers, and their message spread rapidly. As in many other parts of the world Christianity was added to the preexisting stock of ideas and a syncretistic system of thought was the result.

The missions not only attended to the souls of their parishioners. They had to be mindful of the material requirements of the mission. They had to feed their own personnel and to become self-supporting to a significant degree. Thus they acquired extensive lands for farming, not just land on which to build churches and schools. Banana gardens and vegetables were planted, and later coffee. This stake in agriculture meant that the missions had a need, not only for pupils, but for labor. Indeed many of their pupils worked for the mission.[8] The Kilema mission is reputed to have introduced coffee cultivation to the Chagga. But the mission's initial purpose was to grow coffee to sell for its own benefit.

Thus in the effort to sustain itself, the mission had to become an enlarged and transformed version of a Chagga household with gardens. Like the settlers, it recruited Chagga labor to work its lands. It added a cash crop and the Chagga followed. The mission was not far behind the settler-planter.[9] The first commercial coffee estate in Moshi had been started in 1894 (Rogers 1972:167).

Coffee, settlers, missions, and Chagga politics were interwoven from the early days of the century. Chief Fumba of Kilema asked for coffee seedlings in 1901. In 1902, in Marangu, Mawalla, chief advisor of Marealle I, also asked for coffee seedlings (Rogers 1972:166). By 1914, a substantial number of Chagga homesteads had coffee bushes.[10]

In 1914 the Kilimanjaro area had only 105–115 male European settlers (Rogers 1972:171).[11] The most important land for cultivation remained in Chagga hands. It consisted of a highland belt about seventy miles long and five to eight miles wide running at an altitude of 3,500 to 5,000 feet above sea level (Tanganyika Notes and Records [TNR]1965: March, 64:115). A good deal of it was suitable for coffee bushes. The spread of coffee cultivation eventually changed the significance of landholding and the meaning of Chagga land law, but that transformation was not fully felt until well into the British colonial period. The three decades of German colonial rule were just a beginning.

THE SYSTEM OF COURTS AND HEARINGS

As one might expect, the arrangement for the hearing of disputes and the meting out of punishments was significantly changed in German times. Neighborhood, district, and chiefly palavers and hearings continued, but even the chief's court had lost jurisdiction over capital, witchcraft, and political cases (Raum 1965:184). Above the Chagga courts was placed a native court of the Imperial District Office, which handled major matters and had the final say on appeal. In the hearings before this colonial court, the lower court was represented by the chief or his delegates. Since the chief had previously already heard and decided in his own court many (all?) of the cases that came up, the chief did not see his role as "attorney for the accused" but rather as one in which his own prior decision was being justified.

Under the German colonial structure the chief's judicial power was greatly increased. Chiefs began to hear more cases by themselves, and when the age-grade assembly was present, the chief presided over it, and made the decisions. He did not simply announce the decisions of the assembly as had been earlier practice (Gutmann 1926:591–2; HRAF:531). The colonial administration considered that the Native Court of the Imperial District it had established was available to anyone. In fact, only major cases ever reached it. And no wonder, since the white judge was not only surrounded by interpreters, but armed Askaris (soldiers) guarded the entrance and a sjambok-equipped Askari preserved order in the assembly (1926:429; HRAF:386).[12]

Gutmann alludes to a number of law cases handled not by the colonial courts, but by Chagga tribunals. Of some he gives fairly detailed accounts. Some are specified as cases that took place during his stay on Kilimanjaro. Others are clearly precolonial, and were cases he must have been told about. Still others are of uncertain date. Probably the most important historical characteristic of all of these cases is that they did not involve litigation over land. Many concerned cattle, either disputes over the ownership or payment of cattle, or cattle damages claimed for one or another wrong. This central preoccupation with cattle persisted well into the second and third decades of the century. It confirms other indications that the buying and selling of land and land shortage were not an important issue among the Chagga until much later on, roughly 1930, well into the British colonial period, and long after the cultivation of coffee had become a major factor in the economy of the region. Four of Gutmann's cases are described below. His own descriptions are quite garbled, so that clarified versions are offered here rather than direct quotation.

Self-help frustrated: the man who struck another man's wife

Gutmann described this case (one that took place in his own time) to illustrate the nature of the sliding scale of payments of legal fees to the chief in the cases heard on the chief's Lawn of Justice. But it is as much an example of what can happen when self-help is attempted and resisted, and illustrates one of the many ways in which the Chagga used curses. For modern lawyers interested in doctrinal arguments, in the "rule of the case," it shows the inextricable mixture of issues that is commonplace in such disputes, and the absence of any effort to focus on a particular rule to explain the decision.

The case initially concerned three men, A, B, and C. A and B were kinsmen. A intended to collect a debt owed him by C who was the son-in-law of B. A intended to use self-help. It was his plan simply to harvest the grain from C's (the debtor's) field of eleusine.

A went to the household of his kinsman B expecting to find C there, and intending to tell C what he was about to do. C was not there. Instead A found that only the women were at home. A informed B's wife of his plan, and told her to tell C. She refused and they quarreled.

A became angry and cursed her, "May you lose blood." She answered with an immediate counter-curse, "May you and your wife lose blood." A then slapped her. She shouted and her daughter and co-wife appeared. The two women restrained A and prevented him from hitting B's wife again. In the process they, too, were beaten.

B came home later on and was told what had happened. He decided to bring the case straight to the chief without trying to negotiate it.

In his hut he had a he-goat and a fat ox. For a moment he hesitated, trying to decide whether it would not suffice to bring only the he-goat to the chief. But then he cast aside the thought, and said, "I must show that A did not insult a little man. He will not dare do it a second time." And he untied the ox from the halter post and brought it to the chief's residence to start a lawsuit. Consequently A had to furnish an ox as well.

During the trial A denied that he had uttered the first curse, but he could not deny slapping B's wife's face. The chief said, "Not even I would dare to beat somebody else's wife." The chief decided that A would have to pay a goat to the beaten women in compensation. As A preferred to pay cash, the chief decided he must pay ten rupees.

But then B rose before the judiciary assembly and said, "I demand that my head of cattle be slaughtered." He was trying to raise the costs to A. Had B's animal been slaughtered for the benefit of the assembly A would have had to pay the goat, his own ox, and one more ox to compensate B. A asked the chief for mercy.

The chief was so disposed, and told B to take his ox home. A's head of cattle was then slaughtered for the men of the judiciary assembly. (Gutmann 1926:612–13; HRAF:548–9)

It is not clear from Gutmann's account, and indeed may not have been clear from the discussion at the time, whether the compensation was paid for the cursing and the slapping, or only for the beating. A goat paid in compensation in this way could be used for life-preserving sacrifice should the cursed person or a member of her (or his) household later fall ill. The Chagga did, and do, often take curses seriously (1926:554, 690; HRAF:499, 620). What the case does show is the way in which the payment of beasts was a precondition of bringing a case before the chief and the judiciary assembly. It suggests that self-help with notice was a normal procedure and that the privilege of beating a woman was the exclusive prerogative of her husband.

The allocation of an inheritance: the division of agistment cattle among the heirs

Two years before Gutmann wrote about this case the sons of a certain Kirumbujo Mate went to court to settle the distribution of the agistment cattle of their deceased father. He, the father, had been executed by the Germans in 1900 with his chief.

The district magistrate (*mchili*) in conjunction with the elders decided that the eldest son, Ndesaryo Mate, should receive twenty head, the intermediate son, Saluo Mate, two, and the youngest, Mhekye, sixteen head. The intermediate son was still a bachelor and would have to rely on his brothers' help when it came to raising the bridewealth (Gutmann 1926:36–7; HRAF:28).

Gutmann goes on to explain that had it been a matter of cattle within the hut (i.e., not stalled in agistment) these would have been distributed in such a manner that eldest and youngest would have received an additional head, while any intermediate sons would have had to be satisfied with the promise that they would eventually receive a calf from that cow of the eldest or youngest (1926:36–7; HRAF:28).

What seems unusual about this case is that the matter was not handled within the localized lineage, which would have been the normal primary forum. Presumably no resolution was arrived at in the lineage, hence the issue was taken outside. The case is also interesting both in its information about the quantity of a prominent man's cattle holdings and in its confirmation of the secondary place of middle sons.

A girl for a cow; the reluctant bride; the pledge-child who ran away

A case that came before Salema (chief of Moshi from 1900 to 1917; see Stahl 1964:275) follows:

In a famine year Mavin Ovenja slaughtered a head of cattle that had been placed in agistment with him. The owner threatened him. Mavin ran away to the nearby chiefdom of Kilema to the household of his wife's sister. She was married to a man named Moruvera Sajo. Hearing about Mavin's troubles Moruvera gave Mavin a good head of cattle so that he could satisfy his creditor. In exchange, Mavin gave his ten year-old daughter, Ndewuliso Mangowo, to Moruvera.

Moruvera planned eventually to give this child to his son, Mfunguo, as a wife without paying bridewealth for her. During her stay in his household Moruvera financed the girl's cliterodectomy. Having done this and having given her father a head of cattle, he felt he had met his bridewealth obligations.

When she was about fifteen Moruvera betrothed the pledge-child to his son. The girl ran away, and fled to her mother's house. Moruvera demanded that Mavin, the girl's father, return the head of cattle (plus the offspring it would have had in the meanwhile) and reimburse him for the cliterodectomy the financing of which in normal circumstances is a paternal obligation.

After hearing the facts chief Salema decided that Moruvera had the right to one cow only, that he did not have the right to the calves the beast would have had over the years, having forfeited that right by sinning against the laws of growth by marrying the girl off at too early an age.

Moruvera was satisfied and withdrew his other claims when he realized that it was the chief who would pay him the cow, not the girl's father. The father had to cede to the chief the bridewealth guardianship of his daughter, that is, when the daughter would be marriageable (in four years), the bridewealth would go to the chief. (Gutmann 1926:128–9; HRAF:111–12)

In its implications and assumptions this case reveals a number of presumed legal capacities: the right of a father to control the residence or marriage of a daughter; the right of a nonkinsman who pays for a girl's cliterodectomy to demand repayment from her father for having fulfilled in his stead a father's obligation to his child; the "interest" on a cow debt, that is, indemnification calves, which could be demanded if a cow debt was not paid for some years; that the chief in his role as judge could enter a case by paying what the defendant owed and by taking from the defendant in return the bridewealth rights to his daughter; and last, and not least, that the chief had jurisdiction over a case brought in his court against one of his subjects by a citizen of another chiefdom.

A case of false accusation

A theft had been committed in one of the districts, and the supervisor and his deputy searched the local houses for evidence. They also asked the people in the area to give any information they might have that might lead to the apprehension of the culprit.

One woman said that a pot of milk had been emptied in her house a few days before, and that before she herself had even noticed that the milk was missing, her neighbor, a woman named Singia, had appeared and told her that she had seen a man in the house drinking the milk. She also told her that, when the thief realized he had been seen by Singia, he had seized her breasts and suckled them, thus putting her under a sacred obligation not to divulge his identity. Singia said she could therefore not say who he was, but wanted to report the incident so that suspicion would not fall on her.

The neighbor whose milk had been taken said that a boy in the neighborhood had seen Singia leaving the neighbor's house in rather of a hurry, and that he had seen no one else. The district supervisors then began to suspect Singia, and called her in for questioning. They pressed her to reveal the name of the man she had seen. At first she refused, but eventually she said that it was Mkiwa Malisa.

The supervisors then informed Mkiwa Malisa that he had been accused. He in turn took a goat and brought it to the district lawn where he demanded that the accusing woman likewise bring in a goat. This would have been the beginning of a formal lawsuit. But the supervisors persuaded him to take the animal back to his house. The supervisors then made the two confront each other.

The woman, Singia, accused the man, Mkiwa. He denied everything and produced a perfect alibi. On the day in question he had been cutting wood with another man. The alibi was investigated and appeared undeniably true. Singia was then asked what the man she had seen had been wearing and she said she could not make this out. Her husband and brother then realized her case was hopeless, and they stopped arguing on her behalf.

The supervisors worked out a settlement between Mkiwa and Singia. The normal compensation for defamation was a goat. But as Singia was a woman, they decided that Singia was to pay half the value of a goat, that is, four rupees and two barrels of beer. This beer was to repair the honor of Mkiwa and was to be drunk by the participants in the hearing and by the neighbors who would spread the news that Mkiwa had been cleared of all suspicion. In a suit of this kind, the beer had to be delivered in any case to repair the slander, but other forms of compensation could be reduced. Had the case come up before the chief, the reparation of honor would have been a much more elaborate ceremony. (Gutmann 1926:546–7; HRAF:491–3)

CONCLUDING COMMENTS ON THE CASES

The four cases discussed give the general sense of the kind of litigation Gutmann describes as having come before the chief and the judiciary assembly and before the *wachili* in the district courts (*mtaa* courts) during the early colonial period. They reflect Chagga customs and Chagga ideas about right-doing and wrongdoing. All four cases are disputes between individuals without direct political content. As such they do not show the aspects of law that have to do with government, nor the way in which coercion was used in instances of resistance to the exercise of administrative power. For such matters there appear to have been no hearings. As Gutmann explained, the chief (or sometimes even his underlings) could turn any recalcitrant over to the colonial authorities by falsely accusing him of breaking the rules of the colonial government in cases of resistance to his (their) impositions and orders (see note 6 in Chapter 4). They could also manipulate those rules to deprive individuals of opportunities to work for cash by executive fiat. These cases did not come up on the chief's Lawn of Justice.

The "customary law" applied by the chief in his court was a segregated segment of a larger legal-administrative system. But even that segment, one must suppose, was permeated by the knowledge that the colonial government could be relied on to supply coercive force behind chiefly authority. Thus in the colonial period not only was the procedural format of hearings on the chief's Lawn of Justice altered, with the chief taking a new, decisive role, but the changed political-economic ambience in which the "customary law" hearings were held must have significantly reshaped the meaning of the proceedings.

5

The British colonial period and beyond:

an economic overview

POPULATION, CASH CROPPING, AND LAND SHORTAGE

After the British took charge, all the basic processes of change initiated in the period of German rule continued. Some have persisted into the post-colonial situation. The cultivation of coffee increased steadily. Coffee growing, combined with a great growth of population, produced a gradually intensifying shortage of land. From a population of about 110,000 in 1900, the population increased to 289,000 in 1948, 351,000 in 1957, and to 476,000 in 1967. The density of the population is also astounding. Kilimanjaro is a "rururb," a rural area with an urban density. In the 1970s there were 1,000 persons per square mile in the more crowded areas (Maro 1974:76). Children by the half-dozen peer out from between the bushes as one walks up any path. The remarkable population increase may eventually abate slightly, now that birth control methods have become more widely available in the area. But a census of 300 families conducted during fieldwork in 1969 showed that more than 50 percent of the members of those families were persons under eighteen. Of 2,242 persons in the 300 households 245 were about fifty years old or over, and 1,265 were under eighteen. The population has continued to burgeon. How much this population increase has been the result of public health measures which decreased infant mortality and how much to the interference of Christian monogamy with indigenous customs regarding the spacing of children is not clear. It had been Chagga practice to breast-feed children for several years and not to have a new baby until the nursling was weaned. Christian priests and pastors are said to have told the Chagga that it was all right to have a child a year, that polygyny was wrong, and child spacing unnecessary. There is no doubt of the rate of increase.

The most sought-after valuable in the German period was livestock. In the British era land came to be the most desirable scarce resource. In the

1920s it was still possible to obtain a *kihamba* for a cow and a goat.[1] Later on administrative allocation and eventually cash became a means of obtaining land. This shift is visible in the subject matter of litigation as in other indices. From approximately the 1930s on there were some sales of *vihamba* for cash. Nevertheless, for most men, throughout the colonial period, inheritance or allocation of undeveloped plots by the administration remained the principal means of acquiring a *kihamba*. In 1979 kinship was even more important for land acquisition since undeveloped land for allocation no longer existed.

In the late 1920s sufficient pressure on the land had developed to worry the British administration as well as the Chagga. The Chagga chiefs were said to be "very suspicious of alienation of land to non-relatives even where such land lies in the plains some miles below their lowest settlement. At a 'baraza' . . . several chiefs asked if they could bid for land at auctions, and whether the Native Treasury Surplus balance could be used to pay rents of land so acquired" (Annual Report, Northern Province, 1929; TNA 11681:30). It is no wonder they were worried. In 1922 the European population of Moshi District was only 224, but 185 of them were planters (Rogers 1972:246). In 1929 a district officer from Bukoba, A.W.M Griffiths, was called in to make a survey of the local land situation. He was to give attention both to the indigenous customary rules and to the problem of shortage with an eye to determining whether land registration was possible (Rogers 1972:492).

Griffiths reported that the buying and selling of land were not yet permitted, and that the chiefs were against allowing it. Indeed, in 1927, the chiefs had gone so far as to appeal to the governor to ask him to prohibit buying and selling. This implies that the sub rosa sale of land for cash had actually begun, or there would have been no need to prohibit it. The chiefs had good reason for their position on the matter. "Today," says Griffiths, "the control of all land which is not in beneficial occupation is tending to become a perquisite of the chief" (Griffiths 1930:63, 88).

The chiefly prerogative which in precolonial times was essentially an administrative control over unused and unoccupied land was converted in colonial times into something more like a personal interest.[2] Coffee had made unoccupied land valuable, and population growth made it scarce. But even so chiefs did not dare seize unlived-in land once it had been planted with coffee. A basic tenet of Chagga law was that a man who developed bush land by planting trees in it thereby had a permanent interest in it. Bananas were the initial plant around which this doctrine was formed. Then the rule was easily transferred to coffee and to other trees. Because of this rule about planters' rights the Chagga resisted vigorously when, in 1932, the British tried to plant trees on river banks as a measure against erosion.

A certain amount of damage to trees had taken place in the river valleys and it was in consequence decided to replant the banks of some of the mountain rivers with an European species of trees. At considerable trouble seedlings were procured and issued gratuitously by the Government to the natives. The natives declined to plant, for, they argued, when the trees grow up the Europeans will claim that the trees are their own property, having come from Europe, and will also annex the land on which they stand. In short, Government was resorting to a deliberate subterfuge to trick the native of his tribal lands! (Tanganyika Territory, Annual Reports of the Provincial Commissioners on Native Administration for the Year 1933, TNA 19415, 1933:51)

The provincial commissioner seems not to have realized that he was dealing with a conflict of laws situation and that the Chagga had good reason to worry. But he goes on to say that the Chagga were deserving of sympathy in relation to the land question. And no wonder. Land had become a serious issue. Chiefs were using their allocatory privileges over unused land to give plots to their innumerable sons and other kinsmen.

   The sketch maps of Mwika and Kilema (Figs. 5.1–5.3) were made in 1969, but the land situation was substantially the same in 1979. The maps were made only to indicate juxtapositions of landholders. Plots were not measured, and relative sizes of the maps do not reflect relative sizes of plots on the ground. The first of the Mwika maps (Fig. 5.1) shows a section of a *mtaa* in one of the older areas of settlement in Vunjo. The differences in numbers indicate to which lineage the household head belongs. Note the prevalence of the numbers of a once-chiefly lineage. The chiefdom that that lineage had ruled was consolidated into a larger chiefdom in the 1920s. The ex-chiefdom then became a *mtaa* (parish) of the consolidated chiefdom, and its chiefship was abolished. The map is evidence of the allocations made by the then chief to his relatives, probably after 1912 and certainly before 1930, before the chiefship was lost. Land plot histories and local inquiries confirmed this. Small wonder that the chiefs opposed both the buying and selling of land and land registration; both would have made their allocatory control over land more difficult to maintain. Individual objections or challenges to the chiefly rights of appropriation were difficult to mount, since the chiefs controlled the courts of first instance and sat on the appeal court of the division. There did exist formal means of circumventing this procedure and appealing to colonial officials, but this was by no means the easiest nor the most diplomatic thing to do if one intended to continue living in the chiefdom.

   The first response to land pressure was the filling up of all unoccupied or unused land in the already populated areas, inside and surrounding old settlements. Then gradually these settlements extended down-mountain and in some areas up-mountain. New lands were brought under cultivation and allocated to individuals by the Native Administration. Hence the

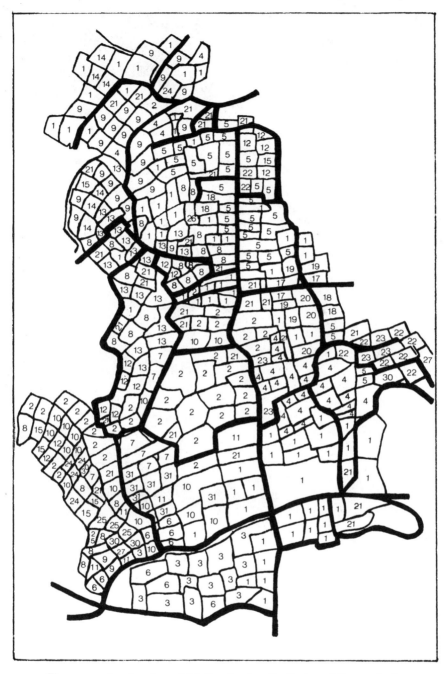

Figure 5.1. A subsection of Mwika showing distribution of lineage lands. Numbers represent lineages. Number 1 is an ex-chiefly lineage. Distance from top to bottom approximately two miles. Not to scale.

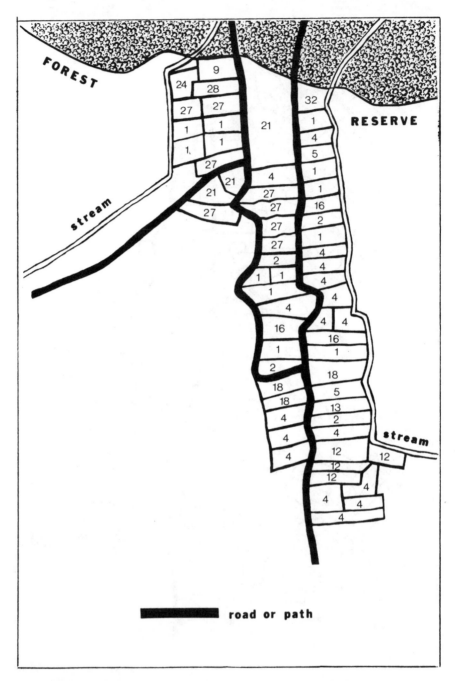

Figure 5.2. Upper Mwika settlement. A recent offshoot of the lineage cores shown in Figure 5.1.

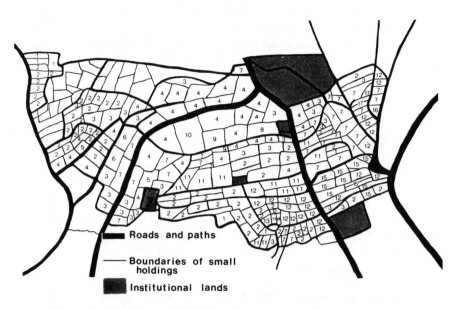

Roads and paths

Boundaries of small
holdings

Institutional lands

Figure 5.3. A subsection of Kilema showing clusters of lineage lands. Numbers represent lineages. (These numbers do not correspond to the lineages in Figures 5.1 and 5.2. There is no connection between lineages bearing the same numbers in the maps of Mwika and that of Kilema.) Not to scale.

localized lineages of the central banana belt come to have scattered satellites, small clusters of kinsmen who had moved from one to four miles away, up or down the mountainside. (See Figure 5.2, Upper Mwika settlement.) Others moved laterally, to less populous *mitaa*. Such sublineage satellites had existed before. Migration was an old Chagga pattern. One assumes that in the nineteenth century people moved in response to wars, local misfortunes, opportunities, political troubles, and the like. But in the British colonial period, the effect of coffee cultivation and demographic increase generated a new reason to move: serious land scarcity in the lineage home territory.

Some of the need for additional food not produced in the *kihamba* was met through the cultivation of *shamba* land near or on the plain. In 1930 most, if not all, households cultivated annual crops of maize, beans, and millet on such lands. Unlike the *kihamba* plots, *shamba* plots were not permanently held. Only the use was given, and that was annually allocated, nominally by the chief. The frequent necessity for fallowing required a form of shifting cultivation. The chief chose the lowland area to be cultivated in a particular year, and then it was divided up among the *mitaa*. Within the plot of each *mtaa*, the land was divided into strips and allocated to individuals (Griffiths 1930:73). Such lands could then be loaned to others by the holder. *Masiro,* the annual gift commemorating the loan of land, used to be given in return. (More recently cash has been paid in some areas.) The same strips were usually reallocated to the same persons as long as the block was cultivated (33). Griffiths explains that this form of shifting block cultivation existed in order to preserve the integrity of grazing areas (74). Random cultivation of little patches throughout the plain would have broken up the grazing pastures. Griffiths does not note an additional explanation that scattered plots would have made protection from animal and human predators much more difficult. Distant as these lands were from the banana belt, it would have been impossible to guard them efficiently except as a block.

In one place Griffiths says that by 1919 Uru, Kibosho, and Machame had no "shifting severalities" because of land shortage. But in another he reports the continued division of maize land in Uru into strips (1930:33). In Uru each person cultivated two strips of about ⅕ acre. Thus a wife and husband each with two strips cultivated ⅘ acre of *shamba* land in addition to their *kihamba* garden.

In 1930 some grazing plots still existed in the banana belt and were estimated to comprise ⅒ of the homestead area (Griffiths 1930:38). The photographs in Dundas' 1924 book show the great spaces of uncultivated land around the ruins of Orombo's Fort (1924:72). At the same site today one can scarcely see the ruins for the bananas and other cultivated plants. Griffiths estimated that the average *kihamba* was about 1½ acres in size, with about ⅔ covered in bananas and the remainder in coffee. He noted that in the newer *vihamba* coffee took a larger share of the land (Griffiths 1930:30). In polygynous households each wife was entitled to a *kihamba* of her own (12). In Mashati where Griffith actually measured the *vihamba* he found that in a household with three wives each had about 1⅗ acres, all of them under bananas except for ⅗ acre under maize and eleusine and ¾ under coffee (18). He gives other, similar measurements. These *vihamba* in Mashati, he acknowledges, were smaller than those elsewhere. In some other places he found *vihamba* as large as 3¼ acres (17).

Griffiths's information should probably be regarded as a serious size underestimate of *kihamba* or landholdings of households, given what he speaks of as "Chagga secretiveness" (1930:26). In 1960 Von Clemm, doing fieldwork in Lyamungo (Machame), describes *vihamba* of both seven acres and five acres, as well as the scattered holdings of a man who had four plots, each of about an acre. He also notes the situation of a man who had only half an acre and of another who was landless (Von Clemm 1964:104). The question how many Wachagga still have several acres and how many have almost no land today is hard to guess, but it is clear that the proportion of land poor persons was seriously increasing and destined to grow.

One may infer that four large-scale processes relating to land use were underway during the British colonial period, but may well have had their inception earlier. First, open plots used earlier for grazing in the populous *vihamba* belt came more and more to be cultivated. Meadowland became *kihamba* land. Second, as more and more banana-growing lands were filled with coffee bushes, and the population continued to increase, the proportion of the diet involving produce from *shamba* land must have become larger. (The marked increase of maize in the diet is a matter of recent memory.) The third process of change in land use was the gradual conversion of what were once *shamba* lands into *kihamba* lands as more and more households moved down-mountain (Griffiths 1930:33). The fourth process was the increasing tendency of the more prosperous land-owners to hold scattered plots. In 1961 Von Clemm observed:

Dispersed holdings are very much a part of the Chagga land tenure pattern at the moment, and I estimate that fragmentation and dispersal are the dominant trends. . . . Dispersal of holdings does not refer simply to the long-standing division between *kishamba* and *kihamba* ownership, but to the relatively new phenomenon of absentee *kihamba* ownership which is the result of over-population and cash economy. (Von Clemm 1964:104)

COFFEE, LABOR, POLITICS, AND LEGISLATION

In the ecological and social circumstances of Kilimanjaro coffee was a crop well suited to the preexisting system of cultivation. Coffee bushes could be *added* to the gardens of bananas and vegetables. Coffee did not at first threaten to replace an earlier way of life, but simply seemed to enrich it. The heaviest labor requirements of coffee, the picking and processing, were spread over a number of weeks, and even at the busiest times, if everyone, men, women, and children, picked, the job could be done without any increase in the labor supply. Individual growers could even process the coffee cherries to the point at which, properly pulped and dried, they could be sold. It was an ideal crop for small-scale production and seemed at first not to involve any serious dislocation of persons or institutions. But the initially invisible changes were fundamental.

No direct evidence about the impact of coffee cultivation on the relationship between husband and wife has surfaced from the early period but the fieldwork permits some informed reconstruction of earlier days. From the start, men took for themselves all right to coffee cash as an adjunct of their heritable rights in land. Although women contributed their labor to the coffee picking and processing, they had no access to the coffee income. Men felt no obligation to share the cash itself with them. Though men recognized that they must provide certain things for a wife that in this century could only be had for cash, such as cloth for clothing, they were not obliged to turn over cash itself unless specifically to buy such items. Today, the amount of money that women are able to make from their vegetable sales in the markets is a tiny proportion of what is available to men from coffee. There is every reason to believe that this was so from the beginning. Thus, even at the level of the household, coffee changed the balance of relationships. It was the more so at the level of politics.

Coffee and politics were intertwined on Kilimanjaro from the moment that the Chagga coffee crop became large enough to generate a substantial aggregate sum, that is, by the mid-1920s. Both the Chagga chiefs and the colonial administration wanted to control coffee affairs. Over time the revenues from the taxation of coffee growers (and eventually through a coffee tax) came to swell the Kilimanjaro district treasury (Lee 1965:36). During the British colonial period these funds were to a great extent expended locally on public institutions and public works, eventually putting many Kilimanjaro facilities far ahead of those of many other parts of Tanganyika. Once simply a source of local revenue, today Kilimanjaro coffee is of national interest as a source of foreign exchange. Because of its economic importance coffee has repeatedly been regulated by government. Again and again legislative, administrative, and executive action organized and reorganized its marketing and production. Over time, Chagga customary land law was transformed by coffee. But that is getting ahead of the story.

In the decade or two after the defeat of the Germans in the Kilimanjaro area in March 1916, Chagga affairs can be followed through the activities of a few remarkable individuals. One of them was a Chagga named Joseph Merinyo, a man from Old Moshi, a pupil and convert of Gutmann, who, even as a young man, in the German period, had had an unusual career. Another was Major (later Sir) Charles Dundas, a British officer in charge of the district from May 1919 to 1924, who appointed Merinyo as his interpreter. Merinyo was suitable for the job because he was experienced in dealing with Europeans. In the early 1900s, in his teens, Merinyo had been the servant of a German settler named Forster (later Gutmann's father-in-law). Forster had taken Merinyo to Germany with him on a trip in 1907 and returned with him in 1908. Merinyo then became Forster's chief clerk and labor overseer, and married a sister of Mangi (Chief) Salema of Old Moshi.

In the year after the German defeat, the British had some anxiety that the Chagga might rebel. Believing that some of their leaders might be a danger to the new administration, Major Theodore Morrison, the officer in charge in 1917, had ordered some thirty-six Chagga deported to Tanga, including nine chiefs, among them Salema, and his brother-in-law, the commoner Joseph Merinyo. When Major Dundas took over from Morrison in 1919, he quickly endeared himself to the Chagga by bringing back all the deported men. Soon recognizing Merinyo's abilities, he placed him in the district office as his interpreter and assistant.

The subsequent rapid development of the coffee crop was not simply a spontaneous growth from earlier beginnings. In the early years of British administration it was government policy to encourage Africans to grow cash crops. Dundas pressed coffee cultivation forward in every way that he could, riding his horse from chiefdom to chiefdom, exhorting the Chagga to plant coffee. He put pressure on the chiefs and the chiefs in turn sometimes encouraged, sometimes ordered their people to do the same (Mwika, Case 26, 1927). Chagga coffee cultivation increased by leaps and bounds. In 1922 money was loaned to the chiefs to buy seedlings for their people. By 1925, all of these loans had been repaid (Rogers 1972:239). Dundas reported that in 1921, there were 125,000 coffee trees in Chagga gardens; in 1922, 175,000; in 1923, 300,000 (Rogers 1972:236). In 1923 twenty tons of Chagga coffee (as compared with 2,000 tons of settler coffee) were exported. In 1925, according to one source the Chagga coffee crop came to nearly 100 tons (Swynnerton et al. 1948:11). In 1927 the provincial commissioner anticipated a crop of 400 tons (Annual Report, Northern Province, 1927, National Archives 1927–8, typescript, p. 21). By 1932, Chagga production had climbed to 867 tons (see Table 1).

It takes several years before a coffee seedling is productive, so there was an inevitable lag between the planting of the 1920s and export tonnage, but a huge steady increase was underway.

In 1924 Major Dundas was transferred out of the area. He was succeeded by Lt. Com. A. M. Clark who was also extremely sympathetic to the Chagga. By 1925 Chagga coffee farmers numbered well over 5,000. With Clark's encouragement, a Chagga organization, the Kilimanjaro Native Coffee Planters' Association (KNPA), was formed "to protect and promote the interests of the native coffee growers on the mountainside." Clark agreed to serve as president and secretary of the association "until such time as a secretary was appointed from the native members of the association" (Swynnerton et al. 1948:11). Within a year Joseph Merinyo had become president, and Clark had stepped down. Nathaniel Mtui (the great Chagga historian and one of Gutmann's principal informants) was made vice-president. In 1926 the KNPA boasted 7,000 members.

The colonial administration was then directing reorganizations. From 1926 to 1929 the chiefs were grouped into three councils (Hai, Vunjo, Rombo) under each of which were the individual chiefdoms of the member chiefs. Each of the three councils was to have its own treasury (Rogers 1972:324). Native Treasuries thus established constituted funds out of which the chiefs were given monthly cash salaries (based on the number of taxpayers each ruled) (Hailey 1938:436).

Table 1. *Progress of African coffee production on Kilimanjaro*

Season (July to June)	Growers (approx.)	Acreage	Green coffee (tons)	Crop value in pounds (F.O.R. Moshi)	Pounds per ton
1923/24	3,300	1,200	32		
1924/25	4,400	1.500	48		
1925/26	5,500	2,000	64		
1926/27	6,600	2,800	80		
1927/28	7,900	3,500	264		
1928/29	9,000	4,000	308		
1929/30	10,000	4,300	416		
1930/31	11,000	4,600	672		
1931/32	11,800	4,900	740		
1932/33	12,530	5,160	867	44,575	51
1933/34	16,800	6,700	716	46,259	65
1934/35	18,550	7,560	1,275	44,728	35
1935/36	21,740	9,380	1,475	45,941	31
1936/37	24,280	12,450	722	25,561	35
1937/38	25,230	14,790	1,177	41,032	35
1938/39	25,730	14,440	1,566	69,762	45
1939/40	26,270	15,170	2,141	85,842	40
1940/41	26,890	16,180	3,250	101,802	31
1941/42	27,330	16,660	1,558	59,457	38
1942/43	27,572	16,860	2,482	163,221	66
1943/44	27,970	16,340	1,691	167,737	99
1944/45	29,310	16,980	3,275	343,474	105
1945/46	29,600	16,830	2,512	256,449	102

Year			Parchment (with husk)			
1946/47	30,450	17,380		1,834	203,543	111
1947/48	31,670	22,460		3,384	439,573	130
1948/49	32,050	22,400		2,623	373,803	143
1949/50	31,590	23,540		3,359	954,713	284
1950/51	32,030	23,010		5,049	1,214,634	241
1951/52	34,390	23,620		5,670	1,396,310	246
1952/53	35,280	25,100		1,949	685,620	352
1953/54	36,880	27,660		6,304	3,724,184	591
1954/55	36,200	27,150		4,361	1,907,084	437
1955/56	37,600	28,200		6,577	3,078,955	468
1956/57	40,420	30,320	5,758	5,522	2,285,695	414
1957/58	44,140	33,100	6,981	5,596	2,191,941	392
1958/59	44,320	33,260	7,370	5,821	1,851,932	318
1959/60	45,130	33,850	8,325	6,798	2,142,143	315
1960/61	45,000	34,000	11,250	8,739	2,499,892	286
1961/62	50,000	34,000	7,239	5,853	1,676,313	287
1962/63	50,000	34,000	6,470	5,182	1,306,135	252
1963/64	53,000	35,000	12,000	9,600	3,105,313	323
1964/65	55,000	35,500	11,308	9,046	3,039,456	336
1965/66	55,000	35,500	21,038	16,831	5,159,543	308
1966/67	65,000	35,500		14,486	4,043,836	279
1967/68	65,000	35,500		11,526	2,862,669	248

Source: Put out by KNCU in July 1969 and given to me by one of its employees, a son of Joseph Merinyo Maro.
Note: Growers and acreages are rough estimates. No records are available for tonnages and value.

Entirely outside of that structure stood the planters' association. The KNPA was a parallel, nonchiefly, nongovernmental organization, mountainwide in its constituency. KNPA coffee was being marketed successfully, and the KNPA was prospering. But it had its detractors. Not all Chagga sold their coffee through the KNPA. Asian merchants in the Kilimanjaro area were buying coffee directly from some of the small holder-producers, as they had in the German period. The merchants were less than delighted by the KNPA. Settler opposition to the KNPA was also growing. Too many signs indicated that the KNPA might become a serious economic force. The existence of Chagga coffee only exacerbated the reluctance of the Chagga to work for the settlers. The Chagga themselves probably experienced a labor shortage during coffee-picking time. When several chiefs raised objections to the use of child labor by settlers the provincial commissioner commented that they probably wanted to use the child labor at home (Annual Report, Northern Province, 1927, TNA 1927–28:13, 34). The report for 1928 confirms that the chiefs of Marangu and Himo forbade children to pick settler coffee because they wanted them for picking native coffee (Northern Province Half-yearly Report for period ending 30 June, 1928, TNA 10902:9).

Certain settlers gave full vent to their anti-African prejudices in relation to the coffee issue, causing the provincial commissioner to remark, "As regards Europeans, it must always be remembered that there is a small section whose views and opinions are in blunt and irreconcilable conflict with the Mandate" (Annual Report, Northern Province, 1927:2; typescript TNA 1927–28). He went on to say that there was an increasing body of Africans who read the local press and noticed the prejudices of Europeans, and their "persistent assertions that Africans who grow coffee are a menace to the good name and safety of the previously established foreign plantations are calculated, in the face of sales on the London market, to create an impression of mere unreasoning prejudice." He continues, "Labour conditions will not, in my opinion, improve appreciably until employers learn that low wages, poor housing and bad feeding of labour are bad business" (3). He said categorically that Africans were better off at home working for themselves than working for many Europeans. The Chagga, on their side, were resisting working for Europeans, and coffee growing made working for themselves an economically viable choice for the Chagga. They even resisted working for the colonial government, though they worked energetically for their own chiefs.[3]

As the KNPA grew wealthier, and came to have more and more members, the chiefs too began to see the KNPA both as a political competitor and as a repository of wealth that they wanted to control. Colonial officials, in their turn, thought that bringing the KNPA into administrative control would be desirable. The district officer who took charge in 1926,

F. C. Hallier, thought it would be useful if KNPA funds went into the Native Treasury (Rogers 1972:361; see also Annual Report, Northern Province, 1928, TNA 1927–8:1, 2). In 1928 Hallier held a meeting with the Chagga to explain a planned Coffee Industry Ordinance which would call for formal registration of all Chagga coffee plantations "to control pests and disease." He also called for the abolition of the KNPA. The political aspect of this plan was that the three councils of chiefs established in 1926 would be consolidated into one which would take over the funds and functions of the KNPA. At this point Merinyo resigned in protest, and wrote a petition to Dundas (Rogers 1972:356).

The dispute reached such a level that Dundas was sent back to Moshi to try to work out some sort of settlement. At the end, Dundas held a public meeting with the provincial commissioner, all Chagga chiefs, and the leaders of the KNPA, including Joseph Merinyo. It was agreed that KNPA funds would remain in association hands, that a 2 percent tax on coffee sales for the new year would replace subscriptions (which had previously been collected from individual member growers to support the KNPA) and that Merinyo would be reinstated as president (Rogers 1972:377). Also conceded was the independence of the KNPA. The KNPA was to survive as a separate body and was not to be taken over by the projected central council of Chagga chiefs. That plan stood. When the central council of chiefs came into being in 1929 it did not take over the coffee growers' association (Annual Report, Northern Province, 1929, TNA 18693, 1929:2).

But the troubles of the KNPA were not over. In 1929 the world price of coffee suddenly declined. From 1927 on Chagga farmers had been paid an advance for their coffee when they delivered it to the KNPA, the rest to be paid after the crop was auctioned (Annual Report, Northern Province, 1927, TNA 1927–28:21). Because of the price drop of 1929, their advance exceeded what was realized when the coffee was finally sold at auction. Other financial problems also existed. To strengthen the KNPA Assistant District Officer A. L. Pennington proposed that there be legislation obliging all native farmers to market their coffee through the KNPA. Such a compulsory marketing ordinance was enacted by the Native Administration (under section 15 of the Native Authorities Ordinance of 1926) and came into force on April 1, 1929 (Annual Report, Northern Province, 1929, TNA 11681, 1929:14). Much coffee continued to be sold illicitly to others (22).

The same year District Officer A.W.M. Griffiths was asked to make a survey of the landholding situation on Kilimanjaro. The Chagga were reluctant to have matters regarding land inquired into (Annual Report, Northern Province, 1929, TNA 11681, 1929:14). They feared land might be taken from them. The Chagga were beginning to experience land shortage in some areas and wanted to acquire more, not give up any.

They managed to do so in some instances. For example, in 1929 the Wachagga of Marangu bought 185 hectares from a European, and the land was then divided among 200 households (30).

Troubles other than land shortage and resistance to land registration surfaced. Allegations were made that Merinyo was involved in financial irregularities and he was jailed. His official connection with the KNPA came to an end. He maintained to the end of his life that he was innocent and had been persecuted for political activity and "uppityness" (as he told me in 1969). In 1932, when the Co-operative Societies Ordinance (no. 7 of 1932) was enacted, the KNPA was dissolved, reorganized, and replaced by the Kilimanjaro Native Co-operative Union, Ltd. (KNCU). The KNCU hired a European, A.L.B. Bennett, as manager. Bennett was married to a Chagga woman, spoke Kichagga well and was a man in between, in every way acceptable both to the Chagga and to the provincial administration (Annual Report, Northern Province, 1931, TNA 11681:8).

Under Bennett's management the KNCU generated sixteen sub-branches in 1932.[4] That is to say, there was a KNCU central office in Moshi Town, but each chiefdom had its own "primary cooperative society" (Annual Report, Northern Province, 1932, TNA 19415, 1932:39). (Eventually populous chiefdoms came to have more than one primary society. By 1960 there were more than fifty primary societies [Von Clemm 1964:100].)

The way in which the primary societies were run is a reflection on the tendency of local political structures to reproduce themselves in new organizations. In Mwika West the first chairman of the coop was Ngao Lengaki Mariki, the son of Lengaki Mariki who had been *mangi* of Msae (chief of the area in which the Mwika West Primary Society was located) until the early 1920s.[5] Ngao Mariki served as chairman of the coop, from 1934 to 1936. His son, Wilson Ngao Mariki, was chairman from 1960 to at least 1969. In the interval between the Marikis there were two other chairmen, one of whom was also a member of a once chiefly lineage from another *mtaa*. The governing committee was formed by having an elected representative from each sub*mtaa* serve. The old geographical/political/administrative framework of the chiefdom was reproduced in the local cooperative society.

One would never go so far as to say that office in the coop, or the office of *mchili* (*mtaa* headman), was invariably hereditary. It was not. But sons often eventually succeeded fathers, a noticeable feature of all sorts of "elected" offices, including the management of some of the primary societies. Nor was it always purely an act of civic benevolence to be chairman of the local primary society. In various periods some allocatory privileges were associated with the office. But there were also economic opportunities. Thus for some years into the 1960s the truck owned by the chairman of one of the primary societies with which I had contact (who was lineal descendant of an ex-chief), was hired annually to transport the coffee of society members to Moshi. Such side business associated with the office was profitable, and some descendants of precolonial chiefs managed to turn their social prominence to advantage in new arenas of economic activity. Insofar as the colonial structure operated through the system of Native Authorities it officially incorporated only the highest local offices into its system, namely, the chiefs themselves. But there was an understructure of suboffices, a web of local officials who headed and ran the *mitaa*, that continued. These suboffices drew personnel from the local lineages that had been used in earlier periods.

Coffee continued to bring prosperity until 1934–35 when there was again a sudden drop in the price. The KNCU was still paying the Kilimanjaro growers in two installments, an advance when they delivered the coffee to the primary society and *mabaki*, a second payment based on the revenue from the crop when it was sold at auction. In the 1934–35 crisis, the KNCU was not able to pay *mabaki*. It could not even cover the payments it had already advanced. The decision was made to cover the existing debt out of the return from the 1936–37 crops. (As it happened the bottom would drop out of the market in 1936.) The Chagga were in an uproar. Some rebelled, resigned, and said they would no longer sell through the KNCU. The "Chagga Rule" requiring compulsory marketing (a new one of 1934) was invoked against them (Annual Report, Northern Province, 1934, TNA 11681).

The law was used in relation to coffee affairs in other forms as well. The courts enforced the administrative rules of the KNCU itself. Thus in Kilema a man who had failed to maintain his coffee grove in proper order, allowing it to be infested with coffee borers, a destructive insect, was brought to court for his negligence by a KNCU inspector and was fined four shillings and told he would be sent to jail for nine days if he failed to pay (Kitabu cha shauri, Kilema, Case 112, 1936. This practice of bringing negligent coffee growers to court continued; see Kilema, Cases 125 and 127, 1947). Once a man planted coffee he was obligated to maintain it under the KNCU rules, and the courts would back the KNCU. The health of the crop as a whole was not to be put at risk through individual neglect.

In the period of the KNCU 1934–35 financial crisis German produce buyers had offered between 10 and 15 percent above market prices if sellers accepted part repayment in German goods, especially agricultural implements (Hailey 1938:1472). Sellers were tempted to leave the KNCU. African coffee brokers, who had been the principal target of the compulsory marketing rule, encouraged the dissatisfaction of Chagga farmers with the KNCU (TNA 41891 Local Government, memo on disturbances of 1936:40). The rebellion had local political dimensions. Some of its force was directed against the chief of Machame (Hailey, 1938:1472).

The central office of the KNCU in Moshi tried to maintain disciplinary control over the primary societies, requiring them to pledge to abide by its rules and rulings. But some chairmen of the primary societies refused to sign anything indicating such a commitment. As Ngao Lengaki Mariki, chairman of the Mwika West Cooperative society, said, "I did not sign that paper which requires me to be under the rules because I am afraid of my own members" (KNCU Minute Book 1932–42, 30 June 1936). And no wonder. At a meeting of the Mwika West society in 1935, Mwalimu Manase, an eminent local lay preacher, proposed that instead of selling through the KNCU, the members sell their coffee to anyone who would pay a single flat price (not an advance and *mabaki*) (Meeting Minutes, Mwika West 31 August 1935). A similarly tumultuous meeting was held a few months later indicating that a delegation had gone to see the provincial commissioner in Arusha to protest the nonpayment of *mabaki* (3 December 1935). At the next meeting a member said, "To sign is like when a person wants to buy something from you and wants you to sign an agreement to accept the price that *suits him*. How can we sign these rules when we don't know the price?" (1 June 1936). Later that year the chief of Mwika, Mangi Herabdieli, appeared at the meeting of the Mwika West society to "explain" the rules to the 166 persons present. He told them that the rules stood for respecting everything that was good. He admonished the members not to heed troublemakers, to remember that "the KNCU is the father of the primary societies and they have to respect orders from the KNCU" (23 July 1936). One member said they begged the *mangi* and the KNCU for forgiveness, and said they were like young children who were wrong and wanted another chance (23 July 1936). But others must not have been so humble, since they refused to sign the rules. A number of primary societies were closed, such as the one in Mwika West (which had only been in existence for two years). It remained closed from 1936 to 1939. Tension in relation to the KNCU continued. Rioting broke out in several chiefdoms of the mountains, and the buildings of a few of the local societies were destroyed. Persons with coffee to sell had to go a greater distance to sell it through other primary societies, or sold it illicitly and privately. The Native Administration defined some of the leaders of the anti-KNCU movement as agitators and they were ultimately arrested and sentenced by the court of the Council of Chagga Chiefs (Report by Acting Provincial Commissioners, Northern Province, 16 January 1937, TNA 19415:2). Several individuals were deported.

Some dissidents brought a law suit against the KNCU to test the 1934 version of the Chagga rule regarding exclusive marketing, arguing that as a private organization it had no power to legislate. Later the Legislative Council fearing defeat in the courts on this point circumvented the problem by enacting the Native Coffee Ordinance (no. 26, 1937). That ordinance established Native Coffee boards as part of the administration. One-third of the members of the boards were to be natives. The boards were empowered to order all native coffee to be sold to them or to any agency they might designate. In November 1937 the Moshi Native Coffee Board was established and it designated the KNCU its agent. But further dissent was averted because coffee prices rose 30 percent from mid-1938 and the general mood changed (Rogers 1972:697).

The KNCU emerged from this period stronger than ever. It expanded its marketing activities to include maize, beans, eleusine, wheat, and the hides of cattle. Its supervisory activities continued and broadened. It concerned itself with standards of production, with coffee diseases, with the distribution of improved seedlings, and in the case of maize and beans, of seed. Not surprisingly such primary societies as Mwika West reopened in 1939 and remained open for decades thereafter, until 1974 when the government abolished all primary cooperatives and in 1976, all secondary coops (Hyden 1980:133). Thereafter the parastatals (government companies) were supposed to deal directly with the peasant. The only effect for the growers on Kilimanjaro was the change of the sign on the primary society building to Mamlaka ya Kahawa Tanzania. It is true that the form of its management was altered, but local Chagga still ran everything, and the farmers still brought their coffee to the same place for sale. I was told (1982) that the decision regarding the primary societies has now been reversed, and the primary societies are to be reopened.

This brief sketch of the early history of the coffee cooperative on Kilimanjaro plainly shows the connection between the cooperative and politics/government both at the most local *mtaa* level and at the level of the Moshi District as a whole. It also shows that the law was a major instrument in shaping its formation, direction, and effect. An enabling law allowed the cooperative to be organized in the first place, and exclusive marketing rules are what made it viable. In the colonial period tax laws siphoned off some of the coffee profits to support the Council of Chagga Chiefs and public works. The immediate dependence of local political units on coffee continued. In the late 1970s a coffee tax collected by the new cooperative villages provided them with their only collective revenue.

But legal controls and exclusive marketing rules and taxes have never succeeded in doing away with certain illegal economic practices between individual growers which have taken place from the inception of the cooperative and continue to this day. Although sales from grower to coop are the only legitimate form, many other sales take place "on the side." A man who urgently needs cash can always find someone to give him a loan if he has a coffee crop to offer as collateral. The seller sells his coffee for a flat sum, advanced immediately, usually at a price substantially lower than he would have been paid had he been able to wait and sell it to the coop. Later the buyer may bring the coffee in to the weighing station as if it were part of his own crop, and is paid accordingly.[6] This is a well-known and old practice, technically illegal, but socially accepted.

Private transactions neither affected coffee production nor did they affect the formal organization of its processing and marketing. The large-scale, formal organizations involved could carry on whether or not individual farmers were involved in dealing in cash loans against crops. The individuals and their petty affairs were inconsequential.

To the extent that law and organizational rules define the proper and the improper in the transactions of individuals, they are only effective if they are enforceable and enforced. The prohibition against private dealings in coffee is neither. As long as these illicit transactions take place on a small scale they are invisible to the authorities. No individual could become a large-scale middleman coffee broker between the peasants and the cooperative without detection. But intervention on the level of individual transactions was and is done. The formal rules inhibited the enlargement of this form of entrepreneurial activity, but did not prevent it altogether. The transactions had other effects. In the long run, such "deals" constitute one of the many factors contributing to the process of economic differentiation between households, intensifying the differences between the relatively affluent and the poor, those who could afford to lend, and those who had need to borrow.

The contrast between the effective legal interventions that concerned the large-scale organization of the cooperative and its taxation, and the ineffective prohibitions of individual, private dealings in coffee raises methodological and theoretical issues. These matters not only bear on the question of the incipient formation of class strata and the process of sorting out relative advantage. They are also directly germane to another question, the tension that can exist between activities in the domain of individual strategy and activities in the domain of law and formal organization. The two can have very different roles in shaping the changing social process. Each can inhibit or enhance the other, as the situation permits. Attention to activities at both these levels of scale and to the way in which they interlock is essential to the analysis of social change. The legal domain and the illegal domain must be approached analytically as parts of a single system.

HOW THE CHAGGA SPENT THEIR COFFEE MONEY

In the British colonial period the income from coffee was spent at three distinct levels: (1) that of the Council of Chagga Chiefs whose collective treasury was filled by taxes on coffee growers; (2) that of the coffee cooperative, which from early days kept funds from the sale of the coffee crop to finance its own expanding operations, and (3) that of the individual growers themselves. Over the years, the Treasury of the Native Administration used its funds to build schools, roads, dispensaries, and courts. It spent money to improve local farming practices and water supplies, and to enhance other public works. The cooperative, the KNCU, not only paid for its coffee-marketing enterprise, its salaried staff and buildings, it invested in auxiliary businesses, and ultimately in an agricultural school, a press, and a hotel. Much of the official collective history, both of the Native Administration and of the cooperative, can be directly documented from public sources, and some of it already has been assembled and described (Rogers 1972). But the expenditures of individual growers and their use of personal cash income is both harder to ascertain and in many ways of greater interest. Part of the story can be pieced together from the past, but of course it can be more fully accounted for from observation in recent years.

One might have expected that once they had a cash income Chagga farmers would spend their money on new things, on objects and services they did not and could not produce at home. To some extent that happened. For example, cloth clothing gradually came to be universal. In precolonial times cloth had come in through the long-distance trade, and at that time it was largely through the redistributory largesse of the chiefs that cloth came into the hands of commoners. But with coffee cash, anyone could buy cloth, and eventually everyone did. Other changes of style manifested themselves. The elite took up tea drinking. The taste for sugar spread. The Chagga purchased cooking oil, as well as soap, metal knives and spoons, china cups and plates. Each of these and many other new items peddled upcountry were trivial, but in aggregate they came to constitute the beginning of a cultural commitment to an external economy. By far the most important cash investment the Chagga made in the new ways was in paying school fees for their children. The demands for education on Kilimanjaro grew from early mission times and a generation later became unremitting (Iliffe 1979:224, 355). The payment for education brought those who had it an economic return. The coffee income of the area was augmented by the salary income received by some of the educated.

Even though certain expenditures on *new* commodities and services were significant, even more striking was the Chagga's use of their cash from the beginning to obtain the very same things that they had always produced themselves. They were ready to buy what they had always given and received through exchange in kinship and friendship, what they had formerly acquired through inheritance and through political patronage. Among the Chagga commerce has operated as a partial process, not as a total replacement of earlier forms of production, transfer, and exchange. The economy of personal gift and loan and the economy of impersonal cash transaction coexist and interpenetrate. The simultaneous existence of the two modes of acquisition of property is visible today. The cash-poor must rely more exclusively then their richer kinsfolk on the system of personal relationship since they have not the cash to do otherwise. But as the poor have less to exchange, it is not the cash-poor but often their more prosperous brothers who figure as the mainstays of the traditional system of exchange. Having cash enhances the capacity to transact in both systems. Without cash one cannot afford to be either "modern" or "traditional."

When elderly Chagga talk about the past these days, they complain, "Today everything is money. In the old days people gave things. Now it is only buy buy buy." That perspective omits the counterobligations that go with all gifts in the indigenous system. Whatever the free gifting ideology of traditional Chagga exchange, there is also realistic calculation. The past may not have been very different from the present in this regard. When coffee money became available a man who could put together the cash to buy a beast was far better off than he might have been had he received it in agistment as a "loan" from a cattle owner, since the owner could always reclaim the animal. If he needed land and could buy an acre rather than borrow it, he ran no risk of its being retaken as he would have in a loan. That much is obvious. But with money in short supply, and cattle and land costly to obtain, the use of the gift-loan exchange system must be understood as an alternative and supplementary way to deploy resources. It was and is a way of stretching a limited amount of cash as far as possible. The choices are complex, and frequently the economic motives for maintaining a stake in both systems are strong. One system has not driven out the other.

THE BUYING AND SELLING OF CATTLE

As shown earlier, the basic productive resources, cattle and land, became available for cash at different periods, cattle early in the century, land much later on, probably after 1930. From early in the century cattle and small stock could be bought, and this avenue seems to have been used for bridewealth, debt repayment, and other purposes. Yet cattle keeping seems to have substantially declined over the century. Cattle are expensive, and the absence of pasture in the banana belt, land shortage, and the

increasing distance women must go to obtain fodder have made the maintenance of cattle much more difficult than it used to be. The alternative is
to buy small stock, goats and sheep. They are cheaper and easier to keep,
and are now much more common. The large herds of hundreds of cattle
said to have been held by some chiefs in the pre-1919 period have not been
held by anyone, chief or not, for many decades.[7] All evidence suggests that
the number of beasts per capita has continuously decreased at least since
the "good old days" described by Gutmann.[8] Thus on the one hand, the
Chagga have carried on commerce; on the other the commodities in question, beasts on the hoof, have become more scarce. Domestic slaughtering
has become less frequent. But there are other ways to obtain meat. Now
there are butchers. Domestic slaughtering still occurs regularly, however,
since it serves substantial ritual, gustatory, and material purposes.[9] But the
commercial butcherings far outnumber the ritual ones.

BEER AND MEAT SOLD IN SHOPS: THE SECULAR PROVENANCE OF RITUAL FOODS

Beer and meat are two of the foods still most valued by the Chagga, as
they were a century ago. Beer is essential to all life-crisis rituals, all
celebrations, all negotiations between kin. Meat is at the core of male
lineage feasting, as is beer. Animals must still be sacrificed when there is
serious trouble. Also gifts of meat must be given on many occasions.
Chagga men sometimes say that they do not feel quite well or strong
unless they eat meat with some regularity. As products of the traditional
basic Chagga resources, land and livestock, beer and meat are infused
with many symbolic meanings. Fundamental to exchanges among kin,
they encode the ideas that connect the living and the dead, and epitomize
relationships among the living. Now that beer and meat are available in
shops as well as being produced at home, the coexistence of those two
sources conveys as few other things could the changes and continuities in
Chagga life.

Meat is now sold by the pound. Since bought meat is cooked by inter-
minable boiling, no great attention is paid to which cut of meat is used.
There is a flat price per pound for all of it, no price distinction being
made among cuts. This indiscriminateness about cuts of bought meat is
striking because the division of cuts is a matter of such extreme importance when beasts are ritually killed at home. Then the distribution of
particular parts of the animal to particular kinspersons is essential. Indeed, it is said that a son eating the father's portion may die of the effects
of this act of hubris. Yet with bought meat, all such distinctions about
cuts disappear. If one cannot afford to keep or slaughter an animal, a
small quantity of bought meat is sometimes a poor but acceptable substitute when obligatory prestations must be made.

Plate 12. Two butchers skin an ox that has just been slaughtered.

Beer and meat exist today as both sacred and secular foods. The selling of them has been one of the most profitable of small businesses on Kilimanjaro for at least fifty years.[10] The cattle slaughtered by the butchers are not the small Chagga cattle that are raised locally for bridewealth and lineage feasting, but a larger type, bought from Masai herdsmen at the Weru Weru market at the foot of the mountain.[11] But the *pombe* brewed for most of the drinking establishments is the same as that brewed at home.

These businesses require small amounts of invested capital for substantial profits. Once the shop is built, the biggest expense is taken care of. Without electricity or piped water, and in the case of the *pombe* shops, often without walls, the shops are not elaborate. The buildings are small, and largely made of local materials, except for the usual corrugated metal roof and sometimes a cement floor. Beyond the initial expenses the investment to carry on the enterprise is limited.

When the coffee harvest comes in each year, the butchers sell more meat, and much more beer flows down many throats than at other times. But even during those months of maximal production, the capital needed by an owner to buy the cattle or to pay for the brewing each week is not great, and is repaid the same week. It is literally a hand-to-mouth operation.[12]

Except at a beer party given to celebrate some special occasion, men do not usually receive visitors at home. Instead, when their work of the day is done, they gather together in the late afternoon at one of the four kinds

Plate 13. Two old women sharing a calabash of beer, 1969. (Photo by D. C. Moore)

of local beer-drinking establishments to gossip with their fellows. There are two kinds of licensed shops where locally brewed beer is sold, there are illegal sales of such beer in unlicensed establishments (at home) and there are "bars" where bottled drinks are sold (see note 12 for details). The salaried, educated men tend to cluster together at particular kinds of beer shops and the farmers meet at others. Some drink a lot, some drink a little. The sociability is more important than the drink itself. For many, cost is a deterrent to heavy drinking.[13]

A year or two after the "villagization" process of 1976 was completed (and not without political pressure), some of these butcher shops and *pombe* shops were rented by, or sold to, the new "cooperative villages" that had formed. How well this reorganization will work remains to be seen. What is certain is that there will be business to be done. The Chagga who can afford it will not tolerate being without beer and meat.

THE MARKETS AND SHOPS

For most farmers coffee money has never produced enough cash to buy more land. But obviously there is enough money to buy smaller things. Beer and meat are among these. But many other things are for sale as well. In 1926 there were twenty-four women's produce markets in the district (Maro 1974:205, 221). In 1969 there were fifty.[14] In the 1968–79 period, in addition to the women selling produce, a few male sellers peddled secondhand clothing, dried fish, and sometimes hardware and utensils. Today male buyers come with pickup trucks to buy bananas from the women for transportation to the towns and cities. Male vendors are more frequently seen in numbers at the larger markets.

Clustered around the markets, and scattered along the main roads, are many kinds of shops: general stores, flour mills, tailor shops, millet-sellers establishments, carpentry shops, and, of course, beer shops and butcher shops. In the past, some shopkeepers who prospered managed to accumulate enough capital to invest either in scattered plots of land (often distant from the *kihamba* of residence) or in service businesses of one kind or another. Some invested in trucks and buses. Occasionally some of the cash was invested in tractors for large-scale cultivation on the plain. Thus for the Vunjo Division (population approximately 126,000) in 1959, the divisional chief reported 353 "trade shops," 95 butcher shops, 13 eating shops, 8 shoe repair shops, 34 carpentry shops and 8 bicycle repair shops in his division (Letter from Divisional Chief of Vunjo to Mangi Mkuu, 21 January 1959, KDC File 1/16). He also reported 21 African-owned tractors, 27 flour mills, 1 carpenter's "power machine," and 4 water mills in his division (Letter from Divisional Chief of Vunjo to Mangi Mkuu, 30 December 1958, KDC File 1/16). The division included territory on the plain as well as in the banana belt, hence the tractors. Given the size of the population the number of tiny shops is not large (see Table 2, p. 136). Many households had little coffee cash to spend, and provided most of what they consumed.

PLAIN FARMERS AND SALARIED OCCUPATIONS

The discussion of cash spending and shops should not be taken to mean that the Chagga were or are fully involved in a cash economy. Quite the contrary. At 1969 prices a man with three or four acres of well-developed land with the maximum number of coffee bushes had an annual cash income from his coffee of under $1,000. Many households had far less land than that, and proportionately smaller amounts of cash.[15] With such incomes the Chagga could not buy much unless, in addition to the coffee money, wages or salaries were coming in. Most families depended, and still depend, heavily on their own food production to survive, and they badly need the maize they cultivate in their *shamba*s on the plain to supplement the bananas from the gardens. For most people, the land remains the center of their lives. It is no wonder that litigation surrounding it should be so bitter.

Plate 14. A clothes-repairer, tailor, at a market in 1969. (Photo by D. C. Moore)

Plate 15. The wife of a smith sells her husband's wares: knives, *pangas*, and the hooked knife used by women for cutting fodder grass, 1969. (Photo by D. C. Moore)

Table 2. *Sources of rural employment in Kilimanjaro District*

Type of service	Total no. in Kilimanjaro[a]	Approx. no. of people in each	Total salaried employees
Primary cooperatives	43	10	430
Primary schools	340	7	2,380[b]
Rural hospitals	5	6	30[c]
Rural medical centers	4	4	16
Dispensaries	44	3	132
Agriculture extension offices	–	–	150
Primary courts	18	4	72
Administration offices	18	2	36
Bars (banana beer)	402	4[d]	1,608
Bars (bottled beer)	141	3	423
Retail shops	1,657	2	3,314
Butcheries	433	3[e]	1,299
Flour mill	75	2	150[f]
Rural tea rooms	92	2	184
Small industries	17	3	51[g]
Commercial vehicles	260	2	520
Missions (nonvocational employees)			60
			10,315[h]

[a]The information was obtained from Kilimanjaro District Council for the years 1960 to 1965.

[b]This is an underestimation because it excludes cooks, who would add another 250 job positions.

[c]There are employees other than Wachagga in medical services in Kilimanjaro but they were not counted.

[d]The figure is based on an estimate of two to three employees and the owner of the drinking place. People who rent the drinking places so that they may sell beer are not counted though they earn some money through such activities.

[e]The owner has been included because he usually works full-time in buying slaughter animals, supervising employees, and doing the planning and accounting work.

[f]The figure 75, is an underrepresentation. The total employment (owner excluded) could be over 200 in Kilimanjaro.

[g]Greatly underestimated. Total employment available could be over 180 in Kilimanjaro.

[h]Excludes local politicians, most of the self-employment categories, casual labor, and some skilled and semiskilled workers.

Source: This table is taken from the Kilimanjaro District Council Records, 1960–65 (reproduced by Maro 1974:185).

Table 3. *Kilimanjaro Region rural population, occupations by sex, 1978*

	Male	Female	Total
Population	403,564	431,274	834,838
Occupation			
Cultivators	104,529	154,385	258,912
Livestock raisers	247	114	361
Fishermen/hunters	5,298	2,671	7,969
Mixed agriculture workers	4,447	8,262	12,709
Agricultural laborers	7,541	2,634	10,175
Craftsmen/machine operators	10,138	273	10,411
Sales/clerical. workers	4,026	855	4,881
Professional/ technical workers	5,571	2,801	8,372
Managers/administrators	603	75	678
Non-agricultural laborers	6,074	1,461	7,535
Other workers	5,129	1,567	6,696
Students	108,520	104,830	213,350
Other unoccupied	141,322	151,310	292,632
Not elsewhere specified	119	38	157

Source: 1978 Census, 4:43.

As for the "other half," the salaried men, Table 2, from the Kilimanjaro District Council, copied by Maro (1974:185), shows the sources of rural salaried employment on Kilimanjaro from the 1960–65 period. Indirectly it also gives a good indication of the way the Chagga were spending their money then. The table does not reveal materials for house construction, used by the prosperous, because the cement, cinderblocks, and tin roofs all come from more distant places, from Moshi Town and beyond, and are not sold through the small businesses on the mountain itself. The table also does not show the large number of persons who live on the mountain but daily go to work in a variety of paid jobs in Moshi Town. Maro estimates that about 3,500 persons from the mountain work at salaried jobs in Moshi, but about 11,000 travel to town each day. Many of these must earn money in the informal sector. See Table 3 for official record of occupations on Kilimanjaro in 1978.

Salaried employment has substantially increased since 1965. But the fact remains that most rural Chagga are peasant farmers, some of whom manage to supplement their incomes as occasional hired laborers or occasionally find work in the informal economy. Many men and women of the younger generation are leaving Kilimanjaro to find jobs elsewhere. This exodus has relieved what would otherwise have been even greater pressure on the land, and has prevented an extreme crisis from developing. So far rural life has proceeded relatively peacefully because the area is increasingly dependent on a larger labor market (and on other areas where land is still available) that can drain off some of its overflow. But whether the outflow will keep pace with the pressure remains to be seen.

6

The formal structure of local government and local courts

UNDERLYING SOCIAL COMMUNITIES, OVERLYING ADMINISTRATIVE STRUCTURES

Two perspectives on the political past of Kilimanjaro are necessary to make the present intelligible: the view from the rural countryside and the view from the administrative centers. The official formal facts of government taken by themselves give the impression that the British colonial administration was founded on indirect rule through traditional chiefs and councils, and that the postcolonial reorganizations have produced a total replacement of earlier forms, being based on an intricate interlock between party and government. In fact the British colonial administration continued the directed remodeling of the indigenous political system started by the Germans. The formal structure of chiefship thus constructed though labeled traditional was largely a new entity. In its turn the postcolonial regime did away with what was left of chiefship and relabeled and revised local administration, at times claiming to be making a total break with the past. Official tables of organization today give the impression that there is no longer anything particularly Chagga about the structure of politics on Kilimanjaro, and indeed that the earlier history of the Chagga is irrelevant to their present situation. But this is not the case.

Even a superficial view from the countryside gives quite another sense. To be sure, chiefship is no more. But the localized patrilineages of the older areas of settlement are still in place, and the old *mitaa* (or sub*mitaa*) to which they belong still exist as significant political entities. They have been transformed by the events of the past century but are still important. In some respects, the *mitaa* are actually more significant than ever now, since in the process of national rural "villagization" made mandatory in Tanzania in 1976, the new cooperative villages of Kilimanjaro were simply formed out of old *mitaa* with some new internal organizational arrangements added.

The focus of rural life is still passionately local with a high degree of

Table 4. *Lutheran church marriages in Mamba*

	1942	1952	1962
Both partners from Mamba	34	26	54
One partner from Mamba	3	4	6
Total	37	30	60

local endogamy. Census information collected in 1969 on 300 households in what was then the *mtaa* of Msae, in the ex-chiefdom of Mwika, showed a remarkable percentage of men married women from the same ex-chiefdom.[1] In 244 of the 425 marriages, the men even found their wives in the same *mtaa*. In 74 others, wives came from other *mitaa* of Mwika. Eighty-six other women came from the immediately adjacent ex-chiefdom of Mamba. Only 21 marriages were with women from more distant ex-chiefdoms, and 12 of these were with women from Rombo, adjacent to Mwika on the Eastern side. An inspection of the marriage registers in the Lutheran Church in Mamba (Table 4) showed a similar degree of marital localism.

No explicit preferential rule or set of prohibitions accounts for the high degree of local endogamy. It is simply the usual practice. The distances involved in these marriages are usually no more than a mile or two, sometimes three.

In 1982 several times a day buses would go from Mwika to some of the other ex-chiefdoms and to Moshi Town. These have existed for years, but such transportation is relatively expensive, and for most rural people there are seldom compelling reasons to go farther than one can walk. In the sample of rural farmers interviewed by Maro only 23 percent of the men had had temporary work experience out of the Moshi District and 12 percent more had been away as British soldiers. Thus 65 percent of the men had "not ventured outside the District" (Maro 1974:190). And half of those who had been away had been away for less than a year. But 20 percent of the men he interviewed said they had children outside the district. Labor migration has not been the occasion for finding a bride. Most men who have been away and return home either already have a wife on Kilimanjaro or have subsequently found one.

Hence every man who lives in and holds lands in these old areas of settlement has dozens and dozens of patrilineal and affinal links to other landholders in his own and neighboring *mitaa*. The relationships between his father and theirs, his brother and theirs, form the background of his own. What interests him when he joins the other men in the late afternoon for a beer and some talk is what is going on in the neighborhood. He may well know the price of coffee on the world market, and may have heard of what the party is saying on somebody's transistor radio, or at a meeting, or even in church on Sunday. But unless he is an official or works in town he is not likely to be preoccupied with what is going on in Moshi, at the administrative seat of the district, and certainly knows little or nothing about what is going on in the other ex-chiefdoms. The ties of the rural neighborhoods are stronger to the administrative center and to the world away from the mountain than to other similar neighborhoods in other ex-chiefdoms on the mountain. The active connections with the "outside" exist through coffee, Christianity, and through government institutions like schools and party. Those "outside" links have personal immediacy to the extent that external institutions have local representatives. The local representatives usually have a double identity, that of neighbor and of link to the outside.

Can life have been any less locally focused in the past? It seems unlikely. Certainly genealogical information suggests that local endogamy is nothing new. Before there were transistor radios, before there were so many educated persons and government jobs, and when there were fewer means of transportation and communication and weaker external economic ties, can the doings of the Council of Chiefs at its monthly meeting in Moshi have been an event of great interest in the rural areas? The way in which the local primary societies of the KNCU rebelled in the 1930s against the discipline of its Moshi headquarters suggests otherwise. Local rural autonomy over many matters was preserved as much as possible. It can be read as a form of resistance to the colonial administration. But it is probably much less regime specific. The same localism exists today in the presence of an African government. The desire to maintain a degree of local control over local affairs continues. Recognizing this localism puts political events at higher levels into perspective. To a great extent the modern integration of the district as a whole is and has been an artifact of its superimposed supralocal organizations, rather than the product of interlocal interdependence.

The character of the central administration in Moshi Town has never been simply a matter of its formal definition by higher authorities, colonial or postcolonial. What such district government can and cannot do, what it consequently is, has rather always been partly defined by the character of the rural districts it administers, and the nature of their connection with the town center and the arrangements negotiated between center and periphery.[2]

The organic relationship between underlying social communities and overlying administrative structures is of theoretical interest because it presents in a clear form the degree to which planned organization is reshaped by practice. Formal organization is accessible to designed social change, is highly public, and always presents a temptation to reformers both from above and from below. If the changes come from above it frequently becomes the peculiar business of the subordinate communities to accommodate themselves in such a way as to allow as little disturbance as possible of those ongoing internal arrangements over which they can preserve their autonomy. That is not to say that subordinate communities are always unaffected or unchanged by alterations at the top, only to emphasize that the dynamic is not by any means simply one of superordinate direction and subordinate conformity, but rather of a tension between direction and autonomy.

When the subordinate communities pressed for central administrative change, as in the colonial period among the Chagga, then a changing government organization negotiated to preserve certain administrative continuities. The economic and social base on which colonial officialdom was superimposed was itself changing. Periodic administrative transformation was not simply imposed on unchanging rural arrangements. The continued existence of localized patrilineages and the local endogamy was important. But the changing demographic situation, the movement deeper and deeper into a cash economy, as well as the effects of new religion, new information, and formal education were working incremental changes that cumulatively had profound effects. Administrative organization and policy have been partly responsive and partly directive in relation to rural change. The present degree of localism and the continuing maintenance of Chagga social and cultural traditions directly play into the dynamic tension between administration and communities administered, between direction and autonomy. Formal administrative reorganizations from above can only be fully understood in terms of the specific local context into which they are thrust.

The process of development of formal units of political organization on Kilimanjaro has been astonishing, and in some ways circular. For a long while change moved relentlessly in the direction of consolidation of small units into larger ones. Now it has swung back to subdivision. At least from the late nineteenth century onward, and perhaps from earlier times the number of chiefdoms gradually diminished. In the mid-to-late nineteenth century, certain consolidations of chiefdoms seem to have been largely loose, sometimes unstable military alliances, often involving tribute-paying arrangements. Small chiefdoms were vulnerable to being dominated by stronger larger ones and were sometimes swallowed by them. From the turn of the century, colonial administrative policies continued and hardened the process of accretion and consolidation. Gradually the several dozen chiefdoms of the early German period (Widenmann lists 37), were reduced to twenty-eight by the time the British took over in 1916 (Widenmann 1899:2; Dundas 1924:279). Later, by 1929, they were further reduced to twenty, and then eventually in 1946 to fifteen on the mountain itself (Annual Report, P.C. Northern Province, TNA 11681, 1929:15; Hailey, 1950:284). After 1961 the new government aggregated the ex-chiefdoms into seven divisions (Maro, 1974:10, 15).

From 1929 until 1946 a Council of Chagga Chiefs collectively functioned at the top of the Native Administrative hierarchy. In a constitutional reform in 1946 the "area chiefdoms," as they then came to be called, were reduced in official status and were grouped onto three geographical divisions, Hai in the west (containing 5 chiefdoms), Vunjo in the center (containing 6 chiefdoms), and Rombo in the east (containing 4 chiefdoms). Each of the three groups was given a superior divisional chief (sing. *mwitori,* pl. *waitori*), making the chiefs of the fifteen "area chiefdoms" effectively subchiefs (Hailey 1950:285). The chiefs also lost their status as Native Authorities. Only the three divisional chiefs were officially listed as Native Authorities. Each divisional chief had a divisional council (composed of his deputy chief, the *mangi* of each area in the division, and two councilors from each of the area chiefdoms, one chosen by the divisional chief, the other elected by the people). The composition of the Chagga Council of Chiefs was radically changed, to consist of the three divisional chiefs and their deputies and six councilors, two chosen by each divisional chief from his own divisional council. The reorganization of 1946 was a major change not only in the direction of consolidation but also in providing (through the position of councilor) an avenue for nonchiefly persons who were able leaders in their communities to enter government.

Additional reforms followed in 1950 increasing the number of commoners in the Chagga Council, and also enhancing the office of the area chiefs to "subordinate native authorities" while saddling them with elected councils (Johnston 1953:135–6). In 1952 the process of consolidation culminated in the installation of a paramount chief of all the Chagga, who was elected to his office. He was an educated grandson of the great Chief Marealle of Marangu who had been a favorite of the Germans fifty years earlier. With his election additional reforms were instituted. Councils, with elected councilors, were established for area chiefs. Increased popular representation on the Chagga Council and the divisional councils was arranged, and the membership of the Chagga Council was increased from eighteen to forty-seven (137–38).

Counterbalancing the development of new and larger political councils in which commoners were widely represented the paramount chief also adopted some traditionalist strategies. During the mid-1950s, as Thomas Marealle gradually met with increasing opposition, he tried to reconstitute the formal political importance of the localized patrilineages. He also aimed to *re*vitalize supposed earlier connections among same-name patrilines in different areas. These may in fact never have had political coherence. In 1956 efforts were made to urge the registration of all the patrilineages of each area as well as the names of their "clan heads" preparatory to giving the "clans a formal role in local political affairs" (Association-Vashari, KDC File 10/27). The advisers of the paramount chief were clearly trying to link his office and government, the highest level of organizational consolidation, with a universal ground-level unit, the patrilineage, on the assumption that mountainwide links among same-name patrilineages were viable, and that there had been an earlier corporateness that could be easily restored. They were wrong about the large-scale political possibilities. The attempt at *lineage* registration had limited success and the plan evaporated with the declining fortunes of the paramount chief. But its failure should not be taken as an indication that the localized patrilineages had lost all their importance.

In the large areas of old settlement the lineages were still very much in place in 1984. That is not so, of course, in the newer areas, both up-mountain and down-mountain, where the clusters of related families are fewer and small. (It might be possible to work out from the 1978 census exactly what proportion of the population lives in the old type of *mtaa* and what proportion in the new.) It is clear that kinship is a weighty factor in the local life of the many older *mitaa*, and some links with satellite spinoff communities are maintained, but local connections unquestionably have more political vitality than any inter*mitaa*.

Throughout the historical process of administrative consolidation on Kilimanjaro, when an independent chiefdom swallowed another, the conquered chiefdom became a *mtaa* of the chiefdom that had ingested it. The process suggests decreasing numbers of chiefdoms and increasing numbers of *mitaa*. This conclusion is true only in a limited sense. Parallel to the process of the consolidation of chiefdoms and the reduction of their numbers was a similar process with respect to the *mitaa*. There were 114 *mitaa* on the mountain with officially recognized headmen (*wachili*) in 1946 (Hailey 1950:284). But many *submitaa* were locally and unofficially recognized as significant entities, which had earlier been consolidated into the officially recognized *mitaa*. Some of these sequences can be reconstructed from local lore and historical documents. For example, in the formation of the ex-chiefdom of Mwika, Fig. 6.1 suggests the sequence.

Mrs. Stahl shows a similar sequence of consolidations in the chiefdoms of Rombo (Figure 6.3) on the most easterly side of the mountain (1964:340). With one exception, the four chiefdoms in Rombo in 1960 had only achieved their fully consolidated form in 1946.

A similar pattern could no doubt be reconstructed for the whole of

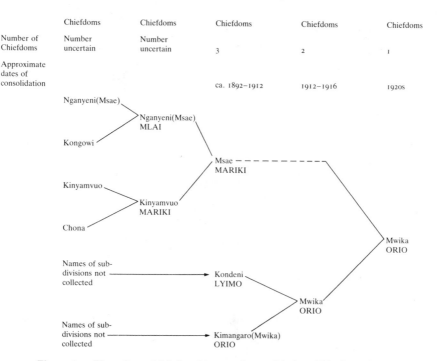

Chiefdoms	Chiefdoms	Chiefdoms	Chiefdoms	Chiefdoms
Number of Chiefdoms	Number uncertain	Number uncertain	3	2	1
Approximate dates of consolidation			ca. 1892–1912	1912–1916	1920s

Figure 6.1. The mitaa of Mwika–history of consolidation. This figure is patently incomplete but gives a sense of the process. Below each mtaa name is indicated the name of the chiefly lineage, in capital letters. This material on consolidation was collected as oral history in Mwika, but the dating is taken in part by piecing together local information with that regarding Marealle I in Stahl (1964:292).

Kilimanjaro; the consolidations in Rombo are more recent than most of those in the other parts, which probably are closer to the Mwika sequential pattern.[3] When independence came in 1961 not only were the local chiefships abolished but the old chiefdoms were broken up into villages, and local administration was carried on village by village. These new villages were consolidated *mitaa*. The 114 *mitaa* referred to by Hailey in 1950 were reduced to 67 in 1963 through amalgamations (Tordoff 1967:117). Seven divisional executive officers were appointed as the nucleus of supralocal organization. Mrs. Stahl seems to think of the abolition of colonial period chiefship as involving the loss of a traditional office and reports that the new administrative arrangements were inadequate replacements for chiefship.

By 1967 nothing had yet replaced this ancient focus in Chagga life. The new situation was that seven divisional executive officers on the mountain, all Chagga, were required to cover the former area chiefdoms, each being responsible for a

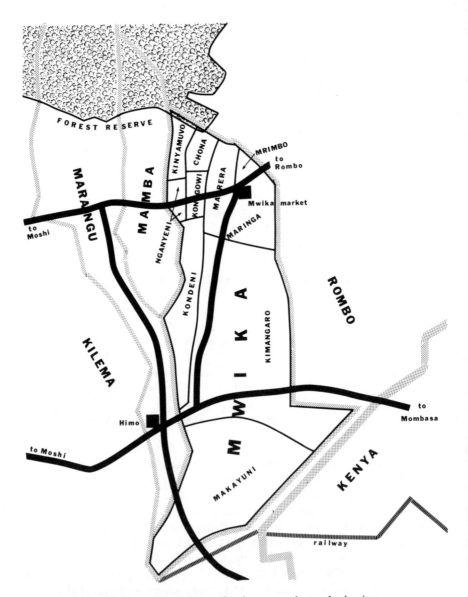

Figure 6.2. Mwika and its environs, showing some mitaa and sub-mitaa.

division containing two or more areas . . . great pains were taken to ensure that each divisional executive officer did not live in his own division. They visited each area once or twice weekly, and departed after office hours. (Stahl 1969:221)

Stahl is certainly right that divisional level supervision at the time was intermittent and limited. Localism was enhanced. Each consolidated *mtaa*

Kishingonyi hills	R. Lumi	R. Mlembea	R. Terakea
1899	Kasseni, Mengwe, Mriti, Keni, Chimbii Mkuu, Ushiri (7)	Kerio, Mrau, Longoni, Kirua, Keni, Mrere, Mbushi, Kitangara, Mashati, Olele (10)	upper Usseri, lower Usseri, Ngasseni (3)	
1945	Keni-Mriti, Mengwe, Mkuu (3)	Mrau, Kirua, Mrere, Mashati, Olele (5)	Usseri (1)	
1946	Keni-Mriti-Mengwe, Mkuu (2)	Mashati, now incorporating Mrau, Kirua and Mrere (1)	Usseri, now incorporating Olele (1)	

Figure 6.3. The mitaa of Rombo – history of consolidation. *Source:* Stahl (1964: 340).

had a village executive officer and a village development committee. These posts were filled by active party men where there were any. Tanzanian African National Union (TANU) had not had much of a foothold on Kilimanjaro in preindependence times. But soon after independence virtually everyone joined. As might have been expected, the local party often replicated preexisting relationships. Even the abolished chiefdoms continued as entities. For some time taxes continued to be collected ex-chiefdom by ex-chiefdom (Table of Taxpayers and Taxes paid for July 1968 dated 7 August 1968, K.D.C.).[4] Given that on Kilimanjaro TANU was formed of preexisting structures, the reorganization of 1964 was rather infelicitously described by Tordoff as breaking down "tribal loyalties."

The strength of local traditions on the mountainside forced TANU in 1964 to work through the traditional parish-like units – the *mitaa* – by appointing the *mtaa* head (who usually controls a water furrow and is therefore a key local figure) as the party representative. This move was fairly successful and only two *mtaa*-heads . . . proved uncooperative and had to be removed. In this instance TANU successfully used the traditions of the Wachagga in order to break down tribal loyalties and by August 1964 had established 47 sub-branches on the mountain. (Tordoff 1967:117)

This TANU maneuver suggested what was to come. From the 1890s until independence, the administrative sequence involved the progressive consolidation of units. Fifteen years after independence the movement toward consolidation into larger and larger units was reversed. In the "villagization" program of 1976 many consolidated *mitaa* of the 1964 reorganization subdivided. Old sub*mitaa* reappeared as cooperative villages. They are now the most significant official unit of present rural reorganization. Because of the population density on Kilimanjaro and the directives limiting the size of cooperative villages, at least in some places the consolidated *mitaa* of 1964 were too large to become the new kind of cooperative villages. In some areas even the *mitaa* from decades earlier were too large. In the ex-chiefdom of Mwika, for example, Kinyamvuo and Nganyeni have become separate cooperative villages returning neighborhood communities to a corporate state of local political significance that they had not enjoyed since the turn of the century.

Thus in a peculiar way, in the recent process of reorganization on Kilimanjaro nineteenth-century entities whose importance was subsequently eclipsed by higher levels, have now been restored to a new life. To recapitulate briefly, the small *mitaa* of the nineteenth century, some of which were once tiny independent chiefdoms, became consolidated into larger and larger chiefdoms both before and throughout the colonial period. The fifteen chiefdoms left in 1946 were then consolidated into three divisional chiefdoms, and the whole ultimately into one paramount chiefdom. The whole process can be seen as a sort of pyramiding. Each time a new level or kind of organization was introduced, it was *added* to the ones already in being. The preexisting ones were left substantially in place. Pyramiding has its political advantages. It maintains continuity, and it does not threaten those in lower level offices in the extreme way that replacement would. It erodes the political significance of the lower levels by transferring to higher levels some of the powers and functions once enjoyed by those below. The same thing is true of adding such entities as councils. They appear only to elaborate. They end by transforming. Then, with a stroke, after independence a great deal of the top of the colonially created administrative pyramid was dispensed with, and replaced. But the community realities at the bottom remained in being. And now, the neighborhood units near the lowest levels of the structure, the *mitaa* of the 1900 period, have become the official resource of rural socialism in the 1980s.

THE COURTS

The closeness of the relationship between the courts and the changing political structure on Kilimanjaro cannot be overstated.[5] Throughout the century changes in the courts have been parallel to the transformation in government administration. Until the 1950s the highest court in each chiefdom was presided over by the chief or his deputy. Yet that element of apparent continuity conceals basic changes. As indicated earlier, in precolonial times the age-set assemblies had a major role in the processing of disputes both in parish (*mtaa*) hearings presided over by headmen (*wachili*) and in those heard on the chief's Lawn of Justice. The role of the age-sets was phased out early in the colonial period. In German times, the judicial role of the chief began to enlarge. He heard cases and decided them himself, consulting with lineage elders and others at his discretion. Over time chiefly power was further consolidated, but its exercise came under closer scrutiny. During most of the period of British colonial rule, the only officially recognized local courts on Kilimanjaro were chief's courts and they came under the direct supervision of colonial officials. Thus until the 1950s, judicial and executive functions were embodied in the chiefly office itself. From the early 1950s on, it became a matter of colonial policy and popular demand that the area chief's powers should be diminished and that chiefs should lose control of the courts. Over the next decade this policy became law. In the last years before independence, magistrates were at first installed in a few chiefdoms, later in more and more. After independence the process was completed. Everywhere the former chief's courts became primary courts, presided over in every ex-chiefdom by an appointed magistrate who sat in the very court building on the very platform where the chiefs had sat in earlier decades.

The changing official definition of the role of the rural courts in the British colonial and postcolonial periods is one dimension of the story within which to consider the cases recorded in the archives. But it is necessary to go beyond formal history to understand what is going on. For one thing the physical and administrative situation is very different on the ground from what it seems on paper. Moshi, the administrative seat from which the chiefly courts were supervised, is miles away from the courthouses on the mountain. Some are as far as eighty kilometers away (Maro 1974:187). The road that leads from Moshi to Kilimanjaro was not paved until the 1950s (233). In the dry season, some of the mountain paths that had been widened for motor vehicles in the 1920s can be traveled with reasonable ease, though they are not the smoothest of dirt roads. In the wet season they are covered with slippery mud, many inches deep. Still no motor road, dirt or paved, connects Vunjo and Rombo directly with the western part of Kilimanjaro. The road network is dominated by an upslope-downslope orientation, and to get from certain parts of the mountain to others, one must go down to the Arusha-Himo road, or to Moshi Town to change buses and go back up the mountain into another one of its subdivisions. An important belt road goes through Vunjo and Rombo in the banana-growing area, but it does not go continuously through the whole of the inhabited area. An inspection of the courts on the mountain by someone coming from Moshi Town, even if one assumes that the inspector had a car (not always the case), is not the simplest of tasks. It can be done, but not efficiently or easily, and takes substantial time. Even today it would be quite impossible to maintain any sort of day-to-day supervision. Today the "courthouse" is the same tin-roofed, open-walled shedlike structure with one or two small closed rooms at either end that has been in use for decades. There is no electricity and there are no telephones. Thus the many formal administrative changes enacted over the years in relation to the local courts must be understood in the light of the difficulties of transportation and communication between the administrative center and the rural areas.

Many changes in the system promulgated in Dar es Salaam in the colonial period were probably not even heard of by, let alone a concern of, rural people. In the pre–transistor radio period the colonial government communicated with the rural population by holding large public meetings and making speeches about innovations. That method still obtains in the postcolonial setting. There were, and sometimes are, direct reactions in the countryside. But it is one thing to communicate new rules and another to monitor the level of conformity to them. Some (but not all) court records were given systematic attention, but the courts themselves could scarcely have been closely supervised in operation.

One immediate concern of the postcolonial government once independence was achieved was to unify the judicial system. In most of the colonial period there had been two structures of courts, one for natives and one for others. That dualism had not always had the form it ultimately took. In 1920 native courts were formally subordinate to the high court (Courts Ordinance no. 6 of 1920). Thus at the outset of the British Mandate native courts were in theory "part of the system of European justice" in Tanganyika (Hailey 1938:441). In practice, the British administrative officers in the provinces supervised the native courts, and the connection with the high court was more nominal than operational. In 1929 the Native Courts Ordinance did away with the unified system of justice under one high court. It created a self-contained system of native courts under administrative supervision. The colonial executive authorities became "the sole avenue of appeal" (Hailey 1938:442).

The Provincial Commissioner – the principal executive officer in each district – was authorized with the approval of the Governor to establish such Local Courts in his province as seemed necessary. He conferred upon them their jurisdiction. With the approval of the Governor he could also revoke, suspend or vary the warrant of any court. (Telford Georges in James and Kassam 1973:13)

The complete separation of the native courts from the European ones obtained until 1951, when the Native Courts Ordinance was repealed (Local Courts Ordinance of 1951, chap. 299). With that repeal a first small step was taken toward reestablishing a single integrated system of courts. From 1951 on, the Central Court of Appeal, the highest court to which cases from the native system could be appealed, had sitting on it a judge of the high court (Local Government Memoranda, no. 2, Local

Courts, 2d. ed., 1957:9; Barnett 1965:64). After independence, the Magistrates Courts Act, no. 55 of 1963 fully consolidated the two systems and made them into one. The process of integration was completed.

In the British colonial period the changing system of appeals and the hierarchy of courts must have made a difference to those few parties who appealed their cases all the way up the ladder. But in general the rulings made in the appellate cases probably had little (if any?) direct effect on the lowest courts in the system. The rulings of higher courts are scarcely ever cited in the handwritten case records of the courts of first instance on Kilimanjaro. (The Kilimanjaro local courtholders never referred back to their own previous rulings either unless the same parties were involved. They never saw the case records of the other courts of the same level. There was no *explicit* attention to precedent.) I very much doubt that in the colonial period the rulings of the higher courts were a matter of which the personnel of the chief's courts (later the local courts and now the primary courts) were even aware, except where it concerned the fate of a particular case appealed from their court. And no wonder. The Digest of Appeals from the local courts published in the 1950s, for example, was in English, which by no means all the court holders on Kilimanjaro understood. At various times during the colonial period some of the chiefs were not literate, let alone English speaking. It is plain that the rulings of the higher courts were to guide the district commissioners in their judgments, not to affect directly what took place in the local courts. In his preface to the Digest of Appeals from the local courts for 1955 and 1956 (which summarized appellate court decisions), the local courts adviser specifically said, "The contents of the three Digests, particularly those cases relating to general principles and those of general application throughout the Territory, should always be borne in mind by District Commissioners when hearing appeals from local courts and reference to them should be made in judgments where they are relevant." In 1968–69, there was very little in the court offices on the mountain, let alone in Moshi (often nothing), in the way of law books or legal memoranda or any other literature regarding the substance of the law. Later, in the 1970s, copies of the Penal Code and of the Primary Courts Manual could be found in Swahili and a more active connection between the primary courts and the higher levels of the judicial system was noticeable. Probably this was related to the postindependence construction of a judicial bureaucracy with a built-in career hierarchy. (See Table 6 and Figure 6.4.)

How much integration of judicial levels had obtained in the system of native courts in the colonial period? Probably very little beyond the province. One can only infer that apart from whatever limited direction and supervision the provincial commissioner and his staff provided, the local courts on Kilimanjaro applied the law as the courtholder, usually the chief or his deputy, saw fit within certain prescribed limits. In general, the native courts were to apply customary law and to enforce the rulings of the Native Authorities, the provincial commissioner, and from 1929 some statutory provisions. The chiefs obviously used their authority to require obedience of their subjects. Their power over the court must have been a significant part of this authority. In 1941 Lord Hailey was still able to write, "In their administrative capacity, Native Authorities have power to make local bye-laws, and to issue legal orders, a breach of which is punishable in the native courts. . . . The position regarding issue of legal 'orders' by native authorities and subordinate native authorities is still somewhat indeterminate." (TNA 41891, Local Government Report by Lord Hailey to the Secretary of State for the Colonies, 1941:38) There was no regular procedure for recording the orders of Native Authorities. Of course many matters were excluded from the jurisdiction of the native courts including all offenses punishable with death or imprisonment for life (Hailey 1950:220). It was also a basic precept of the colonial system that customary law could be applied only so long as it was not contrary to natural justice or morality, was not in conflict with the provisions of any law in force in the territory, and was not unreasonable, the provincial commissioner being considered the best judge of the meaning of those words (see Hooker 1975:130). Thus in theory witchcraft cases could not be tried openly in the courts and magical means of detection and ordeals were not allowed. But clearly, despite these limitations, the office of courtholder had considerable power.

In 1926 not only did each Chagga chief have his own court in his own chiefdom, as he had had before, but three superior native appellate courts were formed. The provincial commissioner grouped the chiefs into three chiefly councils (Hai, Rumbo, and Vunjo). Not only was each council granted its own tax-supported treasury out of which the chiefs' salaries were paid, but each council was designated a first-class court, and was empowered to act as an appeal court from the chiefdom courts which were designated second-class courts.[6] There were differences of jurisdiction between them as courts of first instance, in addition to the appellate relationship.

The ending of tribute and the payment of salaries to chiefs in 1926 were, of course, part of a general attempt to separate the chiefs from their previous sources of income. The courts were no longer to be used as a means of enlarging the chief's wealth, since court fees were to go into the treasury. Chiefs were not supposed to be able to demand contributions from their subjects. In various ways the chiefs managed to get around this ruling. Though they had to forgo court fees, they continued to make their other material demands plain, but they redefined them as "gifts" and labeled them "voluntary." Such gifts were expected whenever land was allocated or transferred. At some point along the way, the date is not clear to me, but it was probably around 1930, the chiefs succeeded in enlarging their control over land transactions by trying to require that all land transfers to be "official" be approved by them. Not only was the information valuable to chiefs who might wish to make their own claims and allocations, but it also enhanced their income. The recipient of the land was obliged to give the chief *upata,* a gift of gratitude, and sometimes *upata* also to the *mchili.* Law cases show that *upata* was paid from 1928 until 1961 (see cases referring to *upata* in the section "The interest of the chiefs and *wachili* in transfers of land"). The variable cost of this practice is evident from the statement in a letter in the Kilimanjaro District File in 1955: " 'Upata' is given to the Mangi as a token of gratitude and need not necessarily be a cow, but anything according to one's power, it can even be a jar of *pombe* or a goat. No limit is fixed." (Letter 26, 10 March 1955, KDC File 9/11)

In 1929 when the Chagga chiefs were reorganized into a single council, the three chiefs' courts of appeal (Hai, Vunjo, and Rombo) that had existed since 1926 were abolished. The single council replaced them and became the Central Court of Appeal. The three treasuries became one. In his report for 1928, the provincial commissioner said optimistically, "The three Appeal Courts have worked very satisfactorily and their functions appear to have been well understood by the people who have invariably obtained justice from them when appealing from a Chief's court. It is anticipated that the Central Chagga Court will function equally well" (Typescript, Annual Report, Northern Province, 1928, TNA 11681:9). The Central Court began operation in 1929. The Central Council had nineteen chiefs. The court sat once a month at the Central Court House near Moshi, which had just been constructed. The court consisted of seven chiefs, one of whom was chosen to be president of the court. Each of the nineteen chiefs constituting the council sat on the court in turn (Annual Report, Northern Province, 1929, TNA 18693). The Central Court was a first-class court. It heard cases beyond the jurisdiction of the chief's courts, cases on appeal from the chief's courts, and cases to which chiefs were parties.

In 1929 the Central Court heard twenty-eight appeals out of 889 cases heard in the chief's courts. The administration pressed the courts to improve their record keeping and to become more correct about procedure relating to the summoning of witnesses, the nonappearance of parties, and the execution of decrees (Annual Report, Northern Province, 1929, TNA 18693:11). In the next years litigation continued to increase.[7]

By 1939 the increasing amount of litigation over land and some uncertainty about the applicable land law was sufficient to engage the attention of the provincial commissioner.

One interesting feature of the Court work of the Moshi district is the great number of suits connected with claims for land. Prior to the introduction of coffee, the issues in regard to such claims were fairly clear cut, but the establishment of this valuable economic crop has resulted in considerable complications. (Typescript, Annual Report, Northern Province, 1939, TNA 19415:6)

The provincial commissioner thought the time had come to frame a uniform land law. He put it to "the Chiefs and Elders" and they promised to consider it, but nothing came of his suggestion. One supposes that the Chagga wanted to retain their existing arrangements and understandings whatever the "complications." In December 1940 a public meeting was held in Moshi to discuss the issue and "it very quickly made up its mind that in no circumstances would it contemplate any change in the present land laws" (Annual Report, Northern Province, 1940, TNA 19415, 1940:5).

Though changes of substance failed in 1940, the postwar period brought further significant changes of organization. The nature of the constitutional reform of 1946, which deprived the local area chiefs of their status as Native Authorities and made them subordinate to three divisional chiefs (of Hai, Vunjo, and Rombo) and their councils, makes apparent the intent of the colonial administration severely to restrict the official prerogatives of the area chiefs. The area chiefs resisted. One mainstay of their remaining power were the courts which they continued to control. They either heard cases themselves, or they appointed *mwakili*, their personal judicial deputies, to sit in their stead.

In 1950 the district commissioner proposed the separation of the judiciary and the executive but his suggestion "had no very great reception from the people" (Annual Report, Northern Province, TNA 19415, 1950:2). In 1950 the chiefs even regained some of what they had lost and were promoted to "subordinate native authorities" (Johnston 1953:135). But change was in the air. The pressure to curtail chiefly powers continued. A commoner political party, the Kilimanjaro Citizens Union (KCU), came to be an important force on the mountain. It was an independent political association which the educated, well-to-do commoners Petro Njau and Joseph Merinyo had been instrumental in organizing. The KCU not only campaigned for a paramount chief, whose existence would further erode the standing of local chiefs, it also demanded "the separation of the native court judiciary from the executive" (Johnston 1953:136). In 1951 a committee of colonial officials and prominent Chagga was formed to consider these constitutional changes. It recommended:

The separation of the judiciary from the executive should be effected by the appointment of divisional magistrates with no executive functions in place of the existing chiefs' deputies. Secondly that a judicial committee of the Chagga Council be set up to hear appeals from the divisional courts. Thirdly that at the lowest level no change should be introduced unless desired by the people of the area chiefdom concerned and that where so decided the functions of the area chief and the area magistrate should not be entirely divorced. (Johnston 1953:136)

Most of these recommendations were accepted by the colonial administration and were put into effect. "In seven area chiefdoms the people asked for area magistrates and these were appointed in place of the area chiefs' deputies who, however, were retained in the remaining nine area chiefdoms" (138).[8] None of the magistrates appointed at the area (chiefdom) level or at the divisional level (Hai, Vunjo, Rombo) had had any previous judicial experience or training (District Commissioner's Report 1952, KDC File 1/16, p. 9).

The separation of the executive and the judicial functions is one of many examples showing that the colonial government had a particular evolutionary model of legal institutions in mind as it encouraged reforms. This particular transformation of the local courts took place during the prosperous period of the "reign" of Paramount Chief Thomas Marealle (1952-60; Stahl 1964:336). It was a time of strong syncretism between symbols of old and new institutions which Marealle himself epitomized. One of his plans along these lines might have had considerable legal implications had it actually borne fruit. In 1952 there was much talk of codifying Chagga customary law. Abraham Salema, the Chagga Council laws adviser was to undertake this work and to use a questionnaire devised for the district commissioners. An American anthropologist, Irving Kaplan, volunteered to help Salema (Judicial-Codification of Chagga Law, KDC File 3/7). Two matters in particular seem to have aroused a good deal of local interest, the Chagga oath and the standardization of bridewealth.[9]

In 1954 there had been a growing demand for the introduction of the traditional Chagga oath on the ground that it would reduce frivolous litigation (District Commissioner's Report, 1954, KDC File 1/16, p. 9). The oath was to be used especially in land cases. It consisted of putting a bit of earth from a disputed *kihamba* on the tongue of the complaining party, while standing in the *kihamba*. He (or, I suppose, she) then declared that all that he/she had said was true. Some versions had it that the oath taker was to say something to the effect of, "May I be struck dead if it is not true" (Circular from Native Administration Headquarters dated 18 February 1955, KDC File on Chagga Oath 3/15). A month later the district commissioner indicated his dissatisfaction with the idea of making this customary oath a part of official legal procedure on the ground that if people really believed they would be struck dead it was not an oath but an ordeal, and as such unacceptable (letter dated 21 March 1955, File on Chagga Oath KDC 3/15). The correspondence continued. The gist of it seems to be that the Chagga thought it would be a marvelously effective way of settling land cases once and for all. The *mangi* of Siha, Hai Division, wrote that any man who swore falsely would surely return the *kihamba* within a year when the oath he had taken *had affected him* (letter dated 7 April 1955, KDC File on Chagga Oath 3/15). Evident from the *mangi*'s comment (and from fieldwork two decades later) is that substantial numbers of rural Chagga believed, as the *mangi* of Siha plainly did, that the oath could have a direct physical effect. As one might have expected from the district commissioner's comments, the oath failed to achieve official recognition. But it is significant that in the very period when the educated and prosperous younger generations of commoner Chagga were coming into their own economically and politically, and taking substantial power away from their illiterate senior kinsmen and the old-style chiefs were losing ground by the day, that there should have been a simultaneous ethnic revival of sorts, in which an attempt was made to gain official recognition for Chagga law. The oath controversy itself is an indication of legal pluralism on Kilimanjaro in the decade before independence.

The British colonial attitude toward "customary law" at the time was clear. Its virtues were formally recognized and odes of qualified appreciation were composed.

Customary law is primarily concerned with the restoration of the social equilibrium, with adjustments and reconciliations, with restitution and the award of compensation; that its procedure is informal but effective, designed to bring about an agreed solution, not an imposed judgment; that its sanctions are the fear of offending public opinion, living and dead, and the fear of magical retribution. But customary law is, in addition, local and popular, it is firmly based on the realities of tribal life and thus understandable to all, it is open to all members of the tribe, and finally, it is cheap. These are characteristics which in any system of law would be admirable and worthy of retention, and care should be taken that, with the inevitable modernisation of the courts they are not abandoned. (Local Government Memoranda 2, Local Courts, 2d. edition [Dar es Salaam: Government Printer, 1957] p. 4)

Immediately after independence "customary law" was given ongoing legal force in civil cases, subject to certain limited exceptions (Cotran 1970:155). Some statutory modifications have since occurred, but in general its official legal place continued and continues as before. "Once a primary court has accepted a proceeding, the issue whether or not customary law applies to a person, or whether or not customary law is the law applicable, shall not be a matter for decision by a primary court, and the primary court should proceed to hear and decide the case in accordance with customary law" (Primary Courts Manual [Dar es Salaam: Government Printer, 1964] p. 5).

Plate 16. Exterior of open-walled courthouse in Marangu, 1973. Closed space at front contains two small rooms, lockup (windowless space to right of entrance), and clerk's office (with window at left). (Photo by D. C. Moore)

After independence the ten provinces of Tanganyika were replaced by ten regions, later seventeen regions (Regions and Regional Commissioners Act of 1962; Barnett 1965:69; see also Cotran 1970). However, the new regional commissioners did not have the power vested in the provincial commissioners in colonial times to establish courts or to appoint court holders. That power was given to the minister of justice who then delegated the power to appoint magistrates to regional local courts officers. In the early years many new magistrates were appointed and some were put through a three-month course at Mzumbe in Morogoro to increase their knowledge of law and procedure (Barnett 1965:70).[10] All local court magistrates were transferred to the judiciary and became primary court magistrates (Magistrates Courts Ordinance, 1 July 1964).[11] The primary courts over which they presided had the power to imprison for twelve months, to impose fines of up to 1,000 shillings or corporal punishment of twelve strokes, and higher criminal powers and penalties in the case of cattle theft (Barnett 1965:75). They had civil jurisdiction in all matters in which customary law was applicable, regardless of the value of the subject matter. They could deal with civil debts not exceeding 2,000 shillings. They had exclusive original jurisdiction with respect to marriage, guardianship, and land matters under "customary law." And

Plate 17. Interior of court at Marangu in 1973, taken from entrance facing raised platform where magistrate sits. In front of his desk, embedded in the cement, is the stone once used by the chief. Behind the magistrate's platform are two small offices, now used by the magistrate and by officials of the ward. The building has neither electricity nor water. An outhouse stands behind it. Parties and witnesses sit on the front benches, spectators on benches behind them. When testifying people stand below the platform looking up at the magistrate who sits at his table writing down their testimony. (Photo by D. C. Moore)

they had jurisdiction over the enforcement of local authority and district council bylaws (Barnett 1965:76; see also Part III, Primary Courts Manual 1964, Civil Proceedings).

In civil cases, two elements of procedure gave the magistrate a great many alternatives if he chose to avail himself of them. He could take steps to promote a reconciliation and he could make "any other order which the justice of the case requires" (Barnett 1965:77–9; Primary Courts Manual, 1964, Part III, Section 9:5). For example, he could order the payment of compensation in kind and had the power to award compensation in a criminal case. This had also been the practice in the colonial local courts.

At first under the 1963 act the primary court magistrate had the discretion to hear cases without the help of local elders. He could call them in or not as he saw fit when customary or Islamic law was at issue. Later, a 1964 amendment made the presence of two assessors (local elders) obliga-

Table 5. *Hierarchy of judicial levels (mid-1970s)*

Courts	Magistrates and judges
High court	Chief justice[a] Judges[a]
Resident magistrates court	Senior magistrate[b] magistrate[b](3 grades)
District courts	Supervisory magistrates Senior magistrate District court magistrate (3 grades)
Primary court	Primary court magistrate (3 grades)

[a]*Have law degree.*
[b]Do not have law degrees.

tory in all cases.[12] The assessors were to give their judgments just prior to the judgment of the magistrate (Barnett 1965:80). He was not bound by their decision, but had to record his reasons in writing if he disagreed with them. The amendment regarding assessors restored a practice that had prevailed throughout the colonial period. Even in the days when the chiefs themselves had ruled their courts, elders whose presence was officially recorded assisted them. Often *wachili* (*mtaa* heads), as well as elders were present.

The unified hierarchy of judicial levels created after independence is shown in Table 5. From the start the day-to-day supervision of the primary courts was in the hands of a district magistrate. Supervision entailed giving attention to personnel, salaries, leave rosters, interdistrict transfers, court advising, court inspection and reviewing decisions, hearing appeals. Each month each primary court submitted to the district magistrate information on the civil and criminal cases heard and pending, and on unpaid fines, if any. In essence the district magistrates took on the supervisory roles formerly performed by the district commissioners.

Criminal "customary law" was abolished altogether (Barnett 1965: 73). "Customary law" pertaining to civil matters was a more complex affair. A Unification of Customary Law Project was undertaken on a national scale in the hope of standardizing "customary" family law for many peoples while instituting certain reforms. Eventually a kind of synthesized restatement of law for patrilineal peoples was produced, and dealt with the laws of bridewealth, marriage, divorce, status of children, and succession (Barnett 1965; see local Customary Law Declaration 4, Rules of Inheritance, Government Notice [GN] 436, 1963; and Local Customary Law Declara-

Table 6. *Judiciary 1973*

Jurisdiction	Courts	Pay
Unlimited original jurisdiction; appellate jurisdiction from all decisions of district courts and resident magistrates courts	High court	Paid out of president's Consolidated Fund (not subject to parliamentary debate)
General original jurisdiction district courts Criminal cases involving not more than (a) 3 years' imprisonment (b) fine not exceeding 3,000 shillings (c) corporal punishment Civil cases in which value of subject matter does not exceed 20,000 shillings Appellate jurisdiction Appeals to district court in both civil and criminal cases from primary courts	Courts of Resident Magistrates District courts	Salaried officials paid by Judiciary Department
Original jurisdiction Civil (a) in which customary law or Islamic law applies (b) other debts, contracts, torts Criminal (a) imprisonment maximum 12 months (b) fine not exceeding 1,000 shillings (c) corporal punishment maximum 12 strokes	Primary courts	

Parallel and complementary system, established in 1969	Arbitration tribunals	Pay	Appeal
All disputes concerning land	Land	Per diem pay for citizen arbitrators; staff salaried	To minister for land and settlement
Any civil disputes	General	Citizen arbitrators unpaid	To primary court

tion, Law of Persons, GN 279, 1963, see also Cotran, 1965, and James and Fimbo 1973:167ff.). It was then ratified and adopted locality by locality. I was told in 1979 that the law had been adopted on Kilimanjaro but was not able to verify it. Some earlier customary practices inconsistent with the new legislation continued to prevail. A clear example exists in the case of the rights of women. Copies of the Law of Marriage Act of 1971 were not to be found in the primary courts on the mountain in 1974, and most of the magistrates I knew at the time did not seem to be familiar with it. Perhaps copies have since been distributed.

Since independence Tanzania has transformed its judicial system and its administrative system. In addition to these internal transformations, the party (formerly TANU, Tanzania African National Union, now CCM, Chama cha Mapinduzi, Revolutionary party) has developed two systems of its own that are parallel to yet involved with the central state structures. Thus, not only has the judicial system of Tanzania been revised, but there are now additional new tribunals run by local party personnel,

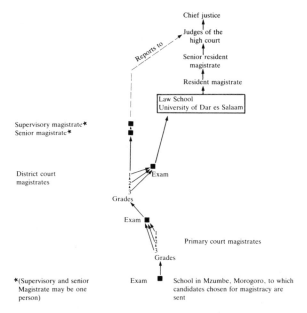

Figure 6.4. Career hierarchy in judiciary, 1973. Career material provided by oral description by resident magistrate in Moshi.

and a new hierarchy of administrative officials concerned with "develop-ment" (see Table 6 and Figure 6.5). These new institutions are defined in terms of a populist ideology, but are often run from the top down. In practice, in the rural areas, this party apparatus sometimes exists only on paper or if it exists seldom functions as planned at the lower levels.

In any case, a few years after independence there was an effort to dispose of much family controversy, and other small-scale disputing, be-fore it ever got to the primary court by creating informal courts run by laymen at an even lower level of the dispute-handling process. They were to be run by local party faithfuls, not by the judiciary. These courts were called arbitration tribunals in the English translation of the legislation but probably a more appropriate translation would be tribunals of reconcilia-tion (GN, no. 219, published 29 August 1969, Magistrates Courts Act, 1963, chap. 537. Regulations under section 154 came into operation 1 September 1969; see also Table 6). All cases arising under the Marriage Act of 1971 had to be initiated in these informal arbitration tribunals. If at the end of any hearing in that forum either party remained dissatisfied with the outcome, he/she was free to go to the primary court. There was to be *at least* one such tribunal in every ward. (On Kilimanjaro there were usually two wards per ex-chiefdom.) The arbitration tribunals consist of

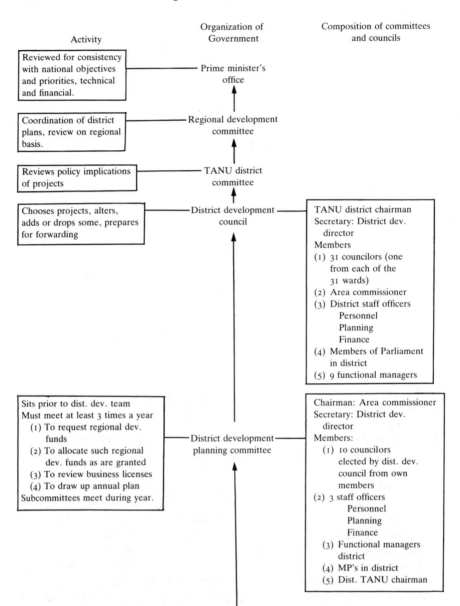

Activity	Organization of Government	Composition of committees and councils
Reviewed for consistency with national objectives and priorities, technical and financial.	Prime minister's office	
Coordination of district plans, review on regional basis.	Regional development committee	
Reviews policy implications of projects	TANU district committee	

Chooses projects, alters, adds or drops some, prepares for forwarding	District development council	TANU district chairman
		Secretary: District dev. director
		Members
		(1) 31 councilors (one from each of the 31 wards)
		(2) Area commissioner
		(3) District staff officers
		    Personnel
		    Planning
		    Finance
		(4) Members of Parliament in district
		(5) 9 functional managers

Sits prior to dist. dev. team
Must meet at least 3 times a year
(1) To request regional dev. funds
(2) To allocate such regional dev. funds as are granted
(3) To review business licenses
(4) To draw up annual plan
Subcommittees meet during year.
	District development planning committee	Chairman: Area commissioner
		Secretary: District dev. director
		Members:
		(1) 10 councilors elected by dist. dev. council from own members
		(2) 3 staff officers
		    Personnel
		    Planning
		    Finance
		(3) Functional managers district
		(4) MP's in district
		(5) Dist. TANU chairman

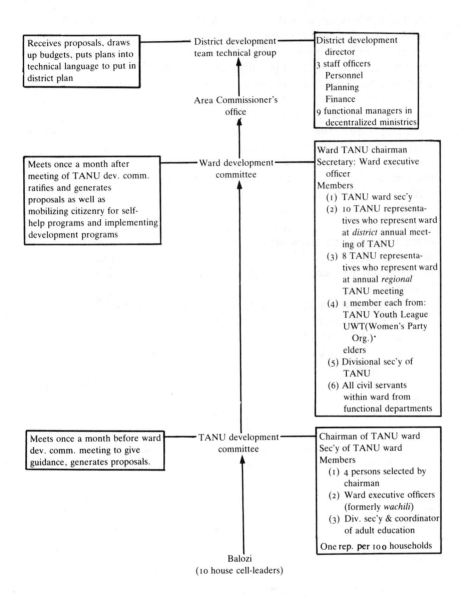

Figure 6.5. Official path of local proposals for development, 1974. Source: oral description by development official in Moshi.

five lay persons appointed by the TANU (Tanzanian African National Union) Branch Committee having jurisdiction over the ward. The five are not paid, and the parties pay no fees. There are no procedural constraints, and proceedings are informal. The citizens on the tribunal have no power to impose any fine or punishment and are enjoined to "endeavor to bring the parties to the dispute to an amicable settlement" (GN, no. 219, published 29 August 1969, Magistrates Courts Act, 1963, chap. 537). In practice, the tribunals have rather freely interpreted their powers and do not always restrain themselves as officially directed. The five members have jurisdiction over any matter brought to them with the concurrence of both parties. And if the tribunal fails to bring about a settlement, the dispute can then come to the primary court. There is no specification of what sort of law the tribunal is to apply. Amicable settlement is evidently conceived of as a sort of negotiated or mediated outcome that could be arranged without any rules more technical than common sense might dictate. These courts have had uneven success and have by no means replaced the informal system of lineage and neighborhood hearings.

In 1973–74 when fieldwork relating to the arbitration tribunals was done, they had been in existence on Kilimanjaro for about three years. The curious thing about them was that some were heavily used and others had practically no cases to hear. The population of potential users of these tribunals were already well served by a variety of existing dispute-hearing agencies: primary courts (one for each ex-chiefdom, hence roughly one for every two wards), and the informal, ad hoc groups of kin and neighbors who heard and decided or negotiated cases, as did local officials, priests and pastors, and even ten-house cell leaders, to be discussed shortly. Why should persons from one locality choose to use the new tribunals of arbitration, and persons from another locality ignore them?

The number of disputes generated in any area of Kilimanjaro can be assumed to be roughly proportionate to its population (see Table "Number of Cases Heard 1956-59" in note 7). Thus extreme differences in recourse to a particular type of hearing must reflect selection by litigants, rather than a local difference in the incidence of dispute. Some wards had many Arbitration Tribunals, others had only one, meeting the minimum requirement. Assuming a fairly steady supply of potentially hearable disputes that varies little from one locality to another, one might expect that a ward that had only one arbitration tribunal would be overloaded with cases, whereas a ward that had many such courts would hear fewer disputes.

Just the opposite was the case. A ward of the ex-chiefdom of Mamba, which had only one arbitration tribunal, had the lowest case-hearing rate of any examined. Yet, not many miles away, in the ex-chiefdom of Kilema, a ward with eighteen arbitration tribunals did a roaring business in each of them. The single court that did little business had no significant problem of physical access. It met under a tree near the main road. As far as could be discovered, there was nothing unusual about the men who sat on the court. What then could explain the many disputes being heard in the ward of Kilema with its many courts and the paucity in the ward of Mamba with only one?

The answer probably lies in the social geography of Kilimanjaro. The most significant social/geographical unit is not that new administrative creation the ward, but the *mtaa* (or the sub*mtaa*). The new arbitration tribunals in Kilema were set up with one per *mtaa*, and their lay judges were recruited from the neighborhood. Everyone could remember when the *mtaa* heads, the *wachili*, and local elders regularly heard cases. The new arrangement was much more analogous to the old, and had more of a foundation in the strong localism that dominates rural life than the one-court, one-ward arrangement. In 1979 some of the primary courts, including the one at Kilema, were not open for hearings every weekday as they had been ten years earlier, but sat much less frequently. The government's intention is clearly to divert as much petty civil litigation as possible into the arbitration tribunals and to reserve the primary courts largely for criminal cases. The primary courts continue to hear civil cases, but in wards where the arbitration tribunals are successful the number may diminish.

A hearing apparatus even lower in the hierarchy than the arbitration tribunals is the system of ten-house cell leaders instituted in the mid-1960s. Each cluster of roughly ten households constitutes a cell and "elects" one person to be its head. This lowest of party offices, the ten-house cell leadership, has many functions. Among them, the leader attends all discussions of dispute that concern his constituents and that are settled "at home." Sometimes he arrogates decision-making powers to himself. Sometimes he is a mediator. Sometimes he is no more than a spectator of the discussions and arrangements of others. He does not preside in a court, but he is a low-level adjunct of the official system.

Another major postcolonial change in the structure of local courts in Kilimanjaro came about through the establishment of customary land tribunals. Here again, a broadening party control of the dispute management process is evident. All freehold lands were converted into government leaseholds in 1963 (Conversion and Government Leases Act, chap. 523). As a matter of political philosophy, the act provided that the people as a whole should own the means of production, that land should belong to the tiller not to a landlord. Thus all "customary leaseholds" were abolished and, on Kilimanjaro, included all loans of land for *masiro*.[13] The right to possession, however, continued for the Chagga to rest on virtually the same grounds as before. *Title* to land could not be sold, but *possession* could be transferred, and cash paid to the seller was legitimate.[14] In effect, land rights continued to be bought and sold, but they were differently labeled in the new orthodoxy. The customary land tribunals were established to implement the new policy. On Kilimanjaro all jurisdiction over land cases was interpreted as having been removed from the primary courts of Tanzania, and given to the customary land tribunals, the Kamati ya Usuluhishi wa Ardhi.[15] For Kilimanjaro the tribunal periodically sits in Moshi and has been there at least since 1971.

The land tribunals are less informal than the arbitration tribunals. They have five members, one of whom must be a lawyer. The TANU and the minister for Land and Settlement in Dar es Salaam appoint the lay members. Any appeals from the land tribunal go directly to the ministry without passing through any other courts, though the courts are sometimes asked to enforce the judgments of the land tribunals (James 1973:189). The lay members of the court are paid per diem, but the court has a considerable staff (about 10) on a regular salaried basis. Case records of some testimony and of judgments are kept, typed, and mimeographed. This investment shows the seriousness with which the government takes an interest in the allocation of land rights. However, despite the procedural modernity and the commitment to socialist ideals the existence of the land tribunal has not substantially altered the basis of land tenure for most persons on Kilimanjaro or the the nature of land disputes.[16]

Family law and land law are surely the two domains of civil law most important to rural people. As has been described, since independence both have been the subject of special legislation which either wholly or partly removes them from the jurisdiction of the normal court system. The purpose seems to be to channel disputes in these domains into avenues under closer control by the party. All proceedings arising under the Marriage Act had to be initiated in the arbitration tribunals run by laymen chosen by the local party branch. Appeals in these cases could be made to the primary courts, but, according to the supervisory magistrate in Moshi in 1973, appeals from the primary court could only be made directly to the high court. In practice, the arbitration tribunals addressed most family matters that came before them with a good deal of autonomy. As for the land tribunals, in the 1970s on Kilimanjaro, their existence was considered to have totally removed jurisdiction over land matters from the primary courts. Appeals from the land tribunal went to the Ministry of Land and Urban Development in Dar es Salaam. Such appeals did not go through the court system. These two procedural transformations diminishing the role of the courts – the one having to do with family law, the other with land law – show the strong political significance attributed to the official system of dispute settlement.

The intention of the government to deal with village land matters through administrative rather than judicial channels is implied in a 1983 pamphlet on agricultural policy which directs the Ministry of Land and Urban Development to work out new land tenure systems, to "streamline the procedures and systems of allocating land," and to develop a Register of Agricultural Land Occupancy (Ministry of Agriculture, *The Agricultural Policy of Tanzania* [Dar es Salaam: Government Printer, 31 March 1983]). The plan is for the government to allocate land to villages on the basis of 999-year leases. The villages are then to sublease their land to village members on a 33-to-99-year basis "while respecting as far as possible . . . traditional land practices and beliefs" (10). On Kilimanjaro, persons who now hold land will continue to do so, one would guess, but the legal theory underpinning their continuing possession will have changed once again! (How the fact of geographically scattered landholdings can be handled is not clear. The mental models that policy planners have of villages are interesting intellectual artifacts in themselves.) Lands leased and subleased under the new policy will not be freely bought and sold but must be returned to the village for compensation and reallocation if the user or his heir wishes to leave the village. Two transformative implications of this projected program are now apparent: that in the future the government may tax land in the form of land rent, and that villages will control the transfer of possession of land to anyone who is not the previous holder's heir under "customary law." The plan alludes to a right to appeal decisions made with regard to the taking of land, but whether this right will involve the creation of yet another set of new tribunals is not clear. How this complex plan can possibly be implemented remains to be seen. The internal politics of the *mitaa* will only be intensified by the plan to give villages power over land allocation. Power blocs organized on a lineage-neighborhood basis will intersect with power blocs organized around the common and competing interest of the salaried class.

What is clear from the recent postindependence history of the judicial system is that the role of the primary courts has already been substantially changed by the creation of new tribunals, even as the role of their predecessor courts had changed in an earlier period. In contrast to the time when most of the cases the primary courts heard were civil cases, they now give at least half of their time and sometimes more to criminal trials. Case records from this level of local courts on Kilimanjaro reflect some of the formal shifts from the 1920s on. But of much broader import, the cases also reflect details of a changing way of life outside of the courts, and some of its ongoing "customary" continuities.

7

The case reports

THE CASE REPORTS FROM THE CHIEF'S COURTS AND THEIR SUCCESSORS, THE LOCAL COURTS AND THE PRIMARY COURTS

An inspection of case reports from the courts of the rural areas from the mid-1920s to the 1970s reveals significant changes in the incidence of certain types of cases. As one might expect, the subject matter of litigation reflects the gradually increasing commitment to a cash economy. Also, over time, the tribunal becomes less and less of a "customary" law court as it develops as a criminal court and a court that spends much of its civil case time on transactions arising from the cash sector.

But much more important to a theoretical understanding of the place of the court in the structure of the society is the extent to which throughout their history the local rural courts have been essentially limited to litigation between individuals, wrongs done to individuals, and the misbehavior of individuals. Organizations other than government (or occasionally a mission) appear neither as plaintiffs nor as defendants. One can only infer that lineages had no standing in court from the beginning. There are no cases brought by or against lineages. Until independence any cases involving non-Africans could not have come up in these courts, so that such organizations as the missions would not have appeared in them as such, though sometimes, as will be shown in one land case, their African lay preachers appeared on their behalf. Disputes between chiefdoms also were handled either administratively or in higher courts, as were contentions regarding the cooperative. The overwhelming body of cases in the local courts specifically concern individuals. The *individualization and decontextualizing of disputes* which this record represents is a central social fact characterizing those courts to which the population of Kilimanjaro had already access. Yet the social reality which they lived, and still do, is one in which certain collectivities, particularly kin-based and neighborhood-based aggregates, were major factors in their lives. Localized lineages never appear in

168

court as such (though their case hearings, decisions, and allocations of property are often alluded to in court), and in some respects this fact has probably contributed toward giving them considerable autonomy over their own affairs. Lineage decisions are only indirectly "reviewed" by any court.

The conception of law that the individualization and decontextualization of dispute involves is in keeping with nineteenth-century European ideas of legal evolution as moving from kin group–based to individual-based systems of rights and duties. Treating an African system of "customary" law as composed essentially of tortlike and debtlike definitions of wrongs to individuals excludes any notion of "constitutional" law other than that concerned with the powers of office. Such a conception of an African system concerns itself only minimally with the question of collective *constitutive units* existing within the society at levels lower than the chiefship. It pays no attention to indigenous ways of generating organizations nor has it any great interest in the way such groups manage their affairs. A reading of the provincial commissioner's reports shows that the overall intention of the colonial administration locally was clearly to remodel and replace earlier structures by concentrating on developing new definitions of office and native government and new organizations such as the cooperative. Missions, too, were part of the new collective scenery. Below the officially recognized offices and organizations the administration perceived only a great sea of individuals, who, to be sure, had their clans and their extended families and their folk ways, but these clans and families were not to be given serious official attention. This disregard was partly because indigenous society was incompletely understood. But this attitude must also have had its roots in nineteenth-century evolutionary ideas about what would be durable and what would fall away, what should be encouraged and what abolished or ignored. The individualization of dispute in the local courts fits well with such assumptions, as well as with the idea of restricting chiefly powers to petty matters, which was certainly an objective of the various limitations of the jurisdiction of the Native Authorities.

What the colonial courts did, in effect, was separate out the question of particular episodes and particular "customary rules" from the local collective social context in which dispute situations were usually embedded. Thus on Kilimanjaro court records, old and new, which involve disputes between persons who are closely associated in long-term relationships, either through kinship or neighborhood or other connection only reveal a small part of the story of any controversy because the official case is separated out of the longer flow of events and the larger set of relationships of which it is a part. In many case records it is impossible even to discern the relationship of the parties, let alone what they are really "doing" in court.

The lineage chronicle which constitutes Part III of this book demonstrates by implication the limited scope of official records in revealing an ongoing context of decades of competition and controversy.

The "customary" disputes brought to the chief's court (and successor courts) in this century were probably decided in precolonial times at home, that is, in the social fields in which they arose. Many are still decided there, but the availability of externally constituted hearing agencies has changed the options. The chief's court in its colonial form (let alone the successor courts) was not a traditional Chagga institution (see Moore 1970). Many subtle changes must have occurred as a result of its existence. For example, one cannot but wonder how the use of the Swahili language might have affected local categories of wrongdoing and obligation. Did any Islamic law concepts penetrate with Swahili perhaps through Swahili-speaking colonial officials who had served on the coast? In recent decades the court clerks who translate factual descriptions of grievances into conventional legal categories have profoundly affected local ideas about the acceptable words that make wrongs actionable.

The colonial (and postcolonial) courts made their contribution toward eroding indigenous institutional structures while giving them explicit recognition in "applying customary law." The decontextualization of dispute and the individualization of dispute were combined processes operating in the courts that altered what they were ostensibly continuing. When "customary law" is treated as a set of mandatory substantive rules enforced by a court rather than as a set of guideline norms used by a primary group to manage the affairs of its members a major reinterpretation is involved. The whole basis on which such groups made discretionary exceptions and modifications is lost in the "translation" from primary group to court, to say nothing of the difference between fact-finding and fact-knowing as the basis of discussion and decision. In the indigenous system the rules had been embedded in a set of procedures administered by a particular category of persons in given relationships. In the courts, new procedures and persons took over. The construction of that durable product, the case record, must be seen in the light of these implicit but unacknowledged changes. The very fact that a written document became part of the process had effects on what had previously been a system of oral law (Goody 1977).

The case reports from the chief's courts of the early British colonial period, their successors, the local courts, and from their present incarnation, the primary courts, reflect these and other changes that were taking place in rural life from the mid-1920s on.[1] Parties appeared (and still appear) in these courts without counsel, pleading their own cases, and the whole performance is very much a local matter. Today as before the parties usually come from the same ex-chiefdom, often from the same *mtaa.* All records are in Swahili. The jurisdiction of the courts includes minor criminal offenses and civil cases involving small amounts of property. Few rural dwellers have more property than can be at issue. Individual plots of land were within the court's scope until 1971, when the land arbitration tribunals took over.

In the first decade of the British colonial period the case reports were kept in large ledgers, each called the Kitabu cha Shauri for the particular chiefdom. Later they were written on separate sheets of paper, pinned together, then sometimes placed in folders. When the chiefs presided, the reports were written by the court clerk. Now each magistrate himself writes virtually all the record of the cases he hears. In the earliest of the records, those from the 1920s, occasional notes from the district officer can be found in the margins suggesting more orderly record keeping, or noting that a particular decision was fair, or improper, and the like. After a few years, such notations cease to be made. It may well be that after the volume of litigation in the chief's courts increased and passed the 1,000 mark for the Kilimanjaro District (around 1930) no one actually read the handwritten records unless a case was appealed or a complaint was made. That certainly was the situation between 1968 and 1979. Some of the case reports are quite jumbled. "So and so stated" and "so and so said," but the relationship of the parties or of the statement to the case is often not specified and must be inferred from clues in the text. Doing so is often possible with some effort. Other case reports are absolutely clear. Some are too brief to be useful for study as case records consisting of a sentence or two, "Complainant claimed Shs/50. Respondent admitted the claim. Respondent to pay Shs/50." Some cases are missing. Some are many pages long.

In short, the records are of uneven quality, but as a whole constitute a body of material useful for analysis if the questions one asks are not the sort that a Western lawyer would ask of an appellate opinion. The case reports occasionally, but not frequently, mention a legal rule, and when they do it is usually to invoke the customs of the Chagga. The reasons why the court holder decided the case as he did are sometimes given, sometimes not. In recent decades some version of "the plaintiff has failed to prove his case" or "there is not sufficient evidence" often does by way of explanation.

Since the early 1970s criminal case records have become more professional, the relevant section under the criminal code is cited for each case, and formally speaking the records are "correct." Yet it is seldom possible to tell from the record what the case was really about. An assault case will dwell at length on the fact of the assault, witnesses of it are questioned (did you see a knife in his hand? did you see him throw the rock?) but rarely is anything said about *why* the defendant assaulted the complaining witness or what the background of their relationship might have been. The more recent the records, the less they say about such underlying matters. The "correctness" is mechanical. The records in the case reports of criminal matters come to be more and more formulaic and alike, whereas the records in many civil cases are more revealing. Since the written records present *plausible* versions of disputes they are interesting as such, but they cannot be taken literally as necessarily reflecting events. In Part III of this book a "behind the scenes" account of a series of disputes shows the importance of the gap between what happens outside the courts and what goes on inside them. Put in place by the state, the courts serve not only the purposes of the government but the purposes of its users and its personnel. The record is a composite byproduct which both conceals and reveals. The case reports of the courts do not ordinarily refer to precedent, or to other cases decided in higher courts. Indeed on one occasion, in 1968, the local court simply ignored a previous appellate decision with regard to the very case before it (Marangu 1968, #85, that oversight emerged in a subsequent appeal).

For most of the period from the mid-1920s to the 1970s the court holders were chiefs or other laymen untrained in law applying "customary law" as they saw fit. Sometimes their acts directly served the political interests of the chiefs and their coteries. Their auxiliary role was to enforce colonial ordinances as directed by the administrative authorities. The level of professionalism gradually changed after independence. In 1968–69 the best-trained of the magistrates had had a three-month course at the administrative school at Mzumbe and many had no training at all. Ten years later the situation was different. The training period became obligatory and longer, and there was some effort to professionalize the primary court level of the judiciary. But the magistrates are not lawyers, nor do lawyers appear before them.

Throughout the 1926–79 period the presence of "elders" or "assessors" at the hearing is always noted in addition to that of the court holder. The practice of having such persons involved in the hearing process continues today. Colonial and postcolonial administrations seem to have always felt the presence of elders sufficient to inhibit the arbitrariness or corruption of the court holder, whatever the relative status of assessors and court holders outside the court. In colonial times the chief or his deputy (who sometimes sat in his place) had much more power than the elders, and these days the assessors are far less well educated and locally prominent than the magistrates. Yet these relations of asymmetrical power did not, and do not seem to disturb the authorities in their belief that the assessors are bound to keep the court impartial and harmonious with local conceptions of justice. In the early days the assessors' opinions are not noted.

Today they must be, and the magistrate, if he differs with them in his decision, must indicate his reasons in writing.

Given the nature of the records, their volume, their state of uneven accessibility during the period of fieldwork, and present purposes, the body of material analyzed involved some selection and some accident. The choices reflected two considerations: the desirability of collecting some materials at roughly ten-year intervals so that changes over time could be studied, and the usefulness of having records from several ex-chiefdoms to discover if there was any substantial difference between localities. Court records from five of the fifteen ex-chiefdoms on the mountain were examined. Summaries and some copies of 2,000 cases from these courts were made and records from other types of tribunals were consulted.[2] Condensed versions of some of these are presented. Most of those chosen have been selected because they shed light on typical and ordinary rural situations. In addition court hearings were attended in five primary courts on the mountain and one in the town of Moshi.

For the present project, in order to develop some simple numerical information, as well as to examine content, data from the total available case record for particular years in certain primary courts were collected (see Table 7). These give an indication of changes in the *stated subject matter* of all disputes, and the proportion of various types of litigation over time. The classifications of subject matter in the tables that follow are my own. Tables 8, 9, 10, 11, and 12 indicate the general trends that are reflected in the case incidence. Frequently the *stated subject matter* is merely the label given an episode in an ongoing series of altercations about other matters. The analysis of case records is thus one in which the "real situation" is reclassified twice, once in the language of the case as written up in the record, and then in the analysis itself. Four things emerge: the relatively small (and in general decreasing) proportion of disputes that concern livestock transactions, the larger and for a while growing proportion of land cases peaking in the 1950s, the general increase after the 1920s of disputes relating to modern cash transactions (including loans and goods and services), and the continuing but uneven incidence of family altercations related to marriage, inheritance, and the like. Since criminal cases were separately filed after 1953 (in some places a few years earlier), and it is important to be aware of their growing significance. Criminal cases were a small proportion of the total cases heard in the late 1920s. The proportion grows over the years. The primary courts have now come to devote at least half and in many courts more than half of their time to criminal matters. No detail is provided here on the criminal case records since with a few exceptions the record-

Table 7. Civil case records inspected

Ex-chiefdom

Kilema

Year	1936	1937	1947	1967
No. cases	114	78	147	88

Mwika

Year	1927–31	1957	1967	1972
No. cases	142	63	95	124

Marangu

Year	1958	1968	1974	1979
No. cases	75	109	40	49

Keni-Mriti-Mengwe

Year	1947	1957	1967
No. cases	180	77	123

Mamba

Year	1930	1933	1940	1951	1963	1972
No. cases	33	78	65	44	179	91

Note: Until the 1950s the case records were in the *Kitabu cha Shauri* in which civil and criminal cases were lumped together. After 1953 the use of the *kitabu* was discontinued (Judicial Circular no. 5 dated 2 April 1953 from district commissioner's office). Thereafter civil and criminal matters were kept in separate files. Thus the figures above before 1953 include both civil and criminal matters; after 1953 the figures reflect only civil cases. Some of the files were complete. Some were not.

Once largely civil courts, the local courts have recently come to be agencies that handle large numbers of criminal cases, often more than the number of civil cases heard. Here are some sample figures.

Criminal cases	Year	Number	Criminal cases	Year	Number	Criminal cases	Year	Number
Kilema	1966	216	Marangu	1968	107	Mwika	1969	332
	1967	182		1972	147		1970	185
	1968	226	Mamba	1968	94		1971	175
	1969	218		1969	87		1972	177
	1970	132		1970	88			
	1971	129		1971	124			
				1972	116			

Table 8. *Mwika court records*

	1930	%[a]	1957	%	1967	%	1972	%
Customary law cases								
1. Transactions in cows and goats	6	23	7	11	5	5	8	6
2. Bridewealth and other family matters (excepting land)	12	46	11	17	18	18.9	29	23
3. Land-related disputes	4	15	14	22	24	25	no jurisdiction	
Noncustomary cases								
4. Loans of cash and other cash matters			16	25	19	20	20	16
5. Transactions for goods and services			8	12.6	17	17.8	45	36
6. Administrative offenses[b]	2	7.6			1	1	6	4.8
Miscellaneous	2	7.6	7	11	11	11.5	16	12.9
Crimes	1							
Total	27		63		95		124	

[a]Since crimes were counted separately from 1953 on, percentages for 1930 were calculated without counting crime. Crime cases appear in a separate file from the 1950s on.
[b]Examples of administrative offenses are failure to pay tax, failure to terrace land, cultivating where prohibited, and failure to pay school fees.

ing methods reveal a minimal amount about the persons involved or their behavior, and by law there are no customary crimes, only statutory ones. In criminal cases, thefts and assaults have dominated the docket for many years, and malicious damage to property, creation of disturbances, brewing without a license, and threats and insults appear occasionally.

The insertion of the ten-house cell leaders into the structure of dispute hearers in the mid-1960s and of the party courts of arbitration in every ward in 1971 probably has diverted some civil cases from the primary courts that might otherwise have reached them. The exclusive jurisdiction of the land court has also taken away a substantial number of cases. The transformation of function of the primary courts in the direction of criminal case work is clear, as is the intention to generate specialized courts for the most policy salient types of civil cases, and to use laymen's courts whenever possible for the remainder. But the recent redesigning of the formal system has not to date altered the kinds of disputes that arise in the countryside, merely the mode of labeling and processing them.

Table 9. *Kilema court records*

	1936	%[a]	1947	%[a]	1967	%
Customary law cases						
Transactions in cows and goats	5	6	5	4.7	2	2
Bridewealth and other family matters (excepting land)	13	15.6	17	16	7	7.9
Land-related disputes	7	8.4	29	27.3	13	14.7
Noncustomary cases						
Loans of cash and other cash matters	13	15.6	17	16	10	11
Transactions for goods and services	12	14.4	12	11.3	13	14.7
Administrative offenses[b]	27	32.5	24	22.6	35	39.77
Miscellaneous	6	7.2	2	1.8	8	9
Crimes	31		41	38.6	separately filed	
Total	114		147		88	

[a]Since crimes were counted separately from 1953, percentages for 1936 and 1947 are calculated without counting crimes, i.e. for 1936 on the basis of a total of 83 cases and for 1947 on the basis of 106 cases.
[b]Examples of administrative offenses are failure to pay tax, failure to terrace land, cultivating where prohibited, and failure to pay school fees.

Summaries of selected case reports follow below. As will be evident from the logic of my organization of the material, I have been particularly interested in issues of power, economic change, and the perpetuation and invention of "customary law" as seen in local court cases.

PROFITS, POWER, AND ENFORCEMENT IN THE BRITISH COLONIAL PERIOD

The use of hearings by the chiefs and their *wachili* to enhance their powers and enrich themselves was still evident in cases in the late 1920s. The taking of livestock as fees for hearing cases seems to have persisted much later in some areas than one might have imagined from the official changes in the formal system. Chiefs also had rights to a share of any found animals. Although chiefs were put on salaries in 1926, for some time thereafter they still found ways to collect beasts, and *wachili* also expected "fees." The chiefs, being native authorities, had official courts, the *wachili* unofficial ones. Chiefs also tried to do away with self-help in cattle cases to force people into their courts, and to require an appeal to

Table 10. *Keni-Mriti-Mengwe court records*

	1947	%ᵃ	1957	%	1967	%
Customary law cases						
Transactions in cows and goats	25	19	12	15	15	12
Bridewealth and other family matters (excepting land)	35	27	6	8	25	20
Land-related disputes	30	23	22	28	21	17
Noncustomary cases						
Loans of cash and other cash matters	4	3	5	6	17	14
Transactions for goods and services	9	7	27	35	35	28
Administrative offenses	19	14				
Miscellaneous	7	5	5	6	10	8
Crimes	25		filed separately			
Total	154		77		123	

ᵃSince crimes are counted separately from 1953, percentages are calculated without crime for 1947.
ᵇExamples of administrative offenses are failure to pay tax, failure to terrace land, cultivating where prohibited, and failure to pay school fees.
ᶜActual numbers noted in *Kitabu cha Shauri* for 1947 are from 8 to 180, i.e., 173 cases. My notes are only adequate to classify 154, because some were dismissed, records were incomplete, parties did not appear, a blank appeared after number, and so on.

their powers. By the mid-1930s when the economic focus had shifted from cattle to land the chiefs and the *wachili* then interposed themselves into all land transfers. They kept as much control over land allocation as they could up to the eve of independence.

A striking practice of the late 1920s reflects an extension of some precolonial modes of enforcement. The chiefs treated it as a matter of course that arrangements could be made so that those who obeyed authoritative orders had the right to punish those who did not by collecting fines from them to their own profit. Incentives both for conformity and for enforcement were built into this process. The procedure may once have been connected with the age-set system, since corvée labor was performed by age-set, and delinquency punished by members of the age-set. (Since independence TANU Youth League members have revived some of these practices.) The courts were also used to penalize disobedience of administrative authority as early as the 1927–30 period. In some matters, such as the requirement that married persons obtain marriage certificates, enforcement sometimes touched on the interests of the missions.

Table 11. *Mamba court records*

	1930	%[a]	1940	%[a]	1951	%	1963	%	1972	%
Customary law cases										
Transactions in cows and goats	4	12	6	9	3	6.8	6	3	6	6.5
Bridewealth and other family matters (excepting land)	17	51.5	21	32	22	50	15	8	5	5.4
Land related disputes	5	15	5	7.6	7	15.9	6	3	2	2
Noncustomary cases										
Loans of cash and other cash matters	2	6	10	15	4	9	33	18	22	24
Transactions for goods and services	2	6	9	13.8	7	15.9	26	14.5	35	38
Administrative offenses[b]							19	10.6		
Miscellaneous	2	6	4	6	1	2	74[c]	41	21	23
Crimes	1	3	10	15			filed separately			
Total	33		65		44		179		91	

[a]Since crimes are counted separately from 1953, percentages for 1930 are 1940 and calculated without crime.
[b]Examples are failure to pay tax, failure to terrace land, cultivating where prohibited, and failure to pay school fees.
[c]These cases are largely reported as follows: Plaintiff claims 3 shillings. Defendant admits the claim. Plaintiff wins. Most probably are loans, or fall into the goods and services category.

Table 12. *Marangu court cases*

	1958	%	1968	%	1974	%	1979	%
"Customary law" cases								
Transactions in cows and goats	7	11	1	1	2	5	2	2
Bridewealth and other family matters (excepting land)	10	16	20	20.8	14	35	18	36
Land-related disputes	4	6.5	10	10			3	6
Washing of the name								
Noncustomary cases								
Loans of cash and other cash matters	9	14.7	9	9	2	5	2	2
Transactions for goods and services	9	14.7	21	21.8	10	25	15	30.6
Administrative offenses	2	3	25	26				
Miscellaneous	20	32.7	10	10	12	30	9	18
Crimes	filed separately							
Total	61		96		40		49	

Note: Numbers analyzed differ from totals in Table I because some case records are too brief for classification, or cases initiated were subsequently dropped, and the like.

[a]Examples of administrative offenses are failure to pay tax, failure to terrace land, cultivating where prohibited, and failure to pay school fees.

By 1979 there were many cases (12) classified as inheritance cases, a category that was seldom used in earlier times. Classifying them under a category that was within the jurisdiction of the primary courts was probably a way of taking up certain land cases. At that time land cases had to go to the land courts, and the primary courts had no jurisdiction.

Livestock and officials: fees, finders, and self-help

A chief's right to a share of a finder's luck when the find was a cow

Mwika, Case 2, 1930, contained in ledger marked Kitabu cha shauri, Mwika 1927 In Mwika, some years before 1930, a man found a lost cow grazing in his *shamba* and gave it to a friend to keep for him. The friend did not return it and said it had died. The original finder of the cow took him to court which told the defendant to pay three beasts to the plaintiff (because in the time that had elapsed the cow would have had two calves). The defendant offered one cow to the plaintiff which the plaintiff refused. The plaintiff returned to court in 1930 saying he was owed a total of four beasts because of the further elapse of time. The chief said that anyone who found a lost animal had to share his find with the chief. He ordered the defendant to pay a total of three beasts to the plaintiff, leaving the defendant with the original one which had not in fact died. The defendant had to pay the court fee of seven shillings, fifty cents. Which of them had to share with the chief is not clear from the text, but the chief several times emphasized his right to a share of a found animal, and one infers that it was the defendant who had to pay. (Chief Solomoni gave the judgment himself, and seven elders were present.)

Mchili's right to a goat of gratitude for a case heard

Mwika, Case 53, 1928 A man sued his *mchili* in the chief's court alleging that he had given the *mchili* a goat as a gift to the chief, but the *mchili* had slaughtered and eaten it. The chief said the plaintiff lost because in fact the goat was not a gift to the chief but a gift of gratitude to the *mchili* for hearing the plaintiff's case against a thief. The plaintiff lost his one-shilling fee. (Chief Solomoni gave the decision, and four *wachili* and three elders were present.)

Mangi receives a goat each from plaintiff and defendant to hear a case, the winner to have his goat restored to him.

Mwika Case 9, 1931 In the time of Mangi Mchili (Mchili was the name of the son of Lengaki Mariki, mangi of Msae; the son inherited the *mangi*-ate briefly from his father just before Msae was incorporated into Mwika in the 1920s) plaintiff and defendant each had brought a goat to Mangi Mchili to hear their case about a cow. The person who won the case was to get his goat back. The defendant lost the case and was ordered to pay the plaintiff a goat, which he never paid, hence the 1931 case. Mangi Solomoni ordered him to pay the goat he owed. (The mangi and six elders were present.)

Chief keeps a cow as a court fee

Mwika Case 24, 1931 A lawsuit in 1927 between two brothers had involved the seizure of eight cows. One brother, the then plaintiff, was awarded six. The seventh was kept as a court fee. The eighth was given to the *mchili* to be returned to the defendant. The *mchili* did not deliver the cow, hence the 1931 suit in which the original defendant's son was plaintiff. The *mchili* was ordered to pay one cow. (Chief Solomoni gave the decision. Six elders were present.)

Self-help: seizure of cows penalized, fined.

Mwika, Case 15, 1929 A man to whom bridewealth was owed appropriated a cow from his debtor. He was ordered to return the cow and fined twenty shillings for taking the cow without the chief's permission.

Mwika, Case 6, 1930 The chief said that if a person has been ordered by the court to pay compensation, he has a period of grace in which to do so. The creditor has no right to seize the property (even if the debtor dies). He must come to the chief's court and cannot use self-help. Creditor is fined twenty shillings, ordered to return the appropriated cow, and directed to bring his case to court if he had a grievance.

The original transaction had occurred several years earlier. The creditor had loaned the debtor a cow. The debtor having no beast with which to repay had given his daughter to the creditor. When she grew older she ran away and returned to her father, thus reestablishing the debt. Enough time had passed for the creditor to claim a cow *and* two calves, which the court awarded him in 1929. Two were to be paid immediately, the third later on. The debtor died before the third beast was repaid. The creditor had then appropriated the cow from the debtor's son.

The enforcement of authoritative orders by giving those who obey profit from punishing those who disobey

A chief's son loses two teeth while trying to confiscate property as a fine

Mwika, Case 12, 1929 In his judgment, the chief said, it was a general custom that an old widow needing assistance (presumably labor) could ask a local teacher for help. The teacher, in turn, would mobilize the pupils under his tutelage to do the work. To insure obedience to the teacher's orders, the teacher could send the pupils who had obeyed to the houses of those who had not turned up for the assigned work to confiscate property (a chicken, a bush knife) as a fine. In the course of such a punitive expedition the children were beaten by the parents of one of the delinquent boys. Among them was the chief's son who lost two teeth in the melee. This case was brought by the chief's son against the man who had broken his teeth. He said it was an accident. He was ordered by the court to pay two cows, and to pay twenty shillings for each tooth. (Chief Solomoni and six elders were present.)

Chief's order on enforcing corvée labor

Mwika "Baraza" in 19– – In a large public meeting between chief and citizenry, among many other matters, the chief ordered all males to go to

Himo and dig the Himo irrigation channel. He went on to say that, if a person failed to go, his goat would be taken, slaughtered, and eaten by those who had done the work. If he had no goats, he would get fifteen strokes in public. (This record was inserted in the 1927 Kitabu cha Shauri, Mwika, after Case 8 in 1930.)

Enforcers are rewarded with a goat

Mwika, Case 8, 1929 A girl slept with a young man and stayed in his house for two days, although she was betrothed to another. She then left. Later she found that she was pregnant, and returned to her lover to give birth to the child. The seducer was ordered to pay a cow and a goat to the father of the girl. He promised to pay but did not. Later he declared that he would not pay. The chief and his elders were angry and ordered two "local policemen" (i.e., two local men) to go to the young man's house and confiscate a cow and a goat for the girl's father. They also took one other goat as a punishment because the young man had refused to obey the court's order. That goat was given to the two "local policemen."

The interest of the chiefs and *wachili* in transfers of land

The chief or the mchili *had to be informed of all land transfers. "Secret" transfers were invalid.*

Kilema, Case 117, 1936 The complainant alleged that he had bought a piece of land for a cow from one Ndetenga. Originally Ndetenga had received the land from Chief Kiritta. At the time of the suit Ndetenga was dead and the *mchili* of the area in which the land was located considered the land to belong to Ndetenga's son. The complainant sued the *mchili* to get back what he claimed was his land. The court held that he had no right to the land because he had not informed the chief or the *mchili* of his land transaction with Ndetenga. The chief or *mchili* had to be informed about any transfer of land in order for such transfer to be valid.

Kilema, Case 143, 1936 The complainant alleged he had loaned land to the defendant who now claimed it back. The defendant said the land was uncultivated public land which he developed. The court held that the land belonged to complainant. Had it been public land, the *mangi* would have provided a witness to the allocation.

Customary payment to mchili *and* mangi *for 1944 allocation of piece of land*

Keni Mriti Mengwe, Case 128, Primary Court, 1967 This case was a dispute over a published will (in a local paper called *Kusare*) regarding the ownership of a piece of land allegedly allocated in 1944. The custom of paying the *mchili* and the *mangi upata*, a gift of thanks, when land was allocated was alluded to by all witnesses in the case. Allusions were made to the gift of *pombe* (beer) (for the witnesses, the *mchili*, and the *mangi*), the gift of a goat (for the *mchili*), and the gift of cash (20 shillings supposedly given to the *mchili* for the *mangi*). Which witness was truthful was irrelevant. But what was significant was that a major part of the evidence of official allocation was the recollection of witnesses of the occasions when the *pombe* was given and consumed by the witnesses. No one denied that such gifts were customary. At issue in the case was which party acquired the right to the land by these means, the gift-giving being an official marker.

Pombe *of* mchili *still being paid, allocation of 1961*

KMM, Case 87, 1967, alluding to land allocated in 1961 To the same effect, that is, that it is Chagga customary law to brew *pombe* for the *mchili* when land is allocated.

Fines for failing to obey the authority of the chiefs and *wachili*

Mwika, Case 56, 1928 A citizen refused to carry a government letter to next village as ordered by *mchili*. Judgment: Chief Solomoni said it was the custom that, when a *mchili* receives a government communication from another *mchili* to be sent on to the next village, he can order any citizen to carry it there. The defendant was fined four shillings. (Present were Chief Solomoni II, three *wachili,* and four *wazee.*)

Mchili *may order citizens to work on public roads*

Mwika, Case 44, 1928 Mchili ordered two defendants to cut trees in an area where a new road was to pass. They refused and came to blows with the *mchili* and broke his horn. (The corvée horn, emblem of office with which the *mchili* called people up for labor was still in use in 1968–69.) Defendants were fined two shillings fifty cents each and five shillings in addition for broken horn. (Present were Chief Solomoni, three *wachili,* and three *wazee.*)

Mwika, Cases 62–81 and 84, 1928 Plaintiffs were two *wachili*. Defendants were men who did not obey orders to cut down trees to clear roads as part of their corvée labor obligation. When they did not do the work, goats were confiscated from their homesteads. The court ordered each defendant to pay a fine of eight shillings and ordered the goats returned.

Mwika, Case 22, 1929 The plaintiff was a man who was ill and did not turn up for communal work. Goats were confiscated from his house and eaten. The case was heard by *wazee*. They told the *mchili* to return two goats. He did not. Plaintiff then seized three goats from *mchili*'s homestead. Plaintiff was told to return those three. *Mchili* was ordered to pay two that were owed.

Irrigation channels could not be cut across road without chief's permission

Mwika, Case 30, 1927 The defendant was fined six shillings for digging furrow across road without chief's permission.

Cultivation near stream used for drinking water prohibited

Mwika, Case 30, 1929 Eleven defendants cultivated near a stream used for drinking water contrary to government orders. Each was fined six shillings and ordered to abandon the plots. The case was heard in November. Defendants were allowed to postpone payment until January because of time of crops. The acting district officer (ADO) commented that punishment was very fair.

Fine for insulting the court

Mwika, Case 8, 1931 The defendant was fined ten shillings for saying all people in the court were "dead people," that is, using abusive language.

Fine for buying meat during hoof and mouth epidemic

Mwika, Case 22, 1930 Defendants were seven women who bought meat from a Masai when government prohibited such purchases because of hoof and mouth disease. They were fined ten shillings each.

The interests of the missions

Marriage certificates required

Mwika, Cases 22, 24, 31, 32, 34, 37, 38, 39; 1927 Defendants were fined two shillings each because they did not register when they married and did not pay one shilling to obtain a certificate.

Kilema, Case 60, 1936 The case is to same effect as the preceding cases. Woman's father was complaining witness. Man was fined for keeping a woman in his house for two years without a marriage certificate. He was fined two shillings and told he would be charged again if he did not obtain one.

Kilema, Case 4, 1937 This case is to same effect as preceding ones. Man and woman had two children, no marriage certificate. Man was fined five shillings. If he did not pay, he must go to prison for fifteen days. Wife must return to her parents until he obtains a marriage certificate.

Kilema, Case 153, 1947 The plaintiff had three children with daughter of defendant. She left him in June 1947. The court held that as they had no marriage certificate, plaintiff could not claim daughter of defendant as his wife, and she was free to marry.

Forcible intercourse as a means of marrying declared illegal

Mwika, Case 28, 1929 Christian ministers in Mwika brought complaint against young man for trying to marry a Christian girl "according to Chagga custom," that is, they asserted, by having intercourse with her by force. She escaped. He was fined twenty-five shillings.

Mwika, Case 29, 1929 The case is same as preceding one. The administrative district officer wrote that it was not proper for the church to bring such a case. It should be brought by the parents of the girl.

Church takes shamba *land to cultivate for widows and poor. Neighbors cannot use it.*

Mwika, Case 20, 1930 Christians from Msae under leadership of Manase Lauo took possession of *shamba* land left by Wamamba to cultivate it for widows and the poor. Court finds for the Christians against a neighbor who tried to encroach.[3]

The use of the courts to enforce administrative regulations

As is evident from the tables, the local courts have been used in civil litigation not only to settle disputes according to "customary law" but to deal with disputes arising from the cash sector, and also to enforce local administrative regulation. Thus the courts on Kilimanjaro penalized the failure to pay taxes, to terrace certain lands, to pay school fees, to observe price controls when these were imposed, to refrain from cultivating land on the banks of streams, to obtain a certificate of marriage, and other similar delinquencies generated by rules promulgated by the colonial administration and the Native Administration. DuBow and Abel emphasize the use of these courts as an extension of the colonial state (DuBow 1973:40–5; Abel, 1979:167–200).

To an important extent the court must also be seen as having once been an arm of personal chiefly power. From time to time the court and the law could be mobilized against a chief's subjects in discretionary ways. Suitable justifications for the record could always be produced for the district officer. Administrative violations were usually punished with fines (with imprisonment threatened if the fines were not paid). An exceptional instance of corporal punishment gives a sense of the implications of a court holder's power. In 1936 a man was sentenced to five strokes (to be administered before the district officer as was required) for failure to come to the *baraza* to pay his tax (Kilema, Case 146, 1936). One gets a glimpse of the way the chief kept his own underlings in line from a case of the same year in which the court fined a *mtaa* headman (*mchili*) five shillings for not having seized the property of a tax defaulter when ordered to do so by the *mangi* (Kilema, Case 168, 1936). In the margin of the report of this case the district officer wrote in red, "Do not enter such cases in this register. . . . This case is neither civil nor criminal."

The same year, 1936, which was in general a year of political disturbance on the mountain, a singularly political case dealt with defendants who were trying to put forward the argument that their *mtaa* (Legho) should not be in the chiefdom of Kilema, but should be under the jurisdiction of the neighboring chiefdom of Kirua Vunjo (Kilema, Case 104, 1936). For such trouble making one man was expelled from Kilema (given one month to leave permanently) and another was sentenced to be imprisoned for six months and given six strokes and was to be expelled when he emerged from prison. Attending this trial were Mangi Kiritta, five *wachili,* and nine elders. The number of persons other than the chief who were counted officially present attests its importance.

The courts were used to enforce agricultural policy, as we have already seen with respect to coffee. This was also the case with other crops. In 1947 several defendants were fined for not planting cotton in the *shambas* of the lower area for which seeds had been provided by the Native Authority (Kilema, Case 144, 1947). The orders of agricultural instructors and veterinary officers were similarly enforced through fines, with imprisonment in lieu of fines always available for the impecunious (Kilema, Cases 115, 116, 1936).

Through the 1960s the courts continued to be used to penalize the failure to pay taxes, to terrace land, to refrain from cultivating certain lands for erosion control, to pay school fees and the like. But since the 1970s, the primary courts have not normally been used for the enforcement of administrative matters, except for the regulations concerning alcohol and drugs which are enforced through the system of criminal law.

Many former rules are now in abeyance, or are honored in the breach. Many roads and irrigation channels are neglected. The party courts of arbitration are specifically prohibited from imposing fines (though they occasionally do so anyway). And the cell leaders of ten houses also lack such powers. There is much talk at local party meetings about persons who fail to appear for communal work projects, or fail to perform other civic duties. Observation and conversation confirm that morale about such matters is low and noncompliance high. Two elements in the postindependence administrative style converge in encouraging such behavior. One is the slacking off of routine enforcement, but perhaps even more important is the absence of conventional rewards. A simple example is the fact that, in the days of the chiefs, work parties ended in beer parties, the drink being provided by the chief or his district heads. Today, in the private sector, when groups of men help one of their number to harvest his *shamba* or do other work, they are invariably given a beer party by the man they helped. But today the agents of the party or the government do not provide beer for public works workers. Such would be out of keeping with the austere philosophy of volunteerism for the sake of ideology that is the current official rationale for community efforts.

A less visible set of rewards available in pre-independence times was the administrative patronage and occasional favor that could be given at low levels of rural administration. Presumably some compliance was given as part of a diffuse system of exchange for indefinite future favors. That diffuse system still exists in some degree. But to the extent that power in the region is closely held at the higher levels of party organization, and people at lower levels have limited authority, there are fewer favors to give or to withhold. Certainly in the 1960s and 1970s low level officials were able to deliver less than in colonial times. What remains to be seen is whether the new cooperative villages will be any more successful in their trade-offs of rewards and controls than their predecessor postindependence organizations. In any case, unless there is a change of policy, the courts will not play the part of exacting administrative compliance that they did in colonial times.

Litigation involving loans and other cash transactions

The cases involving loans and cash transactions for goods and services reflect a sequence of developments in the economy. The contrast is visible if one compares the late 1920s when there was virtually no litigation of that kind with the 1960s, when, depending on the jurisdiction (and local vagaries regarding the number of administrative offenses handled by the court) such cases represented 25 to 50 percent of the civil cases heard. Within these outlines are further nuances.

In the 1940s and 1950s not only did loans often carry exorbitant interest rates, but the courts often enforced them. To this day, outside the legal system, loans continue at very high rates. On the whole, rural people regard the taking of interest as despicable, and something that certainly would not be done between kinsmen or friends. A case in 1958 mentions a rate of 15 shillings per month on a loan of 490 shillings (Marangu, Civil Case 1, 1958). One in Mwika in the same period involved a claim for 5 percent per month interest on a bag of millet worth 92 shillings transferred more than five years earlier. The court was indignant over the hundreds of shillings claimed. It allowed a 6 percent per annum rate (the KNCU rate) on the unpaid balance of the original 92 shillings and reprimanded the plaintiff for his extortionist tricks. But the same court did not balk at enforcing the terms of another loan in which the borrower received 52 shillings, agreeing to pay either 13 *bakuli* of coffee in return or 100 shillings shortly thereafter. The court held him to paying the 100 shillings (Mwika, Civil Case 67, 1957). A subsequent Mwika case involving a loan of 100 shillings also allowed 5 shillings interest per month to stand (Mwika, Civil Case 105, 1967; to the same effect Keni-Mriti-Mengwe, Civil Case 72, 1967). There is no discussion of short-term versus long-term loans, or of any rationale for the distinctions made, but it seems that where the claim was promptly brought to the court, before a large debt piled up, the court was more likely to allow a high rate. The temptation to read in such rationales comes from Western legal training, and may be quite inappropriate. The decisions in these cases may be ad hoc reactions to the total situation in each case, in which the relative respectability of the lender and the borrower and their witnesses may play a significant part.

Serious problems of evidence, and disputes over the authenticity of written receipts in loan cases have occurred. Where the lender writes the receipt and the borrower signs it (the usual arrangement), the borrower may contend that the lender has altered the receipt. So, in a case in 1967 (Mwika, Case 72), the borrower alleged that there had been a receipt for 25 shillings which the lender altered to 525 shillings. He also tried to show that the lender, who was his *mjomba* (category mother's brother) had loaned money to many other persons, thus trying to discredit him by showing him to be a moneylender. The borrower's literacy also became a question addressed by the court. The court held for the plaintiff, the lender, on the ground that the receipts were authentic. Whatever the reality of the facts in this case, the arguments show that cheating, exploitative moneylenders are local folk figures as stereotypical as defaulting feckless borrowers.

Small loans were and are sometimes secured by cattle (Kilema, Cases 5 and 11, 1967). In the first of those cases the loan was of 150 shillings, and a cow was given as security. Subsequently the cow fell ill. The lender returned the cow, but the borrower did not repay the balance at once. The successful lawsuit was to recover the unpaid debt. Other kinds of loans involve a pledge on the part of the borrower to deliver all subsequent harvests of coffee until the debt is repaid. Such arrangements are not uncommon, but they are illegal as sales of coffee are supposed to be exclusively to the cooperative. Because of their illegality they are not usually found in the court cases.

Large loans were sometimes secured by land, and in such instances the lender's intention was probably to get hold of the land, rather than to assure a return of the cash (Marangu, Civil Case 50, 1968; Mwika, Case 72, 1957; Mwika, Civil Cases 12, 44, 1967; see also Part III of this book for an instance). In the 1967 Mwika case just cited, no sooner did it become clear that the defendant, not having paid the debt, would have to hand over his *kihamba* because the court ordered him to do so than his relatives appeared and objected to the sale on the ground that the *kihamba* really belonged to someone else in the same lineage. The court found a way out by requiring the objectors to pay about half of the debt, the defendant the other half. In another Mwika case, an individual "pawned" his *kihamba,* that is, gave possession to a man who had loaned him 1,000 shillings the year before. The owner then was sued by the lender when he failed to pay on the date due (Mwika, Civil Case 96, 1967). The court extended the defendant's time for payment by one year, and ordered the plaintiff to return the *kihamba* when payment was received.

Transactions for goods and services involve either cash payment for objects and work that were once available through the precash system of exchange labor and gifts or payments for new goods and services never previously available. Goods bought, sold, repaired, and borrowed range from harvested crops, especially millet, wood for house building, cooking oil, to blankets, sewing machines, bicycles, and clothing. Most of these appear in the cases from the 1930s on. Later on watches and transistor radios also appear in the cases.

As for hired labor, in Kilema even as early as 1936 a suit arose in a case in which a man paid another to find someone to prepare stones for construction of a house (Case 71). In Mamba in 1940 there were several suits to recover damages for breach of a contract to build a house (Cases 47, 54). By 1967–68 people were being hired to cultivate *shambas*, to dig latrines, to carry loads on buses, roof houses, and clear undeveloped land of trees (Kilema, Case 40, 1967; Marangu, Case 84, 1968; Kilema, Cases 71, 78, 83, 1967). Trucks and cars are hired (Kilema, Cases 76 and 80, 1967). House building cases abound.

Loans and cash transactions involving goods and services account for about half of what has gone on on the civil law side in the primary courts for decades. "Customary law" is generally not considered pertinent. This high proportion of cash-sector cases shows that the court-using Chagga are deeply involved in the cash economy, but a more balanced picture of the many layers of rural life emerges only after these are considered in conjunction with the other third to half of the civil cases that involve kinship affairs and "customary" obligations. But it is, of course, only in knowing much about the disputes that never reach the courts, and the ambiance in which these arise, that the two sides of what happens in the courts can be fully understood.

Since "customary law" is not involved in most cash transactions, the chiefs' and magistrates' decisions over the years were founded on a layman's understanding of the general principles of loaning, buying, selling, and hiring derived from their own experience in the cash economy. They do not go in for finely honed rules. They do not usually feel obliged to indicate the steps in their reasoning. In fact, they usually do not state rules at all, but rather hand down rulings. In the cash transactions cases, the question on what principle a claim is founded is seldom raised. There is a kind of implicit assumption that people ought to be kept to their agreements, but the details are not articulated. Instead, there is much explicit concern with whether a claim has been *proved*. Much weight is given to written evidence and to the testimony of officials. For the rest, it is one witness's word against another, the word of one party against another, and their skill in embarrassing one another when they have their turns at questioning.

SUBSTANTIVE ISSUES CONNECTED WITH RESIDUAL "CUSTOMARY LAW"

Typical cases involving "customary law" questions from the 1920s to 1979 were those involving five general topics: agreements regarding livestock, litigation over land, bridewealth cases, suits involving the legal position of women and children, and cases of false accusation. The issues tend to be quite repetitive. Some illustrative cases involving these issues over a fifty-year period are summarized briefly here to show in what forms questions arose.

Livestock cases

The livestock questions primarily arose before 1930. They still occasionally come up in some jurisdictions, but contracts of agistment are now few and far between and tend not to be agreements typical of the early 1900s

(Mwika, Case 52, 1957). Noting the fading out of the livestock cases from the courts, one might be tempted to suppose that the slaughtering and feasting complex had disappeared since it is never mentioned. That is not the case for many families (as is seen in Part III; "The Modern Uses of 'Customary Law' "). Slaughtering exchanges and meat distributions are simply not matters for public lawsuits. Yet though less frequent than in earlier times strong obligations continue to be recognized in relation to them.

A cow placed in agistment in exchange for goats with an option on the part of the custodian to keep a female calf

Mwika, Case 9, 1930 The plaintiff's father (of *mtaa* Kiruweny) placed a cow with the defendant (of *mtaa* Mrimbo). The agreement, according to the plaintiff, was that the defendant would pay one goat at the time and a second one later to keep a potential calf. If the cow bore a female calf, he was to pay a *third* goat. The first two goats were paid. The cow then had a male calf, and later produced a female. The calves grew and the two men decided to slaughter the male, with a share going to the caretaker. He kept the female. Thus, reasoned the plaintiff's son, he owed one more goat. The defendant refused to pay and was brought to court.

The court ruled that the plaintiff had correctly described a customary arrangement in which a cow was placed in agistment in return for goats, that in such a case two goats were owed at once and one more if a female calf was kept by the custodian provided the meat of any male calf slaughtered was properly shared. The defendant was ordered to pay one shilling court fee and one goat to the plaintiff. (Present were Chief Solomoni and six elders.)

Mwika, Case 13, 1930 The case involved a cow that did not produce sufficient milk both for persons and for her calf. Since the custodian was entitled to milk, he had a right to extra compensation (one goat) for keeping the calf alive. In this case a second calf was born and the cow again did not have sufficient milk. The custodian returned the cow and the second calf. Because he was entitled to a share of the second male calf when it was slaughtered and did not receive a share, he had a right to appropriate a sheep he had also been given in agistment by the same agistor to compensate him for his slaughter share of the bull-calf. (Chief Solomoni and six elders were present.)

A calf lost by one of two cooperating herdsmen

Mwika, Case 10, 1930 Plaintiff and defendant (both of Kimangaro village) agreed to graze their cattle and goats together, taking turns at herding on particular days. A calf of the plaintiff disappeared when the defendant was herding, and the defendant refused to help the plaintiff search for it. It was his duty to help with the search. He was held responsible for the calf lost during his tour of duty and was ordered to pay the plaintiff a beast. (Present were Chief Solomoni and seven elders.)

A herdsman is held responsible for the beasts entrusted to him

Kilema, 108, 1967 Plaintiff employed defendant as a herdsman and gave him fifty-nine head of cattle to tend, in a *boma* on the plain. The defendant said two of the plaintiff's cows were lost. The court held that the defendant stole the two cows and ordered him to pay 400 shillings out of his salary as herdsman for the plaintiff.

Land cases

Litigation over land has varied over the years. In the beginning such cases were few, and seldom, though occasionally, did they involve disputes between kinsmen. Later they became more frequent. Kinship cases invariably are intertwined with questions of customary practice. But on Kilimanjaro land transfers have so long required local official confirmation by the *mchili* (*mtaa* head) or the *mangi* (chief) that in the British period many land cases were not purely customary matters. Yet "customary" elements were inherent in the administrative relationship itself, from the power to allocate to the gift of thanks. The giving of permission to settle in a chiefdom was an old prerogative of the chiefs and their *wachili*. Another old prerogative of the Native Authority was the right to allocate and reallocate *shamba* land in the low-lying areas, to allow for shifting cultivation, and to reassign *shamba*s that had been abandoned. These old arrangements underwent a gradual transformation as land shortage increased. "Permission to settle" had often been given to strangers in a situation of land plenty and low population. Later the chief received direct requests for *vihamba* and *shamba*s from men already living in the area whose fathers could not provide them with land when they married. In the litigation that ensued the issue often was (is) to whom the *mchili* or *mangi* originally allocated the land (Kilema, Cases 8, 62, 158, 1947). Sometimes the question was one of a valid sale, valid if the *mchili* was present or was notified (Kilema, Case 98, 1947). The *mchili* was even sometimes notified of loan agreements for the payment of *masiro* (Mwika, Case 10, 1957). In the 1957 case, evidence of the *masiro* agreement included testimony that, after the possessor's child died, he wanted to bury the body in the *kihamba* and sought the permission of the lender. Permission was given. Burial in a *kihamba* is normally a sign of ownership, thus asking permission was clear evidence that the possessor did not have full rights. The plaintiff in this case was the son of the original lender. Another piece of evidence the plaintiff put forward was that the borrower of the land had sent *pombe* to him (*kumpa pole,* to say he was sorry) when his father (the original lender) had died. The defendant readily admitted that he had sent *pombe* at that time, but said that it was not *pombe* of *masiro,* but merely because he was a neighbor and had heard of the death. The plaintiff won his case partly through the use of such evidence and partly by undermining the witnesses of his opponent by summoning various *wachili* (*mtaa* leaders) who testified against them. Some years later, after independence, the plaintiff became a *balozi* (ten-house cell leader) and continued to be involved in the micropolitics of the neighborhood. Though this cell leader won his case on the evidence of *wachili,* such testimony is not always accepted. In a case in which the defendant had used a *kihamba* for seven years, the plaintiff trotted two *wachili* into court who testified that they had allocated the land to the plaintiff, and that it was therefore his. The court said that had the story told by the plaintiff and his witnesses been true, he would have objected to the defendant's use of the land years earlier. The court accused the plaintiff of trickery and found for the defendant (Mwika, Case 60, 1957).[4]

In addition to burial of kin in the *kihamba* as evidence of ownership, the free planting of trees is also so regarded (Mwika, Cases 33, 40, 1957). Borrowers of land were often not permitted to plant (Mwika, Case 6:1930) not only because compensation would have to be paid when the land was reclaimed by the lender, but also sometimes because of fear the planting might be used to assert that the arrangement was not a loan but a full transfer.

Many lawsuits over land arose as boundary disputes (Kilema, Cases 74, 84, 104, 108, 112, 132, 185, 1947; Kilema, Cases 14, 15, 32, 52, 77, 79, 1967). Since the cost of suing was (and is) proportionate to the value of the claim, it was far cheaper to sue over boundary matters than to sue for a *kihamba.* In one case the court stated that a path is never used by itself as a boundary marker by the Wachagga, that they all plant boundary plants, usually *masale* (dracaena) (Mwika, Case 2, 1957). Such boundary cases often necessarily involve a determination of land rights. Some boundary cases are just what they seem, disputes over tampering with markers and the like, but some conceal larger issues.

Inheritance sometimes gives rise to dispute. Overreaching guardians, competing half-brothers or brothers are found in the cases arguing their better rights (Kilema, Cases 103, 107, 157; 1947). But decisions in such cases do not usually rest directly on customary rules, but on testimony about allocations, and about who used the land over the years. There is sufficient variation in the family constellations (which kinsman dies without sons, who has sons with an inherited widow, what are the accidents of birth order and death order) to leave a great deal to the discretion of lineage elders when they decide who is to receive what at the *matanga*. A good deal also depends on the discretion of guardians in dealing with wards' property. *Vihamba* are sometimes swapped, often subdivided. Normally the courts are quite reluctant to reallocate inheritances of property, guardianships of widows, and allocations of bridewealth if the decisions of the lineage or of testators are clear (Mwika, Case 64, 1957). Such matters are the affair of kinsmen and are not to be second-guessed by the courts. However, they do intervene in some instances of dispute. Seldom, if ever, do all the intricacies of family history involved in these cases emerge in the record. It is often difficult to tell why the court finds one party's story more plausible than the other. Not infrequently the record states "court believed the testimony of X" and therefore decided in favor of Y.

Land sales (for cash) are obviously not "customary," though the right to the land in the first place often rests on traditional claims.[5] Furthermore, the rule that land is not transferred until the full price is paid and that the seller can withdraw from the agreement at any time up to the moment of transfer by returning the purchase price seems likely to have derived from earlier practices (Kilema, Case 35, 1967). In the precash economy transfers of land inherited from or received from agnates to outsiders were contingent on the consent of kinsmen, so that not until the partially ritualized public acceptance of transfer was the transaction complete. One infers that at any time up to that moment, whatever the discussions between primary transactors, the agreement could be broken by either of them or by the donor's kinsmen. This extension and transformation of an earlier practice into a new situation is characteristic of Chagga law. Not fully traditional, but historically rooted and locally generated, the adaptation (and even invention) of "custom" has always been an ongoing enterprise. So have traditional claims (such as inheritance from, or *inter vivos* allocation by, a father) necessarily been mixed into new situations (the right to sell land or to rent). The present patterns of land possession would be incomprehensible without an understanding of Chagga patrilineal kinship and the rights generated under it. But it would be a serious error to suppose that such knowledge would suffice to understand the land transactions of this century, and the legal background against which they took place.

Litigation over land

Unoccupied shamba *land allocated by the chiefs and their* wachili

Mwika, Cases 16, 18, 1930; 2, 5, 1931) These cases concerned allocations of lands recently vacated by Mamba people, then allocated by chief and *wachili* to Mwika people. The disputes were about whether A or B was the person to whom the *mchili* had originally (or finally) allocated a particular plot. They were over the facts. (See also Case 27, 1930, on the mission obtaining part of this land.) The lands were in dispute between Mamba and Mwika before a European magistrate in Moshi at the time (Mwika, Case 20, 1930).

Division of inheritance, the distinction between inherited and self-acquired property

Kilema, Case 170, 1936 A man died leaving one *kihamba* and one cow. His two sons were the complainant (the last born) and the respondent (the firstborn). The cow had four calves after the father's death. The respondent took one cow and bought a *kihamba*. Thus he had two *vihamba*, the one he inherited (as eldest) from his father and the one he purchased. He had given nothing to his brother, the complainant. The court ruled that the eldest brother should divide the inheritance with the youngest and should give him one cow and one *kihamba*.

A man who sells land that is not his must repay all costs that result

Kilema, Case 30, 1967 The litigation was over a sale that took place in 1965. Plaintiff paid 1,400 for the *kihamba,* and claimed 8½ percent interest for two years, plus his costs in building the foundation of a house, because it turned out that the land did not belong to the defendant. The plaintiff won.

A grandfather can will to his grandson land to which his son then has no rights

Kilema, Case 50, 1967 This case involved a grandfather who willed a *kihamba* (in a written will registered in the court) to his grandson. The case states that capacity to make such a will is part of the custom of the Chagga. The grandfather then died. The mother of the grandson and the grandson moved away and the son (the child's father) appropriated the land, which he tried to sell. The lineage reported the action to the authorities who prevented him from selling. He subsequently rented the land for cash for a term of 8½ years. The lineage knew about the rental agreement and one kinsman, the plaintiff, then sued the renter to defend the absent grandchild's interests. The primary court judge ruled that the man was suing the wrong party. The case was appealed, and the appeal court reversed and ordered a rehearing.

Right to masiro

Kilema, Case 38, 1947 The plaintiff said the defendant had used a piece of
land he loaned him for twenty-two years and had not made certain *masiro*
payments. The *mila* (custom) of the Chagga requires that a *pipa* of *pombe*
be paid whenever a house is built on loaned land, and whenever a son or
daughter living in the house is circumcised. The defendant had built three
houses on the land and did not pay. The court held that the defendant
must pay three *mitungi* of beer. (*Mangi* and four *wazee* were present.)

Upholding a decision of the lineage which divided land between two brothers

Kilema, Case 51, 1947 The plaintiff and the defendant were brothers.
When their father died he left only one *kihamba*, half of which was
developed and under bananas and coffee and half of which was undeveloped. The lineage divided the land between the brothers. The brother
who received the undeveloped half was also loaned the developed half
until his share would be developed. He duly planted bananas and coffee
in the undeveloped half. After three years his brother asked for the
return of the loaned share and he refused to return it. The court visited
the property, saw the *masale* boundary the lineage had planted to divide
the *kihamba,* and ordered the defendant to return the half that he had
been loaned. (*Mangi* and four *wazee* were present.)

A father is not allowed to reclaim what was once his land which is then allocated to his son by the chief

Kilema, Case 82, 1947 A man with three wives left the chiefdom of
Kilema (intending to leave permanently). He took with him two wives
and their offspring leaving the third in Kilema with her son. After a time
in the chiefdom of Kirua, the father returned with his family, wishing to
resettle in Kilema once again. The chief said that it was the custom of the
Chagga that when a man left a chiefdom he informed the chief and the
chief reallocated his land. In this case, the chief (through the *wachili*)
reallocated it to the man's son. That allocation was irrevocable and a
matter not between father and son but between chief and subject.

Postcolonial judicial innovation regarding mission land which had once been held under masiro agreement, but then had been turned over to the possessors

Kilema, Case 19, 1967 A sister sued her brother for a *shamba*. The land
had been loaned to their father by the Roman Catholic Mission, for the

payment of *masiro*. *Masiro* had been paid for years. For many years (since 1958) the sister annually cultivated the *shamba*. In 1964 the plaintiff was pregnant and allowed her brother to use the *shamba* that year. Thereafter he refused to return the whole of it to her, keeping a part to cultivate for himself. Her argument was that 1966 was the end of *masiro* payments because the land became the property of all citizens, that each person who had land on loan from the mission came to be the owner of that land, and that with respect to this plot of land, she should be the owner. The court ruled that the *shamba* should remain divided "in order to reconcile the parties." In fact, it shows the strong bias in favor of males as landholders.

A father tries to recover land allocated to an ungrateful son who left

Mwika, Case 80, 1967 A father had two sons. He gave a *kihamba* to son A, with whom he later quarreled. Son A was accused before the lineage of threatening to kill his father. The elders heard witnesses to this effect and fined him four tins of *pombe* and one fatted gelded goat (*ndafu*). Son A paid the *pombe,* but not the *ndafu.* Son A left the area and asked his brother B to look after the land and informed the ten-house cell leader (*balozi*) to that effect. In this case the father sued son B alleging that he was wrongfully planting bananas in the *kihamba* which according to him rightfully reverted to him (the father) when his wrongdoing son A left. The court found for son B.

Bridewealth cases

Bridewealth cases are not uncommon. Among the Chagga the full bridewealth is never paid when a woman marries, the last payment often being made when she dies or not at all. From the 1930s on cash equivalents have often been used in bridewealth awards by the courts. If the marriage did not materialize reimbursement sometimes included gifts given to the girl when she was circumcised. The bridewealth of particular daughters is not infrequently assigned by fathers to particular sons, who then become responsible for protecting that sister's interests. And of course, unpaid bridewealth debts are inheritable as any other property, and pass from father to son or brother to brother, and so on.

Dispute over amount of bridewealth owed

Kilema, Case 62, 1936 The father of a bride said he was owed one cow and three goats. The son-in-law admitted owing one cow and one goat, but disputed over two other goats. Court held he must pay one cow, three goats, four drums of *pombe,* eight shillings, and one goat. "That is the law according to the custom of the Chagga." He was given four months to pay. The case was heard by Mangi Kiritta, four assessors, and four *wach-ili.*

Disputes over unpaid bridewealth; defendants are given varying amounts of time to pay

Kilema, Case 13, 1947 Plaintiff claimed the total bridewealth due from sister's husband was the following:

1. One cow
2. Meat for the sisters of the bride
3. *Pombe* for *mjomba* (mother's brothers) – five *mitungi*
4. *Pombe* for mother of bride – four *mitungi*
5. *Pombe* for father of bride – five *mitungi*
6. *Pombe* for brothers of bride – two *mitungi*
7. One goat for wife's brother
8. Three goats, one cow
9. Twelve *mitungi* of *pombe*
10. Meat of one cow

He had received four goats, one cow, and four *mitungi* of *pombe* and asked that the remainder be paid. The court found in his favor.

Mwika, Case 53, 1967 The plaintiff was father of woman married to defendant. Defendant admitted the claim for bridewealth. He told the court that the marriage agreement was that he would pay seven cows and seven goats for bridewealth, but that he had paid only one cow and three goats. The defendant claimed he had no assets and no job. He was the last-born son and lived with his father. The court nevertheless ordered him to pay six cows and four goats, specifying payments (beasts or their cash equivalent, a cow 200 shillings, a goat 50 shillings) to be made over a two-year period to 1969.

Reimbursement of bridewealth for a marriage which did not take place

Kilema, Case 110, 1936 The complainant was said to have been awarded fifty-eight shillings and sixty cents: twenty-six shillings for thirteen *mitungis* of *pombe,* two shillings for milk, two shillings for meat (bought in shop and sent to bride's father), sixty cents for one bunch of bananas (sent to brother of bride), twenty-seven shillings for one-half cow (half to father of bride, other half eaten by family of husband).

Reimbursement for clothes of bride

Kilema, Case 68, 1936 The plaintiff was brother of the bride. He bought her forty-two shillings' worth of clothes which the father of the groom should have paid for. The father of the groom was ordered to pay forty-two shillings as bridewealth. The case was heard by Mangi Kiritta, three *wazee,* and one *mchili.*

Dispute over which brother is to receive the bridewealth of a sister

Kilema, Case 83, 1936 The plaintiff was brother of the wife of the defendant. He argued that their father had received one cow of the bridewealth. He died subsequently. The plaintiff was the eldest son and heir. The plaintiff and defendant's representative (*mjumbe*) had drunk *pombe* together to formalize the understanding that plaintiff was to receive subsequent bridewealth payments. The plaintiff claimed a cow and three goats. The court ruled that the defendant must pay one cow and three goats, and that the plaintiff must then repay one goat. The case was heard by Mangi Kiritta, three *wazee,* and four *wachili.*

A partial return of bridewealth after six years of childless marriage

Mwika, Case 92, 1967 A man paid 400 shillings of bridewealth to the father of a woman with whom he lived for six years. She produced no children and went back to her father. The husband sued the father for the return of the 400 shillings. This case involved an appeal from a decision by the lower court that the bridewealth should be returned. The father had alleged that at least half of the sum should be kept on the ground that it was Chagga custom that, when a daughter married without her father's consent, the father was entitled to a goat as a fine (a goat for *isale*) and that 200 of the 400 shillings constituted the payment of the fine. The lower court agreed that this was the custom but said that it did not apply in this case because the woman was over twenty-one when she went to live with the plaintiff and had been previously married. On appeal the district magistrate found another ground on which to allow the father to keep half of the 400 shillings; the ground that as she had lived with and worked for the husband-plaintiff for six years and not for her parents, only half of the bridewealth should be returned.

Cases involving the legal position of women and children

Chagga women throughout their lives are considered to be the wards of
men. There must always be a man responsible for any woman to provide
her with housing, care for her in times of illness, and to see that she has
land to cultivate. Since the advent of the cash economy, such a man must
also pay for some clothing for her. Before she marries the responsible
man is her father or his heir, or a brother to whom her bridewealth has
been assigned. After she marries, it is her husband as long as she lives
with him. If she leaves him because he chases her away, and she bears a
child of his, he remains liable for her care and feeding during the traditional three-month period of confinement. If her husband dies while she
is living with him, one of his kinsmen becomes the heir, the *mrithi*. In the
premission days, she became an auxiliary wife of the heir, and any children she bore subsequently were his. In any conflict with her husband, a
wife may leave him and return to the household of her father or brother.
Then a negotiation over her grievance takes place and matters are sorted
out either by the *mkara,* the trustee of the marriage, or in the course of
meetings between the kinsmen of the spouses which may include the
spouses.

Women cannot hold a transferable interest in land. Only one law case
was found in which a daughter inherited land from a father (Keni Mriti
Mengwe 12:1967). The situation and the result were extraordinary. The
plaintiff was a fifteen-year-old girl. Her father had no sons and was said
to have willed a particular *kihamba* to her. The court said that if she paid
compensation to the father's kinsman who had improved the land, she
could have it. It seems unlikely that at fifteen she could pay, so in practical effect unless she was backed by another kinsman she could not recover. In all probability she was a front for interests of a male kinsman.

Women live first in the paternal *kihamba,* later in the *kihamba* of a
husband. If the husband predeceases the wife, she normally continues to
live on the land that was her marriage home. On her death that land is
inherited by her youngest son. The youngest son lives with his mother
throughout her life, and brings his wife to live in his "mother's" *kihamba*
when he marries. If she has no son, the land reverts to the localized
lineage for allocation. Traditional conventions of succession guide the
allocation but the deceased husband's wishes in the matter may also be
relevant as well as the preferences of the guardian.

Although women come to court from time to time to ask for a divorce,
they are normally told to return to their husbands. Women are sometimes
spoken of as "working for" their fathers until they marry and then as
"working for" their husbands. But, in fact, after marriage women have
some property interest in the vegetable crops they produce. It is often
said that they have a right to what is produced over and above that which

is needed to meet a woman's obligation to feed her household. Women may also hold livestock of their own. An occasional law case involves a woman's interest in standing crops or in beasts. Disputes over transactions in the women's markets do *not* seem to reach the courts.

The dependent position of women was made most dramatically evident during a criminal prosecution in Marangu on 7 September 1973. A woman was accused of sending her child out to steal from the house of a neighbor. Male criminal defendants were often kept in the jailroom (lockup) at the back of the courtroom until the hearing, and guarded while they were out. This woman was allowed to walk about the courthouse and its environs freely during the day of her trial. The magistrate asked about this said, "Where will a woman run?" The meaning was that she could never escape, that she could only run to kin, and would easily be caught. Men could run away to town and hope for work as casual laborers. The magistrate was sure that no woman could move easily out of her nexus of relationships.

The legitimacy of paternal control over sexual access to a daughter; seduction of an unmarried girl as a wrong against her father

Mwika, Case 10, 1937 A man must pay a cow and a goat to the father of a girl if he has seduced her and then wants to return her to her parents.

Mwika, Case 55, 1957 This case involved a claim for the return of bridewealth because the wife abandoned her husband. The initial union seems to have been an elopement. Many items of clothing worth 152 shillings and 50 cents had been given to the girl, and a fattened gelded goat (*ndafu*) worth 250 shillings and three containers of *pombe* had been given to the girl's father. The court held that according to the custom of the Chagga the gelded fattened goat had to be paid to a father in a marriage without his consent, but that such a payment was not part of the bridewealth. As for the three drums of *pombe,* one belonged to the father as the payment given to inform him of his daughter's whereabouts and was not part of the bridewealth, two were bridewealth payments. The clothing was judged not to be part of the bridewealth paid to the father. The plaintiff was told he could recover its value from the girl. The girl's father was ordered to pay 70 shillings, the value of two drums of *pombe.*

A promise to marry, intercourse, and a failure to make good the promise

Mwika, Case 20, 1967 A woman sued a man for having intercourse with her after promising to marry her, and failing to keep his promise. He had admitted sleeping with her to two persons who testified against him. The court held that according to the laws of the Chagga of Mwika the man must pay her one cow and one female goat or 250 shillings plus a 13-shilling court fee. (It is not clear whether these beasts then became her property or her father's.)

A father's interest in control over sexual access to his daughter is distinct from a husband's monopoly on sexual access to his wife

Mwika, Case 16, 1957 A father made a claim for a cow and a goat from a man who had impregnated his daughter. The father made the claim as *ugoni* (fine for adultery). The court said in Chagga *mila* (customary law) *ugoni* is only for the husband. But the father can claim *fidia* (compensation) for unlawful fornication if (1) daughter is raped by force, (2) if daughter is taken as a wife for a time and then chased away, (3) if a daughter is made pregnant and then the man refuses to marry her, and (4) if the daughter can prove that the man promised to marry her, then had sexual intercourse, and then refused to marry her. But in this case the father did not recover. The daughter had stayed with the man for four months at about the time she said she was supposed to deliver the child, but she did not give birth then and was sent home to her father. There was no proof that the defendant had impregnated her, and so the father did not recover.

The costs of a father who looks after his sick married daughter should be borne by her husband

Mwika, Case 7, 1957 A woman fled her husband and took refuge with her father. Two weeks later she fell ill. Her father looked after her from August to December and made repeated efforts to have a hearing over the marital dispute (making contact through the *mkara*, the marriage trustee or go-between). The husband never appeared on the days when the dispute was to be discussed. The wife recovered in December. The husband was held liable for the expenses of his father-in-law.

The inheritor of a widow must meet the costs of her illness

Mwika, Case 15, 1957 The inheritor of a woman (brother's widow) must pay for the expenses of her illness. (She sued her husband's brother and recovered.)

*A husband is obligated to underwrite the costs of feeding and caring for his wife during her three months of postpartum confinement (*uzazi*). The funds reimbursed to the woman may often be appropriated by her father.*

Mwika, Case 54, 1957 A married woman bore a child in her father's house. Her husband did not feed her. The husband alleged it was not his child. The woman sued her husband for expenses of 300 shillings and recovered.

Kilema, Case 36, 1967 The plaintiff, a woman, gave birth to a child, and then was sent away by her husband. She went home to her parents. She claimed expenses of 300 shillings. The court ruled that he was the father of the child, that he must pay the 300 shillings, and that he must take his wife back from her parents.

Mwika, Case 45, 1972 The plaintiff, a woman, recovered 300 shillings in confinement expenses from the father of her child.

A woman's property in livestock

Mwika, Case 66, 1957 A woman and man lived together, were husband and wife, and bought one cow together. After separation (case heard before *mchili*) she was allotted a calf and the man was given the cow. The woman now claimed two cows. The former husband said the original cow was his alone. The woman also claimed four goats saying a goat was "loaned to her for keeping." The court said she was entitled to two cows. But *mila* of Wachagga says a woman cannot be loaned an animal while she is living with her husband.

A female child inherits some cattle

Mwika, Case 21, 1930 A woman reared two children, a girl who was her daughter and a boy who was a captured child. She died. Then her husband died. There was a dispute over the cattle left by the husband. The chief's court said, "According to custom, inheritance is only for males." But in fact, the court allowed the daughter three cows and the stepson five cows, "because the daughter is the real child of the parents even though she is female."

A son's right to livestock allocated to his mother

Mwika, Case 14, 1930 A man was married to two wives. Each wife had a son who were plaintiff and defendant in this case. Before he died, the

father transferred six head of cattle from one wife with whom he quarreled to the wife he preferred. Then he died. One of the six beasts was
slaughtered as a sacrifice for the dead man. The son of the despised wife
claimed his six beasts and was given five cows and a calf by his father's
successor, an arrangement ratified by the court. (Chief Solomoni and
seven elders were present.)

*Modern innovation: A widow was appointed co-administrator
of the estate of her deceased husband. The other
co-administrator was his only older uterine brother.*

Marangu, Case 9, 1979 The most interesting figure in this case was a man
of eighty-five who had had four wives and nineteen children. Each wife
had had a *kihamba* of her own. The case concerned the appointment of
an administrator-guardian of the estate, widow, and children of a deceased son (the youngest son) who had recently died, in his forties. At
the *matanga* the kin appointed a full brother who lived in Arusha guardian of the widow and children and made him administrator of the estate.
They gave the old patriarch the responsibility of day-to-day concern with
the well-being of the widow and children. He was to call the Arusha
brother back in case of emergency. The magistrate said that it is *not* our
custom that a father be guardian/administrator of the estate of a deceased
son when that son has married. The magistrate was concerned not only
for the well-being of the widow and her children but also for the "illegitimate" children, the children outside the marriage, *wa nje*, children the
deceased had in another liaison with another woman. The magistrate thus
removed the old man from any official estate-administering role and appointed the widow co-administrator with her husband's brother, admon-
ishing them to follow the general plan of the patriarch, and not to forget
the two "outside" children. The appointment of a woman as co-administrator is out of keeping with Chagga custom which is invariably to appoint
a male guardian-administrator.

*Woman sues her ex-husband for misappropriating her property
in beasts, and wins*

Mwika, Case 11, 1931 When she married the wife had a goat of her own
(given her by a man other than her husband). By means of income
obtained from the goat she eventually was able to buy a cow. The cow
had a heifer which she placed with one Maslayo. The husband took the
heifer from Maslayo and placed it with Marabauya. The heifer matured
and bore a calf. The husband then sent his wife back propertyless to her
parents. The wife sued her husband for three cows and one goat. The

husband denied everything but witnesses persuaded the chief that the wife was right. However, one of her cows had died so that she was only entitled to two cows and one goat. (Chief Solomoni and six elders were present.)

The child of a woman who was separated from her husband does not inherit property acquired after the separation

Mwika, Case 35, 1931 A woman, sent back to her natal home by her husband, lived under the care of her brother for the rest of her life and he buried her when she died, this being a sign of heirship. The brother had built her a house and had looked after her needs. When she died she owned one cow, a calf, and three goats all of which she had acquired during the time she lived near her brother. All the beasts were placed in the households of others. Her daughter appropriated these from them after her mother's death. The brother sued his sister's daughter for their return and recovered. (Chief Solomoni and six elders were present.)

Woman denied requests for divorce

Mwika, Case 16, 1929 A woman complained that her husband did not visit her at night and that he beat her. She threatened suicide if divorce was not granted. The chief ruled she must return to her husband and must pay the costs of the suit.

Woman asks for divorce because she did not become pregnant

Kilema, Case 90, 1936 A woman, married for twelve years, sued her husband for divorce on the ground that she had not become pregnant. The court ordered her to return to her husband for one year. If she did not become pregnant in that period she would be given a divorce at the end of it. If she did she would stay with her husband or not as they may decide. The case was heard by Mangi Kiritta, five *wazee*, and four *wachili*. In a later suit (Kilema, Case 25, 1947) the husband tried to recover bridewealth because of the divorce.

Mwika, Case 13, 1967 A woman asked for a divorce on the ground that her husband was impotent. She was married in a Muslim manner in 1963, remained with him until 1965, and then returned to her father. She had had a child while in the house of her husband but it was the child of another man, the mother's brother of her husband. She alleged that her husband had never had intercourse with her during the period of their marriage. The husband replied that she would hardly have stayed with him for two years without complaining to the *mkara* (marriage trustee) or the sheik who performed the marriage if that were so and that she was lying. The sheik who married them testified that he had heard this case with some elders. The court sent plaintiff and defendant to the medical officer who reported that the husband was both potent and fertile. The case was dismissed.

A woman's interest in the crops she plants

Keni-Mriti-Mengwe, Case 126, 1967 A man and woman who lived together and had two children had a *shamba* of millet (*mbege*). One of the children fell ill and died, and the man's father died. The woman left her "husband" and went to live with another man. In the meantime someone harvested the millet from the *shamba*. The ex-"husband" accused his wife of stealing it, got the TANU Youth League to arrest her and search her new "husband's" house for the millet. They found some, confiscated it, but it proved to belong to her new "husband" and not to have been the missing millet. Meanwhile she was locked up for a day. In this case she was suing her ex-"husband" for the rewashing of her name because he had called her a thief. The court was persuaded that she had taken the millet which she should have divided in half with her ex-spouse since he had provided the seed, and found against her. (The wife had provided all the labor.)

Mwika, Case 64, 1967 A woman and her husband (no marriage certificate) lived together and planted maize and millet (*mbege*) in their *shamba*. The husband chased the wife from his house before she harvested her crops. In this case she was suing him for her share of the harvest. The husband then harvested the millet which she alleged amounted to three bags. He denied this, saying the millet patch had been full of weeds and hence produced only one bag of millet. The court accepted his version, and decided that he owed his wife the equivalent of one-half bag of millet, that the maize *shamba* should be divided in half (each to get 52½ paces of the field), and each was to harvest her/his own share of the crop. The husband was to pay the court fee of nine shillings.

Case showing the attempt of a father to control the marriage of his son

Marangu, heard 15 July 1968 A young woman had a baby at her father's house and sued her alleged husband for 200 shillings' support for her period of confinement. They had no marriage certificate. Her young "husband" was his father's youngest son, that is, he lived in the *kihamba* of his father. The father disapproved of the marriage. The wife was persuaded by the magistrate to withdraw her complaint and try to settle matters "at home." Trying to be even handed, the magistrate required the young man to sign a statement that she was his wife. The father said to his son, "If you take this woman you will have to find a place to keep her yourself," that is, threatening to expel him from the *kihamba* and disinherit him. The case was dismissed because the wife withdrew her complaint.

Parental control over the labor of children

Keni-Mriti-Mengwe, Case 3, 1967 A mother made a contract with a man to give him her daughter as a nursemaid. He was to pay 120 shillings and 2 cents and supply a blanket and a gallon of ghee (clarified butter) for one year's work until the child could walk. She took her daughter back after 5½ months in 1966 because the daughter's legs were infested by chiggers. The defendant had paid the daughter 40 shillings. The plaintiff did not recover because she had broken the contract by taking her daughter back. The magistrate took it for granted that had the daughter worked for the full period agreed to, her mother would have had a right to the payment.

The right of a man to his child

Mwika, Case 11, 1967 The suit was for expenses for *uzazi* and for post-partum illness in a case in which there was no certificate of marriage. The woman sued the child's father. The court held that he must pay 300 shillings for the costs of her period of confinement. He must also pay a cow and a goat when he takes the child away from its mother. He was not to remove the child for a year by which time it would be three years old and could be separated from its mother. The assumption underlying this case is that, according to Chagga law, children belong to the father, not to the mother, provided proper payments are made.

False accusation: suits to rewash the name

Allegations of false accusation tend to be in cases of theft or witchcraft. Few such cases reach the courts, and if they do, lawsuits "to rewash the name" seldom succeed. The court usually goes to a great deal of trouble to ask witnesses whether they specifically heard A call B a thief or a witch in the witnesses' presence, or specifically saw that witchcraft materials were purchased or used. The courts seem to want to find inadequate evidence of slander in order to get the cases out of their courts. No cases treat the accusation of witchcraft as an accusation of something impossible, hence trivial. All take the accusation seriously. Yet witchcraft cases could not be tried in the courts under colonial law, nor can they be today, so the courts were and are, in a difficult position.[6]

By indirection, the suit for the rewashing of the name asks the court to find that the accused person is not a witch, is not a user of witchcraft substance and therefore has been slandered. By finding that there is not enough evidence of *the accusation* to support the claim, the court avoids the question whether the accusation is true or not. The origin of the Chagga's ingenious way out is not clear, but it is frequently used.

This way out has an analogy in the primary courts in some criminal cases having to do with the threat to kill. Such threats can be verbal and can carry the implication that the killing will be accomplished through witchcraft. The courts can slip out of the problem by finding that the threat was not proved. They sometimes do so by taking the position that a weapon or some other material means of accomplishing the purpose must be shown to have been involved, implying that threatening words alone are not enough to constitute the crime.

Claims for the rewashing of the name after an accusation of witchcraft

Mamba, Case 46, 1963 Jumapili had sued Emanueli for calling him, Jumapili, a witch. In 1954 Jumapili paid 700 shillings toward the purchase price of a *kihamba*. The seller, Emanueli's brother, eventually returned the 700 shillings and sold the land to Emanueli instead. Emanueli's son went mad, and Emanueli accused Jumapili of buying witchcraft substance in Tanga, of bringing a *mchawi* (witch) from Tanga into his house, of killing and burying an animal without skinning it, and of saying, "I want you to tell me whether your child got sick or died?" and also of saying, "Where will you send your children?" The case was heard "at home" by fourteen elders and Emanueli was fined a cow and a goat. The case in 1963 was brought to force Emanueli to pay, since he had not done so. The magistrate said that the *mila* of the Wachagga provides that if you call a person a witch and fail to prove he is a witch, you must pay a cow and a goat. But he found that no witness actually heard the defendant call the plaintiff a witch. Complainant's case failed.

Mwika, Case 46, 1967 Plaintiff alleged that defendant had accused him of burying a bottle and a pot and other things in his house, objects that were supposed to be witchcraft instruments. Defendant had gone to the divisional executive officer (DEO) to complain and to ask him to hear the case. The defendant and his mother had brought the witchcraft instruments to the DEO's office. The DEO said unless they had another witness he could not take their claim seriously. The plaintiff then came to court and claimed a cow and a goat from the defendant for the rewashing of his name for having been called a *mchawi* (witch). The divisional executive officer testified that he had seen the plaintiff, defendant, and defendant's mother in his office, that the real dispute was between the plaintiff and defendant's mother and asserted that the defendant had *not* called the plaintiff a *mchawi* in his office. The court decided that since there was no one who would testify that the defendant had actually called the plaintiff a *mchawi*, the case was dismissed.

False accusation as a thief

Mwika, Case 101, 1967 The plaintiff had been convicted as a thief. The defendant was the complaining witness. On appeal the decision was reversed. The plaintiff then sued the defendant for a cow and a goat for the rewashing of his name, under the customary law of the Wachagga. The court decided that the plaintiff could not sue the defendant since technically he was not the one who had prosecuted, but must sue the state. On appeal the court said that customary law was not applicable. The republic is free from such suits. There was no one to sue, and the plaintiff's appeal was dismissed.

Person accused of threatening to kill

Kilema, Case 160, 1947 One brother accused another of saying that he and his wife and children would die. Two witnesses swore that they heard him say this. The defendant admitted making the threat but denied buying witchcraft substance. The court held that the accused must be acquitted because the plaintiff could not prove that the defendant had bought witchcraft substance. (*Mangi* and 4 *wazee* were present.)

Custom inside and outside the courts

The summaries of illustrative cases show the range of types of disputes and accusations that have reached the local courts on Kilimanjaro, and Tables 8–12 show how the incidence has changed over the years. "Customary law" issues are a less and less important proportion of the work of these courts as the century progresses. But that does not mean that all such questions have lost their cogency for the lives of ordinary rural people nor that all is as it appears. What remains to be explored here is the structure of disputation and allocation outside the courts. Its shape and history are embedded in the relationships among kin and neighbors. Once the extramural dimension is added to the history of the official system, various simultaneous levels of transformation can be clearly seen. The peculiar place of any system of official institutions can only become visible in relation to life outside them.

Part III

The modern uses of "customary law": lineage, land, and organizational control

8

The localized patriline in the 1960s and 1970s

CHAGGA LINEAGES IN GENERAL

When independence came to Tanzania in 1961 a new set of party offices and organizations was soon introduced on Kilimanjaro. These reached down to the household level. Party cells of ten households each, a village organization, and a ward organization had been generated by the mid-1960s. The apparatus of local men serving in party roles is a continuing presence on the mountain, most visible on certain official occasions and in certain official places. But it is a construct that lies on top of other local commitments in which the same men are involved. One of the strongest of those commitments in the old areas of settlement is to that durable entity that has no official existence whatsoever: the localized patrilineage. The interconnections between rural political affairs and the institutions of the state are impenetrable if the official hierarchy is the only element examined. The extreme localism of orientation which life often has on Kilimanjaro only becomes evident from attention to the ongoing internal affairs of rural neighborhoods. At work the ward official represents African socialism. At home he is a kinsman, a neighbor, a husband, and brother. In 1974 I came to know Nicodemu L – – who was one of the first men to join TANU in his part of Vunjo. When I met him he was a paid ward official. At his desk at the court building he explained his work and the local structure of party and government in the various "villages" (*mitaa*). Some days later when we walked to his house together I talked with his elderly father and various other kinsmen. One of the young men who appeared was brandishing a *panga* (bush knife) and giggling strangely. After they left, Nicodemu told that the young man, a son of his deceased elder brother, was *kichaa* (mad), but that he had not always been in this condition. "And do you know who they think is responsible?" he asked, "Me. Imagine. They think I bewitched him. And I am not even his father's heir." Thus Nicodemu, accused of witchcraft and sorcery by some of his agnates, supported by others, explained the fatuousness of the accusation by arguing that he was structurally the wrong

213

person to accuse. He plainly believed someone else had worked the witchcraft. Nicodemu no longer shared meat with his accusers, but was on good terms with the others. Such was the lineage life of this upstanding socialist ward official.

What have the great transformations of the past hundred years done to the structure of Chagga kinship organization? Much has changed. But on the surface some things seem the same. Localized clusters of agnatic kinsmen still live in contiguous gardens in the central banana belt, and assemble at large outdoor gatherings to drink beer together to celebrate all the major moments of the life cycle, the births and baptisms, the marriages, the Christian holidays, and to mark the birthdays and the deaths of members and their spouses. Men of the minimal segments still pair off as slaughtering partners, and still butcher beasts for their agnates and take turns at being host. When women marry they leave their natal homes to go to live among the kin of their husbands. But they do not go far. Marriage is usually between persons who were born within two miles of one another. The affinal links in any locality are extremely dense. The common interests are many, the common contacts and celebrations frequent.

But what is left of the larger localized lineage is not all feasting and partying. Externally and formally, kin groups have lost the political role they had a hundred years ago. But internally, for the time being, the localized lineage remains an agency of social control, a source of labor and assistance, an allocator of property rights and guardianships, and a mediator and settler of disputes. The *matanga,* the ceremony on the fourth day after death, remains a major event, involving the assembling of kin and the reallocation of the decedent's property and responsibilities by kin. The courts recognize that a person who is present and fails to make a claim on that day is virtually precluded from doing so later on ([1966] Local Courts Civil Appeal [LCCA] 71 1965, reprinted in Fimbo and James 1973:345–48). Depending on the size of the local lineage cluster, and the importance of the occasion, the resident group occasionally still assembles "as a whole" to do its internal business with or without affines and neighbors.[1] In the more usual matters of less general concern, problems are resolved through the relatively autonomous decisions of its tightly organized subsegments.

The current version of the lineage is short of being a corporate group, having no unitary collective relations with the outside world. Yet it continues to be capable of taking certain kinds of internal action as a body. From one point of view the localized lineage coheres as a bounded universe of overlapping, densely interconnected personal networks. But it is much more than a net of networks. Its members continue to conceive of it as having a formal internal structure based on patrilineal principles, notions of segmentation, and a hierarchy of age. At the base, it is made up of small, parallel minimal lineage segments. Each is usually composed of a living father and his adult married sons, or a group of adult brothers, or the sons of two or more brothers.[2] A group of subsegments sharing a deceased common ancestor (a common great-grandfather, for example) may comprise a higher-level section. If it is a small lineage the whole may be composed of one or two of these higher-level sections. Larger lineages have many more.

The minimal lineage segments are "goat slaughtering groups" because, although the Chagga do not call them that, the levels of lineage structure are explained in terms of meat distributions. If there is to be a small slaughtering, of a goat or a sheep, a father and his sons and their sons are called to share the slaughtering feast. If there is a great slaughtering, of a cow or of several goats at one time, then a set of uncles and cousins and their male progeny are also called. The most intimate agnatic relations are in the goat-slaughtering group, the next range is in the cow-slaughtering group. Beyond that range is the localized group as a whole, which normally does not eat meat together, but drinks beer.[3] Today, the beer-drinking parties, including men and their wives, are frequent. Slaughtering feasts (men only) are held much less often being much more expensive, and are usually confined, as they must have been a century ago, to the smallest subsegments.[4]

Yet today meat sharing remains an important symbol of agnatic relationship, and the failure to provide or share meat regularly according to the rules of reciprocity and distribution is a serious sign of fracture. Withholding meat is one of the sanctions that is available for punitive use within the body of close agnates. It intimates the possibility of general social exclusion, of eventual ostracism.

The shift in the ambiance of meat sharing over this century captures the subtle nature of many of the cultural transformations that have taken place among the Chagga. Some slaughtering feasts continue, and they remain important, but they are no longer the exclusive source of meat. The butcher shops are there. Thus a large part of the element of economic exchange and mundane interdependence for meat food with which the slaughtering feast was once invested has disappeared. But the significance of slaughtering as a material representation of lineage relationships continues. The feeling remains that the keeping of animals should be for slaughtering, festive or sacrificial, not for selling. In that sense kin have an implied lien on eating the beasts of their kinsmen. If a man decides to sell an animal, he must have a good reason and he must make that reason known to his agnates.[5]

Today, the organization of leadership in the localized lineage-as-a-whole is not formalized beyond the principles of seniority and segmentation. The most senior man of each subsection heads his own subsection, and the most senior of those seniors lead the lineage. In each small segment a second person, usually the next most senior male, the putative positional successor of the head (often his eldest son) has a role of importance and leadership. Every time beer is brewed, the most senior man of the segment involved has the absolute right to the first and the last drinks from it. If he is not present at the drinking party, his portion of beer must be set aside for him. Every time there is a slaughtering, he is entitled to the *kidari,* the breast portion. Anyone who takes those shares puts himself in mystical danger. His usurpation may one day kill him. Such was the explanation of the death of one of the men in the village of N – – in the 1970s. In his death-fever his lips swelled and cracked, and he died in terrible torment. His symptoms were taken as evidence that he had once, long years before, no one knew when, eaten the *kidari* of a goat that should have been for his father.

Eroding some of the prestige of lineage seniority is the modern circumstance that certain middle-aged and younger men are educated, salaried, and by local standards wealthy. These men have political force in the lineage because of the place they occupy in the external world. There were such men in precolonial times, men who found favor with the chief, men of outstanding personal qualities, skilled in oratory, respected in judgment, leaders of other men. The chief might reward them with cattle and other largesse, and such men were better off than their kinsmen. It is not a new thing that individual wealth and prominent standing in the public arena should affect internal lineage affairs. But the means of access to status in the outside world has substantially changed and cash does not flow directly or as often into the Chagga distributive system of feasting, ritual, and exchange as cattle once did. Cash that goes into land or into house construction or other amenities does not normally find its way back to the general group of lineage brethren. In most lineages in the 1960s and 1970s the most senior men were the least likely to have status in the outside world. They were unlikely to be literate (though there are a few outstanding exceptions) and they were also least likely to be involved in the modern salaried world. They were hence apt to be available for all lineage palavers for more than one reason. They were qualified by seniority, with all of its ritual implications of closeness to the dead. They were present in the *kihamba,* and not employed elsewhere, and they were likely to have time because younger hands, wives or sons, or hired casual labor, were doing the agricultural work.

Today, there is no individual (was there ever?) who can speak authoritatively to the whole of the localized group and order it to do something. On the whole, lineage palavers at all levels generate decisions about the affairs of individual members, rather than decisions about collective action. The one major exception is the decision to ostracize which still does take place. The decision that comes out of a lineage palaver is enunciated by a senior man. The process of arriving at decisions involves general discussion in which there may be disagreement expressed or unexpressed.

In the literature on collective decision making in Africa apparent consensus has often been taken to mean general agreement. Indeed the notion of such consensus is part of the ideology of many African peoples themselves, including the Chagga. But long contact with Chagga affairs suggests another interpretation of events. When the Chagga say the lineage decided something, they mean that a particular outcome was declared binding at a particular palaver by the senior man present, discussion having reached a point at which enough expressions of agreement from enough key persons gave the leader the social strength to risk being authoritative. Nevertheless, many things simply are not actually settled and seethe, despite the appearance of closure of an episode that may be achieved at a palaver. There are collective dimensions in intralineage disputes.

The appearance of agreement and the appearance of acquiescence are part of the continuous testing of political alignments in a small social field. If disagreements and nonconformity are seen as debits, and agreements and conformity as credits in a long-term history of exchanges of mutual social support, there are risks involved for anyone pressing a point against the tide. Consequently the substantive issues are so often secondary and the personal relationships primary in these kinds of proceedings. The person who wants to express a negative opinion today may tomorrow need the support of those with whom he/she now disagrees. Thus a son who insults his father and is fined beer by the minimal lineage is likely to pay up, not only because of grave supernatural risks, but also because on some tomorrow his status as heir will come up, or his need for bridewealth, or support in a dispute. People may be wary of making someone seriously angry even though in these same relationships people are often driven to rage. In times of illness or misfortune these matters are remembered. Supernatural punishments for misbehavior can be long delayed. Disagreement or disobedience can mean eventual impairment of social or physical capacity. A man must think of the future as he handles himself and his present obligations.

Relationships involve a continuous and subtle reassessment of the question whose fortunes are up and whose down inside the lineage, who is angry with whom, and who is friends with whom, who is well and who is ill. An immense amount of attention, interest, and speculation is generated. Pasts are reviewed as they might bear on the present. Two existentially critical issues involved are land and health or economic and personal well-being. Only endless sociable reassertions of good will and amity can reassure in these conditions, and can keep a person informed. The beer drinking and the exchanges of meat are part of that complex, as are the dispute palavers. A man who offers another a calabash of beer takes the first sip out of courtesy, to show it is not poisoned. To drink together is to show trust. Any rural Chagga will explain that, of course, most beer is not poisoned. But it *can* be used to kill someone, and sometimes is.

Such was the background of a case that came up in 1962 when ten men were prosecuted for assault (Mwika, Primary Court Criminal Case 234, 1962). The defendants were a group of neighbors and kinsmen who had beaten up the eldest brother of several of them, burned his clothes, smashed objects in his house, and presented him with a shroud which they said was for him. Before they could finish him off, the local *mtaa* head and others who were passing by on the road heard the commotion and intervened. They separated the attackers from their victim and carted him off to the hospital. Later in court some of the attackers were fined and required to pay compensation.[6] But locally many thought they were in the right. Some years later the mother of the victim explained what led to the assault. Her youngest son, Fares, had had a beer party for his kinsmen and their wives at which he and his eldest brother had quarreled. (Failing male issue eldest and youngest are still mutual heirs in Chagga custom.) The youngest son became ill after the party and died a day later. The mother and her other sons were convinced that the eldest son had killed the youngest by putting something in his beer in order to inherit his land. The lineage did not allow him to become the heir. And from the time of the *matanga* on neither the mother nor any of the other members of their lineage would receive or speak to the eldest son. He was still living in the area during the fieldwork period, but was ostracized by his agnates and some neighbors.

Residence at the heart of a localized patrilineal cluster is still considered highly desirable, and land in lineage territory is valued above any other. Ancestors are still buried in the banana groves, and their presence, sometimes benign, sometimes malign, is still felt by their descendants. The continuity of the patriline and the continuing occupation of the land are not only closely connected in Chagga thought, but in sociological reality.[7] A son who received a piece of land from his father must give his father a share of beer every time he brews a large *pombe* from the bananas in that garden. For neighboring agnates ritual connections continue indefinitely. Libations continue to be made to the dead. But kinsmen residing at a great distance are not in the effective social circle of the localized lineage, and may seldom or never make an appearance. Some voluntary outmigration has long been part of Chagga practice. But it is different today. Now land shortage has become so serious that many men

Plate 18. A grass house in Old Moshi in 1902. (Photo from M. Merker, 1902)

have had to move away from their natal lineage gardens who might have preferred not to do so. It is the men who remain on the land in the patrilineal cluster (and those who are considered only temporarily away) who constitute the effective localized lineage.

On Kilimanjaro the process of coping with the numbers born in excess of replacement is continuous, and is a central part of current lineage life. This population explosion is part of the background of the deep resentment that the Chagga felt toward the government in the early years after independence when the number of secondary school places open to Chagga candidates was restricted in order to open them to the children of less fortunate peoples. Thus reasons of distributive justice introduced an ethnic element in the choice of candidates in place of ranking by examination results or other ethnic-blind test. The Chagga were also prohibited from building new substitute schools to avoid the effects of the restrictions. The outrage engendered is always seen outside Kilimanjaro purely in terms of the ambitiousness of the Chagga for themselves and for their children. But from a larger economic-demographic perspective success in secondary education and the employment to which it could lead have for decades been one way for a lucky few to avoid the pressures of land shortage. For some time now most Chagga fathers have not had enough

Plate 19. A grass house in 1973. Note modern house at left, with cement floor,
tin roof, and window. (Photo by D. C. Moore)

land in lineage territory to provide several sons with plots large enough to
support a family. But there usually has been enough to subdivide and
enough to give each son space for a house and a small banana-coffee
grove. If the sons had supplementary plots or other resources they could
remain in the main lineage territory in the diminished groves. Some of
the educated men have gone to the city to earn a living and have left their
wives and young children living on their plots in lineage territory to hold
their local social places. Others have managed to get jobs locally, near
enough to return on weekends, or even to live at home. Education has
permitted these men to avoid the hardships associated with the land
shortage and has allowed them to remain in place, among their less
literate and less fortunate lineage brothers. Most localized lineages have
within them the full range of types, from the educated and secure to the
illiterate and impoverished.

A hundred years ago a man, or a pair of brothers, could pioneer new
land and hope to found a new localized lineage through natural increase,
expecting sons and grandsons to settle in adjacent unclaimed land. That
possibility is now closed. Until recent years individual plots sometimes
could be acquired, and it is possible occasionally even now. But there
usually is no adjacent room for expansion, since all contiguous land is
likely to be occupied by similarly expanding families. The most radical

Plate 20. A *kihenge*, a large basket-on-a-platform with a tin roof which contains the household's store of millet (*mbege*) for beer. This is the area next to the grass house in Plate 19. It shows the flat, well-swept center of the *kihamba* area. Behind this open space are the coffee trees under the bananas.

processes of structural alteration of the lineage system have not only been an increasing internal educational and economic differentiation, but the equally fundamental fact that new localized lineages can no longer be formed, or at least that any such new formation would be the rarest case. The reproduction of this structural unit is now possible only where it already exists.

Besides putting a lid on new lineage formation, rising population and land shortage have had two additional effects. The passage of time has generated many "isolated" spinoff families and two or three family clusters settled a distance from the larger localized lineage settlements. Such "isolates" comprise the whole community in the areas most recently opened to settlement, some high on the mountain above the banana belt, and some lower down, nearer the plain. (See Figure 5.2, page 114, for a map of such an area showing lineage diversity.) Such "isolates" also are found in the banana belt itself, scattered here and there between and among the larger clusters of agnates who constitute the territorially localized lineages. Some of these must have always existed, and some must have once represented a stage in the process of new-lineage formation when the population was rising. But "isolates" are now presumably more numerous than they once were, and will not lead to new major clusters.[8]

Plate 21. A *kihamba* on the side of a hill, 1973. Note *banda*, rectangular house of wattle and daub with tin roof and grass house. In background are bananas. (Photo by D. C. Moore)

Population increase and land shortage have also meant that the local-ized lineages of the banana belt are under constant pressure to accommo-date an ever-increasing number of agnatic descendants on the same amount of land, when they cannot or do not want to encourage them to move away. Both processes, subdivision of land and outmigration, are easily observable in the history of any localized lineage. Both are often painful. Survival in the subdivided share has no doubt been facilitated by the old practice of cultivating supplementary strips of land on an annual basis in parts of the lower areas while residing in the banana belt (*ki-hamba* area). Much of what once was *shamba* land has come to be held permanently as *kihamba* land. Individuals now own *shamba*s, and they loan strips or parts by the year.[9] Renewal of these arrangements between the same persons is a common practice. Reliance on produce from the *shamba*s has probably increased over the years, and very likely the num-ber of secondary plots under cultivation has also increased. Supplemen-tary *shamba* cultivation and the importation of food have enabled the banana belt to accommodate denser residential populations than would have been possible if the residential area had been the only one from which subsistence produce was drawn. In 1962 in Lyamungo, Machame, there were 954 persons per square mile, and in Kitandu, Kibosho, there

Plate 22. Young wife of a salaried man in her earth-floor kitchen. She and her husband and children lived in a tiny rectangular three-room modern house of earth bricks plastered over and painted white, with a cement floor and tin roof. Her kitchen was a separate little building of mud-plastered wood. Her stove consisted of three stones in the junction of which she made her fire and placed her round-bottomed cooking pot. On the shelf were all of her cooking utensils and containers. Some years later she was able to afford a larger kitchen of the same type in which she kept two or three goats.

were said to be 3,690 (Von Clemm 1964:100). Consequently Kilimanjaro today is a curious *rururb,* not only a rural area with an urban population density, but an area with pastoral, agricultural, and kinship values that it cannot fully support. The pressure toward emigration from core lineage territories is continuous and intense, and greatly affects not only the emigrants, but those who literally succeed in holding their ground and maintaining the core-lineage life.

Just as in Gutmann's time, today most of the patrilineal clusters are local subunits of named noncorporate patriclans (normally but not invariably exogamous) whose member lineages are scattered all over the mountain. Most parishes (*mitaa*) contain a number of localized lineages and some isolates.[10] Among most of the scattered clan fragments contacts are negligible or nonexistent. There is not even an overarching symbolic genealogy to link the clan together. For the most part what they have in common today is only the same name. This is nothing new. Gutmann deplored the absence of clan connection in his time, assuming that there once had been a unity which had been lost. He thought the breaking up

Plate 23. The sum total of agricultural implements of a well-to-do household.

of clans had been caused by the division of Chagga territory into many mutually hostile chiefdoms, reducing the feeling for clan cohesion to the point that mere local lineage unity was left (Gutmann 1926:21; HRAF:29; see also J. C. Winter's discussion of Gutmann's theoretical ideas, especially those on the "primal ties" 1979:158–211). Gutmann's assumption that there had been a previous period of clan cohesion is largely conjectural. There is no persuasive evidence of a supralocal patriclan organization at any time, at least not above the level of the chiefdom within which there may have been some shared sacred groves.[11]

Gutmann estimated that there were 400 dispersed named patriclans on Kilimanjaro (1926:1; HRAF:1).[12] Most Chagga genealogies do not go deeper than the immigrant who founded the local branch, and often all that is known of him is his clan name, and his "tribal" origin. Sketch maps of parts of Mwika and Kilema made in this study in 1969 (Figures 5.1 and 5.3) and of a part of Machame made in 1930 by A.W.M. Griffiths show lineage localization in these areas.[13] The absence of open space in the later maps reflects the pressure of population on the land. Each outlined unit is a homestead plot. These maps raise the question how long the kind of lineage size and lineage distribution they show has existed. All indications are that in the areas where there are now densely cultivated acres there was once a great deal of unoccupied land, at least until the second half of the nineteenth century.[14]

What is the usual size of present localized patrilines? In Mwika, in the area in which a census of some 300 plus families was undertaken during fieldwork in 1968–69, some 40 patrilines were represented. But these were not of equal size. Twelve of the lineages represented 259 household plots grouped in patrilineal clusters of 6, 8, 10, 15, 16, 17, 24, 23, 23, 29, 31, 57. The rest of the patrilines were composed of under 6 households each. The 57-household group was a cluster of an ex-chiefly line, which, because of the effect of polygyny, was larger than others. The average patriline size of the clusters over 6 comes to 21.5 households per patriline. If one excludes the ex-chiefly cluster, the average goes down to 18.3 households per cluster. For the most part it seems that the localized lineages are relatively small, but there may be substantial downward distortion because of the arbitrariness of the geographical boundary. Several of the smaller clusters are offshoots of larger concentrations nearby.

The average household size in the census was 7.45 persons. This size means that in a number of them more than one adult male was present. (Youngest sons normally reside with their fathers for life.) This size, too, would raise the average adult male membership of the localized lineages above 18.3. The modern lineage sizes in the subareas investigated seem roughly comparable to those yielded by Gutmann's figures for Moshi at the turn of the century, when an average seems to have been 20 adult males (1926:1). In the Vunjo banana belt, all indications suggest that the dimensions of some of the present localized lineages may not be very different from what they were seventy years ago in areas where settlements were already long established. But they are probably geographically much more concentrated. Also there are probably many more such clusters and interdigitated among them probably many more scattered, minute groups of a size under 6 households. The smallest clusters are also found up the mountain and down the mountain in the relatively recently settled parts. (See Figure 5.2 for map of relatively newly settled area near forest.)

Taken together, the maps, the genealogies, and the historical material suggest that the mix of localized lineages that are seen today in the area of Mwika on the map is at most about a hundred years old. The rapid population growth of the past century has closed down the open lands that once lay between the lineage territories, and by doing so, probably has largely limited the concentration of localized lineages to those that had a foothold there around 1900 and the chiefly family which filled up the interstices. Although individual families may have moved in later, the general picture seems to be one of increasingly frozen and immobilized patrilines as this century progresses. We can infer, then, that in many of

its characteristics the particular stable local political arena composed of
the specific lineages now in place, is, in many areas, an artifact of the past
hundred years, not an ancient traditional community that has reproduced
itself for centuries.

The curious thing about this picture is that the Tanzanian "villagization"
program may freeze it in place and perhaps give new political vitality to old
lineage loyalties. As mentioned earlier, in the early 1970s the party made a
decision that all Tanzanians should be organized in cooperative villages by
1976. On Kilimanjaro this decision resulted in the sub*mitaa* (subparishes)
being renamed villages. On the ground, no persons have actually been
moved. The brand new villages have old boundaries which were there long
before the consolidations of the colonial and postcolonial periods.[15] Will
the localized patrilineages act en bloc in village politics? It is not clear
whether the significant political cleavages in the new villages will form
exclusively along the lines of class, with the salaried versus the farmers, the
educated versus the barely literate, or whether localized lineage membership will in some situations have countervailing political importance. For
the time being few collective intravillage issues have been on the table.
That may change. If and when the village ever comes to have substantial
resources to manage, its internal politics will become more of a focus of the
attention of local men than it was in 1979. The Agricultural Policy of
Tanzania (1983) seems to be planning to turn over to the village much
control over members' lands. No doubt unwittingly, the socialist government has provided the lineages with a potential mini-arena of mutual competition which they have not had for a century or more. If the lineages do
not fade away a full circle may close. In the old areas of settlement alliances among local patrilineages may once again become one of the bases of
micropolitical factionalism.

A LINEAGE IN PARTICULAR: THE MEN OF THE M—— LINEAGE AND THEIR WIVES

Far more persuasive than any general statement of the norms of lineage
organization is an account of the particular goings-on in a particular lineage. The chronicle of the localized lineage of the M——s is intended to
show the nature of modern lineage relations through an account of disputes, land transactions, and other allocations and exchanges among
them.[16] It reads like a culturally exotic soap opera, one crisis following
another. The particularities of real situations involving specific individuals
clearly show why certain elements of tradition have been actively continued by as market-oriented and modern a people as the Chagga. In the
economy of social relations and cultural ideas there is sometimes a special
convenience in using existing forms for new purposes. The rural Chagga

have done so with respect to a number of elements of their culture. Although some of the cultural continuities of Chagga kinship are real enough to seem unbroken, the transformations in associated conditions of life are so great that it would be a serious error to mistake the present traditional forms for replicas of the earlier ones they strongly resemble. The lineage chronicle will make that clear.

Case histories of property acquisition and of disputes in the lineage show what issues divide and what alliances bind the local group together today, and what law has to do with it. Many of the disputes and allocations in the M—— lineage invoke tradition to justify a course of action. But these statements must be understood as being made in the midst of a process of change whose manifestations are not always directly translated into precepts of the normative system. What is being said must be understood in terms of what is happening, rather than exclusively in terms of the internal logic of cultural reasoning in which the discourse is carried on.

In 1969 the lineage of the M——s consisted of the households of twenty-nine married men. The eldest was then about seventy-two. Twenty-four of the households resided in the core lineage area. The other five had moved years earlier, four up-mountain and one down-mountain. They maintained intermittent contact with the lineage core. Among the twenty-four households remaining in the core area were dozens of children. Without counting any of the twenty-four married household heads themselves, nor their married sisters, in 1969 there were almost 100 children. By 1979 the count of living offspring was over 110. The population size has reached a point of near crisis. Many of these children, as they become adult leave the mountain.

Between 1969 and 1979, five of the twenty-nine men alive in 1969 died (Kisoka, Mandasha, Lewange, Kiwosi, and Yosia). And one (Lyatonga) moved away from the core lineage lands to a second *kihamba* he owned near Arusha, where he lived with his second wife. Two other men emigrated permanently. But eight newly married men (married between 1969 and 1979) took their places as lineage members (see Figure 8.2). All but one of these young men (Mlatie's son, Simon) have salaried jobs. One works in a dispensary on the mountain, two have a business in Bukoba, another is a mechanic in Moshi, another works for the Tanzanian Tea Authority, two others also work away from the mountain at jobs whose nature I do not know. Thus, though some of the wives of these young men live on Kilimanjaro, the household income does not come solely from the land.

The replacement of dead and departed rural lineage members by a new generation of this kind obviously has transformative implications. To the extent that the new generation is salaried or has cash income other than

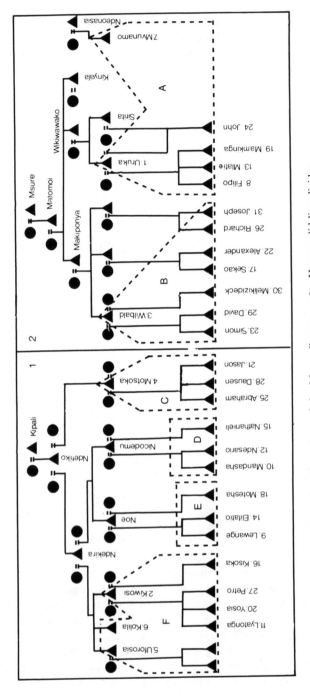

Figure 8.1. Genealogy of the M—— lineage, 1969. Heavy solid line divides cow-slaughtering groups 1 and 2. Broken lines enclose goat-slaughtering groups A–F. Numbers before names indicate order of birth. All unnumbered males are deceased. All numbered males are living adult married men. For reasons of space wives and children are shown only for the senior generation. Paternity disputed for John (24), born to Uruka's wife, who had been Sirita's wife, less than a year after Sirita's death.

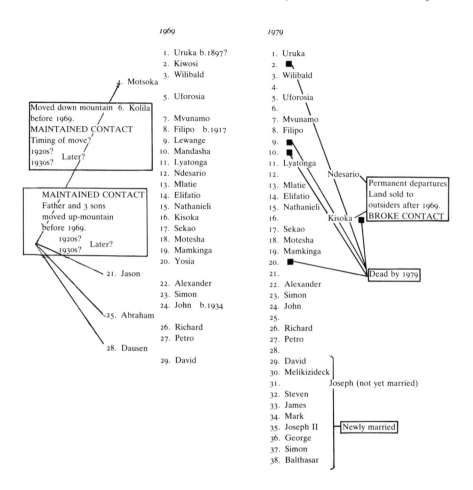

Figure 8.2. Replacement and transformation: married men of the M—— lineage in order of birth, 1969 and 1979. Only married men were full-fledged adult lineage members. Total M—— offspring of men without grandchildren in 1979 (excluding satellite settlements, the descendants of Motsoka and Kolila) numbered 51 male children, 58 female children.

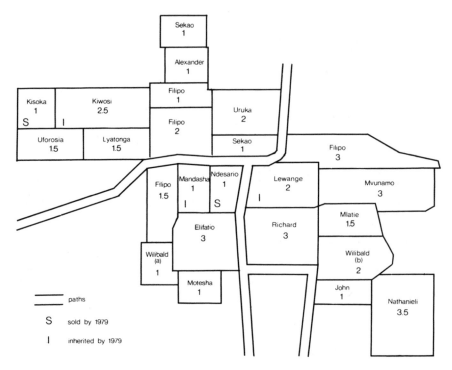

Figure 8.3. Landholdings of the M——s in the core lineage area 1969, and some changes by 1979. Figure is not to scale. Numbers on plots indicate approximate acreage. Of the 29 households counted members of the localized lineage, 5 did not live in the core lineage area. See Figure 8.2. Five adult married males in the lineage did not have separate *vihamba* of their own and resided on their fathers' lands as follows: Mamkinga with Uruka; Yosia and Petro with Kiwosi; David with Wilibald on (a); Simon on Wilibald's second *kihamba* (b).

that derived from coffee, the men are away from the household for work. Consequently the agricultural production becomes increasingly the responsibility of women, supplemented by casual hired male agricultural labor when it can be afforded. The casual laborers are the less fortunate men, usually little educated and unskilled, whose land (or that of their fathers) is insufficient to support them. But some of the men with cash-paying jobs who work in the region, or in Moshi Town itself, manage to get back to their *kihamba* gardens often enough to do the heavy work, and some manage to take a day or two off from time to time when there is work in the *shambas* that requires their attention.

Table 14 shows that in 1969 a change was already evident in the proportion of men who had cash-paying jobs. The table shows that of the men of

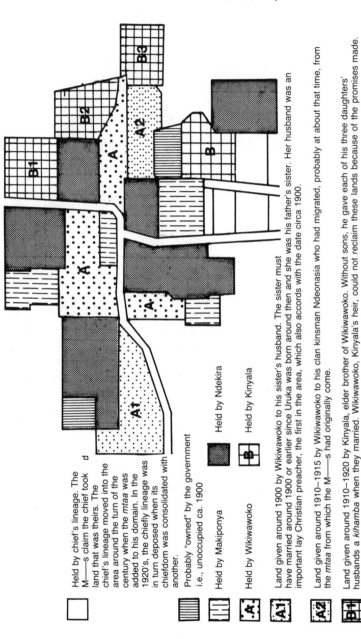

Held by chief's lineage. The M——s claim the chief took land that was theirs. The chief's lineage moved into the area around the turn of the century when the *mtaa* was added to his domain. In the 1920's, the chiefly lineage was in turn deposed when its chiefdom was consolidated with another.

Probably "owned" by the government i.e., unoccupied ca. 1900

Held by Makiponya

Held by Wikiwawoko

Held by Ndekira

Held by Kinyala

Land given around 1900 by Wikiwawoko to his sister's husband. The sister must have married around 1900 or earlier since Uruka was born around then and she was his father's sister. Her husband was an important lay Christian preacher, the first in the area, which also accords with the date circa 1900.

Land given around 1910–1915 by Wikiwawoko to his clan kinsman Ndeonasia who had migrated, probably at about that time, from the *mtaa* from which the M——s had originally come.

Land given around 1910–1920 by Kinyala, elder brother of Wikiwawoko. Without sons, he gave each of his three daughters' husbands a *kihamba* when they married. Wikiwawoko, Kinyala's heir, could not reclaim these lands because of the promises made.

Figure 8.4. Lineage lands of the M——s circa 1900–1920.

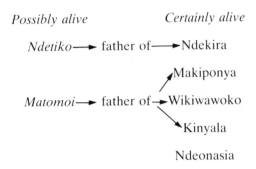

Figure 8.5. The adult married men of the M—— lineage circa 1915. The localized lineage of the M——s in 1915 was less than a quarter of its 1969 size. The increase in the lineage is parallel to the general increase in the population of Kilimanjaro.

the generation 1–15 only two had cash-paying jobs in 1969. In the generation represented by 16–29, there are six, and in fact there may well have been more since the information about the men who did not live in the core area is incomplete. By 1979, the proportion had again changed, and of the eight newly married men only one was a full-time farmer. That last proportion may be distorted because five of those young men were sons of Filipo, the wealthiest man in the lineage. Kilimanjaro still has a large number of men who do not have steady cash-paying jobs, even in the younger generation. Many of these young people drift to the cities in search of work (Temu and Swai 1981:163).

Participation in a cash economy did not change everything. Only three of the wives of the men of the M—— lineage in 1969 had not been circumcised (Table 14, column 4). All the rest (except for two about whom no information was collected) had been circumcised. The three men whose wives were uncircumcised were well-educated men of the younger generation. What is of interest about the prevalence of circumcised married women is that the M——s live in a Protestant area of Vunjo in which the church has discouraged circumcision of women for many years. Female circumcision thus became almost a secret matter. The church has a different view of men. All men are routinely circumcised. Since the circumcision of men is culturally legitimate in the Europeanized world, male circumcision is done in the hospital, usually during late adolescence, or when a man is ready to marry. Because the church and other authorities have frowned on the circumcision of women for decades, female circumcision is done by old women who are specialists in

Table 13. *Amounts of land in 1969 in and out of the core area*

Lineage members in order of birth	Acreage in core lineage lands	Number of plots elsewhere	Size in acres of outside plots
1. Uruka (with Mamkinga)	2		
2. Kiwosi (with Yosia Petro)	2½		
3. Wilibald (with David and Simon)	3	1	2
4. Motsoka			
5. Uforosia	1½		
6. Kolila			
7. Mvunamo	3		
8. Filipo	7½	6	21½
9. Lewange	2		
10. Mandasha	1	2	2
11. Lyatonga	1½	2	3
12. Ndesario	1		
13. Mlatie	1½		
14. Elifatio	3		
15. Nathanieli	3½		
16. Kisoka	1		
17. Sekao	2		
18. Motesha	1	1	3
19. Mamkinga (with Uruka)			
20. Yosia (with Kiwosi)			
21. Jason			
22. Alexander	1		
23. Simon (with Wilibald)			
24. John	1	1	2
25. Abraham			
26. Richard (with unmarried Joseph)	3		
27. Petro (with Kiwosi)			
28. Dausen			
29. David (with Wilibald)			
Total	42	13	33½

Note: The figures given by a lineage member must be taken to be rough estimates. Walks around the relevant plots where possible indicated that the estimates are approximate relative sizes, that is, plausible. No measuring was possible. Underestimates are likely on "outside" plots.

Table 14. *Education, occupation, house type, and circumcision of wives, 1969*

Men in order of seniority	Age	Illiterate	Polygynous	Wife does not speak Swahili[a]	Wife *not* circumcised	School level reached	Cash-paying job[b]	Type of house[c]
1. Uruka	ca.72	X						2
2. Kiwosi		X	X	X				2
3. Wilibald		X	X	X				1 + 2
4. Motsoka		X						2
5. Uforosia		X		X				1
6. Kolila								2
7. Mvunamo						Standard IV		2
8. Filipo	52		X		X	Standard VIII	X	3
9. Lewange			X			Standard IV	X	3
10. Mandasha		X		X				1
11. Lyatonga		X	X	X				2
12. Ndesario		X		X				2
13. Mlatie						Standard IV		2
14. Elifatio						Standard IV		2
15. Nathanieli						Standard VI		2
16. Kisoka[d]						Standard IV		2
17. Sekao[e]		X						2
18. Motesha						Standard IV		1
19. Mamkinga						Standard IV	X	2

No.	Name		Education		House type
20.	Yosia	X	?[g]		2
21.	Jason[f]				2
22.	Alexander		Standard IV		2
23.	Simon		Standard VI	X	2
24.	John	X	Standard X	X	3
25.	Abraham	?	?	X	2
26.	Richard	?	Standard X	X	3
27.	Petro	?	Standard IV		2
28.	Dausen	?	?	?	2
29.	David	X	Standard X	X	2

[a] All men of lineage speak Swahili.

[b] Blank indicates farmer only.

[c] Three types of houses exist on Kilimanjaro: (1) beehive grass house – round; (2) wattle and daub – rectangular, most common type – *banda* (hut); and (3) house of "European style" – cement floor, mud-brick and plaster walls or cinderblock, tin roof. Type 2 predominates.

[d] Occasionally works in *pombe* shop for a pittance.

[e] Occasionally works as a casual laborer, doing farm work on Kilimanjaro.

[f] Had been court clerk, but dismissed for bribery.

[g] Means no information.

the work. Women are thus circumcised under much less sanitary or modern conditions than their male counterparts. How much female circumcision continues in the Protestant areas today is difficult to say, since it has been "underground" for so many decades. An old woman circumciser said in 1969 that there was no dearth of business. But I doubt that there are any new young apprentices in her trade. Circumcision continues in a publicly acknowledged fashion in the Catholic areas where the church has been more tolerant of local custom. But as the operation and the associated festivities are expensive, and as more young girls become more educated and refuse to be operated on, the custom may fade out. It seems plausible that more and more young girls reaching adolescence after 1969 would refuse. But one never knows. A male acquaintance who was a third grade teacher (married to a circumcised woman) told me in 1969 that one of his women colleagues was about to be married, and that he had gone to call on her family and was told that she was in seclusion because of her circumcision. He went on to say, "In the old days this was not such a good thing because it led to infections and troubles. But," said he, "nowadays, we have antibiotics, and so there is no reason not to circumcise." Thus does a knowledge of science serve custom! The new generation may not find such reasoning persuasive.

Circumcision may continue for a while; however there is every indication that polygyny is fading out. In 1969 there were only five polygynous men in the M—— lineage, and they were all of a senior generation. By 1979, none of the previously monogamous men had taken a second wife. Rich, prominent men who are good Christians tend to resort to "serial" polygyny instead. It is possible that monogamy prevails because of the energetic efforts of the Christian church, and the success of the church may have been helped by the land shortage. According to tradition, a man should provide each wife with a *kihamba* for herself and her children. Since that tradition is quite impossible for all but a few men today, there are economic as well as ideological reasons to settle for monogamy. The younger generation of the M——s have obviously done so.

But Chagga traditions continue in domestic life. In most households men and women still do not eat together. A woman eats with her young children and then serves her husband his food separately when he comes home. In some households, when serving him, she routinely takes the first taste to show it is not poisoned. The domain of men and women is largely separate, and friendships are all same-sex friendships. A wife still has the obligation of feeding her children, that is, of raising the food with which they are fed, as well as preparing it. She may sell her surplus produce, and keep the small profit she makes. Such is the arrangement between the husbands and wives in the M—— lineage and in others. A woman can even cut bananas in her husband's *kihamba* and sell them, provided they are not the bananas with which beer is made. Those bananas, *mrarao*, she cannot cut without permission of her husband. Planting bananas is man's work, and it is the husband who decides how many plants and which types to put in.

Both men and women do the work connected with the coffee, but it is the men who get the cash. The money a woman makes at the market is small change compared with the money a man receives from the coffee. There are no big traders among women. Some have small specialties, for instance, selling *magaddi* or tobacco, but their income from these efforts is small, enough to buy beer at the *pombe* shop, not much more.

It is up to a man to decide how much of his cash income he will allocate, when he will do so, and for what purpose. It is his obligation to keep his wife and children clothed, but he is not obliged to give his wife money to spend. He should slaughter an animal when his wife bears a child, and provide blood for the *mlaso*, the blood and butter that she must eat after the birth. He must also provide for his wife's three months of confinement and rest from work that follows the birth of each child. But that period can be arranged quite economically if his mother or sisters-in-law do the work. In 1984 a government official who lives with his wife in Dar es Salaam sent his wife back to his mother on Kilimanjaro for her confinement. "It is our custom," he said.

In the past decade the government has encouraged the women's party organization to go into various businesses that were formerly male monopolies.[17] In the late 1970s in the M—— lineage, the wife of John became the manager of a cooperative shop. The women of two *mitaa* villages put up the capital by buying shares. They collect the profits in proportion to the number of shares they originally bought. John's wife is delighted with this socialist invention, the shareholding company. She has become a person of some importance in her village, and unlike most women can regularly go to Moshi as she must shop for stock. For many decades a few Chagga women have been teachers, but in 1969 none of the wives of the men of the M—— lineage were trained for this kind of work. But by 1979, some of the M——'s daughters had become nurses and teachers. Such is not the lot of most of the wives of the men of the M—— lineage. They remain in rural Kilimanjaro. Most are still cultivating the vegetables and carrying the water that sustains their households. (For the degree of local endogamy among the M——s, see Tables 15 and 16.)

In general, throughout life Chagga women remain the wards of their fathers and husbands. If the father or husband dies, the daughter or widow becomes the ward of the designated positional successor, the heir or *mrithi*. The obligation on the part of the natal lineage to provide emergency protection is lifelong. If the receipt of bridewealth is allocated to a particular brother or other male agnate that brother is the special

Table 15. *The localism of marriage–affinal connections of the M——s in marriage*

Lineage males by seniority	Clan[a]	Wives			Clan[a]	Mothers		
		Same chiefdom	Same *mtaa*	Other chiefdoms (all but 4 adjacent)		Same chiefdom	Same *mtaa*	Other chiefdoms (all but 1 adjacent)
1. Uruka	Soi	X			Ngowi	X	X	
2. Kiwosi	Makundi	X			Matairo[b]			X
	Ngowi							
3. Wilibald	Lyimo			X	Njau			X
	Makundi	X						
4. Motsoka	?			X				
5. Uforosia	Mlai	X	X		Matairo			X
6. Kolila				X	Matairo			X
7. Mvunamo	Makundi	X			Mlai	X	X	
8. Filipo	Moshi			X	Soi	X		
	Mongi			X				
	Mlai-Maanga			X				
	Shirima			X				
	Shirima			X				
9. Lewange	1. ?	X			Mariki	X		
	2. Mbando		X					
10. Mandasha	Lyimo	X			Kawiche	X	X	
11. Lyatonga	Mlai	X			Makundi			X
	Mariki	X						
12. Ndesario	Uiso	X			Kawiche	X	X	
13. Mlatie	Kombe	X			Soi	X		
14. Elifatio	Shao	X			Mariki	X		

No.	Name	Name				Clan			
15.	Nathanieli	Urio	X			Mariki	X	X	
16.	Kisoka	Lekule	X			Ngowi	X		X
17.	Sekao	Nyela	X			Lyimo	X	X	X
18.	Motesha	Moshi			X	Mongi	X		X
19.	Mamkinga	Temu			X	Soi			
20.	Yosia	Mtui			X	Makundi			X
21.	Jason	Shirima	X						
22.	Alexander	Mremi (Matemu)	X			Lyimo	X		
23.	Simon	Lyimo	X			Makundi	X		
24.	John	Ukwai	X		X	Mariki	X	X	
25.	Abraham	Mariki	X		X		X		
26.	Richard	Lyimo	X			Mlai	X	X	
27.	Petro	Chao	X		X	Makundi			X
28.	Dausen	Tarimo	X		X		X		
29.	David	Lyimo	X			Makundi	X		

[a] Some Chagga clans (lineages) have two names, one by which its female members are known and one by which its male members are known. Some of the names are male names and some are female names.
[b] Female name.

Table 16. *The localism of marriage – sisters of the men of the M—— lineage*

Lineage males by seniority	Number of sisters, same mother	Husband from same *mtaa* chiefdom	Husband from different chiefdom	Clan of sister's husband
1. Uruka	o			
2. Kiwosi	1	X		Mlai
3. Wilibald	1	X		Shao
4. Motsoka	o			
5. Uforosia	1	X		Chao
6. Kolilia	o			
7. Mvunamo	o			
8. Filipo	(one dead)	X		Tarimo
9. Lewange	3	X		Mlai
		X		Mghase
10. Mandasha	3 alive		X	Moshi
			X	Mariki
			X	Makundi
11. Lyatonga	1 alive			Towo
12. Ndesario	(same as 10)			
13. Mlatie	(same as 8)			
14. Elifatio	(same as 9)			

No.	Name					Clan
15.	Nathanieli	1 (not married)				Mlai
16.	Kisoka	1	X			Kombe
17.	Sekao	1	X			
18.	Motesha	(same as 9)				Mlai
19.	Mamkinga	(same as 8)				Soi
20.	Yosia	(same as 11)	X	X		Soi
21.	Jason	4	X	X		Mongi
22.	Alexander	(same as 17)				
23.	Simon	1			X	
24.	John	0				
25.	Abraham	(same as 21)		X		Ngomuo
26.	Richard	3		X		Lyimo
27.	Petro	(same as 11)			X	Monyo
28.	Dausen	(same as 21)				
29.	David	(same as 23)				

guardian of the woman and must protect her interests.[18] Guardianship by a woman's own agnates becomes important if she has any serious disputes with her husband or with others. She may run to her father's compound, or her brother's, to take refuge until a settlement is worked out. That right to refuge and protection is often used, as happened in the 1970s in the M—— lineage when Elifatio's sister was accused of witchcraft, and when Filipo's daughter was also so accused. The use of the protection of agnates is by no means a practice confined to the unlettered. Educated women also depend on it.[19]

No women of the M—— lineage or wives of M—— lineage hold any land independent of their husbands. In Chagga law women cannot hold alienable rights in land.[20] A married woman lives in a *kihamba* plot which is her husband's property. Widows have an ongoing inalienable life interest in the land, contingent on occupying it themselves, but problems frequently arise relating to any coffee income the land produces. The heir and guardian may avail himself of the cash, leaving the widow the "subsistence rights." A man who has no sons but has only daughters may choose to bestow land on a son-in-law. He cannot give it to his daughter directly, only to her husband. And he can give freely to a son-in-law only if the land in question is land away from the core lineage area (usually acquired by some means other than inheritance). According to Chagga ideas, land in the core area can be bestowed to nonlineage persons only with the consent of agnates. The formal court system has had other views. In the British colonial period as well as these days a sale can sometimes circumvent the constraints of Chagga custom if the seller is willing to pay the price of being forever ostracized by his agnates.[21] This kind of incident has happened among the M——s.

The domestic unit embedded in its lineage nexus takes its form from the Chagga past. But durable forms do not signify static institutions. To penetrate form and get at the underlying process of transformation it is necessary to look at what happens, at events, not simply at cultural forms. The details of lineage affairs illuminate the playing out of large-scale processes of change, and nested within those, many small-scale ones. The narrative of certain types of events, in this case events of disputation and allocation, reveals the frameworks in which persons conduct their affairs. The discourse on small-scale matters concerns who has a better right, or who has authority, who is morally disreputable, and who is worthy, in a finite universe of interlocked lives. They involve material well-being, personal reputation, and power. Since in reality the "universe" of the lineage neighborhood and village is neither so discrete nor so autonomous as it sometimes conceives itself, it is possible to see through the layer of immediate particulars that deeper layer of larger scale, longer term developments that present the urgent riddles local people must solve immediately with whatever resources they have. Tradition is only one of those resources. The taking on of utterly new ways of doing things has not precluded an invigoration of selected traditional cultural forms. The two transform each other.

In the second edition of *The Judicial Process* Gluckman said, in the spirit of self-criticism, that it would have been better had his data included the events that led up to the court cases he reported, and the incidents that followed, not just what took place in the hearing (1967:372). The lineage chronicle recounted here attempts to provide the kind of contextual detail for which he called. Though a longer, deeper historical setting has already been supplied, the lineage story is intended as more than a simple "case history" parallel in time. The lineage chronicle shows what a finely edited slice of the M——'s story reaches the courts, and raises broad questions about the use of courts and about the place of a system of rules in a changing field of social negotiations. The surface is detail about events in the lives of particular individuals in Africa. The issues are general.

One of the more obvious matters the lineage history illuminates is the relationship between events on the ground and the formal governmental and legal institutions that have purported to control them. The lineage chronicle often shows how little of "what was really going on" came to light in court. Consequently, the court statistics and case reports from the formal system mean both more and less than they say. The lineage chronicle shows the texture of the life that lies behind the court cases that involve litigation between kin. Disputation, allocation, and administration are a small part of the ongoing process of reformation and transformation—sometimes of structure, sometimes of personnel—that the lineage is constantly working on itself. An outsider assessing the sequence of events can see that the lineage of the M——s relentlessly sloughs off some unsuccessful individuals to make room for others. The process of legitimizing the doing of harm in this form, and, indeed, of selecting those who are to fail is connected with the series of disputations and allocations in which kin engage. Let anyone who imagines that life in small-scale kin-based communities today is always more fair, more benign, and less cruel than life in the great impersonal cities of the advanced industrial countries carefully read this chronicle.

9

The chronicle of the M—— Lineage

To preserve anonymity, the names of the individuals have been changed and the particulars of their employment have not been specified, but otherwise the report of matters as they were observed by and/or described to me is exact. In fieldwork inquiry into the affairs of other lineages suggests that the experience of the M——s is far from unique. Some are less prosperous, and some branches of ex-chiefly lineages are better off, but the general character is similar.

LEGAL TRANSACTIONS AND PECCADILLOS OF THE WEALTHIEST MAN IN THE LINEAGE: FILIPO'S STORY

Acquiring free land as an employee of the colonial administration

Filipo is the eldest educated man in the lineage. He retired from a government job in the early 1970s. A vigorous person in his early sixties, he is an important force in local church and village (*mtaa*) politics. He and his wife, his fifth, both have that sleek plumpness of body and face that, among senior Chagga, is usually the mark of wealth. His wife's dresses and her head cloths are always of brilliant colors. They, too, indicate affluence because such an appearance is only possible when the fabric is new or nearly new. Washed and sun-dried clothes soon lose their color and become faded and dull. Not so the clothes of Filipo's wife.

How did Filipo become wealthy? He was a cherished firstborn son of his father. As a boy he was diligent in school. As a young man his reward was a job in the colonial administration. His position as local inspector for a government department obliged him to travel frequently from one part of Kilimanjaro to another. Whenever he saw vacant land that could be had without cost, simply by application to the government, he applied. He acquired three large *vihamba* that way. His job put him in an excellent position to obtain useful information and gave him the influence and skills to make the arrangements. Over the years he also bought three others plots of land. His initial capital came from combining his salary money with his coffee money from the lineage-territory-plot provided by his father. But with every additional plot he bought, he had more income and greater buying power. His many purchased lands are scattered over the mountain and include some *shamba* plots in the lower areas. Since independence one or two of his plots have been confiscated, but he has managed to hold on to the rest. One means of doing so is to place ex-wives, poor relatives, or other landless dependents on the land with the private understanding that they are temporary holders, and that some or all of the coffee money or some of the produce will find its way back to the "owner." This way is not legal, but neither is it unusual, nor regarded as wrong by most Chagga. They see it as a way of maintaining Chagga customs in the presence of an unsympathetic government. Filipo has had five wives. Four are now ex-wives, and each has a separate plot of land which she holds for life — ultimately for her son or sons. Filipo is the only member of the lineage who owns a car, a Volkswagen, a sign of his wealth and importance. He is a key figure in local political organization, a rural socialist leader. As another car-owning Chagga party leader said to me, "You can be a capitalist without property or a socialist with property. It does not matter what you own but what is in your heart."

Acquiring multiple plots in lineage territory: inheritance by a grandson instead of a son, and the reclaiming of "loaned" lands

Filipo's start toward prosperity may have come from his salary and opportunities "on the side" provided by his job. But it was those very means obtained in the modern sector of the economy that eventually enabled him to become the largest traditional landholder in lineage territory (see Fig. 9.1). Through his father Uruka's machinations he reclaimed from "tenants" three *vihamba* plots that had once been his grandfather's. The grandfather, Uruka's father, Wikiwawoko, himself a grandson of the original settlers, once held land that amounted to more than seven present *vihamba* in lineage territory (see Figure 9.1). A long while ago, the grandfather had given each of his two sons (Uruka and Sirita) a grove, and retained a third one for himself. Rather than risk losing the four others to the chief who was in the habit of confiscating desirable unoccupied lands for his own relatives, Uruka's father had "loaned" each of the remaining four *vihamba* to a nonkinsman under the usual condition that they pay him *masiro*, an annual payment of beer. Under Chagga rules the original holder (or his heirs) could reclaim land loaned for *masiro* at any time (from the borrower or his heirs), at will, provided he compensated the possessor for any improvements the possessor might have made.[1] Such relationships

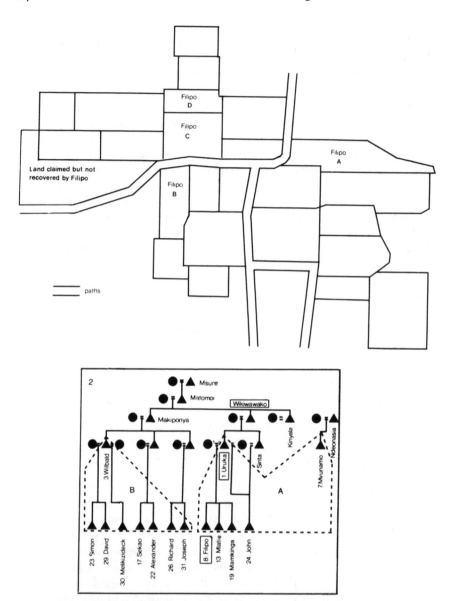

Figure 9.1. Lineage plots of the M——s showing Filipo's land in the core area (A,B,C,D), and Filipo's branch of the lineage showing Filipo, his father Uruka, and his grandfather Wikiwawoko. The paternity of John (24) was disputed. He was born to Uruka's wife, who had been Sirita's wife, less than a year after Sirita's death.

were hereditary and the heir of the original holder had the same relationship with the heir of the original possessor that their fathers had had.

During his lifetime the grandfather did not reclaim the land he had
loaned. After the grandfather's death, Filipo went to live with his widowed
grandmother "to look after her." The implication was that he would inherit her plot when she died as he was to be designated his grandfather's
heir (*mrithi*). It is a Chagga rule that a grandson may be substituted in this
way for a son, if the son already has a *kihamba* and prefers this arrangement. The firstborn son of the firstborn son is the ideal grandson for this
role. In fact, Filipo was the firstborn son of the *second-born* son.[2] Uruka,
Filipo's father, could have been named heir himself but he had no money
to pay compensation for the improvements on the land. Uruka had sent
Filipo to live with his mother and become heir because he knew that as a
salaried person Filipo might soon have the necessary funds.

The grandmother died around 1948, and Filipo not only inherited her
plot but did try to reclaim the four plots that his grandfather, Wikiwawoko, had loaned, offering to compensate the occupiers for their bananas,
coffee trees, and houses. They refused to leave. The case was argued
before members of the localized lineage and members of the lineages of
the occupiers and neighbors and was later reargued before the chief.
Three of the possessors, men from Rombo, eventually acknowledged that
they had no legal right to remain in occupancy, but argued that they were
being offered insufficient compensation. That matter was resolved, and
they left. The fourth argued that he could not be ousted because a commitment had been made when he was installed that he would be given
permanent possession. He was married to a sister of Wikiwawoko (see
Figure 8.4, page 231). Uruka testified for this affine against his son Filipo, and attested to the original agreement. The affine was allowed to
stay. Filipo thus acquired only three of those *vihamba,* plus, of course,
the one he had had from his grandmother. That made him the largest
landholder in lineage territory, holding what was locally estimated to be
about $7\frac{1}{2}$ acres. By 1968 he also had the largest acreage outside of lineage
territory, amounting to about $22\frac{1}{2}$ acres more, thirty all told (see Table 13,
page 233). He continues to try relentlessly to acquire any lineage land
that might be for sale. Thus he approached his relatives Kisoka and
Ndesario when they sold their lands. (See the case histories in this
chapter in the section "The Sale of Land in the Core Territory of a
Lineage to an Outsider, a Nonkinsman.")

The employment of paid labor and the use of kinsmen's services

In addition to his five wives (four divorced) who work in the gardens and
shambas that Filipo has allocated to them, Filipo employs six day laborers

to work his other lineage lands. Three are men who have their own *vihamba,* but need extra cash, and three are men who live with their fathers and have no land of their own. Filipo probably has made similar arrangements for some of his distant nonlineage plots, though now most are actually occupied. When the present government confiscated certain unoccupied lands, Filipo lost one of his lowland *shambas.* He then took measures to prevent any repetition. For example, he put a destitute middle-aged woman in one of his plots officially "giving" her the land. But he is not really giving it away. He adopted her two daughters so that he would eventually receive their bridewealth. As she has no sons, his plan is that the land will revert to his own sons when the widow dies. The government is none the wiser. The management of such quasi-tenants, his day-laborer employees, and the supervision of his wives and children is now Filipo's responsibility. But when he was still away working, his half-brother, John, looked after these matters for him not only in an economic sense but in a personal sense, seeing to the well-being of the dependents.[3] No formal accounts between Filipo and John were kept, nor did John get paid in any direct way for looking after Filipo's affairs. The assumption was that the favor would be returned in some unspecified manner when John might need Filipo's help. But more salient was the matter of seniority and Filipo's authoritative position in the kinship nexus.

Filipo's five marriages, four divorces, and children: his reallocations of land among his sons

Filipo is a Christian, hence he is said to have enjoyed his five wives seriatim. One of the reasons he has been so diligent about acquiring land is that he wants to be sure to have some to give to each of his sons, and he has quite a number. He has nineteen legitimate children, nine daughters and ten sons. He also acknowledges one "illegitimate" daughter in the neighborhood. In this century only chiefs regularly had wives and children in these numbers. Filipo has set himself up in the image of a chief, while accommodating the requirements of Christian monogamy. His state of bountiful paternity is much envied. When I asked his half-brother, John, how he, John, would manage to provide land for his own sons, and whether he had ever considered "family planning," as it is discreetly called, he answered, "why should I have a few children when my brother has as many as he wants?" John's wife had other ideas. Family planning came to Kilimanjaro in the 1970s. After five children, she stopped her annual production, spacing the sixth child some years later.

Filipo has already allocated specific plots to six of his sons. Sons cannot take possession of such lands until they marry, but lands can be allocated in advance. Filipo has indicated who is to receive the four *vihamba* he holds in lineage territory. He is keeping B and C (Figure 9.1) for himself and his fifth wife and their sons. The allocation is a characteristic traditional one, favoring the last, or "favorite," wife and her offspring, rather than being evenhanded. But the practice is not embodied in any rule. Quite the contrary, it is treated as an individual modification. He has subdivided *Kihamba* D (Figure 9.1), which is the plot he originally obtained from his grandmother and in which he originally lived with his first wife, between two of the three sons of his first wife. He allotted half to Steven, the firstborn son, and half to Joseph, the last-born son. (They are numbers 32 and 35, Figure 8.2 page 229.) To Mark, the middle son of that marriage, he has given a *kihamba* in another *mtaa* (parish) which he acquired by purchase (Figure 8.2, number 34). He explains that "according to the *mila* of the *Wachagga*" a middle son has no rights in his mother's *kihamba*. Filipo's arrangement is a modern transformation of the notion that a middle son should cultivate bush and pioneer new lands. Filipo himself actually is providing a developed *kihamba* for his middle son, but as it is not in lineage territory and as it is land he acquired through means other than inheritance he sees what he is doing as the modern counterpart of the old rule.

Kihamba A is allocated to his son George as only son of his second wife, who occupied the *kihamba* (Figures 8.2 and 9.1, number 36). *Kihamba* C is not such a straightforward story. *Kihamba* C was once the land of his third wife, and as such should have become the inheritance of her only son, Simon. But when Filipo decided to terminate that marriage, he sent her to occupy a distant plot he had bought in the next *mtaa,* up-mountain. He wanted to get her and her son out of lineage territory. Her new plot had coffee, but few bananas, being at a colder altitude, so she was permitted to continue to cut bananas in her old *kihamba* when she needed them. However, the understanding was that she was not to live there and that her son would not inherit that piece of land. This withdrawal of land from a married woman whose son was born there is certainly not congruent with traditional values, neither those cited by the Chagga today, nor those indicated by Gutmann. But adjustments have no doubt always been made, particularly by powerful men. The tripartite division of rights — banana rights, coffee rights, residence rights — appears in other contexts as well. The way Filipo made this reallocation and sought to make it legally binding, and the way he divided *kihamba* D on the same occasion is of procedural interest. In 1968 Filipo made these arrangements simply by announcing them at the site before seventeen witnesses.[4] He instructed one of his kinsmen to make a written record afterward. But the witnesses to the oral statement and to the public placement of boundary plants were the key components of legitimation. The writing was plainly secondary. The arrangements were entirely pro-

spective. None of the young sons involved was of a marriageable age at
the time.

The families that make up a localized lineage cluster must each make
painful choices. Certain sons can be kept on the inherited lands. The
number of sons who can be accommodated in the subdivided *vihamba* of
the lineage cluster depends on the landholdings outside of lineage territory and the number of salaried jobs among them. But some have to
leave. For some Chagga fathers the traditional normative preference for
first and last sons in the transfer of property between the generations has
provided an easy rule of thumb by which to select which son shall stay
and which must go (an illustration of this is Filipo's allocation to the three
sons of his first wife, placing the middle son on land away from the
lineage cluster). As in the "stem family" described by Berkner, or the
strategies of heirship examined by Goody, heirs are necessary for each
family in the lineage cluster to hold its own but too many heirs can be a
disaster (Goody 1973; Berkner 1976). The Chagga rule giving property to
first and last accommodates a double heirship, but no more. Among the
families that make up the localized lineage is an underlying competition
about which family will be able to place more of its sons in the local
territory and which will have to scatter its sons. Within large polygynous
families is the question which set of sons will be preferred. The answer
can depend on several factors, including the preference a husband may
have for a particular wife, and, in some degree, how influential a dis-
carded wife's father and brothers are in the community. They may be
able to protect her interests, and indirectly the interests of her sons by
defending her right to property allocated at the time of marriage, should
her husband try to reassign such property to a new wife. But if she is out
of favor and/or her kinsmen have no influence, contrary to the normative
rules her husband may take highhanded action and dispossess her, and
move her to a plot away from lineage territory (an instance of this was the
relocation of Filipo's third wife from *kihamba* C, Figure 9.1).

The internal structure of the lineage is affected by the place the salaried
men occupy in the external world. Because they have access to additional
cash (over and above the coffee money) they have been able to buy land
away from lineage territory, to redeem land once loaned by ancestors (by
compensating the occupiers for improvements), and to make cash loans
and cash offers to kinsmen who may want to sell property.[5] They also
tend to be the men who are prominent in local village politics, since they
have the education, the cash, and the contacts to compete.

The happy fate of Filipo is the chronicle of a good Christian, pillar of
the church in which he holds lay office, who has provided for his five
wives and nineteen children. As the eldest son of the most senior man in
the localized lineage of the M——s, provided he lives long enough, he

will succeed his father, and will be the dominant figure of his generation in his lineage. After 1976 he once again redoubled the joists in the system that supports his prestige by becoming an active unpaid committee officer in the new cooperative village formed by his *mtaa*.

At the time of the reallocation of *kihamba* D, in 1968, Filipo simply stated that he was dividing *kihamba* D to give the two halves to Steven and Joseph (first and last sons of his first wife), and that he was giving C to Balthasar (firstborn of his fifth wife), and that he, Filipo, and his fifth wife would be building on and moving into *kihamba* B. His third wife objected, since C had once been her *kihamba* and her son was born there. She was not shy about speaking up for herself. In fact that very year she had been fined for insulting one of her neighbors when they were both drinking at the *pombe* shop. But on the occasion of the land allocation it was useless to argue, and she left. Then Filipo asked Mlatie to place the boundary plants where he had indicated the dividing line should be between the shares of Steven and Joseph. Mlatie, assisted by his son, planted the dracaena (*masale*) and then the group disbanded. Filipo often says that his sons need not worry, that each will have enough land, because he has so many *vihamba* to give them. But he was plainly making arrangements about which son would have which portion fairly early in the game. Son Balthasar was only nine when the transfer of C to him took place. In 1980 he was married and his right to that land has so far not been challenged. Similarly, though Steven and Joseph were older than Balthasar, neither was married when the allocation took place. The precipitating cause of all of these rearrangements was that Filipo and his fifth wife wanted to start to build a bigger and more lavish house on *kihamba* B. They had been living in a small modern house on D, but wanted something bigger for their myriad children, as it was coming to be time to segregate the older boys from the girls and babies in the sleeping arrangements. In precolonial times a separate hut would have been constructed for the boys and the father would have had one of his own. But today, the well-to-do try to provide a separate room in the house for these needs instead. Therefore at some point in the family cycle, the father is under pressure to build more space.

Banana rights and banana thefts

When a *kihamba* is unoccupied, its crops present an opportunity for theft. Since Filipo's third wife had been given continuing banana rights in *kihamba* C after the divorce yet lived in a *kihamba* a considerable distance away, there were security problems. On several occasions in 1968 she noticed that bananas had been taken. She asked Filipo's kin living nearby if they would watch for the thieves. One of these vigilant neighbors was the daughter of Mandasha, a lineage kinsman of Filipo, who lived in an adjacent *kihamba*.

One day that year Mandasha's daughter saw Elifatio's daughter cutting down a bunch of bananas. She went straight to Filipo's house to tattle. Filipo, of course, was not there. (Filipo was working for the government and was away much of that year.) His fifth wife was at home, and Mandasha's daughter told her about the theft of bananas. The fifth wife then reported the matter to Uruka, the father of Filipo, and senior man of that lineage branch. He, in turn, told the third wife about the theft when she came down-mountain that day to cut bananas for her own household. The third wife went to the leader of Filipo's ten-house cell (the *balozi*), and complained to him. Then the ten-house cell leader assembled a few M—— lineage kinspersons (Lyatonga, Mvunamo, Uruka, and the daughter of Mandasha) for a palaver. Together they went first to the *kihamba* where the bananas had been cut and then to the house of Elifatio. A search party looking for stolen goods in the house of a suspect is not an unusual Chagga procedure. Elifatio asked his daughter whether she had taken the banana clump. She denied having stolen anything. However, the cell leader and his party compared the stem of the banana plant from which a bunch had been cut with the stem of a bunch found in the house of Elifatio, and they found they matched and that both were bananas of a kind called *mchare*. Elifatio's household could provide no adequate explanation of how the bananas had been acquired. The search party was then satisfied that these bananas had indeed been stolen from the *kihamba* as reported by the daughter of Mandasha.

At the later palaver the third wife complained that many bunches of bananas had been stolen from her *kihamba* and said she was sure they had all been taken by Elifatio's family. Elifatio said that he knew nothing about the whole thing, that it was evidently a quarrel between young children and that it was none of his business. Elifatio's wife said her daughter had not brought any bananas home and that everything that was being said about her daughter was a lie. However the assembled M—— lineage kinsmen decided that the daughter had indeed stolen the bananas. Elifatio was held responsible for his daughter's thefts even if he did not know about them since he and his wife should have questioned their daughter about where she had obtained the bananas. Elifatio was initially fined one cow and one goat plus a tin of *pombe*, altogether a heavy fine. But they reduced the fine to one goat on condition that Filipo would agree to the reduction when he came back on leave from his job. Present at this hearing were the third wife, Uruka, Mvunamo, Lyatonga, Elifatio and his wife, Mandasha and his wife and daughter, John, the ten-house cell leader, and an unrelated male neighbor.

When Filipo came home on leave Uruka, his father, told him about the case against the daughter of Elifatio. Filipo called Elifatio to come to see him and warned him that he was angry. He said he had known for a long time that Elifatio was a person of bad character and had been in the habit of stealing banana stems and leaves from this *kihamba* to feed his animals. Wilibald had caught Elifatio cutting some banana leaves from the same *kihamba* and Filipo called Wilibald to attest to this fact and made Elifatio admit that he himself had been taking things from the *kihamba*. Elifatio admitted everything and then Filipo warned him that it was the last time he would get away with a settlement at home, that the next time a complaint would be made against him in the court.

Illegal transactions in ivory: righteous Filipo is caught in criminal activity

After independence, the government made efforts to assign some officials outside their home districts in order to break up the high degree of localism/tribalism that had developed in some areas. As a result, in 1965 Filipo was sent to work away from Kilimanjaro. As the years passed, he proved as ingenious at finding ways of earning money "on the side" in his new post as he had been in his old. He became involved in the illegal traffic in ivory. In 1969 someone must have betrayed him, as his rooms (in the district where he worked) were searched. Two tusks were found and he was arrested. A trial was scheduled. Had all gone as the prosecution expected, he might have found himself in jail for period of time and might have lost his pension. The stakes were high. Filipo called one of his agnates to help him. What eventually happened was that some men were paid to break into the room where the court stored its exhibits at night, and they stole the tusks. It was risky, but it worked. The criminal case against Filipo was dropped for "lack of evidence." There may well have been more to the story, perhaps an "influenced" court. I do not know. But that the case was dropped after Filipo arranged to have the tusks vanish is as much as I was able safely to discover. These events did not damage Filipo's reputation at home. Filipo remains a model of civic respectability and local prominence. It is not clear how many people know about Filipo's brush with the criminal courts. But even if many do, it might not make any difference. The general feeling is that important people are bound to have enemies, and hence run into trouble from time to time. As Petro Itosi Marealle (who did not know of the M——s or their affairs) once said to me about another matter involving tangles with government officials in the 1970s, "There is no matter of importance without there also being problems."

The limits of obligatory generosity

Must a kinsman with a car transport sick agnates on demand?

Since Filipo is the only member of the M—— lineage who owns a car he is often asked to use it for the benefit of his relatives. It is a battered, rather ancient, but brave VW beetle. In 1973 Richard (26, Figures 8.1, 8.2, and 8.3), his second cousin, felt very ill one evening at a time after the buses had stopped running. (They stop in mid- to late afternoon.) He sent Mamkinga, Filipo's youngest brother, to ask Filipo to drive him to the hospital. Filipo refused saying he did not have time and that his car was not in good condition. A neighbor who had a car was pressed into service.

A "case" was made of Filipo's refusal. Mamkinga (who as youngest son lived in the *kihamba* of Uruka, their father) asked Uruka to call a lineage meeting the next Sunday. Uruka thought it a serious enough matter to assemble Richard (26), Wilibald (3), Wilibald's son David (29), and his (Uruka's) sons Mamkinga (19), Mlatie (13), and John (24). (See Figures 8.2 and 8.3. Numbers signify order of birth.) Uruka then sent for Filipo. Filipo said he was on his way to church, had no time to discuss the matter, and refused to come. It is commonplace to hold hearings on Sundays since that is the day most men are available for a palaver, including those with salaried jobs. Filipo could not be effectively accused in absentia, so they resolved to try to meet with him on some other occasion. I do not know what ultimately came of this matter, probably nothing, but it shows what can happen when tradition is invoked to compel a wealthy agnate to be helpful and generous to less wealthy kinsmen, who are not likely to be able to reciprocate directly in kind. The wealthy feel exploited and indignant when faced with their eternally importunate agnates, and are not above taunting them for their failures in reciprocity.

The meat-sharing obligations and modern troubles

One manifestation of tensions between kinsmen is competition and "cheating" in matters of generosity and reciprocity in distributions of meat. Filipo has had a long history of minor contentions of this kind with his brother Mlatie (13). Mlatie, being a middle son, is in an unfavorable structural position. The misfortune of birth order is compounded by the fact that he has had little education (to Standard IV) and that his elder and younger brothers have had salaried jobs for years, whereas he has had no job for the past dozen years or more, and when he worked before that, it was as a laborer. One of the things Filipo publicly grumbled about was that over the years Mlatie had sold some of his small stock (sheep and goats) for profit rather than having shared them with his father and brothers at lineage slaughtering feasts, as, strictly speaking, in the old system of lineage values he ought to have done. Mlatie had overstepped the bounds on one occasion that year when he persuaded an elderly neighbor, a man who was close to his father, Uruka, to sell him a sheep at a bargain price, by giving him to understand that he was buying it on behalf of his father for ritual purposes. Uruka was the neighbor's *mkara,* the trustee-sponsor of his marriage. The neighbor sold the sheep to Mlatie, only to find later that Mlatie had immediately resold it at a higher price to someone he had met casually. The neighbor and the agnates of Mlatie were outraged by this deception and commercialism. To teach Mlatie a lesson, on one occasion Filipo slaughtered three goats for the minimal lineage and did not invite Mlatie. This action was a serious affront. Mlatie was furious. He retaliated in a way he could scarcely afford. He slaughtered a goat and invited everyone except Filipo.

The irritation continued. In July 1969, Mvunamo, a relative attached to their goat-slaughtering group, slaughtered a sheep because his sons were home from secondary school, and he invited Uruka and the sons of Filipo. A Chagga sheep is a small animal, no bigger than a small dog, and this celebration was for a modern occasion, a school holiday, and seems to have involved unmarried young men, all of it modern in ambiance. Mvunamo did not call John, nor did he call Mlatie. However, he sent some of his share of meat (the part he took home) to the house of John and to others, omitting Mlatie. Mlatie sent his son to complain to Uruka. The son said, "We belong to the slaughtering group of Mvunamo. Why were we not called?" Uruka said, "The sheep was not mine. The blame is Mvunamo's," and he gave the boy a portion of his own share of meat to take home. The next day Mvunamo also sent some meat to Mlatie to try to repair matters. Uruka also busied himself with trying to reconcile Filipo and Mlatie. Eventually a temporary peace was made between them and once again they both attended the slaughtering feasts of their minimal lineage when each was host as well as at other usual times. (See note 1, Chapter 9, for another instance in which Mlatie tried to cut corners to improve his economic position and lost).

This set of disputes shows the difficulties that arise in a situation in which the traditional norms of equal exchange and meat sharing are invoked, but for modern reasons the burdens fall unequally on the wealthy and the poor. The problem is met in various ways. Some argue that provided some meat is *sent* to all the men of the minimal lineage entitled to a share, some freedom exists now about who is *present* at a minor slaughtering feast.

The inequality in beasts and fights over meat distributions seem not to be new. Gutmann indicated that substantial disparities in cattle wealth existed in precolonial times and that even then fairness in the distribution of meat was a test of worthiness as a lineage leader. In precolonial times, too, cattle had an exchange value measurable in goats or iron or ivory. Certainly Chagga men used animals in transactions as far back as detailed knowledge extends. But nowadays, the Chagga say that for any sale of an animal to be justified there must be some urgent and unusual family need for cash. It cannot be simply for profit. Thus a man who is ill and sells a beast to pay the diviner-healer (*mganga*) or to pay hospital fees is excused for doing so. Money used to meet school fees is also regarded as justified. Similarly, the sale of a goat or bullock is legitimate if it is to pay for the care of a woman during the obligatory three months' confinement after her delivery of a child. But without such a "special reason" the sale of an animal is frowned on. It should be kept for feasting. So in 1969, when John's baby boy was born and he needed two beasts to slaughter to give his wife meat and blood, John bought one goat in the Keni-Mriti-Mengwe market, and Uruka provided another goat bought from Mvunamo (7). Uruka and his sons came to the slaughtering feast. Mvunamo as a member of that minimal lineage ought to have been there as well. But John explained his absence by saying that Mvunamo might have stayed away because it was his goat Uruka had bought for slaughtering, and he might have felt "ashamed" to receive a share of the meat because he had *sold* it to him.

Financial relations between father and son

Traditional paternal "liens" on the assets of adult sons (not rights, claims supported by lineage authority) are not so easily translated to the cash economy as fathers would like. In 1974 Uruka asked his son Filipo for some cash, and Filipo refused, saying he could not spare any as he was building a new house. Uruka is not only the most senior man in his own minimal lineage, he is the most senior man in the whole localized lineage. He is thus a figure of respect. In his own branch, he is a powerful intermediary with the deceased ancestors of his lineage subsegment when illness or misfortune afflicts one of its members. Nowadays ancestors more remote than the well-remembered deceased are seldom considered responsible for present events. Therefore Uruka, though he is unquestionably ritual head of his minimal lineage segment, does not, as far as I know, normally act as general ritual intermediary for the whole of the localized group, except perhaps in pro-forma matters such as libations of beer. This observation seems to represent a change from Gutmann's time when the localized group as a whole was described as having both a ritual leader and a temporal leader. Collective ritual dealings with the dead may have become less visible and ultimately less actual partly because the church discouraged aspects of these practices. But such ritual manifestations of collective interests may have disappeared for structural reasons. Smaller segments of the localized lineage grew in relative importance as whatever corporateness the localized group as a whole once had gradually dissolved. The limited effectiveness of the lineage-as-a-whole in the public arena is one factor that weakens Uruka's prestige as senior kinsman of the M——s. Another is that he is illiterate and most of his sons are not. He went to adult literacy classes during a campaign to improve rural literacy but the effects of the class on him were limited. He is thus at a disadvantage in dealing with the modern world in comparison with his sons. But he seldom has to do so. Like a number of other old men, he entrusts his coffee cash to his eldest son, Filipo, for fear of being robbed if he kept it himself in his own house. And then, when he needs money, he asks his son for it. When that money runs out, Filipo occasionally gives him some cash out of his own pocket.

The relationship between Uruka and his son, Filipo, can be read in two ways: Uruka as senior, as spiritually powerful, a man whose displeasure may cause misfortune or death, as a figure of respect and authority, as a man whose consent and testimony are weighty, as a man who is a close friend of important unrelated senior men of his generation in the village, or Uruka as the poor, illiterate farmer, father of a wealthy modern man. Both are ingredients in their relationship. Filipo's refusal to give his father extra cash brings out Uruka's dependence on Filipo. But years ago when Uruka testified to the effect that a piece of land Filipo wanted to redeem from a neighbor could not be redeemed because of the conditions under which it was originally given, Uruka showed his secular power as a lineage authority. As a father he is also assumed to possess certain invisible powers over the well-being of his sons and the conduct of their affairs. His own contentions with other men could affect his offspring. In another village, in another lineage not unlike this one, the recent death of a "modern" son in a car accident was attributed by well-educated people to the troubles between his old father and another man over a long-standing land dispute. The situation is mixed. It would be a misreading to assume that Filipo, despite his education and his cash, *always* has the upper hand in the relationship with his father. But elements that undermine paternal authority are certainly visible.

SORCERY, PERJURY, AND WIFE-BEATING

Some economic and structural aspects of accusations of sorcery

Accusations of sorcery are not random and whimsical, but tend to attach to recurrent relationships and situations. In Chagga ideology, having a male heir is essential to a man to maintain his line. A father should be remembered in libations and other ritual acts. A son is the appropriate person to perform these acts of communication and remembrance. A deceased father's power to intervene in the affairs of living descendants is regularly acknowledged. Consequently, in order for a man to have an effective after-life that has this-worldly consequences his wife must bear him a son. If she does not, he may have reason to look to his jealous brothers' wives for the cause. His wife is also motivated to seek the cause, perhaps even more so since her marriage may depend on it.

In these monogamous days, a woman who bears no sons runs the risk of being replaced by another wife. She consequently has strong reasons to have a son to protect her married status and her own conditional life interest in a particular house and *kihamba*. The condition under which she holds house, land, and other property is that the marriage endure. Thus if she is childless some years after marrying or has only daughters, she may begin "suspecting," that is, covertly or overtly accusing one or another sister-in-law in order to fend off the possibility of being sent away. Such sisters-in-law might, in order to enrich their own sons, desire a husband's brother's wife be sterile, or to bear only daughters. If the husband has several brothers and is himself either eldest or youngest, the most obvious candidate for an accusation of sorcery by his wife is a middle brother's wife since a middle son and his own sons are least favored in inheritance and succession by the norms of Chagga law. But any sister-in-law might be accused if there were other contributing factors.

Thus the idea that sorcery might be the cause of sterility or of the sickness or death of children (or adults) remains part of Chagga thought. Suspicions and accusations of this kind figure as part of everyday life. They blight the relationships of particular individuals, often permanently. They affect the micropolitics of the localized lineage and neighborhood. They also figure in the appeals made by individuals to the churches and courts and occasionally to officials. Frequently the individuals involved in sorcery accusations must go on living cheek by jowl in contiguous gardens for life. An injury of the kind that engenders an accusation or that is sustained because of an accusation is remembered long after the cause of the initial episode is removed. Such antagonisms are a continuing element of strain in ongoing local social life. Latent hostilities of this sort are easily reactivated when anything goes wrong either in the economic or in the personal sphere of either party. The early history of relations between individuals thus becomes an important factor in their subsequent interpretation of events in their own lives or those of their children. Structural factors (such as being a middle son or the wife of a middle son) probably predispose certain persons to being vulnerable to the initial accusation of causing misfortune. But once the injurious allegation has been made, relations on both sides often harden into a permanent attitude of mutual suspicion. The particular structural/economic/personal elements that initiated the bad feeling need not have any continuing existence for the bad relations to go on. The interpersonal hostilities have a psychological momentum of their own. Thus land shortage and structural organization greatly exacerbate the general state of competitiveness between brothers (and their wives), and specific and immediate economic causes are by no means always definable as the detonators of specific episodes of dispute. Any incident of misfortune or irritation will do, once a history of mutual hostilities has commenced. Unless there is a better candidate for blame, an old enemy serves.

Another aspect is the way the problem reflects the place of wives in lineage affairs, as extensions of their husband's interests. The women may accuse one another of sorcery or witchcraft, but it is the men who convene the witch-finding rituals and who may carry the dispute into a more public province. A dispute in Chagga lineage life may easily draw outside agencies into its contentions. Thus witchcraft has been a concern of the church as well as of the state. A person accused of witchcraft by relatives who consulted a diviner (*mganga*) in their hour of trouble may choose to turn to the church for help, accusing the accusers of traffic with the devil. Whether the church imposes penalties on the initial accusers may depend on the complainant's standing in the church and capacity to mobilize witnesses. Sometimes instead the pastors or priests exhort and penalize the sorcerer/sorceress or witch.

An alternative for parties who have been accused of dealing with illicit and occult powers is to go to the local primary court to sue for "the washing of one's name," a Chagga version of a suit for slander. Another strategy has been to become a complaining witness in a criminal case. Since the exorcism of sorcery often involves a conditional threat to kill if the sorcery does not cease, the alleged crime can be the "threat to kill." Trials in the courts for witchcraft have been prohibited since the beginning of the colonial period. Hence cases involving witchcraft have had to be dealt with either in other tribunals or in other forms. In the case to be discussed of Mlatie and Mamkinga most of the affair was handled "at home." Mlatie never went further "outside" than to lodge a complaint with the pastor, but hostilities that began twenty-five years ago are still festering.

A case of sterility leads to accusations of sorcery, conditional oaths, and divination

In the late 1950s Mamkinga, the youngest of Filipo's full brothers, had been married for about four years and his wife had not had a child.

Mamkinga suspected the wives of his two elder married brothers (Filipo and Mlatie) for if Mamkinga's wife were sterile, the *kihamba* of their father Uruka on which Mamkinga lived (as youngest son) might ultimately be inherited by one of these brothers (see Figure 9.2). Angry and indignant, Mamkinga went to his father Uruka to ask him to do something to end the bewitchment.

Uruka knew what to do. He obtained a black goat and called his family together, including the three wives of his three married sons, and some of their children. His son Mlatie was away, working in Rombo, but the other sons were there, Filipo, Mamkinga, and John (their unmarried younger half-brother). Uruka killed the goat in his *kihamba* in the presence of this little group, and collected some of its blood in a cup. He offered the blood cup to each of the women and demanded that they drink a draught. They were to swear before they partook that should they be using witchcraft substance or sorcery materials the blood they were drinking would kill them. (Gutmann mentions a similar test for adultery: 1926:223; HRAF:197.)

When word reached Mlatie that such a ceremony had occurred and that his wife was suspected of sorcery, he came back from Rombo where he was working, and stormed over to Uruka's house to ask him what he meant by such a thing. Uruka said he did not particularly suspect Mlatie's wife, but was testing all the women. Mlatie knew very well this was an excuse, that really his own wife was the principal suspect.

And so it turned out. When Mamkinga's wife continued to be sterile, Mamkinga and his father, Uruka, arranged to have a *mganga* come, a diviner/healer from Upare, who would know how to detect the source of the trouble. After he arrived, he dressed in skins and a strange headdress, and unpacked the bones and claws of animals kept in a calabash that were the tools of his trade. Uruka and Mamkinga slaughtered a goat and asked the *mganga* for his counsel. The diviner said that the wife of Mlatie was indeed the one using sorcery, and that Mamkinga's wife could stop the evil that was making her sterile by obtaining and burning all the clothes of Mlatie's wife. At the next opportunity, when Mlatie's wife was away for the day, having gone down-mountain to work in her *shamba*, Mamkinga's wife followed the *mganga*'s instructions. She went to Mlatie's wife's house, took the bundle of her clothes, and burned them on the spot, a potentially life-threatening act against Mlatie's wife.

When Mlatie's wife found her burned clothes, she sent for her husband, asking him to come back as soon as possible from his place of work in Rombo. He returned a few days later. Then, they, in turn, consulted a *mganga*, to discover who had burned the clothes. The diviner took a bit of soil from their doorway and said, "I will do some magic so that the person who burned the clothes will come forward and tell the reason why." His magic was a threat, a means of killing the culprit if he or she did not come

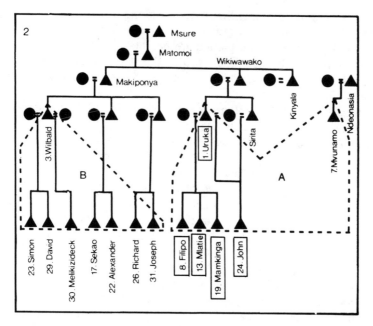

Figure 9.2. Branch of lineage showing Uruka and his sons. The paternity of John (24) was disputed. He was born to Uruka's wife, who has been Sirita's wife, less than a year after Sirita's death.

forward. Needless to say, Mlatie's saw to it that his father, Uruka, heard about the *mganga* and the conditional threat. Uruka, believing that Mamkinga's wife was in danger, counseled her to confess, and ask to be forgiven. She did, and Mlatie responded by telling the wife of Mamkinga that if she wanted to be pardoned, she would have to send a "goat of forgiveness," or else she would die. Such a goat is sent with a necklace of *sale* (dracaena), the same plant that is used to mark the boundaries of *vihamba,* and to mark the graves of the dead. Uruka supplied his daughter-in-law with the necessary goat, whereupon Mlatie increased his demands. He said that the goat earned her their forgiveness, but that the clothes would have to be paid for nonetheless. Mamkinga then paid compensation for the burned clothes. The episode between the two families was thus shifted from its acute, death-threatening phase to a more peaceful state of suspended hostilities, which would continue indefinitely.

A complaint to the pastor and the role of the church in family disputes

Mlatie wanted to punish his father for aiding and abetting Mamkinga's wife in her accusations against his own wife. He went to his father and said, "I am going to report that blood drinking to the pastors." He knew that the report would get his father into trouble in the church, and indeed it did. Mlatie tattled to an immediate neighbor who was a church elder. The elder in turn brought the word to the pastor who called Uruka in, and held a palaver to see what should be done about this un-Christian activity.

Pastors in the Protestant areas and priests in the Catholic ones frequently hold hearings of many kinds. They not only hear accusations of violations of church rules, but also frequently settle disputes between their parishioners. They insist that they never impose fines on anyone, and merely try to reconcile people and to show them the right path. In the Mamba Church in 1968, one of the pastors explained that he heard cases with a congregational council consisting of two or three lay elders and one or more pastors. He said that if matters could not be resolved at this level, they could be sent to a higher church council, but that most matters were not forwarded in this way. He described most of the problems that arose for hearing as "spiritual" problems. The ledger in which records of these hearings were kept revealed that these spiritual matters turned out (for the year 1963) to have consisted of fifty-two instances in which persons were accused of living together in "common-law marriage" without having been married in the church, thirteen cases of fornication (sexual relations outside of marriage without living together), seven cases of polygyny, five disputes between husbands and wives, one woman who failed to pay a pledged contribution to the church, one woman who brought a pagan husband to be told he should become a Christian, and one case of a man accused of consulting a diviner/healer, a *mganga* (Church Ledger, Mamba Lutheran Church, 1963). "People must be taught not to traffic with the devil," said the Lutheran pastor. The priest at a Catholic mission in another village was occupied with similar matters. In 1969 one of the fathers went through his date book to tell me which cases he had heard that year. He, too, heard cases in the company of laymen who were local church elders. There were about twenty such men in the village of K———, *wasimamizi,* two or so per *mtaa.* We may assume that the priest edited what he told me, as I was not allowed to inspect his records. But it is of interest that the cases he mentioned were: a dispute between a father and son, the son being ordered to pay his father a fattened goat *ndafu* by way of apology; several cases of couples living together without being married in the church, also of fornication; five cases or so of polygyny; one of drinking and nonsupport of a wife and family; one accusation of witchcraft between brothers by a sick brother against a well one; and last a complaint about a diviner/healer. The church regards *waganga* as direct competitors, those who deal with the devil instead of with God, and hence do, in fact, have the ability to summon supernatural powers. Thus for Mlatie to complain against his father Uruka to the Lutheran pastor, saying that he had performed an illicit magical ritual, was a damaging piece of evidence and a hearing was held. However, if the churches expelled everyone who consulted the *waganga* there would be no one left in the congregation, perhaps not even the pastor. The churches content themselves with reprimands and temporary suspensions. The Catholic priests deny their parishioners the sacrament in serious cases, impose lesser penalties for minor offenses. The Lutherans exclude miscreants from services for a period of time. In the case of Uruka, the pastor suspended him from the church for several months for invoking the spirit world with the blood of the goat, but he was soon back in the pastor's good graces.

The interminable consequences of an accusation of sorcery

In the M—— lineage the slaughtering of the goats and the various consultations of the *waganga* are said to have had direct effects. For one thing, two years later Mamkinga's wife had her first child, and she has had many more since. For another, within a year after this affair, a married daughter of Uruka died. When Mlatie heard that his sister had died, he went to Uruka and said, "You thought that my wife had witchcraft substance but you have it yourself. You see, your daughter is dead." He meant that Uruka's stirring up of the spirits has rebounded and struck down the young woman.

There were related disputes with affines. Uruka and the father of Mlatie's wife quarreled, since her father thought the accusation of sorcery an outrage against his daughter. In a hearing before various men of the M– – lineage, Mlatie's wife's father brought his complaint, and Uruka was fined in beer, which the two old fathers and the men who had held the hearing later drank together in Uruka's *kihamba*.

But the story was far from the end. In 1979 the wife of Mamkinga and the wife of Mlatie still did not speak to one another, nor did they exchange visits. When one family had a beer drinking, the other did not attend, even if everyone else in that lineage section went. The children of Mlatie were allowed to go to the house of Uruka, but not to the house of Mamkinga, though it is in the same *kihamba*, lest the wife of Mamkinga give them poisoned food. Though the women were hostile the brothers were not so open about their differences.

For many years, Mlatie and Mamkinga continued to be on speaking terms, attended the same slaughtering feasts, and sent each other shares of beer and meat. But that politeness between them was put under unbearable strain decades later, when in the late 1970s Mlatie fell ill. He remained ill for nearly three years. He went to the *waganga*. He went to the hospital. Nothing was of any avail. Convinced that it was his brother Mamkinga who was bewitching him, he took refuge with a daughter who worked in Dar es Salaam, and stayed with her for two years. In the fall 1979 he returned to Kilimanjaro, and Uruka wanted to try to settle matters between his two sons. One Sunday in early November, he called all of his sons, together with the mother's brother's of Mamkinga and Mlatie, and the old sage Wilibald. One of these men told me that there was much discussion, but nothing was settled, and they were to assemble again a week or two later to try again. The old quarrel about the burned clothes and the accusation of witchcraft was mentioned, as were many lesser affronts. I have no idea what the ultimate outcome will be, but the curse of a dead man is particularly dangerous because it can never be retracted. Should Mlatie die, his anger might be dangerous for Mamkinga, so a ritual reconciliation ought to be engineered, and presumably Uruka will try to force Mamkinga to pay a fine in beer and to ask Mlatie's pardon in some fashion. Mlatie has adult sons, so there is no immediate question of inheritance on Mamkinga's part. Though the trouble between them originated in structurally determined rivalries that had economic dimensions, it is a completely noneconomic quarrel in its present form, a case of residual personal hostilities. Its intensity must be counted one of the long-term costs of a severe scarcity of land and the limited freedom of maneuver it has engendered. From the point of view of Uruka and Wilibald, as senior men of their lineage subsegment, it presents an opportunity for them to exercise their authority over their juniors. If all goes well the resolution will provide them with beer as well as deference. This authoritative attitude of the elders should not be construed as simple traditionalism maintained for its own sake. Their attitude is one that their "modern" scornful juniors may well adopt when they become senior men. Many elements interlock in this kinship complex and serve its members well in their current situation.

A lawyer is consulted in order to evade the law more efficiently

Mamkinga is a driver in one of the local government departments. Before he became a government driver, he owned his own pickup truck and had a transportation business. He was involved in an accident in which the truck was completely demolished. There were injuries and a death, and the other vehicle was seriously damaged. At the time of the accident, Mamkinga was driving illegally, his license having been suspended because of an earlier accident. When he had his second smashup, he was not alone. A young helper who had a driver's license was on the truck.

Mamkinga realized that because the accident was so serious, and because he was driving illegally, he would be prosecuted, and probably would be deprived of his license for good. He made an agreement with the helper that if he would say *he* had been driving instead of Mamkinga, and would serve whatever jail sentence was imposed, Mamkinga would pay him 6,000 shillings when he got out of jail. A legal agreement, veiling the whole matter as a loan, was drawn up by a lawyer in Moshi.[6] For the young man, it was a way to earn a nest egg with which he could hope to buy a piece of land.

In fact, Mamkinga had no money, but as he was the last-born of Uruka, and would one day inherit Uruka's *kihamba,* the land was collateral for the "loan." The helper went to jail and did Mamkinga's time for him. Meanwhile Mamkinga tried to work out a way of not paying him. As seen in the case of Filipo and his grandfather, there is a secondary form of legitimate inheritance besides the father-to-son stream, a grandfather-to-grandchild form, which has all the legitimacy of tradition. Mamkinga persuaded Uruka to "will" his land to Mamkinga's daughter as Mamkinga had no sons at the time. That would mean that once the helper got out of jail, Mamkinga would have no interest in the land that the helper could reach. Under local Chagga law no woman holds land, except as a widow and then temporarily. Women cannot acquire a disposable interest. But in the eyes of the formal legal system women can hold land. Under the guise of being a progressive modern man, Mamkinga and his father Uruka re-registered the plot at the KNCU in the name of the granddaughter. They had no intention of ever giving her the land. They did it to make Mamkinga judgement-proof. They hoped to evade land seizure by the helper. They succeeded. When the helper came out of prison; he did sue for the repayment of his "loan" and won his lawsuit. Mamkinga had to pay, but the stratagem enabled him to plead for time, and he paid over a long period of time out of coffee money and some other income from a business partnership in which he was then involved. Subsequently, Mamkinga's wife bore him some sons, so that now whatever happens the granddaughter will never get the land.

Wife-beating and compensation: a bush lawyer is consulted

During the Christmas season in 1968, the ten-house cell leader and several other persons (Uruka, Mlatie, the wife's father, a senior neighbor, crony of Uruka) heard a case between Mamkinga and his wife's father. The wife's father was claiming compensation for taking care of his daughter (Mamkinga's wife) for twenty-one days while she recuperated from a beating Mamkinga had given her. Mamkinga said that his wife had spent money he had given her for clothing at the beer shop instead. He said that he came home one night, late in December 1968, and found his wife drunk and therefore beat her. She then went to the hospital for seven days, while she recovered, and subsequently took refuge with her father for three weeks.

The wife, a lively and talkative woman, contended that she was sober when she was beaten. She argued that Mamkinga had come home drunk and demanded food. She said that she gave him some, but that he did not eat it. He threw it away and assaulted her. She shouted, she said, but no one came because it was the middle of the night. Raising a hue and cry is what is supposed to be done by the victim in such situations, and not to have done so would have tended to militate against her. She said that Mamkinga said he would kill her and was going to marry another wife. She said she managed to get away and went to the hospital for a week. Mamkinga did not come to see her at the hospital, nor did he come to see her at her father's house while she stayed there. Her father took care of all of her expenses during this time.

Mamkinga said that the whole thing was a cock and bull story, that he had not beaten her, that his wife had simply gone off to stay with her parents, and had now constructed this tale of woe. He challenged her version by asking to see a written chit from the hospital giving details about her condition when she was received there. She then explained that while she lay unconscious from her injuries Mamkinga had tried to prevent her from obtaining a written record by telling the medical assistant at the hospital not to give her one. But he did not count on her father's intervention. After the woman had returned to her father's house, her father consulted a local bush lawyer, an interesting and canny man, completely self-taught and unofficially in practice, who, though illiterate, is familiar with the ways of the bureaucracy and the courts, and especially knowledgeable about the kinds of documents they are in the habit of providing. He is busy enough to employ a literate assistant. Much of the time, he simply represents rural people for a fee, by going and speaking to officials for them, usually on errands to obtain written documentation of one sort or another. In this case, he went to the hospital on behalf of Mamkinga's wife, and got the chit she needed to prove the extent of her injuries. Her father then sent word that he wanted the case heard.

Mamkinga and his wife were not married in the full traditional way and did not have a *mkara,* a trustee/sponsor of the marriage. Had there been such a person, it would have been his task to try to settle the quarrel. But as there was no *mkara,* the ten-house cell leader and assembled elders did the job instead. At the hearing, Mamkinga denied everything. But the others all found him guilty anyway. The wife's father asked for fifty shillings' compensation for feeding her for one month. The group decided that he should be paid that sum, and that Mamkinga also should pay his wife fifty shillings to compensate her for her injuries. They also admonished her to move back to her husband's *kihamba* and to stay there, and she did.

THE SALE OF LAND IN THE CORE TERRITORY OF A LINEAGE TO AN OUTSIDER, A NON-KINSMAN

Introduction: the vengeance of poor relatives

The two case histories that follow constitute the two instances (in the period of fieldwork contact) in which men in the lineage have sold their plots, and worse, sold them to outsiders. Both men seem not to have been on the best of terms with their agnates before they decided to sell. But once they had made their moves to alienate land to outsiders the sellers became pariahs. One of the sellers was accused of witchcraft and ostracized. The other eventually committed suicide. Both mini-biographies also involve violence. Similar accounts have been collected from other lineages, and snippets of these kinds of case histories regularly surface in the courts. The circumstances depicted are not extraordinary, however sad.

The customary legal interest of agnates in the lands of other members of the localized lineage described by Gutmann do not seem to have been enforced as such in the courts on Kilimanjaro during the British colonial period. European ideas of freely alienable private individual property in land seem to have replaced indigenous conceptions of the matter.[7] Outside the courts many of these ideas continued. If the courts were to be used, other grounds that would obtain more certain results had to be provided—and were. Internally, the requirement that agnates consent to the sale to outsiders of patrimonial land has, in recent times, been translated into a demand for "first refusal," the right to a first offer.[8] But not all agnates are interested. Only those who can afford to pay are eager for this right, since only they have the means to take advantage of it. In much of the colonial period cash replaced the traditional "cow and goat" as the payment for land. After a time when the value of the cow and the goat was simply paid in cash as a standard payment, cash prices came to vary according to the value of the land. Plot size, quality of soil and improvements, the number and kind of buildings, banana plants, and coffee bushes were all pertinent. In some cases location was also important. It is said that even today cursed land, lands wrongfully appropriated and then cursed by the rightful owner cannot be sold by the appropriator or his descendants at any price if the story of the curse is known and believed. Thus there are supernatural reasons to have a clear "title," that is, in this system, a clear right to sell.

Since the nationalization of land in 1963 (Conversion and Government Leases Act, chap. 523) what is sold is technically not the land itself but the improvements made by the possessor on it. The right to possession is transferred on indemnification for these improvements. In fact, more than anything else, it is the right to possession that is sold, but that concept is not officially acknowledged. The conceptual refinement involved in the abolition of titles, however idealistic, has had limited practical effect on Kilimanjaro, and the price of land-possession continues to rise. Consequently the land-hungry men on the mountain can easily be classified into two categories: a small class of employed, salaried men (or men with small businesses, or pensions, and/or salaried wives) who can afford to buy land, and those much more numerous men whose only cash comes from the sale of coffee, the poorest or most desperate of whom eventually are forced to sell. There are usually both kinds of men in the same localized lineages.

Although subsegmentation within the lineage into slaughtering groups is an important feature of internal lineage structure, the interest of "wealthy" agnates in the potential sale of the lands of their poorer brethren transcends the boundaries of these potential subgroups. Thus a "rich" agnate with a salary may press a poor illiterate unsalaried kinsman to sell to him even if they are not in the same segment of the lineage. Closer agnates may be miffed by this, feeling that their genealogical closeness should give them purchasing priority. But the same traditional rule is invoked, that the land should stay in the lineage. It is impossible to know for certain whether in practice land interest extended in a similar way beyond the minimal segments in earlier times. It seems quite possible.

Land allocated by a father to his son and later reappropriated: Kiwosi and Kisoka

In 1969 a dispute arose between a father (Kiwosi) and a son (Kisoka) ostensibly over the mysterious removal of the plants that marked their common boundary (see Figure 9.3). In fact the son wanted the boundary changed. He wanted the full plot returned to him that had originally been allocated to his deceased mother. He was her only son, and thus in normal circumstances would have been entitled to succeed to the land she had occupied. Some years earlier at the *matanga* of the mother the father had tried to retain the coffee rights to her plot. The kin did not allow him to do so and the coffee went to the son. But the full plot was not given to the son. The father was allowed to keep a portion that he had already appropriated for his own use. In this connection the father had planted a new boundary between his own land and that of his son. The son uprooted the new boundary in 1969. The father then asked that a hearing take place. Those present were resident members of his lineage segment (Uforosia, Lyatonga, Yosia, Petro, Kisoka), a few other agnates from other segments, the ten-house cell leader, the *mtaa* head because the argument concerned land, and several neighbors.

The dispute was decided in the father's favor, and the outcome enraged

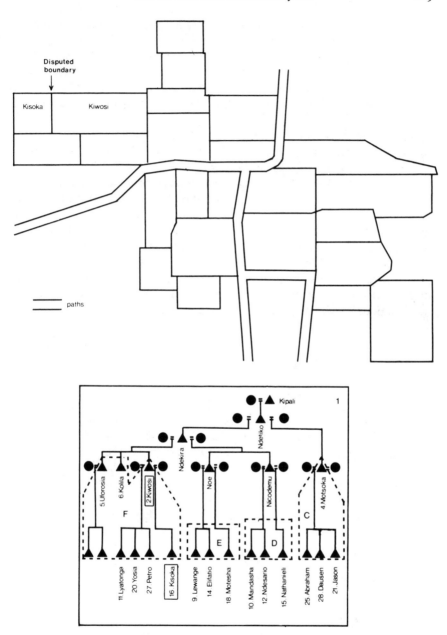

Figure 9.3. Lineage plots of the M——s showing Kisoka's disputed boundary and lineage branch showing Kiwosi and Kisoka.

the son. The father's argument was that as he, the father, had bought the land long ago from a neighbor for two cows (i.e., as it was not originally inherited lineage land) the son did not have a right to it. He also said his son did not respect him. The dislike between them was, in fact, well known and of long standing. The ten-house cell leader acted as chairman of the proceedings, but the *mtaa* head (*mchili*) replanted the destroyed boundary.

The technique of uprooting a boundary to provoke a hearing is not unusual. My sense is that it frequently is used by a junior agnate to force his opponent to bring an accusation against him, rather than overtly take the initiative himself. Destroying the boundary resembles self-help, but may have far less to do with any expectation of allowing a man to repossess land than of properly starting a public intralineage hearing. Once accused of "interfering" with the boundary, the junior boundary-destroyer can play innocent and say he knows nothing about the uprooting of the plants, but that in the circumstances would like to raise the question where the boundary should be. In the background of this 1969 dispute was a long history of bad relations between father and son and bad relations between the father and the wife who was this son's mother.

Episode 1: early intimations of disaster, a son whose father does not forgive him eventually will be punished

Long before the 1969 land quarrel, one day in 1949, Kiwosi (father) and Kisoka (son) quarreled in their *kihamba*. Kisoka (the son) grew so enraged that he cut down a young banana shoot with a *panga* and stormed out of the groves. That cutting of a plant before it bore fruit was a mystically dangerous thing to do, and Kiwosi (the father) shouted after him, "What you have done is bad, and will return to you." Kisoka, the disrespectful son, was the offspring of his father's second wife, a woman with whom the father did not get along and ultimately rejected. Kisoka's eldest half-brother (Lyatonga) tried to mediate the dispute about the cut banana shoot, and a case was heard by a group of agnates. The son was found to be at fault and was told to brew beer to obtain his father's forgiveness. He brewed the beer and it was consumed in apparent amity, but the father still bore a grudge.

Episodes 2 and 3: the son absents himself and returns, a son's right to his mother's land does not die

Kisoka, the son, eventually went to serve in the army in Kenya and remained there for some years. Meanwhile his mother was sent back to her own kin. In 1959 Kisoka returned and so did his mother, and they demanded the *kihamba* that had been allocated to her when she married. The dispute was heard by a group of agnates who said Kiwosi, the father, must return the land to his son. The father obeyed, but only in part. He gave mother and son only a piece of the *kihamba* they had had before. Worse, though the father gave them the banana rights, he reserved the coffee rights for himself. The son then went to the city to look for a job. His father did not take care of the mother in his absence, and she eventually left, to occupy and tend a vacant *kihamba,* for someone else. Then she fell ill, returned to her own *kihamba,* and died. The son came back for her *matanga,* claimed the land, was given it by the agnates present, settled on it, and married. There were several disputes in this period. The son wanted the coffee rights and a larger piece of land (the size originally given to his mother). Eventually agnates, neighbors, and the local *mtaa* (district parish) head, the *mchili,* heard the case, and the father was forced to concede the coffee rights. But he still did not give his son the full-size *kihamba* he claimed. Along the way, the son and his wife had two children who died. (Were these deaths the bitter punishment for the cutting down of the banana plant in the original quarrel between son and father?) The son got a job in the local *pombe* shop, and though it provided him with a calabash of beer a day, his pay was too little to support him and his wife.

Episode 4: Kisoka sells his land and beats his brother

In 1969 the government exhorted land-poor men on Kilimanjaro to leave and pioneer new land within the structure of *ujamaa* villages. Kisoka volunteered to emigrate to one of the new villages. In June 1969 he left for Mwese. He came back some months later having decided that it was too much of a struggle to be a pioneer. Subsequently, in 1973 he decided to sell his small plot of lineage land to a neighbor, a nonkinsman, even though his prosperous lineage brother Filipo offered to exchange a parcel of land elsewhere on the mountain for this one in lineage territory and another cousin, Richard, offered to buy the land for cash. Kisoka preferred the neighbor's cash. He sold his land to an enterprising local businessman, who took it over. Kisoka moved with his wife and with his two small surviving daughters to Kibongoto where he had bought another plot. But on the eve of departure, he was drinking at the *pombe* shop and an altercation developed between him and his eldest half-brother, Lyatonga. They exchanged recriminations. Kisoka complained about not having been given his share of the bridewealth of a sister, and he also complained about not having been given a particular share of meat by his father. The discussion led to blows. Kisoka smashed his elder brother in the face, and the brother went to the dispensary for repair. They ban-

daged his cuts and gave him a chit noting his injuries. He intended to use
this to go to the police and file a complaint against Kisoka. A cousin,
John, intercepted him, and tried to mediate the dispute. John pleaded
with Lyatonga not to go to the police, saying that doing so would make
too serious a case of it, that it would be better to settle it at home. The
next day they met with their father, Kiwosi, the senior agnate of their
lineage section. Also present were Kiwosi's brother, Uforosia, and John,
the peacemaking cousin. The man who had sold the beer was there. He
also happened to be a ten-house cell leader. And some neighbors also
attended. Kisoka was fined twenty shillings which he paid. He then left
and went to live in Kibongoto. In the next couple of years he had two
sons. But life must not have been bearable for him. In 1978 he committed
suicide (so his cousin John told me) by drinking coffee insecticide. His
father, Kiwosi, died the next year, in 1979. The father died a natural
death at the hospital, and was buried in his own *kihamba*.

At the *matanga* of the father, the remaining small parcel of land that
had been part of Kisoka's mother's *kihamba*, the part that the father had
stubbornly refused to give to Kisoka in life, was assigned by the agnates
to Kisoka's children. When I was there in 1979 the mother of the children
still had not returned. I was told that until the children do grow up,
Kisoka's half-brother Petro will be using the land. Why did the agnates
assign the land to Kisoka's children? Did they feel guilty about his suicide? Do they fear a curse on the land? I do not know.

The legal implications of the dispute history

This dispute history raises a number of important legal issues:

(1) *The withdrawal of property as punishment. Is a father's gift of land
to his son a conditional allocation or a nonreversible transfer?* There is a
lingering feeling among the Chagga that a man has some continuing interest in property he has allocated to his wives and sons, and that he might
have some right to reallot it if the composition of the family changes or
some other change in circumstances warrants it. A symbolic indication of
the continuing interest of a father in property he has allocated to his son
is the permanent obligation of the son to give his father a share of any
beer made from bananas growing in the plot. This resembles the *masiro*
payment for loaned land. Normally a father does not take back property
he has allocated. Moreover, the father's possible right to reallocate has to
be balanced against the father's obligation to provide for his wives and
sons. He cannot, without cause, confiscate property without providing a
reasonable substitute plot (see for example Filipo's reallocations in the
first section of this chapter). Indeed, some Chagga say positively that a
father cannot take back a piece of land once he has given it to a son. The

ordinary situation, then, is one in which the original allocations tend to stand, and are deemed by everyone concerned as likely to be permanent. But enough exceptions occur to suggest that full relinquishment does not always take place until death. It would be a misrepresentation of the situation, though, to set out a clear series of rules and the exceptions to them. In this very case, after the mother's *matanga* when the father withheld the coffee rights from his son, and withheld a piece of the *kihamba*, the father was forced to concede the coffee rights at a hearing involving agnates, neighbors, and a local official (Episode 2). Yet he still did not give up the full plot, and got away with it. By the time Episode 3 came up the agnates sided with him on this point, and he did not have to return that piece of land to his son. Lineage opinion may have turned more and more against the son as time went on. I was told that the lineage had come to agree with the father that the son was disrespectful and undeserving, and his behavior warranted treating part of the allocation as reversible. The father's intransigence may also have been a consideration. And there may have been other latent issues which did not explicitly come to the surface. It would be distorting to tidy up these matters too much and present them in causal form. But whether or not the son's behavior was the actual determinant of the unfavorable result in Episode 3, it was the opinion of one of his agnates and it was an argument made by the father; hence they saw the withdrawal of allocated property as *a legitimate punitive sanction.*

(2) *The right of an absentee.* Not only does the father-allocator have a vague continuing interest in land he has given his son, or wife, but the son and his mother have a continuing right to the particular parcel, even if they leave the area temporarily. They lose the land during the period of absence, but can reclaim it on returning to live there. In precolonial times there very likely was no indemnification for produce harvested in the period of absence, as the produce could be treated as the just reward for labor in taking care of the garden. But now there sometimes is controversy over the coffee cash taken in.

(3) *The distinction between coffee rights and banana rights.* It is not unusual for coffee rights to be separated from the "bananas" and for a father to retain the coffee as a source of cash until his death, while giving his son a piece of land for all other purposes. Many fathers are not challenged on this point. A son picking coffee in these circumstances may be accused of theft.

(4) *The distinction between inherited land and other land.* The difference between lineage land, that is, land acquired through patrilineal inheritance in the area of the agnatic cluster and land that was bought or allocated by local officials has to do with disposability. In Chagga law (or in their legal theory, since they seldom can enforce it) "lineage" land can

be transferred to an outsider only with the consent of the local agnates, whereas bought or "granted" land is freely transferable in a modern, individual property sense. This is the modern analogue of the old Chagga rule that the cultivator of unoccupied, unclaimed bush land could freely dispose of such property. It did not become part of the agnatic patrimony in the first generation. There is often no practical distinction between bought and allocated land since not infrequently payment was made to the *mchili* to get him to allocate it. In this series of disputes, the father, Kiwosi, argued that he had the right to withdraw the land from his son, and to control it in ways that were not "customary" because it was not patrimonial land in the first place, but an unoccupied plot allotted years earlier by the authorities. But as far as I know, the fact that it was not patrimonial land should have made no difference to the son's rights which derived from the allocation to his mother. The Chagga are enthusiastic litigants and often throw in dubious arguments on the off chance that they will carry some weight.

(5) *Episodes of dispute and the renegotiation of decisions: decades of reerupting controversy.* Kisoka was involved in controversy with his father over a period of thirty years in his sad life. Disputes specifically referring to his land spanned a twenty-year period. There were at least four dispute hearings before agnates, and two *matangas*, in connection with these relationships. Clearly, intralineage arguments are often not settled in any durable sense, but arise again and again. *Episodes* of dispute are terminated, but the underlying controversy goes on.

It could be argued that therefore the decisions of the lineage (made as a whole or by the persons in the branch concerned) do not have binding force. It could be argued that the lineage does not have sufficient coercive power to make its decisions stick, since they chronically come unstuck. I believe that argument would distort the sociological reality. The lineage can ostracize a member, or can even expel him. It has tremendous power over its members through the control of witnesses. Indeed, if there is enough agreement, it can even mount a violent attack, and beat up a member. It is not because of any lack of coercive powers that decisions of the lineage are periodically challenged by those who find them unsatisfactory. It is one of *our* cultural assumptions that once a case is decided by the proper authorities, it is permanently closed, *res judicata*. But it is one of *their* cultural assumptions that almost anything can be renegotiated after a time. Since, in the long term, deaths have a considerable effect on the composition of the localized lineage and the distribution of its lands (as well as affecting the guardianship of widows and minor children) dispute is not the only way in which rearrangements are engendered. In the past, because of a short life expectancy the turnover in lineage composition must have been fairly rapid, and internal political dislocations frequent. Even for those who lived through the same period together, there must have been ongoing developments in their internal relationships as well as their relations with outsiders. It does not seem at all surprising that what I have called a "life-term" social arena should operate in a mode that permits the reopening and renegotiation of issues after a period of time (Moore 1978). If one thinks of the lineage as much more like a regulatory administrative body than like a court, the frequent re-raising of the same problems under changing conditions is much more comprehensible to the modern Western legal mind.

The misappropriation of a ward's assets by a guardian: an earlier episode involving Kiwosi and his other sons

In December 1973, a palaver was held in the *kihamba* of Kiwosi, called at the instigation of his third son, Petro. The precipitating situation was a sale of a piece of land. Kiwosi's eldest son, Lyatonga, had just sold half of a *shamba* (land down in the lower area) belonging to his mentally ill brother Yosia. Lyatonga said that his father had directed him to sell it, and that the father intended to use the 1,300-shilling proceeds (1) toward building a house for Yosia, the sick man, and (2) to pay for the *mganga* (diviner healer) who had been treating Yosia for years. Petro demanded to know "the real reason" why the *shamba* was sold, alleging that the money received had not, in fact, been used for Yosia, that instead it had been divided between his senior brother, Lyatonga, and their father, Kiwosi.

Lyatonga admitted that this was so, and produced the following explanation: He said that ten years earlier, when the father had acquired the *shamba,* he had paid 400 shillings to the *mtaa* head (*mchili*) to allocate the property. This 400 shillings had been advanced by Lyatonga. Subsequently, the father divided the *shamba* into two parts, half for Petro and half for Yosia, the disturbed son. The father had never reimbursed Lyatonga. When in 1973 Lyatonga sold Yosia's half, he paid himself back by keeping 400 shillings of the proceeds and gave his father the remaining 900. Kiwosi said that this was true and that he would use the 900 shillings for the benefit of Yosia. Yosia's mother then piped up and complained that Yosia had no clothes and seldom had enough to eat. Kiwosi, Yosia, and Petro all lived together in the same *kihamba.* Lyatonga had his own, adjacent *kihamba,* which his father had given him when he married.

Kiwosi was angry, and said that the *shamba* in the lower area that had been sold was his, and that no one could tell him what to do with it. Kiwosi's eldest junior brother, Uforosia, remonstrated with him, saying that once a man has given his son property he cannot take it back. Uforosia said that all the money (all 1,300 shillings) should be kept by

someone other than Kiwosi to be sure that it was used for Yosia. He
proposed putting it in the bank. After a long discussion Kiwosi finally
came around to agreeing to putting the money in the bank, but he asked
that it be done "after the harvest" (meaning that he had already spent his
share). Petro also agreed to bring the 400 shillings that he had kept.
Whether the money was actually ever produced, I do not know.[9]

In Chagga families guardians often take advantage of their wards, and
this is such a case. In principle, entrusting someone with the job of
looking after the affairs of a woman, a minor, or a helpless person, puts
the guardian under an obligation to use all the assets of the associated
estate for the benefit of that person or line. But no records are kept, and
there is no official form of accountability. No one other than interested
parties ever checks on what happens. Thus, enforcement depends on such
interested parties, on their being able to get the necessary information,
and on their taking action. Precisely why Petro acted in this case, I am
not sure. Possibly it was because he had not been "cut-in" on the returns
from the sale. Sheer pity for his sick brother is unlikely to have been the
only factor.

The episode also raises once again the legal problems whether a father
retains some control over land already allocated to his sons. In this instance the situation was further complicated by the mental illness of the
son. The outcome of the palaver was plainly a defeat for the father who
was considered to have abused his position of trust, and to have appropriated property that was not his. The statement of the senior kinsman,
Uforosia, was unequivocally that a man retains no right to property once
he has allocated it to his sons.

Punitive sanctions and the attempt to enforce lineage control over a member's affairs: Mandasha and Ndesario

As indicated in relation to the mental defective Yosia, guardianships can
be lucrative and can endow the guardian with considerable discretionary
power over the property of his wards. Usually the person appointed is the
closest succeeding agnate as defined by the rules of inheritance and succession. But the kinsmen deciding who should serve as guardian can
choose someone else if circumstances persuade them that they should.
Thus the choice of a guardian (or of the trustee of an estate) or the
affirmation of an heir is in some measure subject to the discretionary
judgment of kinsmen. The agnates assembled can use these occasions for
routine confirmation or can use them punitively, to declare someone
disqualified. Arranging the inheritance of property and making the appointment of a guardian is thus rule-enforcing in several senses: (1) it can
enforce the rules of inheritance, (2) it can enforce rules having to do with

disqualifying misbehavior, and (3) it constitutes a reaffirmation of the procedural norms that give the agnates the power to make such decisions. But these rules like most legal rules are in various ways conditional and contingent.

The present case history of the relations between the brothers Mandasha and Ndesario demonstrates this process as well as bringing out a number of other legal issues (see Figure 9.4). The story begins with wrangling about property and ends with an accusation of witchcraft and a death. The potential sale of a piece of land in lineage territory to an outsider, a nonagnate, was at the heart of the conflict during the period from 1968 on. The struggle over this question brought to the fore what the Chagga correctly perceived as the conflict between the law of the public sector in which a sale (technically, of improvements only) to an outsider was entirely legal and the traditional law of the Chagga lineage in which a sale to an outsider was conditional on the consent of the agnates. In this case, the law of the public sector prevailed. But the case history demonstrates the formidable amount of pressure still available to the lineage including material penalties, violence, and ostracism. It also shows the extent to which the modern reference to traditional law is made under entirely changed conditions.

Pledged land, cash debts, and predatory kin

When I first heard about Ndesario in 1968, he was in debt. He had borrowed from a moneylender outside the lineage. Moneylenders loan at wildly high interest rates, and a debt could easily double or triple in a short time. In itself, borrowing from a nonkinsman probably meant that he was not on very good terms with his mother's agnates or with his own. Ndesario's lineage cousins said he spent his money in the *pombe* shop on beer, and was otherwise lazy and improvident. Worse, as youngest son he had the obligation of looking after his mother but did not take proper care of her. She needed special help because she had become blind. To make matters worse her grass house collapsed in the bad rains of 1968. The father, Nicodemu, was not around. Many years earlier, in the 1950s, he had left the area to go to Mombasa to work. He has never returned, nor was he heard from. As the years passed it was generally assumed that he had died. Thus Ndesario's mother was like a widow, and relied on her youngest son. Ndesario had no cash with which to repair the house, or rather to replace it, which was what was needed. Matters became so desperate that the mother moved in "next door" with her elder son Mandasha, on his half of the paternal plot (see Figure 9.4). Some kinsmen said that it was a disgrace that Ndesario neglected his mother. But Ndesario had always argued that even though Mandasha was not the

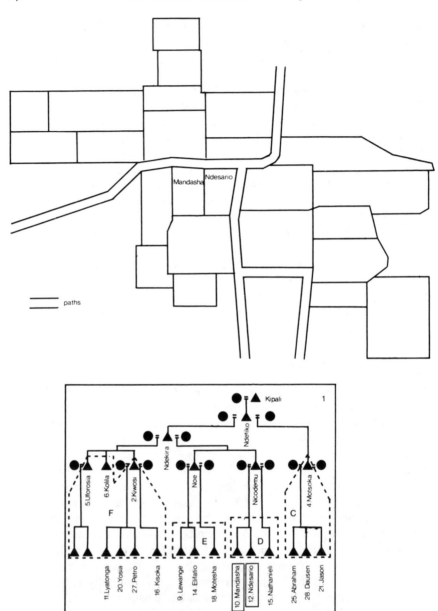

Figure 9.4. Lineage plots of the M——s showing plots of Mandasha and Ndesario and lineage branch showing relationship of Mandasha and Ndesario.

youngest son Mandasha should take more responsibility for the mother than he did because he was better off. Their banana gardens in the lineage area were more or less equivalent, but Mandasha had two other plots elsewhere. Both men were farmers without access to any money other than coffee cash, but Mandasha was a better manager, or so I was told. That Mandasha also had the advantage of extra income (both from his guardianship of the widow, son, and estate of an insane half-brother, and from his extra two *vihamba* away from lineage territory) was not mentioned when people tried to explain how much better a person he was than his brother, Ndesario.

Meanwhile, Ndesario was being harried by his creditors, who threatened to sue. Since his land was his only property, he might be forced to sell. A senior lineage cousin, Lewange, stepped into the breach and paid the debt. Lewange was wealthy by local standards since he had a salaried job as an attendant in a nearby clinic. The usual agreement was made about repayment. Ndesario was to pledge all of his coffee income to Lewange for the number of years necessary to clear the debt. Any such arrangement would be sure to put such a man right back into debt, since some cash is indispensable to a Chagga family. Lewange knew that Ndesario would probably begin to think about selling his land, and he hoped by paying the debt to become the preferred buyer. Another employed cousin, Richard, also approached Ndesario secretly, and asked him to sell to him instead.

Ndesario kept his own counsel and, thinking he would get a better price from an outsider, negotiated with a neighbor, an affluent man who owned a truck. The neighbor made Ndesario an offer of 5,000 shillings, and proposed going to a lawyer in Moshi the very next day to draw up documents. Ndesario accepted. They went and a down payment of 800 shillings was made. In Chagga law, no right to land passes until the full purchase price has been paid. The seller always can change his mind in the meanwhile and nullify the deal by returning such monies as have been paid him. The seller always continues to retain possession until the full price has changed hands. The use of a lawyer is fairly unusual, but the truck owner was sophisticated in business matters and did not want to take any chances.

No sooner had the wife of Ndesario seen money pass from the purchaser to her husband, than she ran to tell his kinsmen about what was going on. From her point of view such a sale would do her son out of his eventual patrimony. While buyer and seller were in town with the lawyer, she went to Lewange and told him what was going on. Ndesario soon heard from Lewange about his moral obligations to sell to him instead. But Lewange did not trust Ndesario and tried other means of blocking the sale as well.

The mobilization of an official to block the sale; the Divisional Executive Officer

At the instigation of Lewange, Mandasha, and Richard, Ndesario's wife, and his mother went to the Divisional Executive Officer in 1970 to beg him to stop the sale of the land. Their argument was that Nicodemu, the father of the two men, might still be alive and might return from Mombasa. In short, they were arguing that Ndesario was trying to sell land that was not his, but his father's. The Divisional Executive Officer (DEO) agreed, succumbed to the appeal of the blind mother and perhaps to other pressures, and prohibited any immediate sale from taking place. The buyer was soon heard grumbling about his 800 shillings and wondering whether he would ever see his money again. Going to an official was not a usual way of handling land disputes. Why they chose the DEO rather than some other local official or tribunal, I do not know. However, their appeal to an official is part of a general pattern of using the authoritative intervention of an individual official if one can. This practice goes back in an unbroken chain to appeals to chiefs, parish heads, and patrons in precolonial times. Colonial policies regarding the powers of local officials must have increased the attractiveness of this mode of procedure, when steps taken inside the lineage by senior elders were not sufficient, and court proceedings seemed cumbersome.

The second attempt to block the sale: the court of arbitration

Time passed. The father did not return. Government was reorganized, and the divisional executive officer moved on. The truck owner resumed his payments, and by 1973 he had paid in full. But nervous, because of the lineage opposition, and because of Tanzanian legislation nationalizing land, he thought he would insure his right to possession by improving the land in a concrete way. Today in Tanzania, the land belongs to those who "put their sweat into it." No fool he, he started to construct a small house with the complicity of Ndesario. The payment could then be explained as a payment for this attached improvement, and/or the house itself might give a right to possession.

Then the various men of the lineage (Mandasha, Richard, and Lewange) tried to mobilize the authorities by using the old blind mother. She went first to the local primary court to try to assign the plot by "will" to her grandson, Ndesario's son.[10] But she had no standing to do so, and under the laws the court had no jurisdiction over land matters anyway, though it did over wills. The court advised her to take her case to the arbitration tribunal, a layman's court of party appointees of the local TANU (now Chama Cha Mapinduzi or Revolutionary party), which hears cases informally and is supposed to try to effect a settlement satisfactory to both parties. Her case was to come up in October 1973.

The accusation of witchcraft

A disaster brought to an end whatever reserves of sympathy Ndesario might have had in the lineage. His elder brother Mandasha, living on the other half of the paternal grove, had fallen ill. The illness went on for some months and did not go away. He called a *mganga* who was not able to cure him. He went to the hospital and still did not recover. Once at home again, he told everyone who came to see him that it was Ndesario who was killing him, and that Ndesario must not be allowed to have anything to do with his corpse, or his family, or his property after his death. Indeed, from a genealogical point of view, Ndesario as the only surviving brother, son of the same mother, would have been the obvious candidate to be the burier of his brother, the trustee of his elder brother's estate, and guardian of his wife, his seven daughters, and his only, very young son, a position of some material advantage. As the only sane survivor of the three brothers, he also ought to have been made trustee of the mad half-brother's land and guardian of his wife and children as well. Mandasha's accusation was to forestall these events.

The second accusation of witchcraft and the use of violence

There were more troubles to come. Getting into the act, another cousin, Elifatio, an immediate neighbor of Ndesario with a contiguous banana garden, told everyone that several of his goats had died and he knew who was responsible. Indeed, chickens from Ndesario's *kihamba* had repeatedly wandered on Elifatio's land, scratching in the manure. He had complained to Ndesario's wife and told her to keep her chickens at home. The implication was that the chickens were somehow transferring witchcraft substance from one place to the other. The chickens did not get the message and continued to roam.

Elifatio, enraged, took matters into his own hands. He went into the *kihamba* of Ndesario and beat his wife so badly that she collapsed. After he left her bruised and bloodied, she sent her young son to fetch the police ten miles away. They came and took her to the hospital, arrested Elifatio, and booked him for assault. Richard, a kinsman, who was an affluent young clerk, bailed out Elifatio, an ordinary full-time farmer, and a date was set for the hearing on the assault.

Ndesario, as the complaining witness, reported at the court on the appointed day, only to find that the case had been postponed. Several times, he walked the miles to the court to testify in the criminal proceedings against Elifatio, his cousin. But every time he appeared at the court, the case was postponed, or the clerk told him he had come on the wrong day. Then he was told the case had been dismissed because of his absence. Another cousin (John) told me the clerk of the court had been bribed. Since Ndesario was illiterate and the situation was being manipulated by the sophisticated cousin Richard, Ndesario could easily have been outwitted with or without a bribe. But even if Ndesario had persisted, he might have lost the case for lack of evidence. As his cousin John said to me, "After all, there were no witnesses except for the wife herself. There cannot be a case. Who will believe her?"

The death of Mandasha and the end of the court of arbitration case

October 1973 came, and the case brought by the old blind mother to halt construction of the house by the buyer of the land was heard by the arbitration tribunal. The tribunal members heard testimony and then ordered construction suspended until they would have an opportunity to inspect the land and hear the testimony of Mandasha and neighbors. As it happened, Mandasha died the very day they came to look at the banana grove. They withdrew without collecting any testimony. The proceeding in that court never continued.

The matanga of Mandasha

It seems to have been accepted by the relevant agnates that Ndesario was responsible for Mandasha's death, because at the matanga of his brother, which he had the wisdom not to attend, the many agnates and affines who were present appointed Elifatio guardian/trustee of Mandasha's property and household. The choice was made by Elifatio's elder brother Lewange. Lewange would have been the correct guardian/trustee if no brother had survived, as he was the most senior of the genealogically closest agnatic kinsmen. But Lewange had used his retirement money (he had recently retired from his job at the clinic) to buy two plots of kihamba land. (I do not know whether Ndesario had repaid his debt in full, but he may have done so and Lewange would have had that cash as well.) One of Lewange's new plots was down-mountain and he had moved to one with his wife. He pleaded that he could not properly carry out the duties of a guardian since he resided at too great a distance and was old and not in the best of health. He proposed Elifatio instead, and Elifatio's appointment was accepted. Other business was also attended to at the matanga.[11]

Postscript 1979

Ndesario and his wife and children left the area shortly thereafter, and the truck owner took possession of the disputed land. He resides in a nearby *kihamba* and only uses his new acquisition for cultivation. For the moment at least the agnates recognize him as the legitimate holder.

A GUARDIAN CHEATS HIS WARDS AND FAVORS HIS SONS: WILIBALD, HIS SONS, AND HIS BROTHER'S SONS

Wilibald has had three wives, but only two have borne him sons, the second gave him Simon and David and the third gave him Melikizedeck. Wilibald wanted to keep his sons near him in his old age, and to provide them with land in the core lineage area. To do so he appropriated the land of his deceased brother which he ought to have been holding in trust for the brother's sons. Wilibald then swapped plots in such a way as to favor his own sons over his nephews, whose guardian he was. Wilibald once had a butcher shop in the village but no longer does. He is a dignified barefoot old gentleman in a battered brown fedora and an old ragged British raincoat and carries a cane. Because he is one of the senior men of the lineage, his views carry considerable weight, and his sons and the sons of his brothers obviously have to abide by his decisions in property matters however much more literate they may be than he.

Wilibald originally had two *vihamba* in the area of the lineage (*ukoo*). He was also the heir-trustee (*mrithi*) of his deceased brother (father of Sekao and Alexander) who had a *kihamba* in the middle of *ukoo* land. The dead brother had loaned the land to a man from Rombo. Wilibald paid the Rombo man the compensation necessary to terminate the "tenancy at will." As guardian of his brother's son Wilibald kept the *kihamba* for a time. Then when the brother's son, Sekao, got married, Wilibald, as guardian, gave him the land but added the condition that he divide the *kihamba* in half, keeping only half for himself (i.e., for Sekao) and giving the other half to Melikizedeck the son of Wilibald by his third wife. The mother of Melikizedeck has a *kihamba* in the lower area, but Wilibald wants to bring Melikizedeck back into the *ukoo* (lineage) area, thus his clever play with Sekao. Wilibald says he will divide the *kihamba* in the lower area into two parts, half for Sekao, his brother's son, and half for Melikizedeck, his own son. Melikizedeck (the son) was not married at the time (1973–74), but Sekao (the nephew) was. The division of the *kihamba* in the lower area had not taken place by 1979 but was simply a declared intention. To claim his half in the lower area, Sekao would have to pay back to Wilibald all that Wilibald paid to the man from Rombo in compensation. Wilibald takes all the coffee from the *kihamba* in the *ukoo* (lineage) area that he has divided between his son and his nephew. Sekao gets only the bananas from his half. Sekao is given coffee from about one-quarter of the *kihamba* of his uterine brother, Alexander (the area where Alexander's mother lives). Wilibald can make these decisions because he is the heir-trustee (*mrithi*) of his brother and guardian of the brother's sons. There are no bananas and no coffee in the *kihamba* in the lower area, only maize, beans, and millet.

It is no wonder that in 1969 Sekao responded to the exhortation of local officials and volunteered to go to Mwese to the new government settlement to pioneer. There he had hoped to overcome the poverty he endured in the village of his birth, and to escape the machinations of his father's brother, Wilibald, which were bound to continue. But he, like Kisoka, became discouraged by the hardships of pioneering and soon returned to Kilimanjaro.

Wilibald's two other sons Simon and David were also favored. David lived in Dar es Salaam where he worked for National Insurance, and his wife and children lived in the *kihamba* of Wilibald's second wife. Simon lived at home on Kilimanjaro with his wife and children, also occupying the same *kihamba* as the second wife. In 1973–74 Simon was building a house in the *kihamba* of the first wife of Wilibald as she had no sons, into which he had moved by 1979. Thus several of Wilibald's sons would eventually have *vihamba* of their own in the core lineage area.

A QUESTION OF PATERNITY: URUKA AND HIS DEAD BROTHER'S POSTHUMOUSLY BORN SON

In pre-Christian days a widow was inherited by an agnate of her husband, usually his successor-heir (*mrithi*). She had the option of refusing the match. But if she accepted, and had more children, those children were the offspring of the actual father, the heir, *not* the children of the dead husband. After conversion to Christianity, widow inheritance took a new form. The inheritor of a widow was supposed to act as her guardian, but not to have sexual access to her. A curious ambiguity arose in the M—— lineage. Uruka inherited his brother's widow in 1934 and some months later she bore a son, John (24). The question was whether John was the son of Uruka or the posthumously born son of the dead brother. It was the widow's choice not to live with Uruka. She took her baby and left her dead husband's *kihamba* and went to live with her mother about a half-mile away. The affines contended that the boy was Uruka's son and that he should take care of him. Uruka denied paternity. Uruka later explained that it was necessary to do so to maintain his standing as a Christian. Uruka had to take the position that the boy was not his son. The boy and his mother remained with the maternal grandmother for

about ten years. Then the mother remarried and went to another chiefdom. At that point Uruka, as John's guardian, brought ten-year-old John
back to the M——'s territory and put the boy into the household of
Uruka's eldest son, Filipo. Then Uruka decided to argue that John *was*
his son, for good strategic reasons having to do with the inheritance of
Uruka's father's lands as we shall see.

Thereafter John lived with Filipo and Filipo's successive wives. When
John did not get enough to eat from one of these wives, who preferred
her own children, or when he was given a beating by Filipo, John took
refuge with his maternal grandmother. But most of the time that he was
not in school, he lived in Filipo's household. Eventually the time came
when he wanted to marry. In his twenties, he went to the hospital and
paid for his own circumcision, something Uruka should have financed.
John decided that the girl he wanted to marry would not get along with
Filipo's then wife and could not be asked to live in that household. It is
normal for a newly married woman to live in the house of her husband's
mother for some months or a year. But as John was not living with his
parents, but rather with his cousin (or half-brother?) Filipo, he felt he
could break with custom. He asked Uruka for the *kihamba* that had been
his mother's, where his father is buried. Uruka gave it to him. John built
a house on it. After the wedding John and his bride went there to live.

It is John's contention that he, not Filipo, should have inherited the
lands of Uruka's father, since his own deceased father was the grandfather's firstborn son and original successor-heir. Uruka was a "secondary" heir after the death of John's father. John's argument runs that as
only son of the original heir he ought to be heir. But as Filipo had
managed to take over the grandfather's land in 1948 when John was still a
boy, and had paid compensation to the holders of the loaned lands, it
would be extremely difficult, in fact impossible, for John to try to undo
all this and get the *vihamba* for himself. Since Filipo is the richest man in
the lineage, and the firstborn son of Uruka, the most senior man in the
lineage, John does not stand much of a chance of turning the matter his
own way. Uruka continues to contend that John is *his* son, hence has no
right to any property through the dead husband of his (John's) mother.
But John holds his resentment in reserve, and thinks about it sometimes
and wonders whether an opportunity to make the claims will arise at
some later date. He has not altogether given up.

WHITE-COLLAR WORKER VERSUS FARMER: THE CASE OF RICHARD'S BOUNDARY[12]

Richard, the lineage brother who came forward to try to buy Ndesario's
acre, is a prosperous man. He wears the white shirt, dark trousers and

pointy black shoes of a clerical worker. The reason he had cash with which to buy Ndesario's acre is quite simple. He went to secondary school. He reads and writes Swahili well and can type. He understands some English, though he does not speak it. This array of skills have made it possible for him to work in Moshi as a clerk-typist and to receive a salary. Richard and John went to the same secondary boarding school and are close friends.

He acquired his first job in Moshi through contacts made on the mountain some years ago. A Lutheran missionary who settled near Richard's *mtaa* hired him as an occasional assistant. Some years later, when the missionary prospered and moved to Moshi, Richard became a quasi-secretary to him in town and eventually moved to another, better-paying, church-connected clerical job also in Moshi. This job, with its steady cash income meant that Richard was, comparatively speaking, a well-to-do man, despite the fact that he, too, has a *kihamba* of only about an acre. Later, another clerical job followed, also in Moshi. Richard must think about the future when his sons will grow up (in 1973–74 he had four daughters; by 1979 he had two sons). Even before he had sons he wanted more land. Land is better security than a salary. Therefore Richard came forward offering to buy Ndesario's *kihamba,* for a man wants his sons to live in clan territory, right near him. It is better that way. There is someone to rely on in old age, someone to respect a senior kinsman, and give him the best part of all the animals he slaughters, and some of the beer he brews or buys. Richard thought of the time in ten or twenty years when he would be, by Chagga standards, an old man. One cannot be too vigilant or foresighted in these matters. Opportunities must be seized when they are presented, and any competitors must be resisted from the start.

In 1968 Richard became embroiled in a dispute with his immediate neighbor and lineage "brother," Elifatio. They come from different large sections of the localized lineage. Their *vihamba* garden plots are right next to each other, separated only by a path on Richard's side lined with boundary plants on Elifatio's side. (See Figure 9.5.)

The path between Elifatio's garden and Richard's was widened in recent years by local government order. The path had formerly passed through the middle of Richard's grove. He had prevailed upon local officials to move it, so that it would pass along the edge of his land. Whether he gained land in this maneuver I do not know, but it seems probable.

Though the path itself is narrow, it seems wide because there is a grassy space of about two feet on either side of it that is without any tall vegetation, and in some places the grass area is even wider. On Elifatio's side of the path, behind the grassy band are tall dracaena boundary plants most

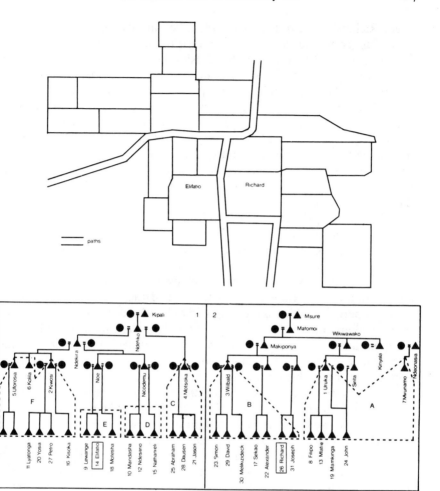

Figure 9.5. Genealogy of the M—— lineage, 1969, showing Elifatio and Richard and lineage plots of the M——s showing plots of Elifatio and Richard.
Heavy solid line divides cow-slaughtering groups, 1 and 2. Broken lines enclose goat-slaughtering groups, A–F. Numbers before names indicate order of
birth. All unnumbered males are deceased. All numbered males are living
adult married men. For reasons of space wives and children are shown only for
the senior generation. Paternity disputed for John (24), born to Uruka's wife,
who had been Sirita's wife, less than a year after Sirita's death.

of the way and a few trees. But in 1968, at one point in the row of
dracaena were several yards where there was a strange gap. Elifatio had
pulled up the dracaena to plant some seedling fruit trees instead. The
fruit tree is doubly useful because its leaves make good food for goats.
Elifatio had put his seedlings all in a tidy row, well back from the path

itself. Richard's side of the path had no boundary of dracaena behind the grass, just coffee bushes. Dracaena itself has no economic use, though it has much symbolic value. As the division between the two *vihamba* was clear enough from the row of plants on Elifatio's side, there was no reason to make it a double row by planting dracaena on Richard's side. Instead, here and there on the grassy border of his side of the path, Richard had planted asteria, a grasslike plant used for animal feed.

The dispute between Elifatio and Richard arose when Elifatio found that all of his newly planted fruit tree seedlings had been uprooted, and he accused Richard of having pulled them up. His complaint was made to the leader of his ten-house cell in August 1968. Richard's pulling up of the seedlings was no doubt calculated to bring this response. It is a form of self-help that provokes the victim to comply or complain. But the true "plaintiff," the person with the initial grievance, by using self-help, becomes the defendant if any responsive action is taken.

At the informal hearing in lineage territory before the ten-house cell leader, kin, and neighbors, lengthy discussion involved many "modern" and "traditional" arguments. Richard argued that the path was government property on which nothing new should have been planted, and used traditional arguments about how the boundary plants had been placed by the grandfathers and should not have been disturbed by Elifatio. Elifatio made modern arguments that it was desirable to increase food production, hence the substitution of useful fruit trees for useless boundary plants was justified, and that the planting was also a measure against soil erosion, and traditional arguments that in places the land on both sides of the boundary had been his, acquired through inheritance, and that he had the right to remove and replace boundary plants on his own property. Spectators argued on both sides as well as the principals. Many other issues were raised. Elifatio continued to demand reimbursement for the uprooted seedlings. Richard eventually asserted that he was righting a wrong when he uprooted them.

Richard won his case. The decision was pronounced by the ten-house cell leader but was congruent with the expressed views of certain lineage elders, and those local white-collar men present, all of whom were Richard's friends. Whether Richard won because he belonged to the stronger lineage segment or because he was a relatively educated salaried man and Elifatio was a simple farmer of little education is not clear. There were persuasive normative rules on both sides. Normative rules did not determine the decision; men did. Three kinds of social relations were significant in the hearing: the lineage, TANU in the person of the cell leader, and the local salaried elite. Richard's victory was congruent with all of their structural interests. He belonged to the more powerful section of the lineage. He was a more useful constituent to the cell leader. He was an active member of the local salaried group which often has contempt for men like Elifatio, their barefoot cousins. This dispute, its hearing in the neighborhood and its later hearing in a court, clearly shows that these particular quarrels between particular individuals are the occasion for assertions of social power. Persons who typify the competition among local organizations and economic categories for control over local affairs often manifest their interests in these situations of personal but public confrontation. The immediate outcome may seem trivial because it affects only the affairs of two rural Chagga men. But the process represents struggles taking place on a much larger scale.

Elifatio did not give up. He brought his case to the primary court as a criminal matter: the malicious destruction of property. He characterized going to the primary court as an "appeal." The reason to bring such a grievance as a criminal case is simply financial. No fee is required of the complainant in a criminal case, whereas a fee is required in a civil case. Nevertheless the magistrate has great flexibility in being able to give civil remedies in criminal cases. This flexibility has been explicitly given by statute at various times and fits very well with the indigenous system of dispute resolution.[13]

Elifatio's court case was heard on August 22, 1968. Thus in less than a month he had two hearings of his case. The picking of the seedlings had occurred on July 28, the hearing before the *balozi* on August 16, and within a week he was in the primary court. The speed was not unusual. Elifatio felt that he had an open and shut case because Richard had admitted to uprooting the plants in the hearing before the *balozi*. As is usual in such proceedings, Elifatio made his complaint. Richard was then allowed to question him. Richard asked, "Why don't you produce witnesses?" Elifatio replied that he thought it unnecessary since Richard had admitted pulling up the plants. Richard then denied having pulled them up. (Note that in the questioning period Richard was not yet under oath, the oaths usually being taken before the formal statement of each party.)

Elifatio's son was, as it turned out, his only witness. He was a thin, sad, and timid-looking boy of seventeen, who looked, as many Chagga adolescents do to American eyes, much younger. He was tall, and his thin wrists stuck far out of his threadbare cotton jacket. He testified that he had seen Richard pull up the seedlings. Richard used his question period rather irregularly, as often happens, and magistrates do not always intervene. Richard not only asked questions but used the opportunity to make a statement, "You did not see me. You were told by your father what to say in this court." The boy seemed terrified. When asked by the magistrate whether he saw the seedlings in Richard's hand, he said he had not. The boy's statement was then read back to him and he signed. The magistrate then asked Elifatio if he had any other witnesses, and he said,

"Yes, there are the people who heard the case before the *balozi*." "No," said the magistrate, "I will not hear them. I want people who *saw Richard* uprooting the trees." There were none.

Richard was then put under oath and asked to make his statement. "I have no statement," he said. Later his kinsman told me that Richard had made no statement because he did not want to lie under oath. It was Elifatio's turn to ask questions, but he, the poor farmer, was no match for his educated kinsman. "What," he asked Richard, "What did you say before the *balozi*?" "I denied doing it." And that of course was true, as Richard had both denied and ultimately admitted it at various stages of the proceedings before the *balozi*. Elifatio's questions turned against him. He kept helplessly insisting that Richard had admitted everything before the *balozi*. "Then why," said the magistrate, "did you fail to win that case?"

In fact, one of Richard's educated friends who had been at the neighborhood hearing visited with the magistrate in his office just before the court session started, and the magistrate probably knew precisely what had happened in the earlier hearing. He was likely influenced against Elifatio. His questioning and verbal bullying of Elifatio and his son suggested partisanship. Richard did not know the presiding magistrate, but the educated friend who visited with him knew both men and probably swayed the magistrate on Richard's behalf. The bond between them was that of men with salaries and white-collar jobs and a stretch of boarding school behind them, men who drink together in the afternoons, and look down on their farmer brothers. They themselves (or their wives) cultivate their groves like any other Chagga, job or no job, but they are more prosperous than any simple farmer, and more worldly.

One of the two assessors put in his opinion. "If Richard had admitted it you would have won before the *balozi*. What is the relationship between you?" The magistrate did not allow the last question of the assessor to stand (the one about their relationship) on the ground that it was not relevant, since no statements had been made during the case about any enmity between Elifatio and Richard. He then asked Richard if he had any witnesses. Richard said he did not. The case was at an end. Poor Elifatio had lost again. Lack of evidence.

A PALAVER ABOUT SORCERY: ELIFATIO'S SISTER

As if poor Elifatio did not have trouble enough with his boundary dispute with Richard, the next year brought him another difficulty. Elifatio has a sister whose bridewealth he received. This sister was accused of witchcraft, and therefore she could be sent away by her husband. She would then have to take refuge with Elifatio. The father of Elifatio had three daughters by his first wife, who also bore Lewange and Elifatio. He divided the bridewealth of his daughters among his sons. Lewange was the firstborn son so he received the bridewealth of two sisters. Elifatio received the bridewealth from the marriage of the remaining sister. When a man is old and cannot otherwise financially help his sons, he may decide to divide his daughters among them in this manner. If he does not do this in his lifetime, then it can be done at the father's *matanga*. In this case, the old man divided up his daughters before he died. Therefore each recipient of bridewealth became ultimately responsible for the welfare of the sister from whose marriage he had profited.

Elifatio's sister was accused of sorcery after the death of her immediate neighbor, her sister-in-law. Elifatio's sister and the dead woman were married to two brothers and lived in the same *kihamba* garden though they had different houses. The illness of the sister-in-law had been long. She had a headache and stomach ache that were severe. Her husband had first taken her to the hospital, but they could not help her. Then he took her to a diviner-healer (*mganga*) in Rombo. She stayed there for two months and came back cured. But the next year she became ill again. She returned to the same *mganga,* but this time she died, in Rombo, and her husband hired a vehicle to bring back her body to bury her at home. When she was ill, she reportedly said, "It is the wife of my husband's brother who is bewitching me." The wife of her husband's brother was Elifatio's sister.

It was not the first time that the woman had been accused of sorcery. Philemoni, an unrelated neighbor of the women, said that he knew about the earlier accusation as he was a close friend of the deceased woman's husband. They drink *pombe* together and they also give each other meat when they slaughter animals. Sometime ago, Philemoni did not remember the date exactly, but about six years earlier (about 1964), a son of another neighbor died. The child had previously visited the house of Elifatio's sister, and she had given the child some food. Philemoni said that Elifatio's sister did not feed this child with her own children, but gave the food to this child separately. From such cases one comes to understand that eating from a common pot constitutes a precaution against poisoning. It is not simply a matter of a lack of separate containers.

The mother of the child had gone to the house of Elifatio's sister to look for her son. When she arrived she found him eating some food in a bowl. He was eating alone. The mother did not say anything, except to tell her son to return home after finishing his food. Then she went home. Her son followed a little bit later. The same day he became sick, suffering from some stomach disorder, and later on died.

Thereafter there was a fight between the mother of the dead child and Elifatio's sister. The mother accused Elifatio's sister of killing her child with sorcery. A hearing took place before members of the M——— lineage and the lineage of Elifatio's sister's husband. Since no one was able to prove that Elifatio's sister was a *mchawi* (witch) the mother of the dead child was fined. She had to pay one goat plus *pombe* (beer) to rewash the name of Elifatio's sister.

Elifatio's sister seems to have quarreled often with her husband, as well as with his brother's wife. As a neighbor and intermediary, Philemoni claims to have settled a number of these quarrels. No witchcraft accusations occurred the first time that the sister-in-law was ill because she recovered. But the second time she fell ill was after she had had a fight with the sister of Elifatio at a *pombe* party. It was said later that the sister of Elifatio had threatened her sister-in-law saying, "Utaona, you shall see," which is a death threat. Philemoni himself had not heard her say it, but he was told that she had said this. At a hearing Elifatio's sister was found guilty of threatening her sister-in-law and was fined.

Then the matter was quiet until the sister-in-law died. At the *matanga* the deceased woman's husband told everyone that his wife had said that Elifatio's sister was killing her. He and his wife had often been on bad terms. For one thing, though she had had five children, they were all girls. On his mother's advice, he had decided to look for another woman because he wanted a son. He found another woman and this woman also had a girl. He and his wife were then expelled from the church because of the bigamous arrangement. The wife asked her husband to beg the pastor to let them back into the church so that their children could be baptized. The pastor readmitted them and the children were baptized. The whole matter was reviewed at the *matanga*.

The husband of the dead woman told the people that when she was ill his wife had said to him, "I am dying. I am warning you. Do not allow my children to be given food by the wife of your brother, and do not let her take care of my children, because she is killing me. After she and I quarreled she said, 'Utaona.' " The dying woman went on addressing her husband, "You cannot marry the girl with whom you have a child. You must marry a woman who has no children. If I die the wife of your brother must not sleep in the house. (During the four days following a death, close relatives and neighbors come and sleep in the house of the dead person.) If this wife of your brother comes, she will bring an animal which will attack her just in the doorway, when she is entering the house." After this warning his wife died.

In fact, everyone knew that on the very day of the death of his wife, the accused woman had gone to the house of the dead woman to sleep there with the other women, and that just as she stood in the doorway, a *kiphaphivi* had appeared. (A *kiphaphivi* is a small animal, I am told, that lives on the mountain. When it is frightened it rolls up into a ball.) When she saw it she ran away.

People said that a few days later, at the *matanga,* Elifatio's sister was supposed to have told Abinezeri the widower, "If you marry another woman I will keep a child in her womb until it becomes as big as a drum," thus threatening him with the death of any new wife and unborn child. The husband of Elifatio's sister did not defend her at the *matanga.* He said he was angry with his wife when he heard what she was accused of, and he told everyone at the *matanga* that he was sorry about what his wife had done and that if he could he would kill her. But as this was impossible he would send her home to her brother Elifatio, that is, he would divorce her and send her packing.[14]

Needless to say, the whole neighborhood was agog about the case. The accused woman went to her senior brother Lewange and complained to him about the things that were being said about her. She denied having any responsibility for this disaster. Lewange told her to return to her husband and to inform him of the date set for a hearing. Lewange told others that he was not sure but that his sister might be a *mchawi* (witch). Interestingly enough, Elifatio, who (because he had received her bride-wealth) would have had to give this sister a haven in his house if it was decided that she was a witch, was the only person who firmly and repeatedly stated that she was not a witch and that the whole story was a fabrication. He said that if her husband did not like her, he should divorce her properly by paying Elifatio a cow and a goat and sending her home to him. (If she was sent away for cause, the payment of the cow and the goat would not have to be made.)

The gossips did not rest. A woman in the neighborhood whose brother was married to yet another sister of Elifatio's said that it was well known that this other sister was also a *mchawi* (witch). The couple lived in another village, where there had also been a case in which that other sister of Elifatio had bewitched a child of her husband's brother, and the child had died. The gossip asserted that all the sisters of Elifatio are called *wachawi* (witches) and that their mother before them was well known to be a *mchawi.*

While Elifatio's accused sister awaited the palaver before a tribunal of kin and neighbors she took shelter in the house of Elifatio, and he made her welcome. The case was heard about six months later, early in 1971. Quite a number of people attended, but no *balozi* was officially present, as, of course, witchcraft trials are illegal. The persons at the hearing were nine male members of the M—— clan, some of whom brought their wives, and six male members of the clan of the accused woman's husband.[15]

The hearing took the form of a complaint by Elifatio saying that his sister had been wrongfully accused, and demanding compensation for her slander. He said that he had asked for a hearing concerning the first accusation over the death of the child in 1964, and neither the *mkara* (trustee-mediator of the marriage) nor the husband had been willing to hold a palaver and he had not pressed the matter. But now he must insist that his sister had been wronged.

The sister then said she had not harmed the child, or her sister-in-law, and that she knew nothing of witchcraft. Her husband then stood up and said he did not believe his wife to be a witch, that he had not been around during this time of trouble because he was sick in the hospital, recovering from having fallen out of a tree. Why his position had changed from the time of the *matanga* is not clear. It may have been a matter of being faced down by his wife's kinsmen.

The *mkara* then mentioned the earlier case of the child who had died. The case had been passed on to the church elders and then ultimately to the pastor. But nothing was done and there was no settlement. The *mkara* also said he had made no effort to settle the witchcraft accusation about the death of the sister-in-law because it was such a grave accusation.

The widower then said he could produce two witnesses who had heard the quarrel between the women and heard Elifatio's sister say, "*Utaona*." He was asked to name the witnesses and he refused, saying he needed a few days. He was given some days to bring forward his witnesses, but did not do so.

Two days after this palaver the wife returned to live with her husband. I was not able to find out what settlement had taken place, but clearly something had been resolved. Shortly thereafter husband and wife were seen drinking *pombe* (beer) together and invited Elifatio to join them. Elifatio's sister was still living with her husband in 1979, but whether there was further trouble, I do not know.

DELAYED PUNISHMENT: THE ILLNESS OF A DAUGHTER-IN-LAW WHO DID NOT RESPECT HER HUSBAND'S MOTHER

In 1974 the wife of Mvunamo was bedridden and had become as small and shrunken as a four-year-old. She could not eat much, could not talk, just lay in bed, and had to be carried out-of-doors. She had been in this condition for four years and the doctors could do nothing for her.

People said that when she was first married, and had just had a child, her husband's mother lived in the same house. The mother-in-law had a swollen leg, and the leg smelled very bad. Mvunamo's wife did not like having her husband's mother cook for her and asked her own mother to come and take care of her during her period of confinement. Her own mother did not share the food with the mother-in-law. The mother-in-law with the swollen leg became angry. "You invited your mother to come so I could not eat the food of my son."

One day Mvunamo's wife assaulted her mother-in-law. The mother-in-law left that house and went to live with another son who lived in a nearby village. She stayed there until she died. When, after many years, the wife of Mvunamo became sick people said, "She is sick because of what she did to her husband's mother."

NEW TROUBLES OVER OLD LAND CLAIMS: WILIBALD'S GRANDSON IS ATTACKED BY SPIRITS

In 1979 there were strains between the family of Wilibald and that of Uruka. A year earlier Filipo had slaughtered a cow at his son's wedding and had shared it with Wilibald and all of Wilibald's family, but there had been no meat sharing since. The reason was that in the interval Wilibald's grandson (David's son), then a slight boy of twelve or thirteen, was alone at home in the evening and he was beaten by some "unknown person or spirits." The whole house was in disarray; chairs were upside down, some thrown out of the house; everything was strewn about. Wilibald consulted a *mganga*. He sought one out in Dar es Salaam and later, with his wife, went to a *mganga* in Tanga. Divination told them that it was a case of sorcery. They suspected Mamkinga and Filipo of buying *jini* in Tanga to bewitch Wilibald's family. Mamkinga and Filipo replied that they were willing to show they were not guilty of sorcery or witchcraft, and would slaughter a goat in the *kihamba,* taking a drink of the blood and swearing a blood oath.[16] The procedure would involve a blood libation to the ancestors, and a call to them by name to strike dead any guilty person who drank the blood and swore the oath.[17] I was told that the goat was not slaughtered, that instead Wilibald and Ndesario had met to try to work out a settlement but had not succeeded.

Another explanation of the trouble is current. An explanation that might give Filipo a claim to the land on which the disturbed house stood was that the land itself was cursed and was making the trouble. Two generations before, the *kihamba* of Wilibald had been the *kihamba* of the widow of Kinyala (a brother of Uruka's father, Wikiwawoko) who died without sons (see Figures 8.1 and 8.4). Wikiwawoko was Kinyala's heir and inherited his land and widow. The widow was badly treated by some of the M——s. They took her beasts and slaughtered them. They cut bananas in her *kihamba* without her permission. She decided to leave and to go back to her parents, but just before leaving she cursed the land, saying, "None of these M—— people will ever be able to stay in this *kihamba.*" Such curses make the land haunt anyone who wrongfully lives there and brings misfortune. She eventually died in her father's lineage territory.

In early October 1979, when Wilibald was at home from Dar es Salaam for a lineage meeting, Wilibald prepared beer for the daughter of the scorned widow, an aged woman, who lived nearby, to come to his house to give witness to the history of the *kihamba.* She said that all problems could be solved if the grandson of Wikiwawoko came to live in this *kihamba,* that is, Filipo. The logic of avoiding the curse by that means implied that the curse was confined to Wilibald's side of the family. The curse-escaping logic may be cloudy but the sociologic is clear. This woman was a daughter of Kinyala M——— whose bridewealth was paid to Filipo. (Her husband lived with another wife in the lower area.) Her tale was that the land had belonged to Kinyala's brother, Wikiwawoko, as heir of Kinyala (who died without sons, leaving only daughters). She said that Kinyala's brother had loaned the land to someone on the other side (i.e., in the other cow-slaughtering division, a descendant of Ndekira) of the local lineage for the payment of *masiro.* Wilibald wanted the *kihamba* and gave the relative a cow and goat and also gave him in exchange another *kihamba,* in another *mtaa.* Wilibald said he thus bought the land. Filipo said it could not have been bought because the occupier had the *kihamba* only on loan and could not sell it. Uruka then said he planted some bananas and coffee trees on the land (indication of right to land) before Wilibald got it. The fat was in the fire, and this dispute was likely to continue.[18] Could Filipo or Mamkinga have beaten the son of Wilibald themselves and messed up the house in order to try to frighten Wilibald's family, to trick Wilibald into surrendering the land to Filipo? Did they hire someone else to do it? Was the old woman bound to support Filipo's claim because he was the receiver of her bridewealth?

DISCREDITING A KINSMAN THROUGH SORCERY ALLEGATIONS

In 1973, three years after Elifatio was made heir/guardian of the estate of Mandasha, he was accused of plotting to bewitch Filipo. Filipo's daughter said that when she was working in the garden she saw Elifatio pass along the path next to it carrying a *panga* (large bush knife). She says he picked up a bit of soil from Filipo's *kihamba* with his *panga,* wrapped it in a banana leaf, and carried it off. Filipo went to the ten-house cell leader and complained that Elifatio was surely planning some act of sorcery or witchcraft against him. There was a hearing that included a number of men from the lineage and the cell leader, and Elifatio was fined a cow and a goat. Filipo waived the payment, saying that he was not so poor that he needed a cow and a goat from Elifatio. Hence nothing was paid. But the bad feeling between them continued, and Elifatio was not invited to the wedding of the son of Filipo, nor, of course, did he contribute anything toward the wedding. The exclusion of Elifatio was portentous since that was the great social event of 1978, to which virtually everyone locally resident in the lineage lands came, as did many neighbors as well. It is hard to see how he could be dislodged from his land and guardianship, but the means seemed to be in preparation. I was told in 1979 that most people in the lineage do not like him, that he "talks ill" of people in the lineage, that he does not "cooperate" properly with them, and so on. The next time I visit, another chapter of this nonfiction soap opera will unfold. I shall hear what has become of Elifatio. Probably nothing good.

IO

The local level and the larger setting

SOME IMPLICATIONS OF THE LINEAGE CHRONICLE: MUTUAL DEPENDENCE AND MUTUAL VULNERABILITY

This chronicle of disputation and allocation reveals on one side of life connivance and cruelty, selection for failure. The other side is the cheerful chatter, the warmth, the laughing and drinking beer together, the common rituals, the exchange of labor, the mutual assistance, the lineage loyalties. They constitute an interlocked existential reality. In its essential exchanges and common history is a submerged system of accounting. The life-term social arena is unforgetting and unforgiving. But it is a system of relative positions, not of absolute ones, and the balances keep moving as the situation changes. The level of potential and actual tension in agnatic relationships today is as high as the continuous mutual involvement. The kinship arena has not disappeared from Kilimanjaro, nor have its conflicts. Dispute, allocation, and litigation in a "customary law" framework display many of the tensions in a raw form. Twenty-seven episodes of dispute in the lineage of the M——s are noted here.[1] There were undoubtedly others that did not come to the surface in the period of fieldwork. In reviewing court case records, for example, I found that in 1968 Mlatie had been sued for a debt he owed to a nonkinsman, a debt of 100 shillings, and that in 1967 Nathanieli who was mentally ill had been taken to court twice by neighbors on charges of assault. As these were not matters of internal lineage disputation, I had not heard about them in any detail. Among the episodes of dispute that did come to light, and which have been reviewed here, were six fully developed allegations of witchcraft and four incidents of violence. Of the witchcraft accusations, three were made against women and three against men. In the incidents of physical violence, three were against women, one against a man. How suitable to many kinship settings is Goran Hyden's characterization of Tanzanian peasant life as founded on an "economy of affection" (1980:18–19)?

In a closed circle in which the dislikes of some become the misfortunes of others, the normal solution for the potential victims is exit. What the demographic, educational, and economic changes of the twentieth century have meant on Kilimanjaro is that for the fortunate there are new opportunities, for others the exits have almost closed. In 1969 when, in an effort both to alleviate the land shortage and develop new areas of Tanzania, the government called for volunteers to pioneer in unoccupied lands in Mwese, the two men from the M—— lineage who volunteered were Kisoka (16) and a son of Mlatie (13). Both knew there was little ahead for them on Kilimanjaro. But even so they found pioneering too arduous and lonely, and they returned some months later.[2] The opportunities to resettle and make a new life are few for the men at the bottom of the heap and for their sons. Yet those are the very persons who need a way out. Disliked by their kinsmen (for bad reasons? for good reasons?) some men are cut out of their patrimony and pushed out. This process must frighten those who generate the pressures, to say nothing of the others who witness the demolition and do nothing to hold out a hand. The penalties for losers are harsh. But the winners can be left with fear of the effects of the anger they cause.

An angry person can use a great range of techniques to wreak supernatural vengeance.[3] But the Chagga may derive some comfort from the notion that many of the methods talked about now require a physical act that involves contact with the victim, and they require special knowledge. Unless the means of bewitching have been inherited in the family, it may be an expensive business, with a journey to Tanga or even farther to buy the necessary ingredients. A bit of bewitched substance may then be put in the path of the *kihamba* of the victim so that he or she will step on it. (The same substance would be ineffective in a public road.) Or some small bit of earth from the *kihamba* may be taken and turned into an agent of misfortune against the possessor. Or something harmful may be placed in the drink or food of the victim. Or a conditional curse may be uttered: "You shall *see*," or "I leave it to God." The curse may be put on the land itself so that there is indwelling vengeance in the very earth. A woman can throw her cloth on the ground of the *kihamba* and bring misfortune to all who wrongfully dwell there later on. The dead buried nearby may also choose to intervene.

The vengeance-prone do not act without risk to themselves, but there is a tight sociogeography associated with such a system. The victim could lose his or her life in an auto accident far away from the location of the vengeance-seeker, or he or she might contract an illness years later when residing in another place. But at the moment the harm is laid on, there is usually some contact with the person or with something intimately belonging to or connected with the person. Since these measures require action and close contact, the departure of the angry one from whom there might be danger is welcome. If the person is never seen again, the danger may leave with him/her. The harm may have been successfully inserted beforehand. But it may not. Or ritual countermeasures or talismans may make it ineffective. God and church may save from harm. Skepticism may even save from fear. In any case, once the harm-wisher is out of sight and far away for good, no new direct damage can be done.

It is obvious from the chronicle of the M——s that worry over the possibility of such vengeance does not necessarily deter anyone from hostile acts. In the eleven years from 1968 to 1979 the M——s hounded two of their kinsmen until they permanently left the lineage area, Ndesario (12) and Kisoka (16), one of them eventually to commit suicide. Both men sold their rights in their land to nonkinsmen. It was the only form of this-worldly retaliation available to them. Whether they took otherworldly measures (or will be thought to have done so) remains to be seen. But the land is lost to the M——s.

CUSTOM AS A LUXURY

Salaried men or "businessmen" or "rich" men buy up parcels of land whenever they can. The better off M——s do this whenever an affordable opportunity presents itself. This process signifies that in this generation some men are still able to accumulate enough land to provide for their sons. But it is only the most prosperous who can afford to meet the traditional obligations of paternity. "Social reproduction" in this sense is a luxury. Meeting cultural conventions about land in current circumstances is something not all can afford.

Failure to maintain tradition on other levels is also something with which the well-off can belabor the poor. The well-to-do can be at once both more modern and more traditional than their less fortunate relatives. The provision for sons, the payment of generous amounts of bridewealth, the holding of large celebrations for baptisms, weddings, and circumcisions, the slaughtering of beasts for feasting, for mourning, the provision of tubs of beer, all these involve substantial economic investments which are less and less possible for poor families. The poor know the techniques of production of all the necessary items of ritual exchange, but they lack the means. The poor cannot afford to be properly traditional and they certainly cannot afford to be modern. How ill conceived are the usual remarks about the nonprogressiveness of peasants.

Disparities of wealth are not new. They existed in precolonial times. The chiefs and their cronies could always be more generous than others. We may be led to ask, "Who made the rules?" Who set the measure of virtue in terms that only some could satisfy? The Chagga seem to have had a cultural preoccupation with that form of obligatory generosity

Fortes so aptly called "prescriptive altruism" (1969:237). But that preoccupation can be variously interpreted. It can have differing meanings in different settings, and at different periods. In one of its crudest forms the capacity to be generous can function as a display of wealth. Does a concern with generosity as a moral value then "euphemize" and conceal a preoccupation with economy and material matters, as Bourdieu (1977) would have it? Or does it emphasize and exaggerate it? The literature on gift-giving from Mauss to Sahlins tends to emphasize exchange, lest gifts be misunderstood as being given without an expectation of return (Mauss 1954; Sahlins 1972). That emphasis should not distract attention from the way in which an ethic of generosity emphasizes the divide between the wealthy and the poor in any system in which there are economic differences. The authority inherent in material superiority is further enhanced by moral authority in which such an ethic prevails. "Prescriptive altruism" translates the many manifestations of the stinginess and craftiness of poverty into moral faults. Filipo's use of competitive slaughtering to put down Mlatie, to shame him for having sold an animal instead of slaughtering it and sharing it with kin, is an example of this. Filipo could afford such action. Mlatie could not.

Among the Chagga to the extent that the basis of differentiation has changed in this century, so also has the meaning of traditional practices. In many situations the observance of tradition has come to serve as an objectification of modern social power. Its dynamic lies in the present even though its form is linked to the past.

COURTS, OFFICIALS, PASTORS, AND DIVINERS: THE USE OF OUTSIDE AGENCIES IN INTERNAL DISPUTE

The lineage chronicle makes it clear that the courts are not the only authoritative agencies used when Chagga disputants choose to try to further their interests by drawing in outsiders. In situations of dispute, the M——s appealed to whatever entity might suit their purposes. The pastors and priests were one resource. They also approached officials high and low. Today, it is obligatory to inform the ten-house cell leader of any local altercation, and there is pressure to include him in any hearing or occasion of public allocation of any size. By no means are cell leaders always included, however. Above that level, the M——s have gone to other party and administrative officials. The *baraza la usuluhishi,* the arbitration tribunals, are one avenue they use little, but other wards use them more often. Instead,, the M——s appeal to any official they know. They also resort to *waganga,* diviners and healers. Since the objective of a disputant, or someone with a grievance (or an allocation to make that will be resisted), is to get someone to do something or to acquiesce, word from any powerful person may be enough. The court is simply one such agency among others. But most matters that can be are handled "at home."

However disputatious the lineage of the M——s may seem, it is not significantly different from many others. Some are larger, some smaller. Some few have more prosperous men, many have fewer. But in general, the processes exemplified by the chronicle of the M——s are taking place in those many parts of Kilimanjaro where localized lineage clusters are still the dominant pattern of residence.[4]

There is an unofficial but efficacious dual (or multiple) structure of incentives and controls in the rural social field. It is not surprising that conformity to requirements that cannot be enforced in the formal legal system may be coerced or induced in the social arena of lineage and neighborhood. But the mobilization (or deflection) of the formal system by the M——s shows the extent to which public institutions themselves can be used as an adjunct of local relationships. This approach is nowhere better exemplified than in the criminal cases mentioned in the chronicle. One, the automobile accident case involving Mamkinga (19), ended with the payment to someone else to serve what should have been his jail sentence. At least three other criminal cases, one against Filipo for dealing in ivory, one against Elifatio for beating Ndesario's wife, one against Richard for malicious destruction of property, came to nothing. Both Filipo and Elifatio used their educated kinsmen to help them out of trouble, and "fix" each of their cases, though both were undoubtedly guilty. And Elifatio was no match in court for Richard. They resorted to the formal system of primary courts in all of these instances, as well as in some of the civil disputes affecting members of the lineage. However, the manipulation of witnesses, of evidence, of court personnel, shows that, though the formal legal agencies at the local level are an adjunct of national institutions, they are often used as the instruments of the local social system.

The practical capacity of the court to obtain independent information, indeed the interest and energy of the court to pursue such questions, is on the whole lacking as observed in the period 1968–79, and likely was so earlier as well. Since independence, there has been an effort to assign primary court magistrates to courts outside the ex-chiefdom from which they come in the interest of impartiality. Such assignments may decrease the vulnerability of magistrates to the local politics that sometimes characterized the chief's courts and their successors during the colonial period. But the other side of the coin is that the magistrates now sitting in the courts, being personally ignorant of the social identities of most of the persons appearing before them, or their common history, tend to rely heavily on clues evident from differences of education, speech, behavior in court, types of witnesses called, and other gross visible characterizations of status and temperament to infer relationships. They are themselves members of the educated salaried class, which is not to say that they always rule in favor of their own kind. On the contrary. But they "hear" their own kind in a different way.

Magistrates also have a particular and rather limited conception of the task before them. They tend to treat each case on its face, often perfunctorily and rather mechanically. Unless the parties are socially matched protagonists, one is likely to control the information that emerges in the court. Even if they are matched, the chances that the magistrate will inquire into the long-term underlying tensions are small. The magistrate is more likely to try to limit the issues than expand them. Within its jurisdiction the technical power exists in the court to subpoena witnesses, to inquire into anything at all it deems relevant, to reach any resolution within its allocated powers that it deems just. But the office is not used to make the work harder. The two "assessors" who sit with the magistrate at hearings are local men who give advisory opinions. The way the hearing is structured, their role is usually limited. All the court officials, magistrate, assessors, clerk, and court messenger, are Chagga. They all come from lineages like that of the M——s. They know life in the countryside. But their highly formal conception of their official duties tends to make them screen out inconvenient aspects of that knowledge for the purpose of the hearings before them. They usually treat cases in terms of the formal category under which the clerk has advised the complainant to file. The issues are narrowed by this process before the case is heard.

In theory the issues could again be broadened during the proceedings. But there are pressures that militate against doing so. No lawyers are allowed to appear in the primary courts. The magistrate is a major interrogator of parties and witnesses and directs the proceedings. He is also both judge and court stenographer. It is he who must write out the testimony of parties and witnesses. He does so in longhand in Swahili, and reads the record back to the speakers after each party or witness concludes. The speaker then is asked if he/she accepts the record as read. The process is slow and repetitious. This method of constructing the record alone would be a brake on extending inquiry. Some case records are quite long as it is, but most are short. The magistrate does not want matters to go on and on, only to achieve a match between the grounds for decision and the nature of the record so that should there be an appeal (unusual), or should the record ever be inspected (extremely unlikely) the magistrate will not be reprimanded. This desirable match is often achieved by saying, "The plaintiff (or complaining witness) has not proved his case."[5] The easiest way to reach an unassailable conclusion is to base it on the question of evidence. Such a decision requires least explanation on the part of the magistrate.

The nature of the contacts of the lineage of the M——s with the formal court system is not unusual. Together the parties and the magistrate construct a record that is inevitably selective and incomplete, sometimes even misleading, and assumes a generally conventional form. The results in the files are records of what the proponents thought were plausible cases, what they managed to marshal in the way of witnesses, and what the magistrate recorded of their statements, and chose to note as the basis of decision. Any reading of the records of the primary courts (or any other courts) must take this process of document construction into account. The case record, once written is fixed, and acquires a degree of immobility and authority. It transforms an oral situation into a written record (see Goody 1977). It becomes an object itself which can subsequently be used. The parties can use it to enforce judgment, to appeal, to foreclose a rehearing of the same issues, and the like. The record in the file also demonstrates the magistrate's work to his superiors. The record has uses in the various social situations that generated it, but it can never be taken as fully describing those situations.

Since independence, the magistrates have had an increased training period of some months' duration. Their technical knowledge of forms and procedures has been enlarged, but they are not thoroughly grounded in the formal system of law. And they certainly were much less so in the past. But of course all magistrates know a good deal about Chagga norms and practices, at least those of the villages from which they come. Their years at boarding school do not separate them completely from that setting. However, as they have become better trained in the national system, particularly in the rules relating to criminal law, the written records of cases have become less revealing of the social facts and more routinely descriptive in terms of the statutory categories. The records are often more "correct" but less informative, a method presumably more and more characteristic as the bureaucracy standardizes and perfects its style.

Knowledge of the saga of the M——s, and of the events of allocation and disputation in which they were involved, puts into perspective those cases that reach the courts and other formal agencies. As in other societies (all?), among the Chagga most events that could be presented to the formal system for disposition are not brought to it but are "settled" outside. That is to say, episodes that erupt in open dispute or threaten to do so often are "closed" by means other than a resort to litigation in the formal system. They are ended in some temporal sense. The episode is ended, but not necessarily the dispute. Nor is there necessarily "settlement." Of these affairs, those that do reach the courts or other formal agencies never appear in their full contextual complication. Most are pieces of a story selected by their proponents in the hope of mobilizing support.

FACTORS AFFECTING SOCIAL STRENGTH IN
THE INTERNAL ARENA OF COMPETITION

The relative positions of social strength of the men in the lineage of the M——s are continuously in the process of being sorted out, and rearranged. The hierarchy of age is a constant, but many less stable factors strongly affect standing. Disputes and allocations are among the more overt expressions of the process of challenging, testing, and selection in which some succeed, some fail disastrously, some just manage to stay afloat, but not without bobbing around in the storms. Among those just managing not to sink, it is hard to predict in advance who will be more secure and who less by the end of a particular decade. Too many chance matters including illness and death enter the list of relevant contingencies. But what seems most certain is that the salaried men who survive are likely to be among the winners. The salaried seem to be the most steadily successful category inside the lineage. They press their poor relatives to give them first refusal on any land that might be sold, and use their positions as creditors to control their kin. They have contacts on the outside that their less well-off kinsmen do not have. They are in position to make loans and to do favors. The poor fight among themselves. Sometimes they are the victims of the manipulations and allocations of their better-off relatives, and the targets of their accusations. But as often as not, they are trying to discredit one another, and to make gains to one another's cost. The well-off are not immune to critical allegations, but they disturb their life course less than others. Filipo was accused of lack of generosity both when he refused to drive Richard to the hospital in his car and when his father, Uruka, asked him for money and he refused. But it is probably not insignificant that Richard is also a salaried man and secure and Uruka is the most senior male in the whole of the localized lineage. One may speculate that they could never have pressed these annoyances to the point of their becoming public knowledge in the lineage had they not been in favorable positions themselves. Less well-situated persons know that it is useless to argue. Thus Filipo's third wife objected when he reallocated the *kihamba* she had been given when they married, and gave it to the first son of his fifth wife, but when she found no support, she simply left the assembled company which proceeded with the reallocation. Acquiescence is frequently the only possible course when the powerful are manipulating the affairs of the weak. Women, unless they are protected by powerful kinsmen, and fatherless young men are in a structurally weak position which they can seldom overcome.

There is more than one example among the M——s of guardians cheating their wards. The "good faith" economy that is sometimes argued to be a general attribute of kin-based societies belongs to the Chagga today more as ideology than as practice. Was it ever otherwise?

Chagga legal rules precast certain persons in difficult roles giving others an opportunity to take advantage of them when there is sufficient temptation to do so. Widows and fatherless youths are not the only vulnerable persons. The traditional rules that disfavor middle sons, requiring them to cultivate bush and giving them the smallest share of any inheritance, also mark them for difficulties. Applied in modern contexts in new versions these rules seem to make middle sons more prone to failure than sons more fortunate in their birth order. One does not have to be a middle son to fail in the lineage arena (viz., the case of Kisoka), but being a middle son may make it more likely.

Genealogies show that in the last two or three generations there have been many three-son families in which all three sons survived to adulthood.[6] If the precolonial population was stable the rules applying to middle sons must have been rarely used.[7] When they were, the hardships implied were different from those today. There was no shortage of land. A middle son might have been cattle-poor, and might have had to settle at some distance from the lineage core. He would have been obliged to develop his own banana grove himself, but he would have had a *kihamba* without depriving any of his kinsmen of land they would otherwise have had. That is no longer the case. Even now middle sons are not ordinarily expected to get as much as their brothers. The corollary assumption is that, when they do not, their envy will be such that they or their wives will be tempted to use supernatural means to obtain more for themselves and their own sons. They are thus potentially dangerous to their agnates.

In the chronicle of the M——s, of those sons with land in the core lineage territory the four middle sons in the lineage seem to have experienced more than their share of trouble. Elifatio (14), Ndesario (12), and Mlatie (13) all are or have been in serious difficulties with their agnates. Allegations of witchcraft have been made about two of them and about the wives of two of them. The fourth, Yosia (20), is a "mental case" who is not well looked after by his brothers. Indeed, his elder brother, with the connivance of his father, sold Yosia's land and tried to pocket the proceeds.

At the moment, unprotected women, fatherless young men, middle sons, and uneducated land-poor men are the most vulnerable persons attached to or in the lineage. Senior and educated, salaried men are in the strongest positions. But whether this particular mixture of "customary" and new criteria for internal lineage power will have any durability over time is as uncertain as the question whether the lineage itself will continue as a significant arena of competition.

Is the legal manipulation, the instrumental activity, the disputation in Chagga life that is evident in the chronicle a transformation that has come with land shortage and population explosion? Was it not also an important element in lineage life when the economic object of competition was cattle? Certainly Gutmann's account indicates that enmity between brothers and disputes over property are not new. Chagga family histories are full of accounts of disputes among agnates in earlier generations. Whether such episodes have always been as frequent or as bitter is difficult to tell. Gutmann saw these matters as evidence of a decline of a peaceful and disciplined collective life which he assumed had once existed. I am not convinced that it ever did. Even the norms as he stated them suggest otherwise. The ranked relationships of brothers, the testing of the slaughtering distributions, the mention of betrayals and fraternal killings, the existence of cattle-rich and cattle-poor men, suggest that internal competitiveness is not new. Has it worsened? Certainly the terms and substance have changed with demographic and economic conditions. Only the general framework of the lineage arena of competition is an old one. The stated norms of "customary law" are a part of that. But this is anything but a pure case of social reproduction.

Is the central process at work today simply a rivalry for land? That is too compressed an explanation though the rural Chagga themselves are most conspicuously concerned with land. The Chagga have also long competed for another resource: money, and land is not the only route to cash. With some important exceptions, it is education that gives access to well-paid jobs.[8] The pressure for education on Kilimanjaro is not only a hunger for knowledge. Such a hunger exists, but education is the path to real economic gains. It leads to salaried jobs. Jobs bring money and money buys land, or enables a household to survive on a small plot. Thus the salaried have access to the very thing the "peasant" needs even more urgently and cannot obtain. Both rely on kinship for some land. But there it stops for the poor. The men with extra sources of cash use the additional means to buy food or to enter the market to buy extra plots. The dream of the most ambitious rural Chagga is to combine some means of access to cash with access to land. No one lives on coffee cash alone. All rural Chagga eat food from their own gardens and shambas. One way or another women, wives of the salaried as well as wives of the "peasants," must still grow the vegetable food that feeds their families. The wives of the salaried may hire casual labor to help them from time to time, and they may have a poor girl resident in the house to help with the children and the domestic work. They may even buy certain foods, but the household is still tied to subsistence production for a substantial part of its basic nourishment.

Under these conditions, given the transformed cultural framework within which the Chagga operate, it is not surprising that the downward trajectory of failure of a rejected kinsman is likely to be marked by disputes and accusations. How else is the doing of harm to be legitimated and made acceptable? Allegations of improper behavior in terms of traditional ideas about reciprocity, cooperativeness, and the like may presage later more serious accusations of financial irresponsibility, bad character, malevolence, and witchcraft. Cases arise. Wives may be accused as surrogates of their husbands. As economic differentiation takes its modern turn, the disparity between the land- and cash-poor and the salaried becomes irreparable, and the ideal of equivalent reciprocity between kinsmen becomes more permanently difficult to realize.

An outsider's first sympathy is with the weak members of the lineage, and their wives and children, the victims of this harsh system and the demographic and economic pressures that make its effects so extreme. But those on top are precariously placed, too. Their resources are not sufficient to carry the poor relatives along without serious risk to themselves. And they know that there is not enough land for their own sons. Compared with Western industrial workers, many Chagga "rich" are poor.

The demands of socialism have added new strains to life in the countryside and have put new pressures on close relationships. Many property arrangements that were legal and legitimate before independence are now against the law.[9] Many illegal or extralegal transactions nevertheless continue.[10] Not all party pronouncements are heeded. The knowledge that kinsmen have of the affairs of their agnates and neighbors now implies a possibility of betrayal to unfriendly authorities. The friendly ones look the other way, and their number is legion. Every man was always his brother's keeper in some sense. Now a new dimension has been added. A multiple-plot landholder has anxieties about confiscation, a new-house-builder about inquiries into the source of his means. The arena of local politics involves many tacit understandings about the new modes in which old business must be done. The general shortage of goods, the limited stocks of the price-controlled government stores, and the exorbitant prices in the private sector make for a peculiarly distorted economic life. Influence is needed to obtain many necessities. Personal networks loom larger than formal organizations, and goods and information move outside the official system. Kinsmen can be useful in these circumstances. The salaried are often useful because of their connections. Those without salaries are their clients, who can be helpful not only because of their current political legitimacy as "simple peasants" but because the salaried are by definition away at work most of the time and need kinsmen at home to look after their affairs and to keep an eye on their wives and children. Seldom do the salaried earn enough to take their families with them. Even if they could, their land would have to be worked, both for profit and to maintain rights in it. By indirection the new socialist laws affecting land have weakened (or perhaps done away with) the old Chagga rules about the permanent land rights of absent kinsmen. Anxiety over the matter and economic good sense keeps wives in lineage territory. Thus do the pressures aided by the new laws reinforce certain of the old relations of agnates.

THE LINEAGE IN LOCAL POLITICS

The new cooperative village structure may restore to the lineages some of their old political significance. By turning the sub*mtaa* into a closed political arena, the most ready-made divisions are the ones most likely to be mobilized. If the village ever comes to have resources and powers worth fighting over, local alignments will involve lineage relations. The salaried take the lead. The cooperative village in which the M——s live has 330 households, and the resident M——s represent 7 percent. The total probably amounts to a population of 2,000. Established in 1976, it has twenty-four ten-house cell leaders.[11] It is something less than a model of universal participation. At a meeting for the whole of the citizenry of the village in 1979, 167 persons turned up. Therefore, those who are active have, of course, a disproportionate say. The village has eight subcommittees with about five officers each. Together they constitute the central committee of the village. Filipo is an officer on three of the committees, and Richard and John are on two, one with Filipo and one without. It is no accident that of the M——s, Filipo is the most prominent person in village politics and holds several offices. But his alliances with others of his "class" is crosscut by his lineage and neighborhood affiliations. Both can be brought into play as the situation requires. The lineage is the primary arena of competition for many less prominent men. The old sub*mtaa*, now the village, is a newly reconstructed secondary arena for those men who operate politically beyond the immediate neighborhood.

The multiplicity of new villages and the nature of the party structure and ward organization will discourage effective political alliances among villages. "Villagization" constitutes the most recent step in fragmenting what was once a growing political coherence in the region. The division into tiny political subunits may or may not have been intended as a further limiting strategy, but it seems likely to have that effect. The increase of local formal structures of apparent democracy simultaneously limits and channels activity away from the regional and national level. The intense local inwardness evident from the lineage chronicle is not likely to be discouraged by such reorganization. Measures to preserve top party monopolies may entrench bottom-level localism.

FORMAL CONTROL THROUGH MEMBERSHIP ORGANIZATIONS

The capacity of a group to control its members has long preoccupied social theorists. Maine and Durkheim both conceived the individual as prisoner of the group in tribal societies, coming into his or her own only in modern settings. To them developments in law were parallel to this change. Many aspects of their conception of legal evolution are no longer theoretically acceptable. But the dynamic asymmetry of power between group and individual remains a central sociological problem.

The shape of the Chagga lineage today is an example of the complexity of organizational controls. These depend not only on the internal structure of the organization, but on the changing environment in which it is located. The very survival of the Chagga lineage today raises questions about the supralineage political organizations under whose formal dominion it has kept its small domain of autonomy. The cohesion of the lineage today fundamentally rests on its control over resources, principally people and land. Beyond its control over resources, how much of the impetus for lineage continuation comes from its convenience as a legitimate form of resistance to the interference of outsiders in local affairs? How much comes from the absence of an attractive alternative? Kinship and neighborhood are the principal ideologically and culturally legitimate resources for necessary forms of mutual support in the Chagga semisubsistence economy. How important are the opportunities for gain for the stronger members that the lineage also presents? The conjunction of all these elements has been congruent with the politicoeconomic setting to date. Will this conjunction continue?

Inherent in the asymmetry between the lineage and its individual members have been some tantalizing correspondences and connections with other asymmetries in the political environment in this century. The major group-individual asymmetrical transactions of male individuals have been of two kinds: the sort founded on indigenous traditional organizational controls and the sort founded on transactions with modern organizations. The essential structural peculiarity of the Chagga situation is that in each case, kin-based or not, modern sector-based or not, the transactor is normally a *member* of the major organizations with which he transacts.

When Americans buy food in a grocery, deal with a corporate landlord, contract with the telephone company, or are arrested by the police, they are not members of the organizations with which they are dealing. Historically that has not been so on Kilimanjaro for the most important organizations in the structure. The usual asymmetry for the Chagga is not between the organization and an individual *outside* it, but rather *inside* it.

At the local level, both the colonial and postcolonial periods have been marked by an emphasis on formal controls exercised through *membership organizations*. There is a certain continuity, a certain sameness in the pervasiveness of this type of control that connects the precolonial indigenous political system with all that has followed, including the structures of African socialism.

Considered in terms of conventional evolutionary ideas about the differences between small-scale and large-scale societies, between simple and complex structures, the various combinations and permutations of the asymmetrical relations between groups and individual members have important implications for the comparative study of politics.

The proliferation and diversification of corporate organizations that are characteristic of complex societies, are part of the formal milieu through which hierarchical relationships are realized. One of the resulting hallmarks of increasing societal scale is an immense multiplication of asymmetrical relationships and transactions. What has not always been so obvious is the degree to which an accompanying structural characteristic of Western industrial societies is not realized elsewhere. In the West as corporate groups have become more diverse and specialized, more and more asymmetrical transactions and relationships have been generated between organizations and individuals who are not legally or socially defined as members of those organizations. As noted earlier, despite long years of involvement in a cash economy, this development has not been characteristic of Kilimanjaro. In the most important controlling organizational relationships in its structure, local political/social arrangements remain basically membership oriented and "segmentary." The explanation evidently derives from a certain political history which has parallels in other parts of Africa, and in other parts of the world.

A fundamental background for present-day control through membership organizations was the indigenous political system for dealing with outsiders. Outsiders were persons belonging to groups other than their own, members of other lineages, or *mitaa,* or age-classes, or chiefdoms. When the Chagga dealt with outsiders individuals transacted with individuals, groups with groups. An individual placed his cattle with another individual, establishing a set of contractual understandings between them. Neither the kin group of the donor nor the kin group of the receiver was involved. But in a marriage transaction, or a transfer of land, individuals negotiated with their kin groups at their sides. Their assent was needed. In normative conception, and perhaps even in practice, Chagga dealt with organizations as individuals only if they were members. In precolonial times a man might have such dealings with his lineage, his irrigation association, his age-set, his district, and in some representative form, the chiefdom. He might have been disciplined by any of these groups. And every man belonged to exactly the same array of groups. If he found himself in any situation that involved an outside group, in indigenous political theory, he could mobilize the comparable group of which he was a member, and then it would be group against group. (See Moore on individual and collective responsibility, 1978:82–134).

The colonial period altered many things about this structure, but certain dimensions of the system of controls continued. Every major organization that was brought to Kilimanjaro during colonial times was in formal definition a "universal-membership organization." Just about all Chagga belonged to all of them. The principal organizations of the period to 1961 were three: the first were the colonially reorganized chiefdoms, which by definition incorporated all the local Chagga. The second was the church, which gradually came to do the same. Since the Lutherans and the Catholics generally had local monopolies on proselytizing, the division between them did not create significant new group cleavages in the population.[12] The third was the coffee cooperative, which similarly came to enjoy nearly universal membership by household. Only men had had formal membership in the cooperative but they represented the products of and, in theory, the interests of their households.

That these were conceived of as universal membership organizations is not to say that within them everyone was equal to everyone else. Quite the contrary. Forms of social distinction reflected differing access to resources, rank, and control, both within and without the organization. There were organizational leaders and organizational followers, persons who dominated and persons who were subordinate. But differences of power and position did not generate a separately designated formal group of the privileged, nor did formal groups of the unprivileged come into being. For example, there was not a church sect of the well-off and a church sect of the poor. Thus, as in some other times and places, differences of class were not expressed in formally ranked groups, but in ranking inside groups, in horizontal networks that crosscut groups, and in vertical ties between leaders and followers, authorities and subordinates. By providing new arenas in which these differences could be played out, the organizations introduced in the colonial period could be said to have contributed to the process of differentiation without creating new formal group divisions to mark them.

During the colonial period the chiefdoms, the church, and the cooperative were the principal instruments of directed social change. Each often dealt with its Chagga members as individuals. The colonial government taxed each hut, not lineages, and the individual household head was accountable. The church proselytized and converted individuals, and solicited contributions of cash, produce, and labor from individual households. The cooperative registered individual landholders as members, and bought the coffee they produced from them as individuals.

Being universal membership organizations, all three organizations lay on top of and did not destroy or replace the preexisting territorial and social divisions at the lowest level. A high degree of local endogamy continued. Lineages, at the bottom of the structure, enjoyed stability and continuity, rooted as they were in the soil itself. No great effort was made to change them directly; rather their existence became unofficial, not politically recognized. They were not dealt with as collectivities. It was at the higher levels that major formal reorganizations were undertaken, always in the direction of greater and greater centralization, always focused on reshaping the nature of public administration, and the character of chiefly and other offices.

Over time, the reorganization of the large-scale organizations and their subsegments contributed more and more to the growth of centralized, supralocal economic and political organization of the Kilimanjaro District as a whole. The more that important decisions were made at the center, and the more that sizable collective funds were amassed and controlled at the center, the more the political significance of small local units diminished. Instead of a formal replacement of noncentral structures from the local chiefdom down to the lineage, their power eroded. In the process of organizational pyramiding, the central organizations arrogated more and more funds and discretion to themselves, while the local chiefships weakened and the lineages lost all political standing. Many stages of this process were the product of policy.

To what extent did local organic economic interdependence grow with centralized administrative unity? The answer is, very little. In fact, Kilimanjaro may have been more interdependent economically in the precolonial period when certain chieftaincies specialized in ironworking and others in herding cattle, when some chiefdoms were better situated in relation to the long-distance trade than others. Precolonial Kilimanjaro had no unitary political structure, but it had some economic coherence. In the colonial period and today, there remains a degree of ongoing interdependence in the subsistence economy, but little in the cash economy. Most foodstuffs continue to be locally produced and exchanged according to variations in the local ripening seasons. The women's markets carry on, and some cash circulates locally, but much of the cash that flows in from the coffee goes out through the shops and traders on the mountain and in Moshi.

It could be argued that both in the cash economy and in the political sphere, the rural subdivisions of Kilimanjaro are more interlocked with the outside centers to which they are attached than they are with one another. Through the government, the coffee, and the church, to say nothing of the schools and the radio, their orientation is outward. The postcolonial reorganization seems to have been designed to increase the intensity of the external and central relationships.

After independence came in 1961, when Tanzania became a one-party state, it was incumbent on all the Chagga to join the national party. Once again a universal membership organization installed itself on Kilimanjaro.[13] In time, when party cells were organized all over the mountain, ten-house cell leaders were to choose their party representatives from among their number in each *mtaa*.[14] These representatives served in the ward organization. (Most of the ex-chiefdoms were divided into two wards each, with a ward development committee and a party committee as their governing bodies.) The ward organization was, in turn, subordinate to a Kilimanjaro District and regional party/government organization. Without going into further detail suffice it to say that, because party representation is based on geographical representation, the composition of the lowest levels of local party organization inevitably reflects preexisting local social groupings.[15] This characteristic is now even more evident because of developments in the "villagization" program mentioned earlier.

The new "villagization" program and all the other changes of the past twenty years are supposed to be part of a general party plan to give power to the peasants and workers. Ideologues all too often conceive peasants and workers as aggregations of similarly situated individuals, not as persons closely tied into networks and groups through previous social commitments. Not only are such matters deliberately played down, but so are the hierarchies within the party structure. They probably hope that these embarrassments will fade away if not much is made of them. In practice, remarkably asymmetrical relations exist even locally between the party higher-ups and their unlettered brethren. The hierarchy between educated and uneducated is central to party structure in practice, though it is otherwise in theory. According to party doctrine and national ideology, all local development plans are supposed to originate with the peasantry. The peasant's proposals are supposed to be polished and put into bureaucratic language, complete with budgets and formal plans higher up in the party, and proposals then compete for funding before regional committees. In 1974, at local party political meetings in different wards on Kilimanjaro, the major items on the agenda of the subvillages were identical. This happy coincidence of "spontaneous" peasant interest had been produced by suggestions emanating from the central regional party organization. When political consciousness is considered insufficiently developed at the bottom levels, it is given stimulation from above. Party meetings are held, but are ill attended. Speeches are made. Decisions are made by acclaim. The top echelons of the party can then later point to the popular source of their own plans. The local party meetings constitute what I call "ratifying bodies public."[16] They give populist legitimacy to decisions made elsewhere.

Decisions about major funded projects in Tanzania are not made at the village level, whatever the ideology. Villagers do sort out some few small benefits. They are given control of decisions minor to the region but still important to themselves about precisely where the site of a new school building or dispensary is to be, or which persons are to do which parts of the construction work, and the like. And there is often a little patronage or private profit for those directly concerned with the execution of these projects. The new village organization is designed to increase small-scale autonomous enterprise. And it will further decrease official opportunities to develop regional political coherence.

Thus precisely coincident with endless propaganda about the peasants and the workers, the importance of self-independence and the benefits of freedom from exploitative domination and the like, the rural Chagga find themselves as distant from the centers of major decisions as ever, more organizationally fragmented than ever in their "cooperative villages," and in many respects more constrained than ever by the official system. But, of course, every formal system has its informal twin.

Many educated Chagga have made their way into the national bureau-cracy and into high levels of the party. The personal networks of many rural dwellers reach from the mountain to those men.[17] For present pur-poses the Kilimanjaro geographical area has been treated as the delimit-ing boundary of analysis. But informal connections with Chagga in the national bureaucracy are an important unofficial link between the moun-tain and the nation. These personal networks operate both to integrate the Kilimanjaro region more closely to the growing national system, and on occasion to give some unofficial activities a degree of political immu-nity and independence from the official system that strengthens certain aspects of local Chagga autonomy.

Today in Tanzania for a person with contacts there are ways to finagle access to jobs, places in schools, to obtain anything from soap to roofing materials. Without contacts everything is much more difficult. The ex-treme shortages of material things mean that supplies and services are distributed in anything but impersonal, evenhanded ways. Though the government passes legislation and uses administrative regulation to try to control these activities, it has not succeeded. At the top, influence can be seen to be used in everything from posts in government services to the uses of the diplomatic pouch.

The convoluted details of official connection and unofficial transactions are not appropriate for discussion here. What the use of influence and the existence of illegal activity signify is commonplace enough. The behavior is likely to continue as long as the perceived advantages outweigh the perceived risks. The social result is a complex multiplication of the layers of publicly evident and privately hidden. If the unofficial activity is widespread, its very existence can undermine the legitimacy and effectiveness of the official political system without any engagement in overt political opposition. Or if the double system endures long enough, the peaceful coexistence of the official and unofficial can aquire a patina of the customary. It is difficult to guess what the outcome will be in the long run on Kilimanjaro, or even to know at this stage whether the unofficial and illegal activities that give individuals advantage have ultimate collective political implications. What is clear is that as long as the relentless intervention of national policy in local affairs is carried on, the rural Chagga will continue to try to insulate certain areas of their lives from it. At the neighborhood-village level, their principal legitimate arena of autonomy at present is the sphere of traditional domestic custom. Lineage affairs are considered to fall into this category. In a large part ethnic domestic custom is considered privileged and generally immune from public intervention. From the Chagga perspective this arena includes some control over access to land. In these circumstances an emphasis on traditional ties of kinship has many quite modern advantages.

As I have suggested, an unofficial autonomy also seems likely to continue. But neither the domestic arena nor, so far as one can tell, the chains of unofficial links are of an organizational kind that could mount any collective political action. The universal-membership organizations of the colonial and postcolonial periods have tended to produce a "segmentary" rather than "organic" local structure, and it is difficult to visualize how the many identical segments could become the springboard for common political action. Segmented structures are convenient for top-down interventions, and for keeping the potential for broad political mobilization at a low level. The party has exacerbated this tendency by embarking on a process of subsegmentation, by dividing the Chagga into collective villages, all of them ultimately administered from a central governmental ministry. Contiguous villages still have some continuing social ties among themselves, but there is no formal organizational milieu in which these can be politically expressed other than within the party organization itself. "Villagization" seems designed to dismantle the potential for effective aggregate political mobilization.

By means of the complex series of changes outlined here, the Chagga have been transformed from a group of autonomous chiefdoms into a politically fragmented ethnic category within a "developing" state. Like many other political and legal systems in the ex-colonial world, the system of law and politics on Kilimanjaro today has several stratigraphic layers. On top are the new, postcolonial inventions. Those rest on and only partially displace the institutions and ideas of law and political authority that were laid down by government in the colonial period. And underneath both lie remnants of the basic foundation of Chagga arrangements of kinship and property whose outlines come from a time before the Europeans appeared, and which have been subtly but deeply altered. A common history has made this present form of Chagga law and politics something uniquely Chagga, but something that is not to be mistaken for the "customary" system that was in being a hundred years ago. There are evident connections with the past, but now is now. Nothing is as it was.

SOCIAL FACTS AND SOCIAL FABRICATIONS: A CENTURY OF CHAGGA LAW, 1880–1980

If one steps back from the details, and looks at the whole century of transformation, three things stand out about the metamorphosis of the indigenous law of the Chagga: the transposition of its place in a political/legal system, the transformation of its economic/social context, and the translation of its meaning.

As for transposition, Chagga law once was an integral dimension of a political totality, the precolonial chiefdom. The entity called "customary law" was constituted out of the residue left after the colonial modification of the Chagga polity. Nowhere was the content of that residue fully detailed. Chagga chiefship of the colonial period was a changed office, not essentially defined by earlier custom. The colonial and postcolonial governments reduced "customary law" for the Chagga to a set of local ethnic conventions largely (but not exclusively) confined to relations of kinship. As such it was a small segment of the plural legal system of the state. Yet "customary law" remained a critical element in the lives of rural people on the mountain because it determined access to land, and because it framed the structure of family and lineage on which the whole system of social support was founded.

The social and economic transformation of Kilimanjaro that occurred in this century radically changed the milieu in which "customary law" was used. But almost by definition, the conventional idea of what "customary law" was seemed not to change. There was no simple mechanism by which the customary corpus could be altered as such. In the colonial period the Native Authorities could make new rules. "Customary law" could be added to, bits of it replaced. It could be reinterpreted. Parts of it could remain unused. But as labeled, it was an entity which was conceived as static.

In fact practices changed freely. In practice land became valuable for cash cropping. Christianity substituted monogamous marriage for polygynous marriage as the prescribed state of affairs for most Chagga. But polygyny retained its ground as an alternative in the traditional set of rules. Widow inheritance was transformed by Christian rules from a marriagelike state to one of guardianship. The heir/successor thus came to have an interest in the widow's property without a concomitant sexual attachment to her person. Schooling changed the control of parents over the education and labor of their children. The cash economy radically restructured the balance of relationships in households, both between husbands and wives and between parents and children, to say nothing of the connections among households in the lineage neighborhoods. Although all of these changes transformed the norms the Chagga lived by, there was no formal means of acknowledging that the entity called "customary law" had been altered to take account of these changes. (Indeed, after Gutmann there were no successful attempts to compile it, let alone to change it.)

As fundamental as was the transformation of land use when coffee cultivation became general, that change was scarcely acknowledged within the conventionally stated rules of allocation, inheritance, and succession. The broad outlines of the rules remained the same. As in other aspects of the system, the most significant changes occurred in changes of practice. Discretionary allocations were made in new ways. To the extent that those discretionary allocations became patterned they could now be restated as rules of preference. Though such rules acquired the legitimacy of general practice, they did not have the patina of tradition. They were the creative, adaptive, changing elements of local mores, but they had not been part of "custom" since time immemorial. These changes have been accommodated with ease without raising the issue of their status as legal rules. This is so because, unlike the higher levels of our own judicial system, the local courts on Kilimanjaro (and even more so, the new informal agencies of dispute settlement) have not been structured as factories for producing and specifying the scope of rules. As a result of discretionary allocations, rights to coffee came to be recognized as separable from rights to bananas and residence in a *kihamba*. In practice more and more fathers divided their land among their sons, and middle sons were often given a share. In practice women were put at a new disadvantage when coffee cultivation became general because their access to coffee cash was limited by the prior rights of men. Rights to the coffee crop were treated as a male prerogative associated with the right to inherit or allocate land. The court records show no trace that these practices were ever an issue for debate. Concomitantly the position of guardian also came to have an important cash component. That these new norms all came in without apparent change in the stated traditions surrounding the rights and obligations of spouses and kin did not conceal from anyone the advent of new conditions and regular new patterns of behavior. They were simply incorporated as part of the system of practice. There was no forum in which the question whether they constituted changes in the "customary law" system could be or needed to be raised.

After independence, aspects of the law of the formal system changed several times, and some local practices changed with them. But the process has not been one in which previous commitments to ideas, norms, and arrangements have simply been abandoned. Far from it. The change in the political environment has not at all altered in the ordinary case the question who lives in which *kihamba* and on what legal basis the right to do so was established. Old rules and old micropolitical arenas are for sorting these matters out, even though new ones are officially in place.

Last and not least in the metamorphosis of Chagga "customary law" has been the translation of its meaning both in the discourse of governments and in the transactions of rural people. The construction of a restricted place for "custom" by governments clearly has been a matter of calculated policy. But some of the operational effect may not have been fully foreseen. The policy has worked to increase the gap between official government conceptions and the realities of local affairs. The domain of local autonomy is not large, but it is carefully insulated from external interference to whatever extent possible. The illusion from the outside that what has been labeled "customary" remains static in practice is patently false.

The supralocal body politic and the rural *mtaa* were always organized on different principles. However, over this century, as supralocal organization lost its earlier indigenous character, and has itself gone through many phases of change the difference between the levels has become larger. Concomitantly a succession of governments have treated residual "customary law" as culturally legitimate but essentially obsolete. The legislated transposition of "customary law" into the "private" sphere has been accompanied by an official vision of government that links innovation with national political leadership, modernism with the top of the political system, archaism and static folkways with the bottom. Meanwhile generations of lively and ingenious rural Chagga have in fact been using their traditions as one of a number of resources out of which to construct new arrangements to suit their ever-changing situations. The Chagga have neither broken with their past nor have they reproduced it.

Epilogue: From types to sequences: social change in anthropology

For decades now the cliché in anthropology has been that process has replaced structure as a preoccupation. Paradoxically the making of structure and its transformation are usually the processes at issue. But now not only the structural results but shifts and continuities in the constituting and transforming processes have themselves become the object of more and more anthropological attention. That is not surprising. Now governments everywhere have large-scale designs to shape and control economies and polities, and "nonintervention" is fully understood to be an active policy in itself. The idea of control on the large scale is matched by a remarkable level of unpredictability or intractability on the ground. Anthropology has something to say about those disjunctions.

In the post-1945 period anthropologists have increasingly focused on the moving parts of the social body. This attention has gradually altered the object of analysis and the perspective of fieldwork. Several theoretical camps have assembled and their lines of print march in hostile columns. Yet, despite strongly declared differences of interpretive premise, in operational fact a common focus of analytic attention has emerged, and it can be called "processual analysis."

Processual analysis is peculiarly appropriate to a changing world, but in itself a processual approach constitutes neither a model nor a theory. It is rather a redefinition of subject matter. Urgent practical and analytic problems have engendered that redefinition. For those who want to create change and for those who only aspire to try to understand it (or its absence), the modes of metamorphosis and their production have become a central focus of interest.

Processual analysis takes as its subject selected social/cultural phenomena seen over time. It makes no attempt at total ethnography in the old manner. But attention to the general political/economic/historical background is considered essential. In that sense holism continues to be served. In the foreground the principal object analyzed may be no larger

320

than the unfolding of a single complex event, or it may concern the dynamics of a larger-scale constellation over a long historical sequence. Within the general frame of processual analysis, the fieldwork moment, the firsthand study of the affairs of a particular aggregation of living persons, is always conceived in temporal terms. The observer is sharply conscious of watching a short part of an ongoing flow. This temporal attitude is there whether or not an actual historical past is known. The fieldwork objective is not simply the inspection of persons embroiled in events but through them to try to discern the cumulative direction of such replications or metamorphoses as may be underway.

Process is not necessarily change. Repetition and reproduction are also processes. But change, rather than process, has captivated the imagination of the model makers. Since 1945, social anthropology has turned more and more of its attention to uncovering the social logic of transformations. Yet the tension between the fieldwork method and the historical questions into which it now inquires continues to be problematic. The quandaries are particularly visible in two approaches at opposite poles of scale: a two-system model and an individual-centered model. Both have had a large place in the model-building literature since World War II. Both are found in Marxist and non-Marxist versions, and both make special claims to revealing the motivity of change.

The perennial two-system model of change has as its dynamic the shattering contact between societies designated as traditional and modern, or precapitalist and capitalist, or some variant of these. The dichotomy has a long theoretical history (Berreman 1978) and had a special place in nineteenth-century evolutionary models. But now the binary contrast has a different explanation. Traditional or precapitalist formations are obviously not becoming modern and capitalist in a process of pristine evolutionary growth. The modern or capitalist is seen to transform the traditional or precapitalist either by penetrating and invading it or, from another point of view, by preserving it as a peripheral backwater and labor pool.

Despite the historical difference of circumstance, shades of earlier evolutionary thinking continue to be seen deeply embedded in the way these binary categories are often used to interpret this complex present. Observed societies are frequently described as if they were in transition between two known grand types. Serious theoretical problems (to say nothing of factual ones) generally lurk in the reconstruction of the earlier phase, before the system became transitional. Other problems lurk in the picture of the future. Sartre notwithstanding, a conjectural tomorrow makes a shaky platform on which to stand a model of the present. Where a single mode of production, the capitalist, is postulated for the postcolonial third world, dualism is reinserted through such concepts as core-periphery, dominant and subservient sectors, and the like. Nor is it altogether satisfactory to see the present as an "articulation" of different modes of production combined in one "real concrete social formation" (Wolpe 1980:35). The notion of articulation implies that elements that originated in one system remain in it even when the general context has changed. Inherent in the very idea of articulation is a presumption of continuing distinctness and separateness of the original systems. This retrospective bias can create intellectual obstacles for the analysis of integrated combinants.

The individual-centered model of change is hardly more satisfactory. In it, transformation emerges from the way people constitute a changing social reality in the course of practice or, in another version, interaction, or in making individual choices that cumulatively have large-scale effects. This model has the advantage of concreteness. It is close to the data of fieldwork and seems to fit the ethnographer's task to perfection. However, it has the crippling disadvantage of a limited conception of analytic field and of causality. In some versions it conflates analytic field with field site, and confuses cause with motivation (Barth 1966:1–11). The external context is all but ignored and the actors are treated as if they made their own fate. In others causality is attributed to highly generalized but largely unanalyzed objective conditions of existence whose broad outlines, "the economic bases of the social formation," are simply postulated (Bourdieu 1977:78, 83).

A number of variants on these two-system or individual-centered models have surfaced over the past several decades, as have a variety of attempts to combine them, or escape them. The new anthropological history is one of the alternative streams.

If one considers how change was addressed in anthropological fieldwork in 1945, the intellectual distance that has been traversed since is striking. In the United States in the early postwar period much print was devoted to describing change in the form and extent of the two-system, two-culture mix found in many Hispanicized and other American Indian communities in their "postcontact" situations. Acculturation was the name given the process (Barnett et al. 1954:974; see also L. and G. Spindler 1959). That most of these situations of acculturation originally involved conquest and political and economic domination by people from one cultural background over people from another was taken as a given but was seldom a point of theoretical interest (Wolf 1959, an exception, was not a fieldwork monograph). In the theory of acculturation the American "melting pot" conception of interethnic contact was extended to quite different circumstances.

By contrast, in British social anthropology, no doubt because of its practical immediacy, the field study of contact transformation unambiguously concerned certain aspects of the colonial encounter (for example, see the works cited in Hogbin 1958; see also Brown 1973). This writing largely concerned the dismantling and disruption of traditional society. At least with regard to Africa shadows of evolutionary models shaded the discourse.

A classic theoretical statement, Godfrey and Monica Wilson's *The Analysis of Social Change* (1945), treated African and European societies as two types of system, "primitive" and "civilized." The terms were applied without pejorative intent, but with evolutionary assumptions. Each type was conceived to have been a coherent system in equilibrium when separate and autonomous. Yet in the 1940s African life was in anything but peaceful equilibrium. Town and countryside were rife with turmoil and conflict. The Wilsons attributed the trouble to "uneven" development produced under conditions of rapid transformation. They saw a destabilizing contact between large-scale and small-scale society in the colonial situation, a case of unbalanced, piecemeal, accelerated evolution in which parts of two systems coexisted uneasily in a temporarily unsteady state, before one would replace the other (167). The Wilsons prescribed as a more desirable transitional period a balanced form of change, a "moving equilibrium" in which everything would be altered in tandem at the same rate of speed. Unlike some of the Wilsons' ethnographic work, their theoretical statement made little of the fact that the colonial contact inherently had a rather special shape of its own, and was not the best material on which to construct a general model of social change.

By the 1960s, in the largely postcolonial world, the nature of the colonial experience was addressed more directly. In some hands, the two-system model was added to and elaborated. Thus, when Meillassoux wrote on the Gouro of the Ivory Coast, he set out not only to reconstruct the precolonial economy of a "self-sustaining" society, but also to summarize the series of transformations worked upon it by specific colonial interventions and the introduction of commercial agriculture (1964). His underlying framework was a precapitalist/capitalist version of the two-system model. But Meillassoux did not leave it at that. He sketched in elements of a particular historical sequence. And he further argued that the continuing elements of the subsistence economy of the Gouro were organically related to the modern capitalist economy, that these were not simply a dogged survival of traditionalism for its own sake on the part of stubborn peasants. He was making the case that the complex and contradictory present had to be interpreted as an interrelated totality (1964:351). Whatever reservations one may have about his conjectural reconstructions of the original form of Gouro society, the attempt to document the effect and *sequence* of precolonial and colonial transformation was a clear departure from the conventions of earlier work.

Development-oriented anthropologists of the same period were equally occupied with the impact of the colonial presence and its residue. In speaking of the disastrous state of the Indonesian economy Geertz said, "Bergson's extravagantly historicist aphorism very nearly holds: there is nothing in the present but the past" (1963:125). When he compared economically backward Java of that moment with rapidly developing Japan, he said of Java, "The existence of colonial government was decisive because it meant that the growth potential inherent in the traditional Javanese economy . . . was harnessed not to Javanese (or Indonesian) development, but to Dutch" (141). "The difference in 'economic mentality' between Dutch and Javanese which Boeke took to be the cause of dualism was in fact in great part its result. The Javanese did not become impoverished because they were 'static,' they became 'static' because they were impoverished" (142).

Though the two-system paradigm was strong, obviously other conceptions were in the air. Political circumstance favored the discussion of national integration in remarkably optimistic terms. Many newly independent countries had a great sense of political hope for a fundamental postcolonial transformation. More and more anthropologists working in the new nations were carried into the discussion of these aggregated totalities, their histories and their possibilities for coherence. Social and cultural recombinants came to be thought of as having their own characteristics and their own generative properties. The two-system paradigm seemed less apt.

The scope of inquiry changed. The articulation of different levels of organization and of different social/cultural fields became a major problem to be addressed. Cultural, social, and structural pluralism was a core issue (Kuper and Smith 1969). The inspection of local communities as closed units of analysis made no sense when nation building was the slogan of the day. Bailey said of the relations between village-level politics and higher political strata in India, "The search is . . . to discover how the different arenas are connected through interaction" (1963:223; see also Bailey 1957, 1960). Still caught in the dichotomous theoretical framework, Bailey conceived of India as an aggregation of *simple* societies using parliamentary institutions exported from a *complex* society. But fortunately this binary conceptual apparatus did not debar him from methodological innovation. Actions, situations, and events rather than normative prescriptions were the data on which he built his analysis. Out of these he inferred the working structure of emerging current relationships. He considered not only the *connections* between the observed social field and the "outside" world important but the metamorphosis caused by the ongoing process of mutual contact equally so. The content of fieldwork was changing. The incorporation of local peoples into national systems became more than a legitimate subject of study, it became a major concern (Cohen and Middleton 1970).

Some explicit attempts were made to escape the two-system framework, and some were a response to practical questions. Could the newly independent countries mount the kind of economic push that would modernize them without having to change all of their indigenous institutions? In answering this question positively Geertz disparaged the kind of thinking epitomized by concepts of *gemeinschaft* versus *gesellschaft*, traditional versus modern, folk versus urban (1963). For him, this typological framework was something *to be broken out of* (147). Geertz's position was the very opposite of the Wilsons'. No necessary incompatibility existed between elements just because they originated in different "systems." "A modern economic system may be compatible with a wider range of noneconomic cultural patterns and social structures than has often been thought" (Geertz 1963:144).

But the assorted recombinations, new arrangements, and odd conjunctions that actually were generated on the ground presented extremely difficult analytical puzzles. Modernization theory predicted that systemic integration would eventually be achieved. Yet the reality was that the culture or society that could be observed was no unitary thing. Geertz's way out of that theoretical dilemma was to dominate all of his subsequent work. He did not construct an alternative model of interdigitated diversity, but settled on explicating the cultural terms in which a particular people "made sense" of their transitional situation. Geertz justified this approach by asserting that the "effort after meaning" on the cultural level was "at the same time . . . an 'effort after order' in social matters" (1965:206). In Indonesia he conceived this effort as unending in a "permanently transitional" society whose culture he found "jumbled" and "kaleidoscopic" (152, 207).

The hermeneutical domain is a fail-safe and interesting intellectual sanctuary in a world in which the coherent total cultural systems of earlier theoretical models are as hard to find as cannibals. Virtually all that can be located on the ground are those culturally kaleidoscopic jumbles that are today's fieldwork sites. By deconstructing the scene into the meanings of particular concepts, icons, symbols, and practices, the social drama can be treated as if it were a temporary amalgam of cultural parts, and the serious consideration of many difficult larger-scale questions can be avoided. That there may be a political economy of cultural diversity beyond the focal range of the inquiry can be gently acknowledged. Such matters as "background" can be recognized in an "out of focus" way without serious analysis. Geertz's argument was and is that the anthropologist's job is to fathom the relation of symbols to behavior through the study of culture. He acknowledged that behavior is "moved by many more forces than the merely ideational" (1965:12). But his work never made explicit the link connecting ideas, other "forces," and behavior.[1] "Interpretive" analysis is art, not method.

If Geertz was unsettled by the kaleidoscopic variety of recombinations he saw in Indonesia, Godelier saw an analogous problem on a purely theoretical plane.

As long as we are unable to reconstruct through scientific thought the limited number of possible transformations which any given structure or any given combination of structures can accomplish, history, yesterday's as well as tomorrow's will tower over us like a gigantic mass of facts with the full weight of their enigmas, and their consequences. . . . It would . . . be necessary to take the analysis far enough to explain these possibilities of alternative action . . . we have been unable to go this far, but at least we have recognized the problem. (Godelier in Seddon 1978:108, 109)

When the limits on the transformational possibilities cannot be defined or explained within a single social setting, let alone in general, theorists of change perforce have to address other topics. Some anthropologists would turn away from grand questions about the repertoire of possible total social transformations to concrete, smaller questions about individual choices actually exercised.

One can see strong intimations of this in Geertz's 1965 analysis. For all the large-scale impersonal causality in his sketched-in Indonesian history-as-background, when he analyzed observed events in his account of the "effort after meaning," he assumed that people were capable not only of reinterpreting, but of *acting on* their situations. Geertz was far from alone in this perspective, which had had special resonance in the decolonization period. How else could the struggles for independence have been acknowledged in the models? How else could the idea of postcolonial directed "development" of economic plans and legislated political structures be accommodated in theory?

In general, in post-World War II fieldwork anthropology, effective persons were put into the model, as events in time were put into the ethnographies. The move in this direction can be seen to have been nascent in England in the 1950s. Raymond Firth talked about social "organization" as distinct from social structure (1951). For Edmund Leach the notion of choice was central to analysis (1954). In Manchester the case method flourished, and individuals were seen to be acting in their own interest, manipulating the normative system (Gluckman 1955; Turner 1957; Van Velsen 1967. See Werbner 1984 for an overview of the Manchester School). Middleton described Lugbara religion through the ritual activities of members of a particular lineage (1960). How much an analysis emphasized that the action of persons was ultimately determined by the conditions in which they lived or stressed options and choices depended on the doctrinal and analytic predelictions of the anthropologist. But the attention to action and to events put the dimension of particular time firmly into the ethnographic enterprise.

It was not a big step to Fredrik Barth's assertion that models could be constructed that represented change *being produced* (1966). When he argued that one should look to the choice-making (generic? actual?) individual "transacting" with his fellows as the site and source of change, Barth was effectively pushing into the background the larger factors that limited and/or determined the available choices.

Over the years Barth has continued to pursue his theoretical concentration on interaction between individuals. But more recently he has completely reversed the telescope. In *Models of Social Organization* he was talking about the way culture is *generated* in the course of individual interaction, but he has recently been occupied with exactly the opposite, how the "scale" of society is reflected in the interaction between individuals (1978). "An exchange between neighbors may well require the context of a world market to be understandable, while a love-letter remains an event in a small-scale system, no matter how much postage is required for it to reach its destination" (1978:256). Barth asks, "Where do the insecurities and ills of modern Western urban life arise?" And he answers, "Perhaps many of the ills of modern life are connected . . . with our situation as the subjects of bureaucratic regimes" (183). The binary categories large-scale and small-scale seem to be offered as conceptual replacements for modern/traditional, capitalist/precapitalist. The change of terms is an attempt to provide the analytic means of handling fieldwork settings in which elements of large- and small-scale systems are found in the very same situation. Where are the transacting individuals and the generative models of yesteryear?

Like non-Marxist thought Marxist analysis has produced its own elaborations and developments on the two-system model on which anthropologists have drawn. Some are refinements on the concept of the articulation of modes of production (Wolpe 1980). Others are variants of the core-periphery dichotomy found in world systems analysis (Hopkins and Wallerstein 1982). Marxist anthropology also has produced its own simultaneous editions of individual-centered models of change. Thus, Bourdieu uses the precapitalist/capitalist duality to characterize two distinct kinds of cultural universe, yet in his theory of practice he locates operational change in the categorical individual. In Bourdieu's paradigm of "practice" dynamic possibilities in the "system" are inserted through the generic individual whose actions reverberate on the plane of culture and social structure, and sound back. In Bourdieu the logical move is from "cognitive and motivating structures" located in individuals, through "thought, perceptions, expressions, actions" to "objective structures (language, economy, etc.)" (1977:85, 86,

95). The circle then closes with "the 'dialectical' relationship between the objective structures and the cognitive and motivating structures" (83). In both respects Bourdieu's approach bears a strong resemblance to many non-Marxist analyses. There are remarkable connections between the pre-occupations of the two anthropologies. Their contemporaneity may have more force than their self-conceptions.[2]

Bourdieu's general model of practice like Sahlins's historical model plausibly and persuasively interposes the generic individual between culture as received and culture as practiced, society as given and society as acted in and on. Sahlins talks about the way signs acquire new conceptual values in the course of human practice, both in the "referential process" and in the "instrumental process" (1981:70-72).

In general, then, the worldly circumstances of human action are under no inevitable obligation to conform to the categories by which certain people perceive them. In the event they do not, the received categories are potentially revalued in practice, functionally redefined. According to the place of the received category in the cultural system as constituted, and the interests that have been affected, the system itself is more or less altered. At the extreme, what began as reproduction ends as transformation. (67)

But by focusing on the universal processes by which cultures and societies may be understood to be continuously produced and transformed through the medium of the generic individual, both Bourdieu and Sahlins have produced models that are of little assistance in addressing nonuniversal regularities. As Sahlins says, "Basically, the idea is very simple" (67).

Analytic dilemmas are evident. The few examples cited in this highly compressed account illustrate some of the tensions in anthropology at the theoretical level. The expansion of subject matter implied in the models of the macrosystem runs counter to the shrinkage of scope implied by models of individual action. If all the minute observations of interaction seen in fieldwork are interpreted only as they manifest signs of the operation of a postulated macrosystem, how much can be learned about either level? The risk of becoming repetitious and formulaic is strong. But if small-scale inter-action is seen primarily as a construct of the actors without systematic reference to some larger context, that conception too is limited and stunted. It is obvious that the full implications of a time-oriented anthropology that integrates small-scale and larger-scale processes have only begun to be worked out. When the extremes of scale, largest and smallest, are the only ones considered, and these are linked largely through a purely theoretical connection, much that is important is omitted. In fieldwork and in analysis the need to address a greater variety of levels of organization and kinds of integrative process is patent. And it is being done in a great deal of the new ethnography, even if it is ignored in some of the polemics of theory.

Somewhere short of a grand universalism, somewhere between the generic individual and the world system, lie many intermediate levels of organization and analysis. In practical fact much work in anthropology now is (and in the past often has been) directed toward addressing questions on those intermediate levels. The methodological commitment to small-scale observation and the intellectual commitment to larger-scale understanding continue. But they prosper most in the quarters in which less totalism is practiced than is evident in the most extreme forms of the two-system and the individual-centered models.

In practice, an emerging anthropology of events and processes attached to large but not necessarily global trajectories of change seems to be redefining some of the tasks of fieldwork, and changing the content of ethnographies. In fieldwork situations the processual approach operates at a level of specificity comparable to that generated by synchronic models, but uses that specificity in the service of diachronic study. Events (ordinary and extraordinary) and event sequences are coming to be the preferred raw data, the logical and processual location of which must then be uncovered.[3]

Common theoretical framework or none, in practice anthropologists are collecting fieldwork materials in a form that reflects the ideas and affairs of people who are very conscious of living through a time of change. But the way those peoples make sense of their own situation is not the only point of interest. Their affairs are one of several routes to inquiring into the larger situation itself. The present object of anthropological knowledge is to address the historical process by combining perspectives that are not normally held at the same time, insider-outsider, local-supra-local, short term–long term, model and event. That is the surprise in the method and the method in the surprise.

At present, within the broad notion of process the metamorphic dimension of these perspectives has become the most riveting. Everyone knows that the dynamics of repetition and "reproduction" are also ubiquitous, but transformative conditions and historical questions have become central ones for anthropology today. Efforts to plan and control the future are central to the present political legitimacy and power of most governments. Yet the semiautonomous social fields of which the social world is composed (including the subunits of what in aggregate is called "the state") have their own embedded agendas. Anthropologists are in a strategic position to observe the product of these conjunctions. Processual analysis is focused on a double problem: the problem of understanding the present in a stream of time and the problem of developing a means of analyzing shifting realities out of the resources of an anthropology founded on typologizing. A profound theoretical riddle is embedded in the empirical task.

Notes

INTRODUCTION

1 These days, in the cultural categories of Western society, "law" seems to mean something quite clear. To a great extent the law is defined by the state and the law is what the state will putatively enforce. The legal also includes institutions that interpret and "apply" the law, others that make, implement, and unmake the law, and an associated body of professions and a corpus of ideas and principles by which the activities and structures of the legal domain are "explained." Such words seem to be a definition, but what they refer to is remarkably open-ended. There is much less clarity about the boundaries than appears on the surface. But even more important for social analysis, the practices of the state are inseparable from the operations of the nonstate, legal ideas and principles from those of other domains of thought. Law is embedded in ordinary life as well as being "practiced" in specialized institutions.

In societies without state institutions, the state-based distinction between the legal and the lawlike obviously has no pertinence, and "law" can be identified only by functional analogy. Descriptions of nonstate societies sometimes try to skirt the problem by calling lawlike phenomena "custom." Unfortunately the overtones of the term "custom" are far from satisfactory. There are inappropriate implications of internalized rules for which no enforcement is necessary, and of unchanging, immutable practices. But the literature is so permeated with the term "customary law" that it is easier to take exception to it and to place it historically than to get rid of it. The universal definitions of law generated by scholars, and conceived to be applicable to any and all societies are usually actually founded on the diagnostic characteristics of law in the West. (See those of Hoebel 1954:28; Bohannan 1967:43–56; Pospisil 1971:95; and the useful discussion in Friedman and Macaulay 1977:1–32.) Anthropologists working in non-Western settings are left with analogy, or are confined to native categories.

2 In their own language and in Kiswahili they are called Wachagga, the prefix "wa" being a plural for "people," Mchagga being the singular, meaning "a Chagga person."

CHAPTER 1. THE NINETEENTH CENTURY ON KILIMANJARO

1 The Chagga have been variously called: Chaga, Waschagga, Jagga, Dschagga, Wa-caga. Wachagga and Mchagga are the forms the Chagga themselves use. But in English the prefix is usually dropped, hence Chagga. The people now designated as the Chagga were divided into many small, autonomous chiefdoms in the nineteenth century, and therefore early accounts frequently speak of each chiefdom as a separate people; the Wakilema, for example, for the people of Kilema (Von der Decken 1869–71, 1:273). The names of the chiefdoms subsequently became geographical names for the various parts of the mountain. There are important dialectical differences between the easterly, central, and westerly divisions of Kilimanjaro (Nurse 1979). For a summary of Chagga ethnography and a comprehensive bibliography, see Sally Falk Moore and Paul Purritt, *The Chagga and Meru of Tanzania*, Ethnographic Survey of Africa, East Central Africa 18 (London: International African Institute, 1977).

2 Fragments of pottery suggest such contacts (Odner 1971).

3 Widenmann (1899:2) says that there were thirty-seven chiefdoms in 1899. There may have been many more in earlier times because the historical process seems to have been one of consolidation of smaller units into larger ones both before and after the beginning of the colonial period.

4 Official statistics of the early German period indicated that there were approximately 28,150 households on the mountain (Gutmann 1926:586; HRAF: 527). Chiefdom sizes varied. They ranged from Machame which was said to have 17,000 inhabitants to Mkuu which was supposed to have had a population of 700. There may have been more organizational variation from one chiefdom to another than was known to Gutmann, but there is reason to believe that many conformed to the pattern he described for Moshi.

5 Using Gutmann's figures, one can guess at the sizes of the patrilineages of Moshi in 1910 or so. With more than eighty lineages in the chiefdom, there would have been an average of 86 persons (men, women, and children) in the territory of each patriline. If half or more of the members were children, and half of the adults were wives of lineage members, then 21.5 was the average adult married male membership of the localized lineages of the Moshi chiefdom. These figures fit with other evidence for an earlier period. For example, Charles New reported that Rindi of Moshi (Mandara) told him in 1871 that he had a force of 700 fighting men (1874:39). Compare also Gutmann's saying that in his time the census indicated that there were 1,240 girls in Moshi (1926:389; HRAF:349). These figures are more or less consistent, which gives them considerable credibility. Compare Rebmann on the size of the chiefdom of Kilema fifty years earlier. He says that in 1849 he saw the 400 or 500 troops of Masaki of Kilema pass before him (Krapf 1860:259).

6 Evidence of localization emerged in fieldwork mapping and in genealogies with landplot histories. Gutmann is also clear on this point (1926:302; HRAF:271). The patrilineages within a chiefdom recognized only very weak ties of clanship with lineages having the same names located in other chiefdoms (1926:29; HRAF:21). They recognized common ancestry, and with it sometimes, but not always, presumed amity, but there was no effective collective patrilineal organization beyond that connecting the related agnatic groups residing inside a single chiefdom.

7 In some of their land the Chagga cultivated beans, maize, eleusine, and various other vegetables, but the basic staples were the many varieties of banana.

They also kept a few cows, goats, and sheep in the huts of the household enclosure and manured their gardens diligently with the cow dung. They also planted and grew trees whose wood was used for construction as well as for other domestic purposes.

8 In most parts of the mountain each district contained a number of patrilineages but in some districts there was only one. The occupation of smithing seems to have been confined to certain patrilineages and still is a hereditary profession.

9 But Gutmann indicates that sometimes the chiefs were afraid of the local political powers of prominent lineage spokesmen and did not like the office of district leader (*mchili*) and lineage spokesman of a powerful lineage to be held by the same man. In 1915 the chief seems not to have had the political power to remove such a person from office easily. Instead he could serve his own interests by appointing as one of the district head's assistants a man from another lineage assigned to spy on him (Gutmann 1926:20; HRAF:17). Chiefs may have been less constrained in precolonial times.

10 In 1973, in the socialist state, it was the party messengers who blew the corvée horns.

11 See Kathleen Stahl's *History of the Chagga People* for a reconstruction of the internecine conflicts, and the rise and fall of the fortunes of various chiefdoms.

12 John Murra has noted the importance of "vertical" political and economic alliances in the Andes. There are significant parallels on Kilimanjaro in a much less advanced economy and a much less sophisticated polity. Clifford Geertz has also described the importance of vertical contacts and political organization in Bali (1980:21).

13 If a cattle debtor and creditor did not live in the same chiefly jurisdiction, the market itself could be used as the locale for staging a public accusation (Gutmann 1926:624; HRAF:560–1). Conditional curses on the debtor were repeated a number of times over several market days with certainty that the message would get back through the market women. On other occasions the chiefs negotiated settlements between them on behalf of their subjects.

14 In the nineteenth century, much as they wanted European goods, the Chagga did not see themselves as powerless against their European visitors. When Johnston complained to Chief Mandara about the endless requests made to him for gifts, and told Mandara the story of the goose and the golden egg, Mandara replied, "And now I will tell *you* a tale. When I plant a seed or a sapling here in my plantation, I let it grow quietly at first – I do not pull it up to look at its roots, and I do not pluck its early blossoms or its tender leaves. I wait until it is mature, and then . . . if it fails to bear abundant fruit, I cut it down" (Johnston 1886:133–5). Mandara was imperious, calculating, and on his own territory threatening.

CHAPTER 2. PRACTICAL NORMS AND MYSTICAL IDEAS IN CHAGGA LAW

1 Gutmann was invited to participate in a German government project to investigate the laws and customs of the peoples under its rule in the colonies. A questionnaire had been devised for the study by a committee of eminent scholars, including Josef Kohler and Albert Hermann Post, but Gutmann found the questionnaire format too confining, and decided to write his own account of Chagga law and custom in his own way (Winter 1959:52, 87). Anyone who knows Gutmann's work will be aware that a lot of the original seems jumbled and rambling to the modern eye. My fieldwork made it possible to make sense of many passages that are not otherwise clear. Some remain unintelligible. The reinterpretation of his material offered here is shaped by current theoretical concerns. His concerns were entirely different. The account given here though heavily based on his writings is not the account he gave. Readers interested in the difference between what he says and what I have made of it will have to go back to his text. I have tried to facilitate doing so by making many specific references to passages in his remarkable works. When I quote, I have used the HRAF translation except that I have changed the word "sib" to "lineage."

2   Over recent decades legal anthropologists have increasingly recognized that in many nonliterate societies, in the course of *dispute* resolution, frequently statements of normative rules cannot be shown to "determine" the particular outcome even though they are part of the common cultural background, and may even be explicitly invoked (see Gulliver 1973; Comaroff 1981).

3   "Each chieftaincy had to send several interpreters to the native court of the Imperial District Office . . . their original function, to interpret, has been discontinued. Nowadays they act as intermediaries between the Office and the persons that are asked to appear and between the Office and the chieftain. The natives call them *wasu* (envoys). . . . If a person brings a law case before the chief, he not only has to pay the chief and the spokesman but also the *msu* from his district. . . . In Moshi each party has to pay one rupee . . . to the *msu* (Gutmann 1926:594-5; HRAF: 533-4).

4   Gutmann's work is invaluable and extraordinary. But some of the questions that preoccupied him no longer seem paramount. Gutmann's theoretical models are thoroughly described by his biographer, J. D. Winter (1969). Gutmann thought in evolutionary terms. He was as preoccupied with the development of ethics and the existence of "survivals" as Edward Burnett Tylor, and as concerned with stages of clan evolution as Lewis Henry Morgan. A conception of the primitive mind shaped his interpretation and informed his descriptions. He was concerned with such issues as whether the Chagga had a fully developed conscience and sense of guilt, whether their conception of truth was unlike the European, whether the ethical ideas of the individual Chagga could be considered independently of the group, and the like. His questions all postulated some notion of stages of moral development. And he often thought the "original" Chagga practices morally more sound than those introduced in the colonial period.

5   For the Chagga, as for many other peoples, male and female human beings and the familiar objects of the natural and cultural environment served as the visible signs of a great and continuous cosmic drama in which life-giving and life-sustaining elements were intermixed with life-destroying and death-bringing ones. To humans, the maintenance of life, the task of insuring that the procession of men and animals and plants, would go on, their fertility and reproduction and renewal would never cease, was an endless concern, from season to season, from year to year. The riddle of life

and death was joined with the puzzle of sexuality. All that lived died. All life was tied
to death. Though life and death were two "opposites," they were part of one process.
Male and female together made new life through sexual acts. Man and woman were
two. They were separate and different. They, too, were "opposites." But they were
one in the very act that generates life, and one in their humanity. The two that could
be one and the one that was two were among enigmas and paradoxes that Chagga
ritual addressed. Powers awakened could engender good fortune or disaster depending on the circumstances.

   In Chagga culture, the laws of society and the laws of nature were intertwined
in a single system of causes and effects. The proper combination of male and
female in marriage was in keeping with social order and produced healthy new
life. The wrong combination, out of wedlock, incestuous or anomalous in some
other way, made disorder, sickness, and death. One of the practical and philosophical problems was to keep separated that which should not be in contact, and
to combine that which could be connected, each at the right time and in the right
way. Just as male and female were different, but the same, necessary to each
other, but essentially separate and distinct, endowed in timely combination with
the greatest possible powers of life-giving, but separately, or too soon or too late,
incapable of procreation, so the principles of separation and combination, of
similarity and difference, and of timeliness had to be applied to all attempts to
control the powers of creation and destruction, of fortune and misfortune. The
powers of destruction could be used against an enemy for protection of self.
Hence the powers of destruction were not unambiguously evil, merely dangerous,
and the direction in which they were sent determined whether they were operating positively or negatively for a particular person. Similarly ambiguous were
some of the most fundamental of the life-maintaining processes such as the taking
in of food and drink. What entered the body could nourish and sustain it, or it
could poison and kill. Thus the persons with whom one shared food, drink, and
physical contact were the most trusted and intimate, and yet were the very persons to whose bad intentions one was most vulnerable.

   The symbols that figure in Chagga cursing ritual reflect some of these cultural
ideas and categories. Objects and words were used to evoke the cosmic implications of all that might otherwise seem ordinary. Their "collective representations," their cultural associations of ideas, their conventions about significance
gave subtle and special meanings to mundane things: maleness and femaleness,
water and fire, right and left, blood and milk, the colors red, white and black,
heat and cold, clay, stone, and iron, and all the animals and plants of Kilimanjaro. Such qualities and objects and creatures were treated in ritual and sayings as
if they were knowable quantities in the basic equations that summed up the life
and death processes:

The pots that have the cursing power are made of unfired clay. Their shape is either that of
a regular pot or that of a human being. There was a strict distinction between the two forms.
The size varied, but it was never unwieldy. The most striking feature of the pot-shaped
cursing instrument was a wreath of wart-shaped protuberances below the rim of the pot.
These wart-ornaments made the pot rather decorative. The human figure – in the other form
of the cursing instrument – had a length of from 12 to 15 centimeters with a head that was

carefully shaped. The mouth was open as if the person was shouting. The arms and the legs were only stumps so that the whole looked like a fetus. The sexual organs were done with the greater elaboration. The Chagga used male and female figures. To intensify the curse a female figure was swung after the male figure, and the female cursing form was regarded as being more effective. (Gutmann 1926:620; HRAF:556)

The clay vessels and figures have the color of the earth out of which they were formed. . . . (Gutmann 1926:620; HRAF:556)

One side of the cursing pot was a wide vertical band of soot, on the other side a corresponding stripe of red clay. To the left and to the right of this red stripe, somewhat to the side of it, there are two whitish stripes of ashes. The soot side is the back of the cursing pot. The swinger of the pot must see to it that the black side is turned toward his body. For the side which is painted red is the side of attack, the side from which the pernicious power emanates. The red side must be turned toward the dwelling of the opponent when the pot is swung and the curse pronounced. Typical once more the term for the red side: *ora lo modo* i.e. the side of the fire. The clay figure has the soot stripe on the back, while the red stripe runs from the open mouth down over the whole front. There is one stripe of ashes at the left side. The right side was either left unpainted or had a blue stripe which protected the swinger. (Gutmann 1926:620–1; HRAF:556–7)

Gutmann describes the cursing bell used in the Moshi District of Mahoma.

In an ordinary cow bell only the mantle is split, whereas in the case of this particular cursing bell the clapper was split, too, "like the tongue of a snake." The ring in which the clapper hung had four points which were called teeth. In the middle of the one half of the split bell mantle, brass was inserted, and this brass was the transmitter of the curse since brass was called *menja ja modo*, "iron of fire." The other half was of pure iron, *menja ja mringa*, "iron of water." The water-iron side was the curser's, the fire iron side corresponded to the cursed person. (Gutmann 1926:663; HRAF:596)

Cursing stones were perforated stones of the size of a fist. They were not necessarily ring shaped. . . . One eye witness who had seen such stone . . . described it to me as having the shape of a bolt, the upper end of which was perforated. Below this ring perforation the bolt tapered off to a neck, while its lower end formed, so to speak, the body. The neck part had a vertical groove. This stone is said to have had the male sexual organ on the one side and the female sex characteristics on the other. Even simple ring-shaped cursing stones sometimes seem to have had crude indications of these characteristics. (Gutmann 1926: 658; HRAF:592)

The source and distribution of the perforated cursing stones are not too clear. Gutmann seems to have thought them a remnant of Bushman occupation of the region. Gulliver reports that the Arusha Masai and Meru use them and say they came from Pare, Kahe, or Taveta (1968:291), and Dundas thinks them like *Kithathi* of the Kikuyu, round pieces of lava with a hole in the center, as he saw one meeting that description which had been dug up in the village of the great chief Horombo (1924:174).

The cursing stone was manufactured. A groove divided the ring into halves, one being the side of the curser, the other the one of the cursed.

Only stones from the bed of a cursing stream (mringa fo iwawa, i.e., "water of pain") were regarded as suitable. A brook may be designated as cursing stream if it dries up regularly, or if it has no tributary, or if it has become, for some unknown reasons, the site for mourning ceremonies. . . .

The stone was traditionally kept in the opening of a tree trunk. It had to be a tree that had milk sap (especially mfumu and mseseve) since these trees were thought to have special protective powers. The stone is given its function with the following incantation: . . . "I bore a hole for the mouth: may it spout ire like a human being. Stone. May your mouth cause pain. May your heart be painful and burn like a nettle." (Gutmann 1926:659–60; HRAF:593)

When it comes to the cooling of the stone and to the expiation of the persons concerned, the stone is scraped with a snail shell. The scrapings from the female side are mixed into the blood of the female sacrificial animals, while the scrapings from the male half are put into the blood of the male animals. (Gutmann 1926:658ff.; HRAF:592ff.)

The dangers in the combination of male and female could be kept in check by keeping male and female domains separated and by permitting sexual connection only under regulated conditions. Family and lineage exogamy defined the basic prohibitions. There was also a proper order in time. The age-set system had sexually regulatory aspects as well as political and economic implications. The warrior age-grade alone had the right to father children. Each man in it had to resign from the warrior grade as soon as he had a circumcised child (Gutmann 1926:358; HRAF: 324). In the ritual in which he was welcomed into senior age, a man was cautioned against seeking another child from his wife. Were he to have a child after his own son's circumcision, or were his wife to bear a child after her daughter's marriage, it was said that the old parents and their child might die, killed by the ancestors (1926:359; HRAF:325). Thus individual men left the age-grade one by one as their children reached the age of marriage. The age-grade consequently disintegrated over a period of years. However, the age-set officially and collectively surrendered the Lawn of Justice to the next age-set in a ritual whose timing was determined by the incumbent chief. At that time the chiefship might be handed over to the chief's son.

The proper order of things was to have the generations procreate in succession. Even a mother cow and her female calf could not go on living in the same homestead. If they became pregnant at the same time the owner would die (Gutmann 1926:405; HRAF:451). There could be no mixing up of the order of things, or disaster would follow. Part of that order was an order in time, a sequence of replacements that continued the line. Parent and child could not occupy the same position in the series at the same time. Like doing things backward or upside down, doing them in the wrong order was chaotic and evil, and brought misfortune and death.

Similarly, the efficacy of a ritual depended in part on performing the ritual acts in proper succession and the correct number of times. The rituals of malediction performed with the cursing pots, bells, and stones, and the rituals to pacify these instruments, had specified sequences in which some of their power was inherent.

For a more detailed discussion of the Chagga system of classification and explanation see S. Moore, "The Secret of the Men," *Africa* 46(4) (1976).

6   The case has been paraphrased and is not a translation.

7   "Utaniona," or "Mtaniona" says literally, "You'll see me" but means something more like "You'll see what I do about it." I have heard accusations in court of threats to kill in which these were the only words allegedly uttered.

CHAPTER 3. THE POWERS AND OBLIGATIONS OF CHIEFS AND COMMONERS

1 Gutmann describes an example. He says that several important men of the lineage could go to the chief and tell him that the whole lineage wanted to get rid of their brawling brother, since they were having to pay too much bloodwealth on his behalf. They might then say, "But we do not dare kill him. This is your country, oh chief. We shall turn him over to you, you are the lord. We are willing to throw the colocynths upon him" (Gutmann 1926:247; HRAF:220). (Colocynths refers to plants put over the corpses of men killed in a fight or battle.) The chief might then be obliging. One way was to arrange for a false battle alarm. The warriors, including the lineage brother to be killed, would all respond and rush out to the chiefdom boundary that was supposedly being invaded. An ambush could be set up so that the brawler might seem to have been killed by accident by one of his fellow warriors. This stratagem made a better story to tell his wife, and also assured that he would not be killed on lineage lands. The killers would thereby avoid the dangerous pollution of lineage land and the possible wrath of the ancestors (1926: 247, 249; HRAF: 220, 222).

Gutmann comments that the involvement of the chief in such a planned homicide shows that the lineage could not freely execute its own (1926:247). Nor could blood vengeance against a killer from another lineage be taken without the chief's permission, but evidently on occasion permission could be obtained on request (1926:243; HRAF:216).

2 Interlineage feuding is said by some informants to have continued deep into the colonial period and may well have been one of the causes of the killing of Nathaniel Mtui in 1927. Mtui was a major Chagga historian and informant for Gutmann, Raum, and Dundas.

3 The types of homicide Gutmann cites as requiring either vengeance or bloodwealth payment were: (1) killing in a fight (1926:247; HRAF:220), (2) accidental killing (1926:245; HRAF:218), (3) drunken killing (1926:245; HRAF:218), (4) homicide through negligence (1926:245; HRAF:218), and (5) the death of a wife who died during her first pregnancy (1926:250; HRAF:223).

4 That the chief was appealed to in cases of homicide and violence, and that he had to make serious political choices if he intervened is neatly illustrated by the account of the exhortations supposedly made to Rindi when he became *mangi* of Moshi in the early 1860s. I interject "supposedly" because the verbatim description was collected by Gutmann more than forty years later. Despite the fact that persons in an oral tradition tend to remember oratory better than the literate, what was told Gutmann is probably not very good evidence of what literally was said to Rindi so many years earlier. But it is probably reasonably good evidence of the way the chiefship was conceived and the kinds of ideas that were entertained about killings by chiefs, and vengeance killings by others. It also has passages that strongly suggest the political dangers to the chief that could ensue from unpopular action, and suggests that chiefs be wary, keep themselves well informed, and seek advice and indication of political support before any major decision, including killing a subject. The significant passages are several:

One part of the exhortation and instruction of the young chief reads:

Protect the poor against the pressure from the rich. The aristocrats think in terms of the wergild (makara). They are able to say, If I kill one of these poor ones, it will not harm me, because I have enough brothers who will help me to raise the wergild. If you let this sort of people rule the country, your country will fall into misery. (Gutmann 1926:350; HRAF:316)

This passage surely suggests that in reality some were better able to "get away with murder" than others, that the aftermath of homicide depended on many factors including wealth and political position, and that this kind of lineage power was seen as a danger to the chiefship.

As for approving of or helping lineage members to kill a lineage mate, Rindi was said to have been admonished to try to stay out of such cases,

If somebody comes to you and deposits the "stick of death" (a head of cattle) for his lineage mate, do not eat it. Keep it and call in two elders and two advisers and share the meat with them. You should not obey if a man asks you, with the help of a cattle-present, to give orders for the killing of a lineage mate; remember, not all the lineage members will agree with the killing. But do not reject the head of cattle either, but stall it and call in four trusted advisers with whom you discuss the matter. They will advise you. (Gutmann 1926:355; HRAF:321)

The passage goes on to suggest the way that the chief should force the lineage brothers to settle the issue peacefully is to publicize the threat by calling an assembly of the men and informing them of the homicidal intentions of one agnatic kinsman against another.

Other homicidal attacks are also mentioned in the hortatory address:

Beware of quick decisions . . . if someone comes bleeding to the "lawn of justice" and says to you, "Mangi, . . . I am dying." Listen to both sides in a regular law suit. Perhaps it may be that the bleeding one started the quarrel and that you may have to say to him: Keep your cuts to yourself. (Gutmann 1926:354; HRAF:320)

However, treason was rightfully punished with death by the chief. Gutmann explains that the "mouse that gnaws at the borders" is the traitor who goes to another chiefdom to plot with a neighboring chief against his own, and that "throwing the stick" means condemning to death. "If someone leaves his country and turns into a mouse that gnaws at the borders, the stick shall be thrown for him by the chief. And the stick shall also be thrown for one of the chief's advisers if he intends to cut the sleeping chief's throat" (Gutmann 1926:356; HRAF:323).

The young chief is warned to be careful to keep himself informed.

We say that you have the eye of an eagle that spies into every district. But if you remain too self-reliant, you remain blind in the end. You must place a spy in every district, a spy whom you pay for his services with meat and cloth. He will tell you whatever is worthy of note. Then you can call in the district officials and the elders. (Gutmann 1926:350–1; HRAF:317)

Again and again he is admonished not to come to any fatal conclusions alone. "If you should hear of people who want to betray you, do not make any decision alone, but call in the people whom you can trust" (Gutmann 1926:352; HRAF:318).

The chief must not have someone killed wrongfully, lest supernatural punishment fall on him from the dying man's curse, a curse that cannot be undone, and that could affect not only the chief but his whole lineage.

It is impossible to dig up the root of the baobab tree. And it is just as impossible to propitiate a dead man who left his last wish in the form of a curse. . . . Do not have a design upon another person's life. A single crime in your house may become responsible for the extinction of the entire lineage, for who can propitiate a dead man's thirst for revenge? (Gutmann 1926:352; HRAF:318)

5   The reports of travelers who visited Chagga chiefdoms before the colonial period tend to depict the chiefs as powerful and autocratic, but though they came earlier, they did not have close knowledge of the inner workings of local politics (Krapf 1860:243; Von der Decken 1871, 1:274ff.; New 1874:377–433; Johnston 1886:87–156). Chagga chiefship probably had its origin in the age-class system. A chief was expected to step down from office before his death and hand his place to his son, and also a Chagga chief could be deposed by the warrior age-class. But despite its age-class origins, if origins they were, by the mid- to late nineteenth century, the office seems to have developed a definition of power apart from the age-class system, and to have been held remarkably longer than the chief's age-class stayed in power, at least in certain chiefdoms of which Moshi was one.

6   In 1921 Sir Charles Dundas collected figures on 34 chiefs who had 285 wives among them (Griffiths 1930). Gutmann speaks of the 70 servant girls of the wives of the current chief of Moshi, saying each wife had from 5 to 8 such servants (1926:388; HRAF:349). Petro Itosi Marealle showed me a newspaper interview that said his father had had 60 wives. That seems implausible because only 13 children survived. In 1917 in an effort to curtail chiefly polygyny the chiefdom of Kiwoso limited its new chief to 5 wives (Gutmann 1926:389; HRAF:350). Whether chiefs had more wives in the early colonial period than they had ever had in precolonial times is not a question that can be answered, but it may be worth a moment of speculation.

7   Chief Rindi of Moshi (chiefship from ca. 1860 to 1891) is said to have carried raiding to a new level of refinement by dividing his military force into warriors and looters (Gutmann 1926:538; HRAF:486). After a raid, the looters had to turn over all the captured livestock to the chief for division and redistribution. Unless he was feeling especially magnanimous, at least one half of all captured animals belonged to the chief (1926:538–41; HRAF:486–8). The rest was divided among the men. Some objects taken in the course of looting, such as iron tools, hoes, axes, and sickles or wooden pots and barrels belonged to the captor. The same rule pertained to captured cloth, cattle skins, and butter. But any quantity of brass and copper rings, or lead and iron ones, as well as chains of iron had to be offered to the chief who repaid their value in goats. Captive women and children were sometimes incorporated into the family of the captor, but were often taken by the chief for sale as slaves (1926:542; HRAF:489). Ivory tusks belonged to the chief but he had to pay half their value to those who had captured them (1926:543; HRAF:490).

Among the captured items livestock was surely one of the most important. A whole series of elaborate rules surrounded the distribution of these beasts, which the chief could, of course, amend at will. In theory, if there were enough animals to go around, each looter would have received one head, each warrior two, each district head three, and a few especially fine animals would have been reserved for prominent senior men of the lineages the chief wanted to reward. It was probably more often the case that there were not so many animals as men, and in that case, additional rules about the division included rights to calves the captured cows might have later on and preferential rights to booty from subsequent raids (Gutmann 1926:538–41; HRAF:486–8). The chief himself could later claim one of the offspring of booty–cattle allocated to his warriors as tribute (1926:381; HRAF:342).

8 The *isumba* could place his cattle with others "by day," that is, openly and publicly placing cattle as the chief did. In theory such a man had no need to conceal assets from the chief since he contributed so much to him. But in fact *masumba* did place cattle secretly, to hide them from overreaching chiefly greed (Gutmann 1926:442; HRAF:397). Sometimes, cattle-wealthy men even exchanged animals for this purpose. If an *isumba* saw that his "placed" cow or calf was going to be confiscated from the man with whom he had placed it, he could speak up, and neither the district head nor anyone else would dare to take it away (1926:447–8; HRAF:402). Indeed, an *isumba* might extend this kind of protection to all the animals held by his "borrower," even to animals that did not actually belong to him. Thus it would seem that the chief had cattle clients whom he protected, and they in turn had cattle clients to whom they could extend their own protection.

9 Scattered references exist in Gutmann to the lineage slaughtering feasts (1926:40–50; HRAF:31–9), to skin rings (1926:54, 81–2; HRAF:43, 68), and to bespitting animals before sacrifice (1926:13–14, 97; HRAF:11, 81). Dundas has a longer but somewhat garbled account (1924:123–50). Both of these writers treated lineage feasts essentially as evidence of a strange system of religious belief. These earlier writers scarcely subjected slaughtering to any social and economic analysis.

When animals were slaughtered at the chief's behest for foreigners the *kishongu* rings were also fashioned for them (Krapf 1860:238; Von der Decken 1871, 1:273). Evidently the meat-sharing, blood-of-the-animal–sharing, and skin-ring–sharing symbols that were part of kinsmen's patrilineage feasts were extended to nonkin with whom alliances were desired. There is no way to know whether in the 1860s these might have been pro-forma gestures, or material symbols of supernatural significance calculated to bring misfortune down on the breaker of the compact of friendship. Certainly as enacted within the lineage, a clear ritual relation existed among the common killing, the common eating, the common ancestry, and the common vulnerability to the caprices of the spirits of common ancestors. The practice carried many of the characteristics of the blood feasts of other peoples that would have gladdened the heart of William Robertson-Smith.

10 After a steer was dead, an artery in its throat was cut and the blood caught in a bowl. Later on in the butchering, blood was also collected from the lungs and heart. The blood was a delicacy. Part of it belonged to the owner. If the animal had been placed in agistment, some of the blood was reserved for the man who had been taking care of the animal. The rest was shared by the men at the slaughtering feast.

After being killed and bled, the animal was skinned and the internal organs were removed. The *kiuno,* the loin or flank was the part that was eaten at the slaughtering place. If it was fatty enough, it was roasted in the fire; otherwise it was boiled. Then it was cut into small pieces, dipped in the salted blood, and eaten. It was of paramount importance that these small pieces of meat be distributed by seniority, eldest first. Even in distributing the beer which was consumed at the slaughtering place, seniority was recognized. The senior elder had the prerogative of having the first drink. The foam from the top of the beer, associated as it was with semen and fertility, and the continuity of male descent in the patrilineage, belonged to him. He was also given the last drink of beer, and the dregs were then poured out as a libation for the ancestors. But it was the meat distribution of the small pieces to be eaten at once that completely replicated the birth order of the men in the lineage.

The ancestors' share, which was put on the ground for them, consisted of the contents of the stomach and intestines, *mra,* and some tiny token slivers of the share-to-take-home of each man present. The ancestors' share was called *nedaso.* The most important cut of the animal was the *kidari,* the breastbone and surrounding meat, from the throat to the navel. The *kidari* had to be given to the senior elder of the lineage branch. If someone else took it and ate it, doing so was sure to kill the presumptuous fellow sooner or later. The second most important share, the *ngari,* went to the second senior man. It consisted of the middle ribs and the hump. Part of the lungs, head, and five ribs on both sides, the portion called *longu,* belonged to the married sister of the animal's owner. The *mgongo,* consisting of the last few ribs together with the kidneys, was reserved for the mother of the owner, or to his wife's mother. The slaughterer received the meat from the rump and one foreleg. The owner of the animal kept the head, saving the lower half and tongue for himself, but the top, with the brains was for his unmarried daughters and nieces. They were also to be given the genitals, as well as some parts of the stomach and intestines. The large stomach was shared by everyone, the smaller ones being saved for the women. The owner kept the small intestine. He saved the large intestine for his mother and the rectum for his father. Men of procreative age were forbidden to eat the rectum of animals. The beast's neck belonged to the owner's wife, who shared it with female neighbors and sisters-in-law. The owner kept one of the forelegs if he had raised the animal himself. If it had been placed in agistment, the custodian received that leg. The owner gave each of the two hind legs to one of his brothers. As for the entrails, it was important that some small bit of the heart, lungs, liver, and intestines be given to each person along with his slaughtering share. If the man entitled to a slaughtering share was away, and unable to attend the feast, his share had to be sent to his household anyway. If there was no living relative of a particular category, a substitute of the appropriate relationship and sex received the meat.

Some of these allocations varied slightly from one lineage to another and from one chiefdom to another, but the *kidari* and the *ngari* seem not to vary (cf. Dundas 1924:184–5; Gutmann 1926:40; HRAF:31). In the course of this field-work, 1968–79, informants in the two ex-chiefdoms of Kilema and Mwika gave similar information about present practice.

11 In some lineages the internal "legal trustee" worked out most matters of internal dispute, as well as representing the lineage to the chief in tax matters, and dealing with other external lineage debts. Other lineages without a legal trustee were more inclined to go to the chief with their troubles. If the chief did not want to be bothered with their internal lineage quarrels, he might appoint one of their number to act as mediator (Gutmann 1926:15 ff.; HRAF:12 ff.). But sometimes the chief himself heard complaints and made decisions.

12 He must have been a relative (possibly the grandfather, since a son named Merinjo is mentioned) of Joseph Merinyo Maro, who married the Gutmanns' housekeeper, became Dundas's interpreter, and later the first president of the coffee cooperative and an important figure in Kilimanjaro politics.

13 Gutmann says it was rare for a livestock thief to slaughter and eat the stolen animal, even if it was a goat. To slaughter and eat a stolen animal was regarded as an unutterably reprehensible form of misappropriation, so wrong that doing so carried, it is said, much more severe penalties than homicide. In fact, if the act occurred secretly and privately, it would have been hard to conceal because of the lack of privacy in a household. It amounted to compounding the theft by violating all the obligatory norms of meat sharing and sociability that surrounded slaughter-ing. Theft plus concealment in another household makes much more sense.

14 Whether the right to reclaim was frequently exercised or not in the dim past is hard to know. Without either land shortage or population increase, there would have been both less motive to do so and less hardship to the occupier if he had done so than in the later conditions of land shortage.

15 There seems to have been a good deal of migration of this kind in the second half of the nineteenth century. Lineage genealogies combined with land-plot his-tories, if obtained on a large enough scale, could provide much broader historical evidence than now exists. Part III shows some of the potential.

16 Jack Goody's paper "Strategies of Heirship" has a table on family size and the likelihood of a male child predeceasing his father in preindustrial conditions. It indicates a two-thirds chance then that the son will die before his father. As for numbers of sons, it indicates a 7.2 percent chance of having two or more sons if the average number of children is 2.5. The chances of having two or more sons goes up to a 28.3 percent chance if the average number of children goes up to 6.0 (Goody 1973:17–18). See also the demographic discussion in the first section of Chapter 5.

17 Indeed, a grandfather who had provided separate *vihamba* for all of his sons and still had one or more banana gardens might well indicate which grandson should inherit them. Informants in Vunjo stated some preference for the firstborn son of the firstborn son.

18 The burier of a man assumed his assets and obligations. If he left an adult son, the burier was normally the decedent's son (Dundas 1924:183). Gutmann says the contrary, that the eldest son could not bury his father (1926:34; HRAF:26). But elsewhere he says that the burier inherits the debts and the son buries his father's skull (1926:483, 486; HRAF:434, 437). The burier-heir of the brother who left no sons, or only minor sons, was that brother who was his slaughtering partner in life. This brother was also the preferred inheriting husband of the widow. If she married him, he assumed the guardianship of the estate and the care of the widow. But if the widow did not agree to marry him, the roles of guardian and widow's husband could be separated and occupied by two different brothers (1926:50; HRAF:39). If the son of the decedent was adult, he inherited the estate, but the decedent's brother inherited the widow-mother. (In the western parts of Kilimanjaro, a son could inherit the wives of his father other than his mother. In Moshi, he could inherit such a wife only if she had not borne any children to his father.) In any case, the youngest son inherited the *kihamba* occupied by the mother.

19 If the sons were minors, the youngest was still supposed eventually to receive his mother's *kihamba*. Older sons were to be helped to acquire land by the father's brother in his role as guardian. That guardian-uncle when possible was the one who had been the decedent's slaughtering partner. He might also be the widow inheritor, but did not have this last role unless she agreed.

20 If eleusine was the crop grown exclusively on a plot, the land required a year and a half of fallowing between crops. But if maize, eleusine, and beans (intermixed with maize) were rotated, one crop being grown per year, only one year of fallow was required in four years of cultivation. (Land Tenure Report, Moshi District, 1930, A.W.M. Griffiths, district officer, p. 27)

21 Gutmann speaks of sixty-five canals in the Moshi and Mbokomu districts in his time (not counting the government canal), and says that of these only ten flowed permanently, the others being operated through the reservoir system. The reservoirs could be opened and closed as could the channel branches themselves. During the rainy season everything was left open so that the damming devices would not be carried away. If the land that was flooded for the purpose of making a reservoir had once been cultivated, the owner was thought to be sufficiently compensated by receiving a water share. But if he lived elsewhere and did not benefit from the water community, he had a right to a tub of beer every third year from the grain collected by the canal head, and in the intervening years had a right to a calabash full.

22 Each marriage usually had a sponsoring couple who were "trustees" of the marriage. They counted and witnessed the transfers of bridewealth and were supposed to mediate or adjudicate all quarrels arising from the marriage. The "trustee" is called *mkara*.

23 In some chiefdoms, the scale of these activities was small. In Moshi chiefdom, the *mangi*'s domain was small enough – 7,000 persons and 80 lineages – for him to exert personal influence widely. But insofar as the chief's power rested on his economic means and his military arm, it depended heavily on the efficacy of an underlying structure of local social discipline in the districts and the patrilineages.

CHAPTER 4. THE GERMAN PERIOD: CHIEFS, CATTLE, CASH, AND COURTS

1 It is difficult to know for certain with Gutmann whether his evolutionary ideas and his enthusiasm for the precolonial Chagga way of doing things might have affected his sense of the change in economic values or not, but it seems to fit with other evidence that the value of cattle had increased.

2 Gutmann tells us that when a European asked the chief for milk, thinking that it would be easy for the chief to provide it, given the size of his herds, the European did not realize that the chief's wives would object if he took milk from their cows, and that rather than tangle with them, the chief would send for milk from one of his subjects (1926:393; HRAF:353).

3 The lawsuit alleged that the chief had failed to return certain of these beasts. Fifteen cows had originally been placed in the chief's *boma* (cattle fold) by a commoner, Lemama, whose son was involved in the suit. When some of the animals were withdrawn by the original agistor, one bull was paid to the chief as his share for their care. These facts in the lawsuit were not disputed. There was disagreement over whether the last few head of cattle had been returned. In an earlier suit one witness had testified that the chief had not returned all the animals. In the later case of 1931 that witness acknowledged perjuring himself, to the chief's detriment, explaining that he had done so because at the time he wanted to get back at the chief who had previously taken two of his own cows away. The chief (now ex-chief, who was present) acknowledged that he had once taken two of the perjurer's cows. The self-acknowledged perjurer then said there had been no genuine claim against the chief. The claim was fictitious. The self-confessed liar was fined thirty shillings. (Who knows which of the statements was a perjury?) The parties to the suit were the son of the man who had originally placed his cattle in the ex-chief's *boma* and the son of the ex-chief.

4 There is no way to know from the materials I have seen whether this shift to chiefly *boma*s (cattle folds) took place in many chiefdoms or only in Mwika. In precolonial times such *boma*s on the plain probably would have been much harder to maintain because they would have been vulnerable to cattle raiding.

5 They were not unfamiliar with cash transactions before 1898. When Sir Harry Johnston offered to pay Mandara the equivalent of 12 rupees a month for the land he was using, Mandara said he wanted 100 rupees (Johnston 1886:191).

6 Gutmann states:

At one time taking care of someone else's cattle was a blessing for the poor. Now cattle lending had become a necessity for the rich. . . . Still more important . . . the rich regard the chief's tax as the only means for maintaining the splendor of the chief's household. . . . The naked historical fact . . . is that, in the majority of chieftaincies, after the colonial pattern, the cattle tax for the chief was extended to every homestead where there were any cattle at all, and from now on this tax is to be collected every three or four years. (1926:384–5; HRAF:345)

Gutmann reports that in 1912 the "supervisors" of the *mitaa* (*wachili*) and the rich men went into conference with the chief and said:

"Chieftain, we beseech you to give orders that everybody, rich or poor, should pay taxes to the chieftain . . . consider the situation: the poor people now have their own livestock everywhere. Where are we supposed to place our cattle? We cannot find a person willing to undertake the care of our cattle since they all have but one thought: to work and to buy livestock with wages. . . ." This was the cause for the chieftain's order that his tax had to become as general [i.e., falling on rich and poor alike] as the colonial tax. . . . This was different at the time of Rindi [precolonial period]. . . . No cattle tax was expected of people who had only one head of cattle or two. Now even the owner of one head of cattle is asked to pay the cattle tax. . . . This demand stirs the anger of the elders and the poor. They know: this is robbery and not taxation. And whoever declines to pay such a tax is, under some shady pretense, accused. . . . For instance, he is accused of having refused to work for a European. And when the Governor hears about this he appoints the man as a mail carrier who has to carry the mail to Arusha (which is a dreaded assignment in view of the Askari escort . . .). On the other hand, if someone wants to work for a Westerner, they retain him at home and say to him, "You have to stay home, since you are too old." (1926:383–5; HRAF:344–5)

This use of false accusations to manipulate colonial officials into penalizing disobedience to the demands of the chiefs was well remembered in the 1960s and 1970s as one of the onerous aspects of the colonial period. As we shall see, false accusation remains a powerful weapon of administrators, even in the postcolonial period.

7 One Marangu market is shown in its present location on an early German map of Hans Meyer's travels in East Africa in 1887, 1889, and 1898 (map hangs in Kibo Hotel, Marangu).

8 Shann describes the curriculum, "There was also some practical activity. . . . In the early days at Kilema children assisted a Lay Brother in introducing livestock and planting vegetables and fruit trees. A parcel of coffee beans from Reunion reached Kilema in about 1895" (1956:29–30).

9 The missions and the settler community had their intermarriages and other connections. Gutmann was married to the daughter of a settler in Moshi, Dr. Emil Theodor Forster, who among other things, started a coffee plantation in Machame (Winter 1972:54–5).

10 Kilimanjaro Native Coffee Union booklet printed in 1948 says that by 1916 there were 14,000 coffee trees owned by Chagga growers (Habari zote za Kahawa KNCU 1948:11). This is not really a great number considering that an acre of good land may hold as many as 350 to 400 coffee trees interplanted with bananas, and that in the early days of the century each Chagga homestead had several acres of land available to it. But 14,000 coffee trees were a start. (The figure 14,000 may not be reliable either. There may have been more. See Rogers 1972:177.)

11 Europeans held 24,644 hectares of land, 2,267 of which belonged to the missions. In 1912 the government called a halt to further alienation (Rogers 1972:171).

12 This show of force, and the use of force was an inherent part of the initial relationship between the colonial government and the Chagga.

At first some of the officials treated Africans cruelly. The founder of the colony set the worst possible example in this respect. In 1896 the Socialist deputy August Bebel told the Reichstag that Carl Peters had been guilty of great cruelty when he was Reich Commissioner in the Kilimanjaro region in 1891-2. It was said that he had ordered the hanging of a native servant called Mabruk for petty theft. . . . Peters appeared before a disciplinary court, which decided that the case against him in the matter of Mabruk had been proved. He was also found guilty of. . . . "conduct unworthy of his official position." (Henderson 1965:146)

CHAPTER 5. THE BRITISH COLONIAL PERIOD AND BEYOND: AN ECONOMIC OVERVIEW

1   In 1929 in Mwika the daughter of Chief Solomoni was involved in a lawsuit regarding a *kihamba* for which, five years earlier, she had agreed to pay three goats. In fact she had paid a calf and owed a goat (Case 26 in Kitabu cha Shauri, Mwika, 1927). She lost the case and the *kihamba,* the argument of her opponent being that she had bought a house on the land but not the land. In any case, the plausibility of paying a cow and a goat for land at the time was accepted by all concerned. That was not the legal issue. The land was the property of a member of her father's clan, and was transferred by him to another man, who was trying to oust her. Her argument probably failed because Chagga women do not hold land independently in this way. During the course of the case, the record mentions a government order to everyone to plant coffee!

2   The chief had the right to allocate [or refuse] land to strangers wishing to settle in the chief's territory. He also had allocatory power over all unoccupied land in his territory and could grant plots to his subjects and/or approve their appropriation and cultivation of it. See also chief Kirita v. Salema Fumba (1953), Digest 16, the Central Appeal Court, cited by James and Fimbo 1973:67.

3   The following reports of the provincial commissioners speak for themselves:

To obtain labour for government without conscription has been exceedingly difficult in Moshi as in Arusha, but with the exception of porters, it has been done. . . . [But the chiefs called out communal labor successfully, and paid beef and beer to the workers from funds taken out of Native Treasuries.] (National Archives 10902, Northern Province Half-yearly Report for Half Year Ending 30 June 1927, p. 18)

The Public Works Department do not seem able to recruit labour in Moshi and Arusha Districts. The Governor's sanction was obtained for conscription of 200 men for road work for 3 months. Great care has been taken by the District Officers to see that this labour is fed and housed up to the best plantation standard and in accordance with regulations on the subject. This should tend to popularize work for the Government. (National Archives 10902, Northern Province Half-yearly Report for Half Year Ending 30 June 1928, p. 9)

Chagga of their own volition are constructing a truly wonderful road at a high altitude round the mountain from West to East thus making access easy between the various mangiates and providing a motor road via Old Moshi into Moshi for their produce. Eastern Chagga in the past have had to come down to the Taveta Road and thence to Moshi. . . .

[Beef and beer is given for most work but carpenters and masons who build bridges get paid.] . . . It is entirely for the benefit of the natives and is being paid for from their treasuries. There has been very little European supervision and the work done is remarkable. (National Archives 10902, Northern Province Half-yearly Report for Half Year Ending 30 June 1928, p. 4)

Labour boycott of all European plantations was threatened by Chagga. (Annual Report, Northern Province, 1928, p. 2)

Only a very small percentage of Chagga work on non-native plantations. (Annual Report, Provincial Commissioner, 1929, TNA 11681:37)

The following incident is of interest as indicating the attitude of the Chagga towards head porterage. A Coffee Officer required seventeen porters to carry his loads a distance of five miles to a new camp at 40 cents per porter. The porters subscribed an additional Shs. 3/20 between them, hired a lorry for Shs. 10/- and sent the officer's kit to the camp on it. (National Archives 11681 Annual Report, Provincial Commissioner, Northern Province 1931, p. 10)

4 Rogers interprets the breaking up into primary societies as an attempt to disband a political force (1972:508). But it seems more plausible, since the central office continued in being, and controlled substantial funds, to see the establishment of local societies as a response to the continuing growth of coffee production and to the practical utility of having centers of collection and administration near the farms of the coffee growers.

5 At that time Msae became a *mtaa* of Mwika, the Msae chiefship came to an end, and the Marikis became subordinate to the chiefs of Mwika, of the Uriyo (Orio) lineage. But the Marikis continued to be one of the preeminent lineages in the *mtaa* of Msae. The information on the Mwika West Primary Society was garnered from its handwritten minutes of meetings and other files.

6 It may be for this reason that cordial as the primary society people were about the inspection of some records they frequently insisted that they had lost or mislaid many of the records of coffee sales by individuals to the coop. These practices were as commonplace in 1961 as they have been more recently (von Clemm 1964:109). In any case, this sidetraffic in coffee is not easily susceptible to detection except at the cost of extremely painstaking checking of handwritten records, whose accuracy may not be all that might be desired in the first place. Yet I did not come across any cases in the local courts concerning these illegal sales of coffee to individuals.

7 The Tanganyika District Books, vol. 3, a typescript in the library of the School of Oriental and African Studies in London, indicates on page 13/23 that while the chiefs banished by the British were away their herds were misappropriated, and when they were reinstated in office they asked that they be restored. The numbers given there were 150 head of Kisarika of Uru, 24 of Salema of Old Moshi, and 600 of Tengia of Keni-Rombo. Restitution seems not to have been achieved in either Kisarika's case or Tengia's, and the numbers, being claims, may have been exaggerated.

8 An animal census of beasts in 100 households in Vunjo (beasts actually kept in the *kihamba*) made in 1969 showed that 87 households had animals. (Eight had no stock. For 5 there was no reliable information.) No household had more than four head of cattle, or eight goats. None had other stock placed elsewhere. Five households kept chickens. The total figures for 100 households were 146 cattle, 239 goats, 25 sheep.

Estimates of cattle in the district suggest that though their absolute number has increased, the human population has increased more rapidly. Figures given by Maro (1974:85) show:

	1946	*1970*
Cattle in the district	95,000	147,000
Human population	231,000	522,000

Even if the total figures are not fully reliable, the general process depicted fits with all other evidence.

9 Figures indirectly indicate the proportion of beasts killed at home. A random survey of the disposition of 128 cattle hides in Moshi and Rombo made by MacKenzie in 1972 showed that 56 of the beasts had died a natural death, 51 had been slaughtered by butchers, and 21 had been slaughtered at home. Thirty-five of the skins were kept for domestic use, 82 were sold, and 11 were thrown away (William MacKenzie, *The Livestock Economy of Tanzania,* Nairobi, Dar es Salaam, Kampala, East African Literature Bureau, 1977).

10 In 1934 the provincial commissioner remarked that "the small butcheries scattered along the slopes of Kilimanjaro . . . have done much to encourage meat consumption amongst the local tribes." (Annual Report of Provincial Commissioner for 1934, Tanzania National Archives 19415, 1934:2) He must not have been aware that the Chagga need no encouragement to eat meat. He commented, too, on legislation prepared or approved that year dealing with liquor control and cattle markets (8). Administrative regulation of Chagga enterprises kept pace with their development.

11 The butcher shops are tiny, one-room buildings. Meat hangs inside and is sold through a windowlike opening. Customers do not enter. They simply approach the window. Other than a knife, the most important piece of equipment is a scale. Attention to the standardization of weights and measures on Kilimanjaro seems not to have been a matter of colonial concern until 1938 (Maro 1974:221).

12 According to my calculations in 1968–69 from indirect evidence, a butcher I knew, who had two butcher shops, grossed over 100,000 shillings a year from an investment that never exceeded 3,000 shillings at any one time (apart from the investment in the buildings). In other words, for an investment in livestock that never went very much over $425 at one time, his shops took in over $14,000 a year (at the then exchange rate of seven shillings per dollar). In the few good months he slaughtered about a beast a day in each shop, in the slower months, only about three animals a week in each store. The butcher insisted that his profits were entirely from the sale of the skins. On that basis alone – and he probably was minimizing – he would have made about 9,000 shillings per year, that is, about three times his ongoing investment.

Prices paid by Tanzania Hides and Skins Company in 1969

Skin	Grade (no.)	Per pound
Cattle	I	1/70
	II	1/20
	III	0/70
	IV	0/50

Per skin (not weighed)

Goat	I	4/50
	II	3/00
	III	1/50
	IV	0/50
Sheep	I	4/00
	II	3/00
	III	0/50
	IV	0/25

Expenditures of two butcher shops owned by the same man, 1969

Estimated cost factors per year

448 beasts at average 200 shs. each	89,600
driving 448 beasts up-mountain at 2 shs. per head	896
Two employees, 30 shs. per week apiece	
in cash and kind	3,120
Rent of shop paid to kinsman (1 sh. per head	
slaughtered in shop)	224
License	50
Total	93,890[a]

Expenses at harvest time

14 beasts at roughly 200 shs. each	2,800
Drivers' fee at 2 shs. a head	28
Employee salaries, part paid in cash, 3 shs. a day, 6 days	36
Total	2,864[b]

[a]*About $13,000 per year at 1969 exchange rate. Incidentals not taken into account: meat paid to unofficial helpers at slaughtering, paint for shop's occasional rehabilitation.*
[b]*About $400.*

Beer shops operate in a somewhat different way, but the proportion of profit to ongoing capital investment is probably even greater. There are four kinds of drinking establishments on Kilimanjaro. Two of them are licensed beer shops that sell locally brewed banana beer.

There are many types of bananas. The basic division is between food bananas and beer bananas. The most important as far as the Chagga are concerned are those used only for brewing beer (Swahili: *ndizi ya ng'ombe;* Kichagga: *mrarawo*). Beer can be prepared by men or by women. It is made out of the ingredients: bananas, millet, *msesewe* bark, and water. The process takes a number of days. The ripe skinned bananas are boiled with water on a wood fire, nowadays usually in a metal container. The length of time they are cooked depends on how the bananas look. They should be red when finished. Then they are put in a wooden container (*mtungi*) and allowed to stand for four or five days. On the fifth or sixth day water is added to the bananas, and they are stirred, and left to stand one day. The next day the banana mash is put into a gunny sack and strained. In the meanwhile the second major ingredient, *mbege* (millet), has been prepared. The millet is washed and then put into a container wet. After four or five days, when it has just begun to sprout it is removed and dried. The drying process takes about two or three days. Then the millet is ground, nowadays by a miller who has a gasoline engine–powered mill. He is paid with cash. In 1969 the cost was fifty cents a tin. Then the millet is cooked mixed with water as if porridge is being prepared. When it is ready, it is combined with the banana liquid. The third ingredient, which makes the beer ferment, is bark from the *msesewe* tree. It is washed, cut in pieces, dried, and stone ground. It is boiled with a half gallon of water or so, and then added to the bananas and millet. Twenty-four hours later, the *pombe* is ready to drink.

One of the two kinds of beer shops that sell local brew legitimately is an open, roofed, but usually unwalled rough structure called a *pombe* shop. The other, called a *mwafrika,* is a closed more finished building in which there is normally a radio playing dance music as well as beer. The *mwafrika* is always near a *pombe* shop from which it buys all the beer it serves. Banana beer is also illegally sold in private homes. Commercially bottled drinks, alcoholic and soft, brought in by truck, are sold in a fourth type of establishment called a *bar.* The *pombe* shop is the least expensive of the two legitimate beer shops. Or to be more exact, prices are everywhere the same, but less beer is served per drink in the *mwafrika* than the *pombe* shop, and still less in the illegal beer houses. (This distinction follows the model of the women's markets in which prices are often standard for a particular day for certain produce, but the quantity varies seasonally and from seller to seller.)

A clear class structuring is perceptible in the clientele of the *mwafrika* and *pombe* shops. The *pombe* shops being open-air establishments and cheapest have the largest daily attendance. Drinkers are often so numerous that they spread out over the surrounding meadow or hill and sit on the grass in the afternoons sipping from their calabashes. They are the farmers of the area and some women from local households. Differentiated from them are the young salaried males who patronize the *mwafrika.* Men in their twenties and thirties, they have had sufficient education to qualify them for posts as teachers, dressers in the dispensary, typists, veterinary assistants, and the like. They usually hold local civil service jobs of some kind.

Some of the beer that is sold in the *pombe* shop is brewed by the owner. Some of it is not. The shop serves as a place where anyone can brew and sell beer. If a man wants to make some beer to sell, he goes to the *pombe* shop owner and tells him that he wishes to make so and so many drums of *pombe* on such and such a date. He registers his name and pays a fee to be able to do his brewing and selling. In 1969 he had to pay the owner of the *pombe* shop five shillings for twelve tins. The individual assembles the bananas and millet with which the beer is made at his own house, and the preliminary stages of the preparation take place there. On the day of the final brewing, he brings the "makings" to the *pombe* shop, and on the next day he sells his beer. Fewer than ten such outsiders normally brew in addition to the owner.

The people on the mountain were angry in July 1969 when, in an effort to encourage people to work more and drink less, the government further restricted the drinking hours, permitting the shops to be open only from four o'clock in the afternoon on weekdays, and from two on Sundays, instead of from two o'clock every day.

To give some idea of the quantities of beer that are sold on a Sunday: on August 18, 1969, the following amounts were noted. One *pombe* shop had on hand two barrels of 24 *debe*s each, two of 12 *debe*s, one large *pipa* of 8 *debe*s and one small *pipa* of 6 *debe*s. A *debe* is a four-gallon tin, the standard liquid measure for sizable quantities. Thus all told, he had on hand 248 gallons of beer, of which the owner of the nearby *mwafrika* bought 32 gallons. In all, the *pombe* shop had 1,984 pints of beer, of which it would sell 1,488 pints and the *mwafrika* 496 pints. Not all the beer would be consumed on the spot, since some people would buy a *debe* of beer and take it home. Nevertheless, the staggering number of pints gives one an idea of the magnitude of the business, on its best day of the week. The *pombe* in question is probably one of the most prosperous, being on the main road.

Two men were in business together in this *pombe* shop. One of them had several businesses and was only at the *pombe* shop from time to time. The other regularly ran the *pombe* shop. He employed three men continuously to help him with the preparation and serving of the beer. These men were paid, I was told, ninety shillings a month each, and a free calabash of beer a day. The other partner in the business occasionally brewed the Sunday beer. When he did so, the regular man and his employees were out of the picture. He employed his wife and two "turn boys," young men who work loading and unloading his trucks and doing odd jobs. The pay for being a turn boy is also about three shillings a day, and food. I was not able to discover what the financial arrangements were between the two partners.

Beer spoils rapidly and cannot be kept, so every day, the sellers try to calculate exactly how much is likely to be sold, and they calculate conservatively. The owner of the *mwafrika* goes to the *pombe* shop before opening time to buy his supply of beer. The *pombe* shop later sells all it has left to its many customers. The *pombe* shop runs out of beer earliest every afternoon, and then some of the farmers take their trade to the *mwafrika* to finish its stock. In 1968 and 1969 these *pombe* shops and *mwafrika*s were open every afternoon including Sunday. In fact, Sunday was their biggest business day. In 1969 for fifty shillings it was possible to rent the whole *pombe* shop for a day, so that no one else but oneself could sell beer.

13 In 1969 the pombe shop had two sizes of calabashes, a fifty-cent size and a one-shilling size. A tin (*debe*) of beer cost eight or nine shillings. See note 12 above for economy of a beer shop.

14 List of produce markets from Kilimanjaro District Council, 1969:

West Hai	Central Hai	East Hai
Sanya Juu	Kalali	Mkoringo
Lawate	Kyalia	Ongoma
Naibilie	Sambarai	Mrawi
Langata Mbalelo	Kombo	Kidia
Mola	Kindi	Kinyange Kya-Mamfundo
Kware	Narumu	Sahoni
Kyuu	Manushi	Arusha-Chini
Majengo	Malanja	Kiboriloni
Boma Ngombe	Suungu Mweka	
Rundu Gai	Nkuringa	
Sanya Chini	Ndereni	

West Vunjo	East Vunjo
Uchira	Himo
Lyamwombi (Kilema big mkt.)	Lyangoyo (Mwika)
Kyamo (Kilema small mkt.)	Kinyange (Marangu)
Rindima	Kisambo (Mamba)
Nanga Pumwami	
Kahe	
Chekereni	

South Rombo	North Rombo
Mkuu	Mnamu Kitirima
Shimbi	Tarakea
Keni	Mrere
Mriti	
Holili	
Kitalo	

Cattle markets are located at Weruweru and Uchira.

15 To give an idea of the economics involved: in 1969 a well-developed acre, in which all coffee trees were over five years old, might have 350 to 400 coffee trees producing 10 to 12 hundredweight bags of coffee per annum. There would also likely be about 200 bananas. Such a garden would have brought in an annual income of about 1200 shillings in 1967–68. At that time coffee prices were 112 shillings for one hundredweight (112 pounds) of coffee. The price of bananas in the market are variable. In the same period they ranged from 2 shillings a bunch in times of plenty to around 6 shillings in times of shortage. About three-quarters of the banana crop is eaten for subsistence, only one-quarter or so is sold.

CHAPTER 6. THE FORMAL STRUCTURE OF LOCAL GOVERNMENT AND LOCAL COURTS

1 Msae was composed of two sub*mitaa*, Kinyamvuo and Nganyeni. The two have become separate cooperative villages. The census was completed with excellent local assistance. I had hoped to repeat the census in 1979 to measure changes that might have taken place on a larger scale than was possible from conversations with the persons I knew best, but in the anxious political climate of the time this plan proved to be impractical. I was also curious to discover to what extent Kinyamvuo and Nganyeni themselves were endogamous. More scattered census data from the ex-chiefdoms of Kilema, Mamba, Machame, and Uru produced similar indications.

2 See Samoff 1974 for a study of politics in Moshi Town.

3 Locally resident Chagga interested in their own history could easily complete this set of reconstructions and should do so before the information disappears. But awareness of the recentness of these changes is not universal on the mountain. Thus the scholarly geographer Maro, who is a Chagga, presenting a map of the 1961 reorganization of the mountain into seven subdivisions says, "The subdivisions shown in the map are the former chiefdoms whose boundaries have not changed since the late 19th century" (1974:10).

The old consolidations should be discoverable not only for the chiefdoms, but also for the *mitaa*. The more recent ones certainly are. But the reconstruction cannot be casually done. I was told that Mwika just before independence had seven *mitaa* and that between 1961 and 1962 these were consolidated into three.

Immediately before independence	*1962–76*
Kimangaro	Kimangaro
Shokonyi	
Makayuni	
Kinyamvuo	Msae (name of one sub*mitaa*)
Kondeni	
Maringa	Maringa
Marera	

From 1976 the consolidated *mitaa* were subdivided into "villages." Thus, for example, two sub*mitaa* of Msae Kinyamvuo and Nganyeni became separate villages. The task of working out a proper historical map of all the *mitaa* and sub*mitaa* of Kilimanjaro at various dates has not yet been undertaken. In the normal process of consolidation the newly consolidated *mtaa* or chiefdom carried on the same name as one of the merged subunits. In the colonial period the name was taken from the one whose leading lineage retained the office of *mchili* or *mangi*. Consequently in a historical context great care must be exercised to identify the unit alluded to. A placename may be the same in 1960 as it was in 1860, but the geographical entity of 1860 may have been but a small subpart of the area encompassed by the 1960 chiefdom.

4 Number of taxpayers, July 1968:

Mamba	2304
Mashati	4311
Mwika	3701
K.M. Mengwe	3500
Siha	5517
Uru	6214
Arusha Chini	641

Usseri	7518
Masama	5892
Marangu	4073
Machame	9562
Kiwoso	6602
Old Moshi	5031
Mkuu	3510
Kahe	1141
Kirua Vunjo	3349
Kilema	3214

Source: (Mimeographed list, Halmashauri ya Wilaya ya Kilimanjaro, Moshi, 7 August 1968.)

5 S. F. Moore, "Politics, procedures and norms in changing Chagga law," *Africa,* 40 (October 1970): 321–44.

6 The jurisdiction of two classes of courts was defined by the ordinance limiting the value of the subject matter of the cases before them or the severity of the punishment they could mete out. Class A courts could hear civil cases in which the subject matter did not exceed 600 shillings; in criminal cases they could impose a sentence of up to six months' imprisonment with hard labor, a fine not exceeding 200 shillings, or corporal punishment of eight strokes. In Class B courts the limits of value of the subject matter were 200 shillings in civil cases; in criminal cases they could impose up to one month's imprisonment with hard labor, a fine of 50 shillings and or six strokes. The fees charged in civil cases, uniform throughout the territory, were 5 percent of the value of the subject matter with a minimum fee of one shilling and two shillings for cases in which the value could not be assessed. There were later revisions of the court classes, values, punishments, and so on. (Local Government Memoranda no. 2, Local Courts, 2d. edition, 1957:6)

The judicial reforms for all Tanganyika, which were the goal of the postwar colonial regime, were spelled out in a 1957 government memoranda no. 2, on local courts. The general state of the local courts in Tanganyika at independence can be judged from the many matters the memorandum identifies for repair. Among other objectives the memorandum declared a desire eventually to phase out corporal punishment, but in the meanwhile:

Care must be exercised to ensure that the instrument in use is not such as will inflict brutal treatment but, on the other hand, it must be such as will admit of reasonably severe punishment. No doubt many of the instruments at present in use are of an entirely suitable type, but it should be remembered that, for sanitary reasons and for the maintenance of their efficiency, instruments used for administering corporal punishment should be replaced by new ones at fairly frequent intervals – a point of important detail which is very often overlooked.

It must be remembered that Government is committed to a policy of restriction in the use of corporal punishment, with a view to its eventual abolition. . . . Every sentence must be executed in the presence of a medically qualified person and of the District Commissioner. (Local Government Memoranda, no. 2, Local Courts, 2d. ed., 1957:15)

The practice of flogging offenders, begun in German times, before there were prisons to house convicts, continued throughout the British colonial period and is one of the punishments allowed by the Penal Code of Tanzania (Chap. 16, sec.

28; see also Hailey 1938:443). I have heard several cases in which offenders who were minors were sentenced to be flogged. This practice is a small indication of the substantial continuities between the form and function of the local courts of colonial times and their successors in the early years after independence, but step by step since, more and more changes have been instituted.

7   In 1931 the chief's courts heard 1,099 cases of which 44 were appealed to the Central Court and 19 to the District Officers Appeal Court (Typescript, Annual Report, Northern Province, 1931, TNA 11681:9). In 1933 the provincial commissioner reported that in 1932 criminal prosecutions represented about 30 percent of the total cases brought before the native courts. Of these 41 percent were offenses against the person such as assault, 36 percent offenses against property, and 23 percent offenses relating to marriage, customary law, and orders issued under the Native Authority ordinances (Annual Report for the Year 1932, TNA 19415, 1932:39). Figures for the first nine months of 1933 showed that 1,221 cases had been heard (200 more than in all of 1932). The proportion of criminal cases remained the same (Annual Report for the year 1933, TNA 19415, 1933:53). By 1936, 1,816 cases were heard in the chief's courts; 116 were appealed, and only 16 appeals were taken to the court of the district officer (Typescript, Annual Report, Northern Province, 1937, TNA 19415:3). Skipping two decades we present the district commissioner's reports for 1958–59 (KDC File 1/16).

Number of cases heard, 1956-59

Seventeen Area Courts and Moshi Town Court

	Criminal cases heard				Civil cases heard			
	1956	*1957*	*1958*	*1959*	*1956*	*1957*	*1958*	*1959*
Hai	1265	1202	1452	1531	571	537	459	546
Vunjo	692	733	923	988	356	412	469	562
Rombo	418	428	625	920	308	243	295	522
Liwali (Moshi Town)	606	604	734	659	107	83	84	79

Chagga Appeal Court

	1956	*1957*	*1958*	*1959*
Appeals heard	387	287	379	595
Appeals allowed	139 (36.9%)	95 (33.1%)	171 (45%)	250 (42%)
Appeals pending	68	107	89	90

District commissioner's appeal court

Appeals heard	84	52	147	213
Appeals allowed	23 (27%)	22	53 (36%)	73 (34%)
Appeals pending	22	43	45	42

Note: In 1955 (District Commissioner's Report 1955, KDC File 1/16, p. 11) the number of taxpayers for the divisions were given as follows: Hai, 33,366; Vunjo, 16,675; and Rombo, 16,517. The taxpayer figures account for the much heavier proportion of cases in Hai.

8 In 1952 divisional magistrates were appointed. The appellate system was modified so that appeals from the area courts (chiefdom courts) went directly to the Chagga appeal court which consisted of the three divisional magistrates who took turns being chairman. Appeals from the Chagga appeal court went to the district commissioner's court.

9 Replying to a request from the paramount chief, the mangi of Murika wrote his proposal for the standardization of bridewealth (Letter dated 7 March 1953, Letter 85, KDC File 3/7 II, Codification of Chagga Law). The bridewealth arrangements proposed as the standard were:

Payments before the wedding
    mitungi of *pombe*   62
    goats (meat)   4
    milk – calabashes   15
    meat   1/2 cow   goats for *mahari* 3
Payments from the wedding day until bridewealth payments completed, all to go to the father of the bride
    cow to be slaughtered (all parts for the bride's father)
    4 goats for father of girl
    1 cow, 1 goat as final bridewealth payment
Distribution to relatives other than the father to be standardized
    (a) Bride's mother
         8 *mitungi* of *pombe* 15 *shisangu* (bundles of meat) 15 milk (calabashes) 1/2 cow (meat), 1 goat (meat), 1 live goat
    (b) Bride's mother's brother
         5 *mitungi* of *pombe* (or if not paid, one goat)
    (c) Brother of bride
         5 *mitungi* of *pombe* (or if not paid, one goat) [There is some lack of clarity about a goat to be sent by the husband to the wife's brother, but which the brother should slaughter and share with him.]
    (d) Mother of bride's father
         1 goat
    (e) Bride's father's brother
         1 goat
See also case reports concerning bridewealth.

10 For the law relating to them see Sheria ya Mahakama za Mahakimu 1963 (Magistrates Courts Act, 1963) and Kanuni za Mahakama, Sheria ya of Mahakama, no. 55, ya 1963.

11 Act no. 67, 1964; also Memorandum from the District Court, Kilimanjaro to the Executive Officer of the Kilimanjaro District Council, 20 January 1965, KDC File 3/10/II. The position of Local Courts Officer was soon abolished, and magistrates were chosen out of a list of candidates recommended by a regional board. A judicial special committee then chose the magistrates subject to approval by the minister of justice (Barnett 1965:71).

12 The assessors were to be chosen from lists locally generated of middle-aged or elderly men, and they were to sit for a minimum of a month and were paid three shillings per day. A letter from the KDC 8 November 1967 changed the policy and prescribed that assessors be changed two or three times a week (KDC File 3/10/II). The letter alludes to some difficulty in getting assessors to serve. A memorandum of 13 February 1965 from the KDC to the Divisional Executive Officers on the choice of assessor specified that they must be chosen by the village development committees (KDC file 3/10/II). The memorandum also includes a list of employed persons ineligible to serve ranging from government personnel to pastors, from members of the police to persons of unsound mind. The extensive list of exclusions virtually prescribed that the assessors be local farmers.

13 Customary Leaseholds (Enfranchisement) Act (no. 47/68). This policy was extended to Moshi District in 1969. Government Notice 263/1969 cited in James and Fimbo 1973:374.

14 In the Kilimanjaro District in the first ten years after independence, in theory, at least, an application for sale of a *kihamba* had to be made to the village executive officer (VEO) in the locality of the land. Then the VEO had to publicize the sale in the ward and transmit the application to the District Council through the district executive officer (James and Fimbo 1973:452–3). James and Fimbo confirm that the government acknowledged and approved much buying and selling of land (450).

15 Notice from Mahakama za Wilaya, Moshi, 13 October 1971, Ref. no. C 1/7/26 to all Primary Court Magistrates of the Kilimanjaro District.

16 Both the basis of land tenure and the outcome of land dispute continued to rest heavily on a "customary law" basis. Indeed, a formal procedure was established by means of which persons wishing to remove land from the customary system could apply to the Regional Land Office through the executive officer of the District Council to ask that the land rights held be converted into a statutory right of occupancy. See James and Fimbo 1973:496 for a discussion of this procedure and its use in the Kilimanjaro District. They seem to think it was commonly used. That is not my impression. Most land where I have worked has not been removed from the customary system.

CHAPTER 7. THE CASE REPORTS

1 The records of these courts were not all in one place. Some were in dog-eared heaps on shelves in the offices of the court clerks in each of the rural courthouses of Kilimanjaro. It seemed a matter of chance which files happened to remain on the mountain and which did not. Another collection was shelved in the faculty library of the Law School at the University of Dar es Salaam, but at the time they were inspected, they were not arranged in any particular order; indeed a good many had fallen onto the floor. The period studied in the chief's court/primary court records is 1927–79. A great many of these and other court records have now found their way into the Tanzanian National Archives where they really belong.

2 It was neither practical to copy them all *in extenso,* nor did it seem useful. Microfilming was impossible at the time and place these were examined. Few of the records were of a kind that invited fine-grained textual analysis. An analysis of the whole corpus of all the case records from all the ex-chiefdoms is a project to be taken up, one hopes, by faculty and students at the Law School of the University of Dar es Salaam.

3 See Nkuu v. Thobias Mesaki (1958) Digest 122 as cited in James and Fimbo (1973) to the effect that a Lutheran mission could not hold land under Chagga customary law.

4 See also (1962) Local Courts Civil Appeal (LCCA) 6/1962, an appellate case involving a Chagga *kihamba* cited in James and Fimbo 1973:341 in which long possession and use are deemed a sound basis for the presumption that the occupier had permanent rights, thus putting a burden on any competing claimant to prove a clear and unequivocal claim. A shadowy claim could not be allowed.

5 Allusion was made earlier to the conditions under which individual plots could be alienated in precolonial times. It is not the alienation itself that is not customary, but the cash and the implications that surround it.

6 Cases having to do with accusations of witchcraft were heard, and spoken about throughout the period of fieldwork. These took place inside and outside the courts. One was heard in the Marangu Primary Court in 1979.

CHAPTER 8. THE LOCALIZED PATRILINE IN THE 1960s AND 1970s

1 In important matters that draw agnates from more than one subsegment, the group that holds a palaver is most often a rather ad hoc assemblage of all of the men of the localized lineage cluster who happen to be around and are available and interested. They act for the lineage as a whole, empowered to do so by the underlying assumption that at an open meeting of the "lineage at large" anyone who wanted to have a say would have attended. Most of these meetings are fairly small. But they can be sizable. During the fieldwork visits two meetings of a local section of an ex-chiefly lineage which had lost it chiefdom in the 1920s, drew crowds of affines and neighbors as well. At one, which had to do with the allocation of a piece of land, there were at least forty-five agnates present, and more may have been in the crowd of spectators. At the other, the *matanga* of two young men who had been killed by the police in another region where they worked, at least 200 persons were present and a substantial number of these must have been from the local agnatic cluster.

2 In size the localized lineage is like the unit that Gulliver called the "inner lineage" for the Arusha (1973). But the Arusha inner lineages were geographically dispersed since it was commonplace for sons to pioneer new land wherever they could find it. The Chagga by contrast, whenever feasible, live in aggregations of localized subsegments on the same lands once occupied by their grandfathers.

3 If the local lineage is one of the extremely large ones, the beer-drinking group may be merely a large section of the whole. Gutmann does not mention the two levels of meat-eating group, but he describes a similar subsegmentation, illustrating it by saying that if each of two brothers had five or six sons, they might separate into two slaughtering units, and thereafter get together only for lineage beer for births and weddings (Gutmann 1926:46; HRAF:37).

4 One of my young prosperous friends in the M—— lineage told me that he slaughters a cow no more than once in two or three years, but that every year he slaughters at least three goats. This represents a major drop from Gutmann's estimates of slaughtering rates early in the century when wealthy men slaughtered cattle five times a year and only poor men once every two or three years (1926:390; HRAF:350). Then a poor man was defined as one who had five head of cattle or fewer (1926:382; HRAF:343). At that time if, in a lineage of twenty adult men, each slaughtered three head of cattle a year on average, and goats twice a year, someone slaughtered every three or four days, and everyone got a bit of meat. When old Siara of Kilema sadly told me that *zamani*, long ago, there were never three days that passed without someone slaughtering, he was probably factually correct.

5   "Good reasons" have been the need to pay school fees or to pay for care for the sick. Sometimes there are other rationales. If an ox kicks a person and draws blood, the ox must die. Thus in 1973 when Uruka, senior man of the M——— lineage, sold his ox to the butcher for cash instead of saving it to share with his agnates during the holidays, he explained that it had kicked him and the wound had bled so it had to be killed immediately. (Who knows whether it really had.) He promised to buy a goat or two with the proceeds so that, when the time came for feasting and his eldest son Filipo was on leave, he would have something. But he clearly used some of the cash for other purposes. The cash economy is there, and Chagga avail themselves of it in innumerable ways. But the feeling is still strong that some areas of life should be reserved from it, and segregated from its calculations. It seems to be increasingly difficult to do so.

6   One was fined 100 shillings (or three months in prison), three others were fined 50 shillings each (or two months in prison). The compensation was a cow and two goats and 29 shillings and 15 cents for the burned clothes. The six other defendants were acquitted and warned that they would be severely punished if they repeated the offense.

7   James and Fimbo acknowledged this continuity in 1973:428 when they asserted that clan control had faded out in many areas but remained strong in Machame, Vunjo, and Mkuu "for example."

8   I cannot estimate what proportion of the total population of Kilimanjaro is in localized clusters (six households or more) and what proportion is in "isolates." I have collected precise data only for a few areas. See Figures 5.1, 5.2, 5.3 (see discussion of patriline sizes in Mwika in the section "Chagga Lineages in General" in Chapter 8).

9   The conversion of *shamba* land into *kihamba* land gave rise to a good deal of litigation over the issue which lands were which. See Chagga cases reprinted in James and Fimbo 1973:78–83: Appeal to Governor, no. 78 (1944); Appeal no. 20/1950, 30 March 1951; Appeal no. 1/1955 (1955); (1946) Appeal to the Governor no. 120 (4/1946); (1964) Local Courts Civil Appeal (LCCA) 27/1963.

10   There seem to be some special exceptions in Usseri. There, Mrs. Stahl reports, whole parishes are occupied by a single clan, each containing from 60 to 300 families, and all parishes acknowledge descent from the Tarimo clan (1964:343). This form of organization is not characteristic of much of Kilimanjaro in this century, and was not in Gutmann's time.

11   As mentioned in Chapter 5, in the late 1950s, when its fortunes were fading, the political party called the Kilimanjaro Chagga Citizen's Union embarked on an

ill-advised attempt to organize and revitalize what it, too, presumed was an earlier form of the coherent clan. It tried to establish authenticated genealogies, the sacred place of each clan, to appoint clan heads, and the like. (Two typed letters from N. P. Njau, addressed to various clans were found in the political correspondence folder in the courthouse at Keni-Mriti-Mengwe: 71 [13 January 1958] and 72 [25 January 1958].) Although some meetings were held, the effort soon fizzled out, a fact that confirms the lack of connection to build on at that time. Why Njau and other advisers of Thomas Marealle, the then paramount chief, did not realize this situation in advance is not clear. They may have mistakenly assumed that the vitality of the localized lineage branches implied some latent larger-scale organization that could easily be stimulated. This traditionalist political gesture was made at a time when Thomas Marealle was increasingly under attack by TANU and may have involved more of an element of desperation than reasoned calculation.

12 See Chapter 1 for clan sizes in Gutmann's time. The list of clan names reported by T. F. Figgis in 1957–58 (the period of clan "revival") comes to approximately the same number.

List of clans and their locations

Clan	Chiefdom[a]	Clan	Chiefdom[a]
Assenga	4, 7, 9, 14, 15, 16	Kavau	17
Assey	7, 8	Kavishe	see Kalshe
Bureta	5, 14, 15	Kawa	4, 9
Chaki	7	Keembe	5
Chami	3, 4	Kenda	16
Chawo	7, 8	Kenyi	9
Choo	3	Kerti	17
Chuwa	4	Kesi	7, 8, 9
Fota	1	Kiara	5, 7, 10
Hamaro	17	Kibosi	17
Hondo	17	Kichili	9
Ibaleni	17	Kifumu	1
Inchini	17	Kilalo	8
Iringo	6	Kilana	1
Isowe	1, 9	Kilawe	5, 6
Kaale	5, 15	Kilenga	15
Kaialu	6	Kileo	2, 3, 4, 5, 7
Kalanga	4	Kilimu	1
Kalshe or		Kimambo	6
Kavishe	15, 14, 17	Kimaro	2, 3, 4, 5, 6, 7, 9,
Kamde	6		14, 15, 16, 17
Kamosho	9, 17	Kimbori	4
Kanje	17	Kimei	9
Kanza	6	Kimura	1
Kaole or Kaale		Kingola	17
Karia	5, 7	Kinini	17
Kasha	3	Kinjaka	17
Kasharo	16 (see also Masharo)	Kinyara	9
Kashora	16	Kioro	4
Kasinga	17	Kirere	1
Kauki	14, 17	Kireti	9

Clan	Chiefdom[a]	Clan	Chiefdom[a]
Kirua	16	Makishe	8, 9
Kisabi	1	Makonyi	6
Kisaka	7	Makunda	7, 9, 13, 17
Kisanga	3, 5, 6, 16	Makundi	(see Kundi)
Kisarika	16	Makuri	9
Kisasi		Makwai	4, (see Kwai)
Kisela	15, 14	Makyao	1, 8
Kishe	8, 9	Malami	9
Kishimbo	6	Malamsha	9, 14, 15
Kisima	4	Male	8, 9
Kisoka		Maleko	2, 3, 9
Kitale	9	Malewo	4, 9
Kitefure	17, 15	Malisa	8, 6
Kiwelu	6, 9	Malyawere	9
Kiwera	1	Mambali	9
Kiwia	4, 5, 6	Mamcharo	9
Kiwisha	9 (Kavishe)	Mamiro	9
Kiwori	9	Mamjo	7
Kombe	3, 9	Mamri	6, 9
Komu	4	Mamsenga	8
Koteva	16	Mamuya	9
Koyu	8	Manba	9
Kulaya	4	Mandana	7
Kundi	7	Mangesho	16
Kwai (Kwayu)	5, 4, 9, 3	Mangowi	9
Kweka	2, 9	Mangya	4, 5
Kyaasio	9	Manjo	17
Kyaawa		Manko	1
Kyambo	4, 5, 6	Manyanga	9
Kyooki	17	Maole	9
Lekule	9	Marandu	9, 14, 15, 16, 17
Lema	2, 3	Marawite	7
Leto	7	Maresa	6
Limi	7	Mareshi	7
Limo	5, 6, 7, 8, 9, 16	Maria	9
Lokosi	9	Marika	6
Lola	1	Marima	6, 7
Lomali	16	Mariwa	7, 8, 9
Luave	17	Maro	(see Kimaro)
Lyakurua	17, 14	Marucho	6
Lyamashawi	9	Mashayo	(see Shayo)
Lyamuya	5, 7, 9	Masakimaski	3, 7
Lyaruu	8, 9	Masamu	9, 6
Lyatuu	6	Masanjuo	9, 14
Maasare	1	Masao	(see Maswe)
Macha	5, 6, 7, 9	Masaro	1, 9
Machua (Mashua)	9, 15	Masaua	15
Maeda	6	Masaule	9
Maembe	7	Masawe	2, 3, 4, 5, 6, 9, 14, 15, 16, 17
Mafue	3		
Maharo	17, 15	Masenge	1, 5, 15
Mahoo	7, 9	Mashina	6, 9
Makata	15	Masoi	9
Make	9	Maswai	14

Clan	Chiefdom[a]	Clan	Chiefdom[a]
Mashayo	(See Ngobi)	Mnene	5, 9
Matari	9, 16	Mnganya	15
Matee	5, 6, 7, 8, 9	Mnyia	9
Mateemba	5, 9	Moine (Maena)	8
Matem	4, 7, 8, 9	Mokila	6, 17
Materu	5, 6, 16	Mola	6
Matilya	5, 6, 9	Monangu	17
Matingo	4	Mongi	5, 6, 9
Matoi	(See Kundi)	Moose (Mwaasi)	4, 6
Mauki	4, 5, 6 (see Kauki)	Morio	9
Mbando	7, 8	Mosha	See Mwasha
Mbasa	2, 3, 4	Mote	9
Mbasi	13	Mpuru	13
Mbishi	4, 8	Mramba	17
Mbomba	5, 7, 8	Mrecha	6
Mbonge	7	Mreme (Mremi)	6, 9, 14
Mbonyo	4	Mrina	4, 9, 15, 17, 14
Mboro	1, 14, 8, 6, 2, 17,	Mrinde	7
	9, 7, 3, 4	Mrongoma	17
Mbowe	3	Mroso	9, 14
Mboye	7, 9	Msaki	3, 5, 6, 7, 9
Mbughu	7	Msangi	7
Mbushi	17	Msara	7
Mbuya (or Mboya)	4, 5, 6, 7, 8, 9	Msechu	9
Mborio	17	Msei (Assey)	15, 17
Mchaki	9	Msele	4, 9
Mchau	5, 6, 9	Msendo	7
Mchome	7	Mshanga	5, 9, 14
Mchovu	7	Msilemwa	17
Mchowe	7	Msoma	4, 5, 7
Mdakama	13	Msumanyi	13
Meela	9	Mtani	14
Meena	1, 5, 7	Mtefu	17
Mende	4, 5, 6, 9	Mtei	15, 17
Mfoi	4	Mtena (Mtina)	7
Mfuru	3, 4, 7, 9	Mtenga (Mtengo)	14, 15, 16
Mikirie	7	Mtesha	6, 11
Minde	4, 5, 6, 7	Mtesu	17
Minja	5, 6, 7, 8, 9	Mtui	9, 17
Mkadi	15	Muheny	1
Mkenda	9, 15, 16	Mumburi	4, 5
Mkera	16	Munishi	1, 3, 4, 5, 9
Mkindi	7	Munuo	2, 3
Mkonyi	6, 8, 9	Murangu	1
Mkumbi	5	Murio	9
Mlasawe	9	Muro	2, 3
Mlay	5, 6, 7, 9, 14, 17	Mwaase	3
Mlinga	6, 7, 15	Mwanga	2, 3, 6, 5
Mloviri	13	Mwanjo (See Manjo)	17
Mmanyi	6, 13	Mwarie (Mwaria)	1, 4
Mmario	13	Mvungi	7
Mmasi	(See Chuwa)	Mwowo	6, 8
Mmbo	5, 6, 7	Nambuo	7, 17
Mmru	13	Namfu	1

Clan	Chiefdom[a]	Clan	Chiefdom[a]
Nanyaro	I	Sangara	I
Nashuu	I	Saria	I, 6
Natai	2	Sarita	17
Natema	I	Saro	3
Ndanshau	3	Sauro	16
Ndashuwa	3	Sawe	3
Ndasiwa	3	Seka	9
Ndau	7	Sembule	17, 16
Ndosa	2, 3	Senya	4, 5
Ngalo	6, 8	Sereha	17
Ngeleshi	16, 17	Shalo	15
Ngila	3	Shau	14, 15
Ngoi	9, 16	Shayo	5, 7, 8, 9, 17
Ngoja	17	Shio	5, 4
Ngola	4, 9	Shirima	5, 9, 14, 15, 16, 17
Ngonda	17	Shoo	See Choo
Ngoti	3, 5 (see Kilawe)	Shori	7
Ngowi	2, 3, 6, 7, 15, 17	Showe	9
Ngowo	4, 6, 7, 15	Shuma	3
Ngulia	17	Siao	2
Nguma	4, 7, 8, 17	Silaa	2, 16
Ngunda	I	Silayo	5, 14, 17
Njau	2, 5, 6, 15, 16	Sohankite	3
Njuu	6	Soka	3, 4
Nkya	1, 2, 3	Somi	3, 9, 2
Nyange	7, 8, 9, 17	Sore	15
Nyaki	6, 7	Swai	3, 2, 4, 14, 15, 16, 17
Nyambo	7	Tairo	14, 15
Nzawo	9	Tarimo	3, 4, 5, 6, 9, 15,
Ochiwa	8		16, 17, 14
Oiso	15, 16, 17	Teemba	5, 9, 10, 14, 15, 16, 17
Okama	4, 6	Temba	4, 7, 9, 17, 14
Okotu	3	Teete	5
Olomi	2, 3, 4, 5	Temu (Mtemu)	4, 7, 8, 9
Omari	1, 5	Tenga	6, 8
Orio	4, 5, 7, 9, 11, 14, 15	Tesha (Tashia)	1, 5, 7, 9, 16, 17, 14
Orassa (Urassa)	2, 3, 15, 16, 17	Teti	5, 7, 8, 9
Oshoa	17	Tilya	5, 6, 7, 15, 17
Ramale	17	Tira	9
Reye	8	Towo	9
Rimoi	8, 6	Tuni	I
Ringo	6	Uiso (see Oiso)	
Riwa	5, 8	Ukoka	7
Ruati	17	Ulotu	3, 5, 4, 6, 9
Saiwo	I	Umbela	7
Sakaya	3	Umburi	3
Sala	4	Uroki	3
Salema	2, 3	Uronu	3
Samba	9, 15	Usini	3, 2
Sambaya	16, 17	Usoki	5
Samki	7	Utou	14
Sandi	8, 9	Uwowa (Owoiwa)	5, 8
Sangana	16, 17	Yawi	4, 5

Source: Chagga Land Tenure Report, 1957-58 by T. B. Figgis, borrowed from Philip Gulliver. Moore's fieldwork data suggest that there are omissions in Figgis's list.

Please note that Figgis makes cross-references to items that are not in the list. This is his list, not a corrected list.

ᵃCode numbers indicate chiefdoms: (1) Siha (Kibongoto), (2) Masama, (3) Machame, (4) Kibosho, (5) Uru, (6) Old Moshi, (7) Kirua Vunjo, (8) Kilema, (9) Marangu, (10) Mamba, (11) Mwika, (12) Arusha Chini, (13) Kahe, (14) Keni-Mriti-Mengwe, (15) Mkuu, (16) Mashati, (17) Usseri.

13 The maps made in this study are not accurate measures of plot size, but were made freehand to show social contiguity rather than size of landholding.

14 For example, one subpart of what is now Mwika, the Marikis, whose numbers are now great (the largest lineage indicated on Figure 5.1, page 113.) moved into the Nganyeni area about that time. The Marikis were originally chiefs of the up-mountain *mtaa* of Kinyamvuo. They subsequently became chiefs of a consolidated Kinyamvuo-Nganyeni chiefdom under Marealle I during the early part of his reign (Stahl 1964:291). The genealogies of many descendants of the first chief of the consolidated unit who live in Nganyeni confirm this history, tracing back to him four generations from the present.

That some Marikis settled in Msae after 1892 suggests that at least until then the area had open unoccupied space. Some of the neighbors of the Marikis say that *they* were there first, and some even assert that the Marikis appropriated lands they had considered theirs. Be that as it may, the other lineages cannot have been there long. One substantial neighboring lineage that claims prior residence in the area traces itself back six generations to the two founders of the Msae patriline, and therefore would have arrived in the 1860s. Some Marikis must already have been there, as Marealle I's own stepfather was Makiponya Mariki, and Marealle himself grew up in the Mariki household in Msae-Nganyeni (see Stahl's summary version of Mtui's material on the Marealle-Lyimo genealogy in Stahl 1964:317–19). Around the same time that the Marikis moved in, Marealle I is said to have placed some of his Lyimo kinsmen nearby in Kondeni as chiefs. There must have been ample space in which to settle.

15 In the 1956–61 period there were 133 *mitaa* which had been consolidated to that number in the government reorganization of 1946 (Stahl 1964:13; see also her list of these in her Appendix II). These were further consolidated after independence. Then, in relation to the 1976 "villagization" some (all?) were redivided, the new cooperative villages being the old sub*mitaa*.

16 The names of the individuals have been changed, but otherwise the report is of matters as they were observed by or described to me.

17 Thus in Kilema, the women's organization has managed to buy a bus, and is running passengers from Kilema to Moshi and back every day.

18 Bridewealth is often paid throughout the life of the "bride." Bridewealth is usually not paid in full and the final payment is sometimes made when the "bride" dies.

19 In 1979 a retired Marangu man who had once had a salaried job used his retirement (and pension) to organize a thriving business selling eggs and milk and other produce. His wife was a teacher, and he wanted her to leave her job and supervise the household. There were eleven children to worry about, and casual laborers who did some of the farm work. I do not know precisely what he did to make his wife's life unbearable, since I had the story from him. But whatever it was, she took refuge with her brother for many weeks, and said she would not return until she was compensated for his mistreatment, and her brother for the cost of her care, and until he agreed to allow her to continue as a teacher. The matter was eventually settled and she returned home.

20 See Dausen F. Sawe v. Oforo Semu Swai (1967) Civil Appeal 4 (1967); (1967) High Court Digest 429, reprinted in James and Fimbo 1973:201–2, which declares that even under the postcolonial modifications of Chagga law a woman could not inherit full alienable rights in land, but only the usufruct, unless there was no living male of the clan.

21 In the British colonial period Siara of Kilema tried to give land to a son-in-law, and his kinsmen withheld their consent. He took the matter to the chief's court and the chief upheld the kinsmen. In the early 1950s he sold the land to a nonkinsman and helped his son-in-law to buy a plot with the proceeds. He calculated that, given British colonial policies regarding purchases and sales, the courts would not be willing to support the interests of his agnates if there was a sale as opposed to a gift. The sale went unchallenged. But it is not surprising that Siara does not find himself the recipient of meat from his kinsmen. For Siara's life see S. F. Moore, "Old Age in a Life Term Social Area," in *Life's Career: Aging,* ed. B. Myerhoff and A. Simic (Los Angeles: Sage Publications, 1978).

CHAPTER 9. THE CHRONICLE OF THE M—— LINEAGE

1 Melishoni bin Maimbi v. Mzee bin Kombo (1949), Appeal to Governor no. 117 (no. 1 of 1946). There is no time limit to redemption of pledged land provided improvements are compensated for. Cited by James and Fimbo 1973:409.

An interesting strategy that derives from this rule has come in with the cash economy. A person who has the inherited right to redeem a piece of loaned land and who does not have the money may secretly (because lineage land should not be freely sold) try to locate a monied buyer. The person with the right to redeem sets the buyer a price that is higher than the sum he needs to redeem the property. When the buyer gives him the cash, he redeems the property, and later passes it on to the buyer having made a profit in the meanwhile. This was attempted in the M——lineage by Uruka's middle son, Mlatie. In the 1950s Uruka was ill and thought he was going to die and wanted to assign all his unallocated properties. Having given Mlatie, his middle son, very little land, the father wanted at least to appear more evenhanded. Thus he gave Mlatie the redemption rights in this parcel of land, a segment that his own father, Wikiwawoko, had loaned under an agreement that the borrower pay *masiro*. Uruka then recovered from his illness. When Uruka later heard that his son Mlatie had secretly sought a buyer for the land, he reassembled his sons and withdrew his gift to Mlatie saying that from then on the land would be held as the property of Mlatie's son, Uruka's grandson. This effectively prevented Mlatie from selling it and kept the loaned land vested in a lineage member for another generation. Sometime later Uruka thought better of it and himself sold part of that land.

The interesting part of this from a legal point of view is the ongoing ability of the father-donor to retract gifts of land to his sons and grandsons. A father's gifts of land are in some sense conditional.

2 John, who asserts that he was the proper grandson because he was the post-mortem child of Sirita, Uruka's elder brother, was too young at the time to make his claim (see the section "A Question of Paternity" in this chapter).

3 This included looking after Filipo's wife and children. When a child was ill, John took the child to the dispensary. A sick child is supposed to be the concern of the father, not the mother, since the child belongs to the father's patrilineage and should be under the protection of his ancestors. There is always the chance that any child has been made ill by some malign influence emanating from the mother or her kin. In the past farmer fathers were almost always the ones who took their children to the dispensary. Now, because of labor migration and a situation in which men are often absent for a variety of other reasons this practice is no longer as prevalent as it once was. However, a child's illness remains a common enough excuse for men who do not want to appear for work or for corvée labor or for a party meeting.

4 Present at the time were Filipo's father Uruka (1), Filipo (8) and those three of his sons who would be most directly affected, Joseph (youngest son of first wife; her eldest was away at boarding school or he would have been there as well), Simon (son of third wife) and Balthasar (firstborn son of fifth wife). Filipo's brothers also were there, namely, Mlatie (13), Mamkinga (19) and John (24) as well as a son of Mlatie, and also old crochety Wilibald (3) and Richard (26) from the other most closely related minimal lineage. Filipo's third and fifth wives were there (his first wife has remarried and lives elsewhere), also the ten-house cell leader, a senior neighbor, and one of the unrelated laborers who worked on the land of Filipo, who happened to be present.

5 Note, for example, that in the instances shown in the case histories on Kiwosi and Kisoka and on Mandasha and Ndesario Filipo approached his agnates secretly, hoping that they would sell to him.

6 Land of a judgment debtor could be attached and sold under an order of the court. Civil Procedure Code 49/1966, Part II, and Magistrates Courts Act, chap. 537, 4th schedule 3(2).

7 The Report of the Royal Commission on Land and Population in East Africa in 1955 recommended that the individualization of land ownership replace customary law. The argument was that it would improve the economy by permitting progressive farmers to buy up the land of the less progressive. (See Fimbo 1974.) But such ideas were probably embedded in the policies of the provincial commissioners in much earlier times.

8 See James and Fimbo 1973:244 in which they also allude to the obligation of any Chagga who wants to sell a plot of inherited land to offer it first to his agnates. Land prices varied substantially. P. H. Johnson reports that in 1946 it

was still possible to obtain an uncultivated *kihamba* for a cow and a goat, but that a cultivated one in Kilema with a good stand of coffee and bananas three acres in size with a good house might go for 1,400 shillings and the same *kihamba* without a house in Kirua Vunjo might vary from 400 to 1,000 shillings (1946:4). Prices have now risen to many times what they were in 1946.

9 Those present at this discussion included the resident members of Kiwosi's minor lineage segment, that is, three of his sons (Kisoka was away), and his eldest junior brother Uforosia. Petro also assembled a number of other kinsmen including Elifatio and John. He tried to get Richard to come, but Richard was also away. Petro obviously was trying to get representatives from as many of the five local minor lineage segments as he could. Members from three came. The most senior man present who was not a litigant (Uforosia) was also a senior member of the lineage minor segment whose affairs were at issue and he "pronounced judgment."

10 See (1962) LCCA 44/1962 Chagga case cited by James and Fimbo 1973:229 indicating that during late colonial times heirs could be disinherited by means of a written will. The *Local Customary Law (Declaration)* (No. 4) Order GN 435 of 1963: 3d. schedule Rules on Wills also granted the power of testation, but in general Chagga do not use written wills. This widow was doing something not only unusual, but irregular since she was not the "owner" in Chagga law, but only had a life interest. However, it is one of many instances in which new legal rights, often incompletely understood, are used when it is advantageous to do so.

11 Other business attended to at the *matanga* included:

(a) A brother of Mandasha's widow said that Mandasha had agreed to sell him a *shamba* in the lower areas, and that 500 shillings had already been paid toward the purchase price. He wanted to make this a matter of record at the *matanga* so that when the full price would be paid the land would be his. The widow testified that there had been such an arrangement with her brother. The matter was settled as he requested.

(b) Mandasha's mother's brother (*mjomba*) claimed that one beast was still owing of the bridewealth of Mandasha's mother, and that was agreed to, and Elifatio was directed to pay it.

(c) Elifatio said he had borrowed 30 shillings from Mandasha, hence owed it to the estate.

(d) The old blind mother of Mandasha and Ndesario said that when her husband Tenguo had gone to Mombasa there had been three head of cattle in the house and that Ndesario had sold them and had not divided the money with Mandasha. The agnates all agreed the Ndesario's deed was a terrible thing, that they would demand the money from Ndesario, would accuse him in court if he did not pay it. (In fact nothing came of this threat.)

(e) The mother also went on to say that Mandasha had ordered his sisters never to enter the *kihamba* of Ndesario again, and all those present agreed that they should never again set foot in Ndesario's *kihamba*.

(f) The husband of Mandasha's sister stood up and told of the financial troubles in the house of Mandasha. He had left seven daughters and one very young son. Some of these children had been baptized that very year, an expensive business. Mandasha's widow said that she wanted one of the children to go to live with her grown-up daughter in Arusha, and that her son-in-law should support the child. This request was arranged, though the son-in-law said he could not pay for advanced schooling.

(g) Then the wife of mentally ill Nathanieli (15) said that as Mandasha had been guardian of her family, he owed Nathanieli's family money, because he had taken and sold the coffee from Nathanieli's *kihamba* for years. She also claimed that he had taken a sheep and a goat from Nathanieli's house as well as one wheelbarrow, one wooden barrel, one hoe, and a coffeepulper. The senior agnates inquired into these matters. Nathanieli's wife, of course, had no record of the coffee sold. They asked her who had paid the school fees of her child, and who had sprayed the coffee in her *kihamba* with insecticide, and the like. She had to admit that all these matters were attended to over the years by Mandasha, and that in fact her son was in secondary school. The elders agreed that Mandasha had behaved properly, and that he had used the coffee money for the correct purposes, including using some of it to pay hired hands to pick the coffee in Nathanieli's *kihamba*, and that no coffee money was owed the widow. As for the sheep and goat, they agreed that in the time that these had been in the house of Mandasha they had given birth to other sheep and goats and she was owed some beasts. As for the wheelbarrow and other things, those were to be returned to the wife of mentally ill Nathanieli. By the time of this *matanga* Nathanieli had been taken away to a mental hospital. But during his time in the neighborhood he was frequently taken to court on criminal charges of assault. He was brought into court twice in 1968, and on both occasions he was found guilty and fined.

(h) Finally those present took up a collection for the benefit of the dead man's family. They collected 160 shillings and gave the money to the widow. The *matanga* then concluded as it had opened, with a prayer.

12   A more detailed description of this case appears in S. F. Moore, "Individual Interests and Organizational Structures: Dispute Settlements as Events of Articulation" in *Social Anthropology and Law*, ed. Ian Hamnett, Association of Social Anthropologists Monograph no. 14 (New York: Academic Press, 1977), pp. 159–88.

13   See section on procedures in this book; also Local Government Memorandum no. 2, Local Courts Government Printer 1957, 2d. edition; SS134 of the Criminal Procedure Code, Chapter 20 of the Laws (Dar es Salaam: Government Printer, 1961); and Primary Court Manual (Ministry of Justice Government Printer, 1964) Part IV Criminal Proceedings SS21, (2) a and b; also Part III Civil Proceedings.

14   When I asked why the husband joined the accusers of his wife, why he believed the things that were being said about her, I was told, "Perhaps he *knew* she was a *mchawi* (witch)." The husband of Elifatio's accused sister had, in fact, been away for a long while, and had just returned home at the time of the *matanga*. Some months earlier he had fallen out of a tree, and this accident has left him terribly injured, and he had been hospitalized during the whole period of the fatal illness of his brother's wife. His brother had helped him while he was in the hospital, by paying his children's school fees, so he was deeply indebted to him. When I heard about Elifatio's sister's husband falling out of the tree, I asked

whether this might have been caused by his wife's witchcraft, and my informant responded at once, "No. *That* was an accident." But he did tell me that the man stopped eating food prepared by his wife after he returned, once he heard people saying she had killed her sister-in-law.

15 Persons from the wife's side (*i.e.*, the M—— lineage and affines) attending the witchcraft palaver were: Elifatio and wife, Lewange and wife, Motesha and wife, Mandasha and wife, Ndesario and wife, Kiwosi, Lyatonga, Uforsia, Wilibald and one of his wives. Persons from the husband's side were husband of accused woman, his brother, the *mkara*, the mediator of the marriage between Elifatio's sister and her husband.

16 In this book I use witchcraft and sorcery loosely and interchangeably because the tidy anthropological distinctions sometimes drawn between them do not fit present Chagga ideas with any neatness. The literature draws the distinction that a witch's malevolent capacities are an inherent, almost physiological characteristic of the witch, whereas sorcerers are simply skilled professionals who use their technical knowledge of rituals, spells, and the special properties of things to achieve their ends. In Chagga discussions of these matters, they say that the functions of persons we conceive of as witches, sorcerers, exorcisers, and healers are sometimes performed by the same person. It is clear that there are hereditary lines of Chagga witches, but it is uncertain whether or not the witchcraft knowledge is a technique taught from one generation to another in a witch family or whether it is somehow built in, or both. Chagga witches may be male or female. There are mundane bewitching techniques that are said to be in wide use, and there is reason to believe they are. Those who want to make sure that their manipulations reach their target may hire a sorcerer or witch to instruct them or sell them objects that will convey misfortune or ward it off. An important distinction for the Chagga is the difference between cursing and witchcraft. Cursing is something done in public; witchcraft is performed in secret. But the difference between witchcraft and sorcery made by anthropologists is not made by the Chagga in the same way, at least not when they are speaking Swahili. Perhaps in Kichagga there is a neater classification, but I doubt it, particularly now that the idea of the Christian devil is also involved. See also the first section of Chapter 10.

17 Such calls are made to remembered dead, grandfathers and great-grandfathers, not to remote ancestors. (The same procedure was followed in "A Case of Sterility Leads to Accusations of Sorcery.")

18 Late in 1979 a quarrel emerged that is probably related to the bad feelings between Wilibald, and Mamkinga and Filipo. John, half-brother of Mamkinga and Filipo, had a *kihamba* immediately adjacent to the one Wilibald shared with his adult son David, the very one in which the mysterious attack by spirits took place. Ordinarily John got along well with David's family. David's wife used John's watertap to wash her coffee. Her child walked through John's *kihamba* when he took a shortcut. Formally speaking, John was also on good terms with Wilibald. But John was more than a little annoyed about paying the cost of cutting up a tree that had been on their common boundary and had fallen on John's side. John argued that the tree really belonged to Wilibald, and *he* should have had it cut down, let alone cut up once it had fallen. (John said he had given Wilibald some money a year earlier to hire someone to cut it down, but that Wilibald had kept the money and done nothing.)

After the tree fell on John's side (damaging one or two coffee trees) Wilibald said the firewood from it belonged to him. John said he would not give him a single piece of the firewood. A few days later John had half of the tree cut up by a hired hand and the logs neatly stowed in the rafters of his wife's kitchen hut. John then told Wilibald he could have the rest of the huge log if he cut it up. But John also took the precaution of sending Wilibald two calabashes of beer to try to assuage his inevitable anger.

CHAPTER 10. THE LOCAL LEVEL AND THE LARGER SETTING

1 Since the episodes come in connected chains, one may count more or fewer depending on the criteria used.

2 During fieldwork, I obtained from several local officials lists of those in each of several villages who had volunteered for the pioneering effort. Those few whose family situation I was able to explore in detail were all in some kind of trouble in their lineages, or were the sons of men in such trouble. Since land shortage is widespread and relatively few men volunteered, some explanation for their having chosen to leave is in order. For those whose histories I know it was not socialist idealism in any form that motivated them to volunteer, but the land shortage and their family situation.

3 For an account of older techniques see P. I. Marealle. He says there is no witchcraft, but there is much fear of it (1947:78). In 1979 in conversation he again said there is no practice of witchcraft despite witchcraft beliefs. It is difficult to tell to what extent such statements are made for public consumption but do not represent private views. Certainly for many Chagga farmers witchcraft is real enough and techniques to ward it off are continuously employed. There is every indication save public demonstration that in addition to invoking God to bring misfortune to one's enemies other methods are regularly used as well. Educated Chagga like to say that witchcraft is not a traditional practice of the Chagga but has somehow come in from other peoples.

4 Field materials gathered from several lineages in each of five ex-chiefdoms substantiate this. As for the use of the courts, court records in Mwika were consulted to see how many of the 300 households studied in the household census used the courts in the years 1967 and 1968. In 1967 there were four criminal cases and thirteen civil cases. In each case at least one and often more than one local householder was involved. In 1968 there were thirteen criminal cases and seven civil cases drawn from the same 300 households.

5 This statement was often used in the old days in both civil and criminal cases. Now in criminal cases the magistrate usually alludes to one or another section of the criminal code, but this practice is quite recent. In civil cases the evidential ground for decision is still used frequently. Allusion to legal rules is occasional, not surprising since the magistrates do not have any substantial legal training, and

few cases are customary law cases. Ideas about rules are, of course, implicit in all of these cases, in the arguments, the testimony, and the opinion, but rule construction and interpretation are not the focus of much explicit attention.

6 In one of the Mosha sublineages of Kilema, of thirteen men of the grandfather generation who had sons, eight had three or more. Of the Nguma lineage, also of Kilema, of seven men of the grandfather generation who grew to adulthood, three had three or more sons.

7 Attached to Jack Goody's "Strategies of Heirship," *Comparative Studies in Society and History* 15 (1973): 3–20, there is a table on family size and the likelihood of a male child predeceasing his father in preindustrial societies. It indicates that there is a two-thirds chance that a son will die before his father. As for numbers of sons, there is a 7.2 percent chance of having two or more sons, and the average number of children is 2.5. The chance of having two or more sons goes up to 28.3 percent, and the average number of children is 6.0 (17–18).

8 Some craft and service businesses do not involve very much formal education, but require an apprenticeship and/or some capital. For a few these also may be the route to affluence.

9 After title to land was nationalized in 1963 it could not be bought and sold from then on, and landlord-tenant arrangements were restricted. However, the right of occupancy could be transferred, reimbursement for improvements paid, and there was considerable room for manipulation of the realities of tenancy. In practical fact, then, land continued to be bought and sold at least to January 1984, the time of my last visit before publication of this book, though by then a new policy was in place to give villages control of land through a system of long-term leases and subleases. See under Official Publications, *The Agricultural Policy of Tanzania* (Dar es Salaam: Government Printer, 31 March 1983).

10 The ideologue's abstract conception of the agrarian cooperative village, the group of peasants living together in a bounded territory in which they farm, did not fit the Kilimanjaro situation from the start. The division between *kihamba* land (bananas and coffee) high on the slopes and *shamba* (millet, maize, and beer) land near the plain meant that though the community of persons was concentrated, the lands were not all in one place. In the precolonial and early colonial periods a Chagga rich in cattle could conceal his assets by placing them with many individuals far away. Now a Chagga rich in land can conceal his assets, because his plots of land are scattered and, where necessary, he can place persons on those lands who are beholden to him. He may also use political office and community institutions to obtain commodities for himself or for others that otherwise either are not obtainable at all or are more costly. I know that the decisions of officials can be influenced and in some instances, I am told, bought.

11 Most of the budget of the village comes from two sources: contribution by the citizenry, and the eighteen cents per kilo of coffee from the *baki* payment withheld by the *Mamlaka ya Kahawa* (successor of the KNCU). This eighteen cents can be turned over to the village if it makes an approved request. In 1979 the village had just installed a new public water tap which cost 18,000 shillings and had 31,000 shillings left in its budget. Eventually the village may also have some income from a *pombe* shop it has taken over and from other similar small enterprises.

12 Christianity is nearly universal on the mountain today. There are a few Chagga Moslems and some Seventh-Day Adventists, but the Lutherans and Catholics strongly predominate.

13 The national party was then called TANU, the Tanzanian African National Union, now the *Chama cha Mapinduzi*.

14 The ten-house cell leaders also have minor administrative functions, collecting "voluntary" contributions for government campaigns, reporting all births and deaths, all unusual events in the area, mediating in quarrels that arise among their constituent households, and summoning ambulances or police or other officials when necessary. They are supposed to be a source of continuous political vigilance, and indeed, the ten-house cell system was instituted after an attempted coup in 1964.

15 The cumbersome design of some development aspects of party/government in the 1970s is shown in Figure 6.5, p.162. By no means did it function exactly as designed. See Maeda 1976 for a broader account of the structure as then conceived.

16 See "Political Meetings and the Simulation of Unanimity," in *Secular Ritual*, S. F. Moore and B. Myerhoff ed. (Assen: Van Gorcum, 1977), pp. 151–72.

17 In the 1973–74 period President Nyerere, fearing a military coup, removed a Chagga army general from office, a son of Petro Itosi Marealle, and sent him off to the Far East. He was later permitted to visit Tanzania, where he still maintains a home on Kilimanjaro. Many other Chagga remain in positions of substantial national influence. They are found in many high offices in the party and in other parts of the bureaucracy, and they are found in innumerable lower-level administrative and clerical positions.

EPILOGUE

1 Geertz has recently put the "interpretive" position succinctly, "Social events do have causes and social institutions effects, but it just may be that the road to discovering what we assert in asserting this lies less through postulating forces and measuring them than through noting expressions and inspecting them" (1980:178).

2 Giddens has put the matter as follows:

Let me put the facts of the matter as bluntly as possible. If by "historical materialism" we mean that the history of human societies can be understood in terms of the progressive augmentation of the forces of production, then it is based on false premises, and the time has come finally to abandon it. If historical materialism means that the history of all hitherto existing society is the history of class "struggles," it is so patently erroneous that it is difficult to see why so many have felt obliged to take it seriously. If finally, historical materialism means that Marx's scheme of the evolution of societies (from tribal society, Ancient society, feudalism, to capitalism; and thence to socialism, together with the "stagnant" offshoot of the "Asiatic Mode of Production" in the East) provides a defensible basis for analysing world history, then it is also to be rejected. Only in historical materialism of human *Praxis*, snippets of which can be gleaned from the diversity of Marx's writings, does it remain an indispensable contribution to social theory today (Giddens 1971:1, 2). "Pure Marxism is an impossibility in the contemporary context" (Kahn and Llobera 1980:91).

3 "Events" is not used here in the historians' sense of events that change the course of history.

Glossary

Non-English terms are Kiswahili unless Kichagga is specified.

age-grade, age-set Of a social category whose members are all of the same sex and socially defined generation, for example: youths, warriors, elders. An **age-set** is a cohort of particular persons who move through the successive phases of the **age-grade** system together. Among the Chagga there were six named **age-sets,** which were subdivided into senior and junior levels (Gutmann, 1926:328, 344; HRAF: 296, 311). **Age-class** is a term sometimes used for **age-grade,** sometimes for **age-set.** Only context can indicate which is intended.

agistment the taking in of another person's cattle to be fed and cared for

baki (pl. **mabaki**) remainder, residue; among the Chagga: the second payment made on a coffee harvest

bakuli a metal bowl or basin used for measurement at the market. A **bakuli** contains about two quarts

balozi ten-house cell leader (new use); conventional meaning: political envoy, consul

banda hut or house; today usually rectangular made of wattle and daub

baraza place of public audience or reception; used on Kilimanjaro to allude to the courthouse

baraza la usuluhishi tribunal or arbitration or reconciliation; an informal "people's court" run by laypersons in Tanzania

boma stockade; also used to refer to forts and government offices

debe four-gallon tin can in which gasoline and kerosene are imported, normally used for carrying water or beer in the countryside and as a unit of liquid measure

fidia ransom, redemption, compensation

isale (derived from **sale**) (pl. **masale**) (Kichagga) dracaena plant used for fencing and marking boundaries of the **kihamba** garden, and to mark the burial place of ancestral bones as well as for a variety of ritual purposes; the plant of peace-making, it was sometimes draped around the neck of a goat offered as an apologetic or peace-making gesture, or to accompany a request

jini fairy, spirit, genie, but used on Kilimanjaro as means of bewitching

kichaa crazy

kidari the breast portion of a slaughtered animal to which the male head of a sublineage or lineage was entitled

kihamba (pl. **vihamba**) (Kichagga) permanently held inheritable cultivated plot, usually planted in bananas; see **shamba**

kihenge the large roofed basketry storage "tank" for millet

kishari (pl. **vishari**) (Kichagga) lineage or clan

kiuno loin, flank, waist, the part just above the hips

kumpa pole to soothe or encourage or express sorrow, condolence after an accident, shock, misfortune, bad news

longu (Kichagga) the lung and rib portion of a slaughtering share

mabaki see baki

magaddi soda

mahari bridewealth, money or property paid to the bride's relatives

mangi chief

masale see isale

masiro (Kichagga) annual gift from the borrower to lender commemorating the loan of land

masumba (sing. **isumba**) (Kichagga) the prominent men who made regular cattle contributions to the Chagga chiefs in the nineteenth century

matanga period of mourning, the ceremony on the fourth day after death at which the property, debts, and responsibilities of the decedent are reallocated

mbege (Kichagga) millet, eleusine

mchawi witch, male or female

mchili (pl. **wachili**) (Kichagga) head of **mtaa** (district, parish)

mganga (pl. **waganga**) native doctor, diviner, medicine man

mgongo back, back part, backbone of a human or animal

mila custom

mjomba mother's brother, sister's son

mjumbe representative, messenger, ambassador

mkara (Kichagga) marriage sponsor, trustee of marriage

mlaso (Kichagga) combination of fat, blood, and milk, a special food given to women after childbirth to make them strong and to make the milk flow. The Chagga do not normally eat milk and meat in the same meal.

mra (Kichagga) the contents of the stomach and intestines of a slaughtered animal

mrarao (Kichagga) a type of banana out of which beer is made

mrithi the inheritor, heir

msesewe (Kichagga) a tree, the bark of which is used to make beer ferment

mtaa (pl. **mitaa**) district, parish

mtungi (pl. **mitungi**) container for beer, holding three or four **debe** (four-gallon tin), traditionally among Chagga a wooden container

mwafrika literally "African" but on Kilimanjaro the name of one type of beer shop that sells locally brewed banana beer where men gather in the late afternoons

mwakili the chief's deputy in colonial times, literally a brainy person

mwitori (pl. **waitori**) (Kichagga) divisional chief

mzee (pl. **wazee**) elder

ndafu fatted gelded goat

ndaso (Kichagga) the ancestor's share of the slaughtering feast consisting of the contents of the beast's stomach and intestines and some small slivers of meat

nduo (Kichagga) yellow fruit used in ritual of expulsion in which a man was disowned by his lineage

ngari (Kichagga) the slaughter share of the second most senior man in the lineage

panga large bush knife used for cutting brush and trees

pipa barrel for beer

pombe beer

prestation offering or gift

sale (pl. **masale**) dracaena plant used to make a hedge around the **kihamba** compound, also planted at the grave of the dead, and having various symbolic uses (see **isale**)

shamba cultivated plot, planted in annual crops, distinguished by the Chagga from **kihamba** in that **shamba** tenure was temporary, though annually renewable until fallowing was necessary

shisangu (Kichagga) bundles of meat

ugoni fine imposed for adultery

ujamaa socialism

ukoo (Kichagga) lineage or clan

upata the gift of thanks given to the district head (**mchili**) or chief (**mangi**) for a favor done, often for the allocation of a plot of land

utaona literally: you shall see, but is a threatening statement meaning "You'll see what will happen to you"; an implied death threat

uzazi confinement, period of three months of rest and withdrawal by Chagga women after giving birth to a child

waganga see **mganga**

wasimamizi (sing. **msimanizi**) supervisors

zamani in past time, long ago

BIBLIOGRAPHY

GENERAL PUBLICATIONS

Abel, Richard. 1979. Western Courts in Non-western Settings: Patterns of Court Use in Colonial and Neo-colonial Africa, pp. 167–200. In *The Imposition of Law,* ed. Sandra Burman and Barbara Harrell-Bond. London: Academic Press.

—— 1979. The Rise of Capitalism and the Transformation of Disputing. *UCLA Law Review* 27(1):223–55.

Ahmed, Akbar S. 1980. *Pukhtun Economy and Society.* Boston: Routledge & Kegan Paul.

Althusser, Louis. 1970. *For Marx.* New York: Vintage Books.

Asad, Talal. March 1972. Market Model, Class Structure and Consent: A Reconsideration of Swat Political Organization. In *Man,* 7(1):74–94.

Augé, Marc. 1982. *The Anthropological Circle: Symbol, Function, History.* Cambridge: Cambridge University Press.

Bailey, F. G. 1957. *Caste and the Economic Frontier.* Manchester: Manchester University Press.

—— 1960. *Tribe, Caste and Nation.* Manchester: Manchester University Press.

—— 1963. *Politics and Social Change.* Berkeley and Los Angeles: University of California Press.

Barnett, H. G., Leonard Broom, Bernard J. Siegel, Evon Z. Vogt, and James B. Watson. 1954. Acculturation, an Exploratory Formulation. *American Anthropologist* 56:973–1002.

Barth, Frederik. 1966. *Models of Social Organization.* London: Royal Anthropological Institute, Occasional Paper no. 23.

—— 1981. Models Reconsidered. *Process and Form in Social Life.* London: Routledge & Kegan Paul.

—— ed. 1978. *Scale and Social Organization.* Oslo: Universitetsforl (Bergen: John Grieg).

Benda-Beckmann, Franz von. 1979. *Property in Social Continuity.* The Hague: Nijhoff.

Berkner, Lutz. 1976. Inheritance, Land Tenure and Peasant Family Structure. In *Family and Inheritance,* ed. Jack Goody, Joan Thirsk, and E. P. Thompson. Cambridge: Cambridge University Press.

Berreman, Gerald D. 1978. Scale and Social Relations. In *Scale and Social Organization,* ed. Fredrik Barth. Oslo: Universitetsforl.

Bohannan, Paul J. 1957. *Justice and Judgment among the Tiv.* Oxford: Oxford University Press.

——— 1967. *Law and Warfare.* Garden City: The Natural History Press.

Bourdieu, Pierre. 1977. *Outline of a Theory of Practice.* Cambridge: Cambridge University Press.

Brown, Richard. 1973. Anthropology and Colonial Rule. In *Anthropology and the Colonial Encounter,* ed. Talal Asad. London: Ithaca Press.

Burman, Sandra B., and Barbara E. Harrell-Bond. 1979. *The Imposition of Law.* New York: Academic Press.

Cohen, Ronald, and John Middleton. 1970. *From Tribe to Nation in Africa.* Scranton: Chandler.

Collier, Jane. 1973. *Law and Social Change in Zinacantan.* Stanford: Stanford University Press.

Comaroff, John. 1982. Dialectical Systems, History, and Anthropology: Units of Study and Questions of Theory. *Journal of Southern African Studies* 8(2):143–72.

——— and Simon Roberts. 1981. *Rules and Processes.* Chicago: University of Chicago Press.

Cotran, E. 1962. East Africa. In *Judicial and Legal Systems in Africa,* ed. A. N. Allott. London: Butterworth. pp. 98–105.

——— 1965. Integration of Courts and Application of Customary Law in Tanganyika, *East African Law Journal* 1:108–23.

——— 1970. Tanzania. In *Judicial and Legal Systems in Africa,* ed. A. N. Allott. London: Butterworth. pp. 145–69.

Diamond, A. S. 1971. *Primitive Law Past and Present.* London: Methuen & Co.

DuBow, Frederick L. 1973. Justice for People: Law and Politics in the Lower Courts of Tanzania. Ph.D. diss. University of California, Berkeley, Sociology, Criminology.

Dumont, Louis. 1972 [1966]. *Homo Hierarchicus.* London: Paladin.

Dundas, Charles. 1924. *Kilimanjaro and Its People.* London: Witherby.

Engels, Frederick. 1942 [1884]. *The Origin of the Family, Private Property and the State.* New York: International Publishers.

Fallers, Lloyd. *Law without Precedent.* 1969. Chicago: University of Chicago Press.

Fimbo, G. M. 1974. Land, Socialism, and the Law in Tanzania. In *Towards Ujamaa, Twenty Years of Leadership,* ed. Gabriel Ruhumbika. Dar es Salaam and Nairobi: East African Literature Bureau, pp. 230–70.

Firth, Raymond. 1951. *Elements of Social Organization.* London: Watts.

Fortes, Meyer. 1969. *Kinship and the Social Order.* London: Routledge & Kegan Paul.

Foster, George M., Thayer Scudder, Elizabeth Colson, and Robert V. Kemper, eds. 1979. *Long-Term Field Research in Anthropology.* New York: Academic Press.

Friedman, Lawrence M., and Stewart Macaulay, eds. 1977. *Law and the Behavioral Sciences.* Indianapolis: Bobbs-Merrill.

Geertz, Clifford. 1963. *Agricultural Involution*. Berkeley and Los Angeles: University of California Press.

1963. *Peddlers and Princes*. Chicago: University of Chicago Press.

1965. *The Social History of an Indonesian Town*. Cambridge, Mass.: MIT Press.

1968. *Islam Observed*. Chicago: University of Chicago Press.

1973. *The Interpretation of Cultures*. New York: Basic Books.

1980. Blurred Genres. *American Scholar* 29:2:165–79.

1980. *Negara*. Princeton: Princeton University Press.

1983. *Local Knowledge*. New York: Basic Books.

Georges, Telford. See James, R. W., and F. M. Kassam. 1973. *Law and Its Administration in a One-Party State*.

Giddens, Anthony. 1971. *Capitalism and Modern Social Theory*. Cambridge: Cambridge University Press.

1979. *Central Problems in Social Theory*. Berkeley and Los Angeles: University of California Press.

Gluckman, Max. 1955; 2nd ed. 1967. *The Judicial Process among the Barotse of Northern Rhodesia*. Manchester: Manchester University Press.

Godelier, Maurice. 1978. The Object and Method of Economic Anthropology. In *Relations of Production*, ed. David Seddon. London: Frank Cass.

Goody, Jack. 1971. *Technology, Tradition and the State in Africa*. New York: Oxford University Press.

1973. Strategies of Heirship. *Comparative Studies in Society and History* 15:3–20.

1976. *Production and Reproduction*. Cambridge: Cambridge University Press.

1977. *The Domestication of the Savage Mind*. Cambridge: Cambridge University Press.

1982. *Cooking, Cuisine and Class*. Cambridge: Cambridge University Press.

1983. *The Development of the Family and Marriage in Europe*. Cambridge: Cambridge University Press.

Gray, Sir John. 1963. Zanzibar and the Coastal Belt, 1840–84. In *History of East Africa*, eds. Roland Oliver and Gervase Matthew. Oxford: Clarendon Press, pp. 212–52.

Gulliver, Philip. 1973. *Social Control in an African Society*. London: Routledge & Kegan Paul.

Gutmann, Bruno. 1909. *Dichten und Denken der Dschagganeger*. Leipzig.

1926. *Das Recht der Dschagga*. Munich. English translation by A. M. Nagler, Human Relations Area Files, New Haven: Yale University Press. (Cited in this study as HRAF.)

1913. Feldbausitten und Wachstumsbrauche der Wadschagga. *Zeitschrift für Etnologie* 45:474–511.

Hailey, Lord William. 1938. *An African Survey*. Oxford: Oxford University Press.

1950. *Native Administration in the British African Territories*. Part 1. London: His Majesty's Stationery Office.

Hannington, Bishop James. 1885. Bishop Hannington's Visit to Chagga. *Church Missionary Intelligencer* 10(n.s.):606–13.

Henderson, W. O. 1965. German East Africa, 1884–1918. In *History of East*

Africa, ed. V. Harlow, E. M. Chilver, and A. Smith. Oxford: Clarendon Press.

Hoebel, E. A. 1954. *The Law of Primitive Man.* Cambridge: Harvard University Press.

Hogbin, H. Ian. 1958. *Social Change.* London: Watts.

Hooker, M. B. 1975. *Legal Pluralism.* Oxford: Clarendon Press.

Hopkins, Terence K., and Immanuel Wallerstein. 1982. *World-Systems Analysis.* Beverly Hills, Calif.: Sage.

Hyden, Goran. 1980. *Beyond Ujamaa in Tanzania.* Berkeley and Los Angeles: University of California Press.

Illiffe, John. 1979. *A Modern History of Tanganyika.* Cambridge: Cambridge University Press.

James, R. W. 1971. *Land Tenure and Policy in Tanzania.* Nairobi, Dar es Salaam, Kampala: East African Literature Bureau.

———— 1973. Implementing the Arusha Declaration – the Role of the Legal System. *African Review* 3(2):179–208.

———— and G. M. Fimbo. 1973. *Customary Land Law of Tanzania.* Nairobi, Dar es Salaam, Kampala: East African Literature Bureau.

———— and F. M. Kassam. 1973. *Law and Its Administration in a One-Party State* (selected speeches of Telford Georges). Nairobi, Dar es Salaam, Kampala: East African Literature Bureau.

Johnston, H. H. 1886. *The Kilimanjaro Expedition.* London: Kegan, Paul, and Trench.

Johnston, P. H. 1953. Chagga Constitutional Development. *Journal of African Administration* 5:134–40.

Kahn, Joel, and Josep R. Llobera. 1980. French Marxist Anthropology Twenty Years After. *Journal of Peasant Studies* 8(1):81–100.

———— 1981. Towards a New Marxism or a New Anthropology. In *The Anthropology of Pre-Capitalist Societies,* eds. Joel S. Kahn and Josep R. Llobera. London: Macmillan Press.

Kimambo, Isaria N. 1969. *A Political History of the Pare of Tanzania.* Nairobi: East African Publishing House.

Krapf, J. L. 1860. *Travels, Researches and Missionary Labours during an Eighteen Years' Residence in Eastern Africa.* London.

Kuper, Hilda, and Leo Kuper. eds. 1965. *African Law, Adaptation and Development.* Berkeley and Los Angeles: University of California Press.

Kuper, Leo, and M. G. Smith, eds. 1969. *Pluralism in Africa.* Berkeley and Los Angeles: University of California Press.

Lamphear, John. 1970. The Kamba and the Northern Mrima Coast. In *Pre-Colonial African Trade,* ed. Richard Gray and David Birmingham. New York: Oxford University Press, pp. 75–101.

Leach, Edmund. 1954. *Political Systems of Highland Burma.* Boston: Beacon Press.

———— 1961. *Pul Eliya, a Village in Ceylon.* Cambridge: Cambridge University Press.

Lee, Eugene C. 1965. *Local Taxation in Tanzania.* Oxford: Oxford University Press.

Lewis, I. M., ed. 1968. *History and Social Anthropology.* Association of Social Anthropologists Monograph no. 7. New York: Tavistock Publications.

Mackenzie, William. 1977. *The Livestock Economy of Tanzania.* Nairobi, Dar es Salaam, Kampala: East African Literature Bureau.

Maeda, Justin. 1976. Popular Participation, Control, and Development. Ph.D. diss., Yale University, Political Science.

Maine, Sir Henry. 1894 [1861]. *Ancient Law.* 10th edition. London: John Murray.

Makler, Harry, Alberto Martinelli, and Neil Smelser, eds. 1982. *The New International Economy.* Beverly Hills, Calif.: Sage.

Malinowski, Bronislaw. 1951 [1926]. *Crime and Custom in Savage Society.* New York: Humanities.

Marealle, Chief Petro Itosi. 1947. *Maisha ya Mchagga hapa Duniani na Ahera.* Marangu.

Maro, Stephen P. 1974. Population and Land Resources in Northern Tanzania, the Dynamics of Change 1920–1970. Ph.D. diss., University of Minnesota, Geography.

Mauss, Marcel. 1954. *The Gift.* Glencoe, Ill.: Free Press. (Original *Essai sur le don,* 1925.)

Meillassoux, Claude. 1964. *Antropologie économique des Gouro de Côte d'Ivoire.* Paris: Mouton.

⸻ 1980. From Reproduction to Production: A Marxist Approach to Economic Anthropology, *The Articulation of Modes of Production,* ed. H. Wolpe. Boston: Routledge & Kegan Paul, pp. 189–201.

Merker, M. 1902. Rechtsverhaltnisse und Sitten der Wadschagga. *Petermanns Mitteilungen* (Gotha), Supplement 138, 30:1–40.

Meyer, Hans. 1891. *Across East African Glaciers.* Translated from German by E. H. S. Calder. London: George Philip and Son.

Middleton, John. 1960. *Lugbara Religion.* Oxford: Oxford University Press.

Moore, Sally Falk. 1970. Politics, Procedures and Norms in Changing Chagga Law. *Africa* 40(4):321–44.

⸻ 1977. Individual Interests and Organizational Structures: Dispute Settlements as Events of Articulation. In *Social Anthropology and Law,* ed. Ian Hamnett. Association of Social Anthropologists, Monograph no. 14. New York: Academic Press, pp. 159–88.

⸻ 1977. Political Meetings and the Simulation of Unanimity. In *Secular Ritual,* S. F. Moore and B. Myerhoff, eds. Assen: Van Gorcum, pp. 151–72.

⸻ 1978. Uncertainties in Situations, Indeterminacies in Culture. In *Law as Process.* London: Routledge & Kegan Paul, pp. 32–53.

⸻ 1978. Old Age in a Life Term Social Arena. In *Life's Career: Aging,* eds. B. Myerhoff and A. Simic. Beverly Hills, Calif.: Sage, pp. 23–76.

⸻ 1981. Chagga "Customary" Law and the Property of the Dead. In *Mortality and Immortality,* eds. S. C. Humphreys and H. King. New York: Academic Press, pp. 225–48.

⸻ and Paul Purritt. 1977. *Chagga and Meru.* Ethnographic Survey of Africa. London: International African Institute.

Morgan, Lewis Henry. 1963. *Ancient Society.* New York: Meridian Books (first published 1877).

Moser, Michael. 1982. *Law and Social Change in a Chinese Community.* Dobbs Ferry, N.Y.: Oceana Publications.

Nader, Laura. 1965. Choices in Legal Procedure. *American Anthropologist* 67(2):394–9.

⸻ and Harry F. Todd. 1978. *The Disputing Process – Law in Ten Societies.* New York: Columbia University Press.

Needham, Rodney. 1975. Polythetic Classification: Convergence and Consequences. *Man* 10(3):349–69.

New, Charles. 1874. *Life, Wanderings and Labours in Eastern Africa*. London: Hodder & Stoughton.

Newman, Katherine S. 1983. *Law and Economic Organization*. Cambridge: Cambridge University Press.

Nurse, Derek. 1979. *Classification of the Chaga Dialects*. Hamburg: Buske.

O'Connor, Richard A. 1981. Law as Indigenous Social Theory: A Siamese Thai Case. *American Ethnologist* 8(2):223–37.

Odner, Knut. 1971. A Preliminary Report on an Archaeological Survey on the Slopes of Kilimanjaro. *Azania* 6:131–49.

Posner, Richard A. 1980. A Theory of Primitive Society, with Special Reference to Primitive Law. *Journal of Law and Economics* 23(1):1–53.

Pospisil, Leopold. 1958. *Kapauku Papuans and Their Law*. New Haven: Yale University Press.

1971. *Anthropology of Law*. New York: Harper & Row.

Raum, O. F. 1965. German East Africa. In *History of East Africa,* eds. V. Harlow, E. M. Chilver, and A. Smith. Oxford: Clarendon Press, pp. 163–207.

Rey, Pierre Philippe. 1971. *Colonialisme, neo-colonialisme et transition au capitalisme*. Paris: Maspero.

Roberts, Andrew. 1970. Nyamwezi Trade. In *Pre-Colonial African Trade,* eds. Richard Gray and David Birmingham. New York: Oxford University Press, pp. 39–75.

Roberts, Simon. 1979. *Order and Dispute, An Introduction to Legal Anthropology*. Harmondsworth: Penguin Books.

Rogers, Susan Geiger. 1972. The Search for Political Focus on Kilimanjaro. Ph.D. diss., University of Dar es Salaam.

Rosen, Lawrence. 1980–81. Equity and Discretion in a Modern Islamic Legal System. *Law and Society Review* 15(2):217–45.

Sahlins, Marshall. 1972. On the Sociology of Primitive Exchange, in *Stone Age Economics*. Chicago: Aldine.

1976. *Culture and Practical Reason*. Chicago: University of Chicago Press.

1981. *Historical Metaphors and Mythical Realities*. Ann Arbor: University of Michigan Press.

Saltman, Michael. 1979. Indigenous Law among the Kipsigis of Southwestern Kenya. In *Access to Justice,* eds. Mauro Cappelletti and Bryant Garth, Vol. 3. Milan: Giuffre, pp. 313–40.

Samoff, Joel. 1974. *Tanzania, Local Politics and the Structure of Power*. Madison: University of Wisconsin Press.

Schapera, I. 1938. *A Handbook of Tswana Law and Custom*. London, Oxford University Press for the International African Institute.

1962. Should Anthropologists be Historians? *Journal of the Royal Anthropological Institute* 92: 143–56.

1970 (rev. of 1st ed. 1943). *Tribal Innovators*. London: Athlone Press.

Seddon, David, ed. 1978. *Relations of Production*. London: Cass.

Shann, G. N. 1956. The Early Development of Education among the Chagga. *Tanganyika Notes and Records* 45:21–32.

Smith, M. G. 1962. History and Social Anthropology. *Journal of the Royal Anthropological Institute* 92:73–85.

1974. *Corporations and Society*. London: Duckworth.

1978. *The Affairs of Daura.* Berkeley and Los Angeles: University of California Press.

Snyder, Francis. 1981. *Capitalism and Legal Change.* New York: Academic Press.

Spindler, Louise S. and George D. 1959. Culture Change. In *Biennial Review of Anthropology.*

Stahl, Kathleen M. 1964. *The History of the Chagga People of Kilimanjaro.* The Hague: Mouton.

1969. The Chagga. In *Tradition and Transition in East Africa,* ed. P. H. Gulliver. Berkeley and Los Angeles: University of California Press, pp. 209–22.

Starr, June. 1978. *Dispute and Settlement in Rural Turkey.* Leiden: Brill.

Stuhlman, Fr. 1909. *Beitrage zur Kulturgeschichte von Ostafrika.* Hamburg: Friedrichsen.

Swynnerton, R.J.M., A.L.B. Bennett, and H. B. Stent. 1948. *Habari Zote za Kahawa ya "KNCU."* Moshi, Tanganyika: Moshi Native Coffee Board.

Tambiah, S. J. 1976. *World Conqueror and World Renouncer.* Cambridge: Cambridge University Press.

Tanganyika Notes and Records, March 1965. Number 64, Dar es Salaam.

Temu, A., and B. Swai. 1981. *Historians and Africanist History: A Critique.* London: Zed Press.

Terray, Emmanuel. 1972. *Marxism and "Primitive" Societies.* New York, Monthly Review Press.

1978. Event, Structure and History. In *The Evolution of Social Systems,* eds. J. Friedman and M. Rowlands. London: Duckworth.

Tordoff, William. 1967. *Government and Politics in Tanzania.* Nairobi: East African Publishing House.

Turner, Victor. 1957. *Schism and Continuity in an African Society.* Manchester: Manchester University Press.

Van Velsen, J. 1967. The Extended-case Method and Situational Analysis. In *The Craft of Social Anthropology,* ed. A. L. Epstein. London: Tavistock, pp. 129–49.

Von Clemm, Michael F. M. 1963. Trade-bead Economics in Nineteenth Century Chaggaland. *Man* 63:13–14.

1964. Agricultural Productivity and Sentiment on Kilimanjaro. *Economic Botany* 18:99–121.

Von der Decken, Carl Claus. 1869–71. *Reisen in Ost Afrika 1859–1865 Bearbeitet von Otto Kersten.* 2 vols. Leipzig and Heidelberg: C. F. Wintersche Verlagshandlung.

Werbner, Richard. 1984. The Manchester School in South-Central Africa. *Annual Review of Anthropology,* pp. 157–85.

Widenmann, A. 1899. Die Kilimandscharo-Bevolkerung. *Petermanns Mitteilungen,* Erganzungshafte, Gotha, 27(5):1–101.

Willis, Roy. 1974. *Man and Beast.* New York: Basic Books.

Wilson, Godfrey, and Monica Wilson. 1968 [1945]. *The Analysis of Social Change.* Cambridge: Cambridge University Press.

Winter, J. C. 1979. *Bruno Gutmann 1876–1966.* Oxford: Clarendon Press.

Wolf, Eric. 1959. *Sons of the Shaking Earth.* Chicago: University of Chicago Press.

1981. The Mills of Inequality: A Marxian Approach. In *Social Inequality,* ed. Gerald Berreman. New York: Academic Press, pp. 41–58.

Wolpe, Harold, ed. 1980. *The Articulation of Modes of Production*. London: Routledge & Kegan Paul.

OFFICIAL PUBLICATIONS

The Agricultural Policy of Tanzania. 31 March 1983. Dar es Salaam: Ministry of Agriculture.
Digest of Appeals from Local Courts 1955–1956. 1957. Dar es Salaam: Government Printer.
Kanuni za Mahakama. 1963. Dar es Salaam: Government Printer.
Local Government Memoranda No. 2 (Local Courts). 1957. Second edition. Dar es Salaam: Government Printer.
Maelezo ya Mahakama za Mwanzo. 1964. Dar es Salaam: Government Printer.
Primary Courts Manual. 1964. Dar es Salaam: Government Printer.
Sheria ya Mahakama za Mahakimu. 1963. Dar es Salaam: Government Printer.

UNPUBLISHED DOCUMENTS

Annual Reports, Northern Province Tanzania National Archives (TNA) (typescript with one exception):

Report for Half-year	
ending 30 June 1927	TNA 10902
Annual Report for 1927	TNA 11681 1927
Annual Report for 1927	TNA 11681
Report for Half-year	
ending 30 June 1928	TNA 10902
Annual Report for 1929	TNA 18693 1929
Annual Report for 1931	TNA 11681 1931
Annual Report for 1932	TNA 19415 1932
Annual Report for 1933	TNA 19415 1933
Annual Report for 1934	TNA 11681 1934
Annual Report for 1935	
(printed, 1936, Dar es	
Salaam, govt. printer)	TNA 19415 1934
Annual Report for 1936	TNA 19415
Annual Report for 1939	TNA 19415
Annual Report for 1940	TNA 19415
Annual Report for 1941	TNA 19415
Annual Report for 1942	TNA 19415
Annual Report for 1943	TNA 19415
Annual Report for 1949	TNA 19415
Annual Report for 1950	TNA 19415
Annual Report for 1952	TNA 19415

Associations – Vashari, Kilimanjaro District Council File 10/27.
Barnett, T. E. Based on interviews from August 1964 and January 1965. Report on local court systems in East Africa, Kenya, Tanganyika and Uganda. Typescript in library of University of Dar es Salaam.

Case Notes, Arbitration Tribunals (Baraza la Usuluhishi). Kilema 1972–73, Mamba 1973, Mwika 1972, Uru 1972.

Case Records, Land Court (Baraza la Usuluhishi wa Ardhi). 1972.

Case reports from courts of Mwika, Mamba, Marangu, Kilema, Keni-Mriti Mengwe, and Moshi Town. 1927–79. Located in local courthouse buildings, in faculty library and Law School of the University of Dar es Salaam.

Church Ledger, Mamba Lutheran Church, 1942–68. Records of marriages and of cases heard before the congregational council.

Figgis, T. F. (n. d.) Chagga Land Tenure Report 1957–58. Copy in possession of Professor P. H. Gulliver, York University, Ontario, Canada.

Griffiths, A. W. M. 1930. Land Tenure Report Moshi District. Copy in possession of Professor P. H. Gulliver, and in the Manuscript Collections of Africana in Rhodes House Library, Oxford, MSS Afr. s. 1001.

Kilimanjaro District Council (KDC) Files

Letter #26, 10 March 1955, KDC File 9/11

Commissioner's Report, 1952, KDC File 1/16

Judicial Codification of Chagga Law, 1952, KDC File 3/7

District Commissioner's Report, 1954, KDC File 1/16

Chagga Oath, 1954–55, KDC File 3/15

Memorandum from the District Court, Kilimanjaro, to the Executive Office of the Kilimanjaro District Council, 20 January 1965, KDC File 3/10 II. Assessors in Primary Courts

Kilimanjaro Native Cooperative Union, Minute Books, 1932–33, 1937, 1942–50, 1950–54.

Local Government Report by Lord Hailey to the Secretary of State for the Colonies. 1941. TNA 41891.

Memorandum on the disturbances of 1936. 1937. TNA 41891 Local Government.

Minutes of Mwika East Cooperative Society, 1950, 1951, 1952, 1961, 1966.

Minutes of Mwika West Cooperative Society, 1934–36, 1940–1969.

Notice from Mahakama za Wilaya, Moshi, 13 October 1971, Ref. C 1/7/26 to all Primary Court Magistrates of the Kilimanjaro District.

Political correspondence. Folder relating to 1950s in Keni-Mriti-Mengwe courthouse.

Tanganyika District Books. From 1919 to 1940s. Vol. 3, library of School of Oriental and African Studies, London.

Ulipaji wa Ushuru (Local Rate) Mwezi Julai, 1968. List of taxes paid. Halmashauri ya Wilaya ya Kilimanjaro.

Index

Abel, Richard, 11, 51, 186
absentee, rights to land, 273
access, to women and children, 59–61
accretion, of groups, 54
acquisition, of bush land, 79
"acculturation," 322
administration (*see also* government), 95, 141
administrative consolidation, of chiefdoms, 97
administrative regulations, use of courts to enforce, 185–87
administrative reorganization, 97
administrative structures, 139; overlying, 139–48
adultery, 260
age-grade system, 19, 32, 53, 54, 55, 63, 90, 104; military aspects of, 96; assemblies, 42, 54, 55, 88, 89, 90, 104, 148, 177
agricultural instructors, 186
agricultural policy, 167; use of courts to enforce, 186
agricultural production (*see also* food production), 230
allocations, 11, 242, 298; of land, 318; of livestock, 66; of productive and political resources, 55
Althusser, Louis, 8
ancestors (*see also* the dead), 218, 256, 258
appeals, 151, 152
annual-crop lands, 62
anthropological history, 320–29
anthropological method, 329
arbitration tribunals, 161–65, 166, 167, 175, 187, 280, 301; powers of, 164
archaeology, 26
arenas, of action, 91
arenas, of competition, 54, 97, 226, 305, 306, 309

"articulation," 322, 327
Arusha, 126, 149
Asian merchants, 122
Askaris (soldiers), 104
assault, 218
"assessors," 172, 173
asylum, chief's hut as place of, 57
asymmetry, between group and individual, 53, 310, 311
Augé, Marc, 7
autonomy, 315, 316, 319; local, 141, 142, 315, 316, 319; of lineage, over own affairs, 169

Bailey, F. G., 324
banana, 15, 32, 111, 116, 117, 134, 271, 273, 318; rights regarding, 251–53; theft of, 251–53
banana gardens, 62, 80, 83, 101, 103; as burial ground, 81
Barnett, T. E., 157, 159, 322, 356n
Barth, Fredrik, 322, 327
beads, 28, 29
beans, 115, 127
beer, 59, 60, 61, 62, 63, 68, 69, 75, 85, 89, 90, 97, 108, 131–33 216, 218; bananas as men's property, 230; brewing, 85, 132, 349n, 350n
beer parties, 60, 132
beer shops, 349n; types of, 132–33
Benda-Beckmann, Franz von, 10
Bennett, A.L.B., 124
Bergson, Henri, 324
Berkner, Lutz, 250
Berreman, Gerald D., 321
birth control, 110
blood brotherhood, 57
blood vengeance, 57, 58

385